This boo may be kept

W9-AEZ-927

OUR BIBLE AND THE ANCIENT MANUSCRIPTS

PLATE I.

The Byble in Englyshe, that is to saye the content of all the holy scrypture, bothe of ẏ olde and newe testament, truly translated after the veryte of the Hebrue and Greke textes, by ẏ dylygent studye of dyuerse excellent learned men, expert in the forsayde tonges.

Prynted by Rychard Grafton & Edward Whitchurch.

Cum priuilegio ad imprimendum solum.

1539.

VIVAT REX

GOD SAVE THE KYNGE

THE GREAT BIBLE—A.D. 1539.

(*Original size*, $13\frac{3}{4}$ *in.* × $9\frac{1}{2}$ *in.*)

OUR BIBLE AND THE ANCIENT MANUSCRIPTS

by

SIR FREDERIC KENYON
K.C.B., M.A., D.Litt.
Formerly Director and Principal Librarian of the British Museum

05885

BS
475
.K37
4th ed

ST. JOSEPH'S UNIVERSITY STX
BS475.K37 4th ed.
Our Bible and the ancient manuscripts,
3 9353 00005 1456

EYRE & SPOTTISWOODE: LONDON

First Edition, December, 1895
Second Edition, 1896
Third Edition, 1898
Fourth Edition, revised, rewritten and enlarged, 1939
Reprinted, 1941
Reprinted, 1948

BS475
K37

This book is produced in complete conformity with the Authorized Economy Standards and is made and printed in Great Britain for Eyre and Spottiswoode (Publishers) Limited, 15 Bedford Street, London, W.C.2, by Billing and Sons Ltd., Guildford and Esher

INTRODUCTION TO THE FOURTH EDITION

DURING the forty-three years that have elapsed since the first publication of this work, great additions have been made to the evidence bearing on the history of the Bible text. Some of this evidence is direct, in the form of newly discovered manuscripts of portions of the Bible. In particular, a whole new section has been added to the story by the discovery of Biblical papyri in Egypt. In 1895 only one Biblical text on papyrus was known, and that of quite late date. Now the papyri have gone far to fill the gap between the dates when the New Testament books were written and the earliest extant vellum manuscripts. The recently discovered papyrus manuscripts in codex form have supplied a new chapter in the history of book production, and their contents have thrown much light on the conditions under which the New Testament Scriptures circulated in the earliest times. Further, new vellum manuscripts of importance have been brought to light, such as the Freer manuscripts of both Old and New Testament at Washington, or the Koridethi Gospels at Tiflis. Much work has meanwhile been done on textual theory, notably by von Soden, Streeter, Burkitt, Lake and Clark, and while the controversy between Hort and Burgon over the merits of the " received " Byzantine text has receded into the background, the character of the so-called " Western " text has been the subject of much study, and its problems have been elucidated, though not finally solved.

But in addition to this purely textual matter there have been great increases in the indirect evidence, the archæological data which form the background of the Bible story, and particularly of the Old Testament. The spade has been busy, both in Palestine itself and in the surrounding countries, in Syria, in Mesopotamia and in Egypt. References (necessarily brief) will be found to the recent discoveries at Jericho, Lachish and elsewhere, and especially to the very remarkable results of the excavations at Ras-Shamra. These enable us to appreciate much better the surroundings among which the books of the Old Testament came into being. In particular we know far more than ever before about the origins of writing and the forms in which books were written and circulated in the Near East during the centuries in which those books were produced

It has been necessary, therefore, largely to rewrite or rearrange the introductory chapters of the previous editions. In their original form a start was made from the existence of " various readings," and the book was planned to explain the existence of such variants and the means of judging between them. At that date the controversies arising out of the appearance of the Revised Version were still fresh, and formed a sufficient basis for such a volume. Now the point of view has somewhat changed, and it seems desirable to widen the basis. The Bible student wants to know something more about the origin of the Scriptures, before considering the details of the text. It is matter of general knowledge that there have of late been many discoveries which affect, in greater or less degree, the history of the Bible as a book, and the non-specialist reader, for whom this work is intended, may (and indeed should) wish to know something of the nature of these discoveries and of the opinions held about them by scholars. The attempt is therefore made in the early chapters of this new edition to lay the foundations of the history of the Bible according to the present state of our knowledge; after which the manner of the tradition of the record will be pursued as before, the discoveries which have been so plentiful in the last half-century being worked in in their proper places.

In the Introduction to the first edition I acknowledged, as in duty bound, that I had been indebted to the labours of others at every turn; and though the work of forty-three years may have enabled me to add something from my own knowledge nevertheless the statement remains essentially true. In addition to the scholars then named, I have derived much from those mentioned in the first paragraph of this Introduction; and for information and many courtesies I am indebted to Professors Campbell Bonner and H. A. Sanders, of the University of Michigan; to the late Cardinal Gasquet, Cardinal Mercati, and Dom H. Quentin, of the Vatican; to Drs. Nestle (father and son), von Dobschütz, Lietzmann, Rahlfs, and Kappler, of Germany; and others whom I have mentioned in the text. It is the results of their labours that I am trying to bring to the knowledge of the ordinary student of the Bible. I have also to thank the Librarian and Trustees of the John Rylands Library, Messrs. Emery Walker, and Prof. H. A. Sanders and the Trustees of the Freer Collection for the new illustrations added to this edition.

I hope that a new Appendix will be useful in enabling the reader to appreciate the meaning and character of the "various readings" that are found in manuscripts of the Bible, and to realise that, interesting and important as they are, they do not affect the fundamental doctrines of Christianity, nor the general authenticity and integrity of the records, which, on the contrary, have been notably confirmed by the discoveries of the last forty-three years.

F. G. K.

December, 1938.

CONTENTS

LIST OF ILLUSTRATIONS

CHAPTER I

NCIENT BOOKS AND WRITING

ook.

n of all study of the Bible, with which the reader n imself if his study is to be securely based, is the kı its history as a book. The English reader of the Bi le knows that he is reading a translation of books written in other languages many centuries ago. If he wishes to assure himself of the claim which these books have on his consideration, he must know when and in what circumstances they were written, and how they have been handed down through the ages. He needs to be satisfied that he has the text of them substantially in a correct form. He is concerned, therefore, first with their production and transmission in their original languages, Hebrew and Greek, and next with their translation into the languages in which they have been made known to the inhabitants of these islands, which are Latin and English. It is this story which the present volume aims at telling.

Canon and Text.

There are two main divisions of the story. There are first the questions how and when the books under consideration came into existence, and how and when they were marked off as possessing special authority. This is what is known as the history of the Canon (*canon*, a Greek word meaning primarily a rule, and thence, among other things, a list of books designated by order as authoritative). There is therefore a Canon of the Old Testament and a Canon of the New Testament, both of which will have to be briefly described. Next there is the question how these books, thus recognised as authoritative, haofe been handed down to us. This is known as the history of the Text; and again it is a different story for the Old and the New Testament respectively. Indeed, there is a marked contrast in respect of both Canon and Text between the two Testaments. In the case of the Old Testament the history of the formation of the Canon is obscure, while the history of the Text is comparatively simple; but in the case of the New Testament the history of the formation of the Canon is in most respects clear, while the history of the Text is involved and often obscure.

Origin of Writing.

There is, however, a preliminary inquiry which lies behind both the composition of the books and their transmission. This is the history of writing, without which these books could not have come down to us. The fundamental fact in the history of all ancient literature is the fact that before the invention of printing—that is, until about the year 1450—every copy of every book had to be separately written by hand. The whole history of ancient literature, including that of the Bible, is therefore conditioned first by the invention of writing, and next by the materials and forms of books in the various countries in which they were produced and circulated.

Now here we have at once occasion to realise how greatly our knowledge has been increased by the many marvellous discoveries of our own age. We have learnt very much of late years with regard to the antiquity of writing. It is not long since it was commonly maintained that the books of the Pentateuch could not be based on contemporary records, much less be attributable to Moses himself, because writing was not known at that time. Eminent scholars in the last quarter of the nineteenth century, such as Wellhausen and Graf, held that writing was not known in Palestine before the time of the kings. Here archæology has come to our assistance most decisively.

Recent Discoveries of Writing in Mesopotamia.

In Mesopotamia the excavations of American scholars at Nippur in 1888-1900 brought to light thousands of clay tablets, including many bearing literary texts (among them the Sumerian narrative of the Flood) which can be dated to about 2100 B.C. or earlier. To about the same time belong the tablets found by Sir Leonard Woolley at Ur, containing temple records and accounts in the most minute detail; while earlier tablets at Ur, and those found at Kish by the Oxford-Chicago expedition under Langdon, are said to go back to the middle of the fourth millennium or even earlier.

Egypt.

The evidence from the other side of Palestine is equally impressive. From Egypt we have actual manuscripts, written on papyrus, datable to about 2200-2000 B.C., and containing texts which claim to have been written at a much earlier period. Probably the earliest of these are two ethical treatises, the Teaching of Kagemna and the Teaching of Ptah-Hetep, works of gnomic philosophy akin in character to the Proverbs of Solomon, which are attributed to about 3100 B.C. and 2880 B.C.

respectively. There are also several copies of the great ritual work, the Book of the Dead, dating from the XVIIIth Dynasty (about 1580-1320 B.C.), which may be contemporary with Moses; while portions of the Book of the Dead existed many centuries earlier.

Hittite and Cretan.

Hittite and Cretan writings of the second millennium B.C. have also been discovered by the German excavators at Boghaz-Keui in Asia Minor, by Sir Leonard Woolley at Atchana in Northern Syria, and by Sir Arthur Evans at Knossos in Crete.

The Tell el-Amarna Letters.

All round Palestine therefore we now have evidence, unknown to our fathers, of the free use of writing back to a time far earlier than that of Abraham. We can also bring new evidence from Syria and Palestine themselves. In the year 1887 an Egyptian woman found, amid the ruins of an ancient city about half-way between Thebes and Memphis, a collection of some 350 clay tablets inscribed with strange markings.[1] The city is now well known as Tell el-Amarna, the capital of the remarkable king Amenhotep IV, or Akhenaten, who made a vain attempt to revolutionise the religion of his country, and was the father-in-law of Tutankhamen, the discovery of whose tomb by Lord Carnarvon made such a sensation at the end of 1922. The tablets of Tell el-Amarna, however, raised an almost equal sensation among Oriental scholars; for here, in the middle of Egypt, were documents written not after the manner of the country, in the Egyptian language and upon papyrus, but engraved upon clay in the unmistakable *cuneiform*, or wedge-shaped script characteristic of Mesopotamia (see Plate II). Nor did their surprise lessen as the writings were deciphered and their meaning ascertained. For these tablets proved to be the official correspondence of Egyptian governors or vassal-princes, from various places in Palestine and Syria, with their overlord, the king of Egypt. Their date is about the year 1380 B.C., which, according to the view now generally accepted, and which seems to be confirmed by the recent excavations at Jericho, is the period when Joshua and the Hebrews were overrunning southern Palestine,[2] while the Hittites were

[1] The tablets are now mainly divided between Berlin and the British Museum.

[2] There have been two main views of the date of the Exodus, some scholars assigning it to the time of Amenhotep IV (1380-1362), and others to that of Merenptah (1233-1223), the successor of Rameses II. The excavations at Jericho, conducted by Professor J. Garstang for Sir Charles Marston in 1930-36, seem to show that Jericho was destroyed by violence early in the fourteenth century, and thus strongly support the earlier dating.

conquering Damascus, and the Amorites were invading Phœnicia, Jerusalem, Lachish, Hazor, Megiddo, Gezer, are mentioned by name; and complaints are made of the assaults of the Habiru, who have been generally regarded as the Hebrews, though the identification is not accepted by all scholars.

Early Hebrew Writing.

In the Amarna tablets, therefore, we have actual documents written in Palestine about the time of Joshua. They show that writing was then familiarly known and freely used, and consequently that historical records may easily have been composed and preserved from that period. They are, however, not in Hebrew or in any other dialect of Palestine, but in Babylonian, which was apparently the official medium of correspondence, even with Egypt, much as French has been in modern Europe.

The Moabite Stone.

For Hebrew writing it was until recently necessary to regard the celebrated Moabite Stone as the earliest known example. This is the famous monument on which Mesha, king of Moab, recorded his war with the kings of Israel and Judah about the year 890 B.C. It was found by a German missionary, Herr Klein, in the possession of some Arabs in 1868. It was then perfect, but before it was acquired by M. Clermont-Ganneau for the Louvre the Arabs had broken it up, and large portions of it have never been recovered. Fortunately a paper squeeze had been taken of it before it was broken, and from this the text can be restored. This is written in what is known as the Semitic alphabet common to the Phœnicians, Aramæans and Hebrews.

The Serabit Inscriptions.

The earliest form of this alphabet appears to be that found in some inscriptions at the turquoise mines of Serabit, in the south of the peninsula of Sinai, first copied by Sir Flinders Petrie in 1904-5, and claimed as the ancestor of the Hebrew alphabet by Alan Gardiner in 1929, in the light of new copies made by Kirsopp Lake. These, which appear to be datable to the XIIth Dynasty of Egypt (*c.* 2200-2000 B.C.), are written in an alphabet derived from Egyptian hieroglyphs, which may well be the ancestor of the Phœnician, and therefore ultimately of the Greek alphabet. Several other recent discoveries help to close the gap between these proto-Phœnician signs and the inscription of Mesha.

Plate II.

CLAY TABLET FROM TELL EL-AMARNA—*circ.* B.C. 1380.

(*Original size*, $5\frac{5}{8}$ *in.* × $3\frac{3}{4}$ *in.*)

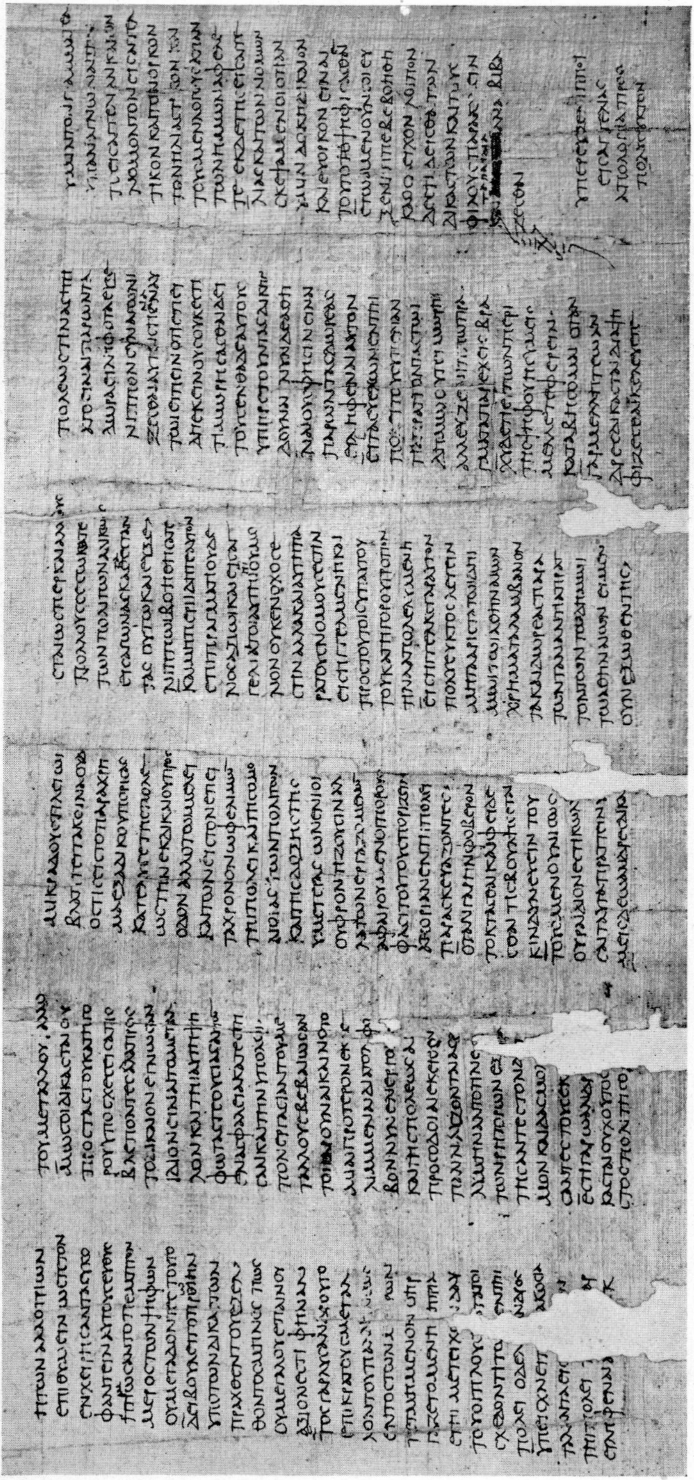

Plate III.

PAPYRUS ROLL OF FIRST CENTURY A.D. (*Brit. Mus. Pap.* 115, *Hyperides pro Euxenippo*).

(*Original size of portion reproduced, with full margins,* 17 *in.* × 12 *in.*)

Other Proto-Hebraic Writings.

A fragment of pottery found at Gezer in 1930, dating about 2000-1600 B.C., bears three letters in characters similar to those of Sinai. In 1926 an inscription was found at Byblos, on the Syrian coast north of Beirut, on the sarcophagus of King Ahiram, which is generally considered to be not later than 1200 B.C., and is certainly earlier than 1000 B.C. Still more recently, in the excavations conducted for the Wellcome-Marston expedition at Tell Duweir (the ancient Lachish) by Mr. J. L. Starkey from 1932 to his lamented death at the hands of Arab murderers in January, 1938, several characters in this Sinaitic-Hebrew script have been found on pieces of pottery datable about the beginning of the thirteenth century B.C. (Starkey's date is 1295-1262 B.C.). The exact dates and interpretation of these inscriptions are still matters of discussion among specialists, but the cumulative effect of their evidence is to assure us that writing was known and practised in Palestine, not only in Babylonian cuneiform but in the script from which Hebrew eventually developed, from the time when the Hebrews entered Palestine after the Exodus.[1]

The Ras-Shamra Tablets.

Still more remarkable, for their bearing both on the history of writing in Syria and on the intellectual and religious background of the Hebrews, are the results of the excavations which have now for some years been proceeding at a place called Ras-Shamra, a site on the coast of north-west Syria, not far from Alexandretta. Here a chance discovery in 1929 led to excavations which were so fruitful that they have been carried on continuously since that date by M. Claude Schaeffer and his colleagues. The site was identified as that of the Phœnician city of Ugarit, a flourishing settlement from about the beginning of the second millennium B.C. Among the ruins was found a building which had apparently been a library, containing quantities of clay tablets bearing cuneiform writing; and the liveliest interest was aroused when it became known, first, that this was not the ordinary Babylonian cuneiform, like the Tell el-Amarna letters, but was alphabetic in character; secondly, that the language was an archaic form of Hebrew; and, thirdly, and especially, that the texts included a number of literary and religious writings, among which occurred names familiar to us from the Old Testament.

The decipherment and publication of the Ras-Shamra texts is still in progress, but the general results at present arrived at

[1] For fuller particulars see Sir C. Marston, *The Bible Comes Alive* (1937), p. 171 ff.

by the scholars who have worked at them (Schaeffer, Virolleaud, Dhorme, and others) are of the highest interest, both in themselves and for their bearing upon the ancient Hebrew records and religion. They may be briefly summarised as follows. The library of Ras-Shamra seems to have been, if not founded, at least considerably developed about the middle of the second millennium B.C. by a king of Ugarit named Nigmed, whose name appears on several of the tablets. It was housed in a building between the two great temples of Baal and Dagon. The writing is a cuneiform alphabetic script with twenty-nine characters. The exact relation of it to the Sinaitic and Phœnician scripts has still to be worked out. The language is Semitic, and can be fairly described as proto-Phœnician or proto-Hebrew. Many of the texts are non-literary, including Sumerian-Babylonian vocabularies, the former being the language of ancient literary texts, the latter the language of diplomacy (as in the Tell el-Amarna letters) and commerce. Another dictionary is of Sumerian and an as yet undeciphered tongue. In addition, inscriptions in Egyptian, Hittite and Cypriot have been found, showing that Ugarit was a place where many languages met and were in use. Other texts are commercial, medical, legal, diplomatic and private. But by far the greater part of the library of Ugarit was composed of religious writings; and it is these that are of the greatest interest for our present purpose. No one can question their relationship with the early Hebrew religion. They are by no means identical; but it is clear that analogies existed between the beliefs and rites of the Canaanites and those of the Hebrews, and the names of the gods of the Philistines, the gods to whom the Israelites from time to time fell away, recur repeatedly. The supreme god at Ugarit was El, who rules over the other gods. His symbol is the bull. His home is in the " Fields of El " in the far west. His wife is Asherat, a sea-goddess. Next to these the most important god is Baal. Reference is also made to a great serpent with seven heads, whose name Lotan seems to be a contracted form of the Biblical Leviathan. The struggles between the gods, their downfalls and their uprisings, form a large part of this literature, as in Mesopotamia and in Egypt, and in singular contrast to the purer form of monotheism which was developed among the Hebrews. Of history there is little, though one group of tablets records a campaign against the Terachites, a name which recalls Terah, the father of Abraham. Altogether, no more remarkable discovery, for the light which it throws on the religion of the Canaanite peoples before the invasion of Joshua, has ever been made. We must not expect to find exact parallels with the Old Testament; but this Canaanite literature alike in its strong points (for it has much sincerity and beauty among its extravagances and its crudities) and in its weak shows us amid what surroundings the religion of Jehovah grew up and developed, and so helps us to appreciate the vast superiority which it achieved.[1]

Forms of Books.

We have now seen that, when the Hebrews left the land of Egypt, they left a land in which writing had been practised for hundreds of years; and when they entered Canaan under Joshua, they came to a land already possessing a literature and an alphabetic writing, available alike for secular and religious purposes. This has an intimate bearing on the origin and credibility of the books of the Old Testament; and the recent discoveries bearing on it have therefore been mentioned in some detail. It remains to examine the external form of the books which were used by the authors of the writings of the Old and the New Testament, and by the scribes who handed them down from their origin to the invention of printing.

Many materials have been used by men in different parts of the world to receive writing—stone, leaves, bark, wood, metals, linen, baked clay, potsherds—but for the main transmission of the Scriptures three only are of prime importance—namely, skins, papyrus and vellum. Of these, and especially of the last two, something must be said.

Leather.

With regard to leather, we know that prepared skins were used as writing material from a very early date. In Egypt there are references to documents written on skins in the fourth millennium B.C., and actual specimens are extant from about 2000 B.C. Ctesias, the Greek historian of Persia, refers to royal chronicles written on leather, but does not specify their precise dates. They may include those to which reference is made in Ezra vi. 1, 2 and Esther vi. 1. Herodotus records that once, when papyrus was scarce, the Ionian Greeks used sheepskins and goatskins in its place; and he adds that many of the "barbarians" still did so in his day. More important for our present purpose is the traditional use of leather for the books of the Law in Hebrew. In the Talmud it is laid down that all copies of the Law must be written on skins, and in roll form. This rule still continues in force, and many examples of such leather rolls are in existence. A specimen is shown in Plate II.

[1] The best summary account of the Ras-Shamra discoveries is in M. Schaeffer's Schweich Lectures before the British Academy for 1936, published in 1939.

The Talmud regulation no doubt represents a long-standing tradition, and it is therefore probable that the "rolls" from time to time referred to in the Bible were written on this material. In Ps. xl. 7 and Ezek. ii. 9 there is no decisive indication of material; but in Jer. xxxvi. 23, where it is said that Jehoiakim used the scribe's scraping-knife to cut to pieces the roll of Jeremiah's prophecies, the use of such an instrument seems to show that the roll was of tougher material than papyrus. A knife was, in fact, part of the equipment of a scribe writing on leather or vellum, for the purpose of erasures, as we know from medieval pictures. Further, it is recorded that the copies of the Law which were sent from Palestine to Egypt in the third century B.C., for the purpose of the making of the Septuagint translation of the Hebrew Scriptures into Greek, were on skins. At what time papyrus came into general use in Palestine cannot be ascertained. What is certain is that for formal copies, intended for use in the synagogues, leather was the regular material, and it may be presumed that this goes back at least to the period of the prophets.

Papyrus.

Far more widespread was the use of papyrus. The home of this material is Egypt. It was manufactured from the pith of the papyrus plant, which then grew plentifully in the Nile. The pith was cut into thin strips, which were laid down in two layers at right angles to one another, so that the fibres lay horizontally on one side and vertically on the other. The two layers were fastened together by pressure and glue, and in this way sheets were formed, which were then fastened together side by side, so as to form a roll. The height of the roll is limited by the length of the strips of pith; specimens exist which are as high as 15 inches, but about 10 inches is more usual for works of literature. The length could vary according to taste and convenience; several Egyptian liturgical rolls exist of 50 feet and over, and one is known of 133 feet; but such rolls were too cumbrous for ordinary reading, and Greek literary rolls seldom, if ever, exceed 35 feet—a length which is sufficient for a single book of Thucydides or one of the longer Gospels, but not for more. A sample may be seen in Plate III, which contains some columns of an oration (otherwise unknown) by Hyperides, from a papyrus of the later part of the first century in the British Museum.

Papyrus was used in Egypt as far back as the third millennium, if not earlier. How early it was in use in Greece we cannot say. The evidence of Herodotus, quoted above, shows that by the middle of the fifth century B.C. it was so well established that he cannot conceive a civilised people using anything else. We may therefore take it that at least from the sixth century onwards (and possibly much earlier) the papyrus roll was the regular material for book production in the Greek world. When, therefore, in the course of the third century B.C., a demand arose among the Jews settled in Egypt after its conquest by Alexander for a translation of their Scriptures into Greek, it was on papyrus rolls that the translation was produced; and when the books of the New Testament were written, in the first century after Christ, papyrus must again have been the material. For our present purpose, therefore, papyrus is the material of first importance.

Papyrus had many merits as a writing material, and for the best part of a thousand years, at least, it met the requirements of the Greek and Roman worlds. But from our point of view it lacked one very important quality, that of durability. Originally a material of about the same consistency as paper, it is destroyed by damp and, if kept dry, becomes very brittle with age. There is only one country where the soil is so dry that papyrus manuscripts buried in it have a chance of survival, and that is Egypt.[1] It is only comparatively recently, however, that this fact was discovered, and until then it could be said, with almost complete accuracy, that all manuscripts on papyrus had perished, and that works written in Greek or Latin could only have come down to us from the time when papyrus was superseded by the far more durable material known as vellum. All copies, whether of the Scriptures or of works of classical literature, earlier than the first half of the fourth century after Christ were assumed to have perished. It is only within the last half-century that a flood of new light has come to us from Egypt.

Discoveries of Papyri in Egypt.

The first discovery of papyri in Egypt was made in 1778,[2] when some natives in the province of the Fayum discovered a jar containing a little hoard of forty or fifty rolls. They could, however, find no market for them, and destroyed all except one, which was taken by a dealer as a curiosity. This turned out to be merely a list of labourers employed on irrigation works in A.D. 191, and was published in 1788. During the next hundred years a few score of papyrus documents turned up, including a few of literary character: two or three portions of Homer, and (more important because new) portions of four lost speeches of

[1] A very few sporadic discoveries of papyrus manuscripts have been made elsewhere, in southern Palestine and at Dura, on the Euphrates, where the climatic conditions are similar.

[2] Some charred rolls of papyrus were found at Herculaneum in 1752, which had been buried by the eruption of Vesuvius in A.D. 79, but it was not until their publication began in 1793 that it was known that they contained portions of the works of Epicurus and other philosophers.

Hyperides, the contemporary and rival of Demosthenes, and an ode by Alcman. The first discovery on a large scale was made in the Fayum in 1877, when a great mass of papyri was brought to light by natives, and was for the most part acquired by the Archduke Rainer of Austria for his library in Vienna. These, however, were mostly of late date and of non-literary character, and it was not until 1891 that the great era of papyrus discoveries began. In that year a number of fragments of papyrus, extracted by Professor Flinders Petrie from the cartonnage wrappings of mummies, were found to include a few portions of Plato and of a lost play of Euripides, with a number of non-literary documents, all of the third century B.C.; while a batch of rolls acquired by Dr. E. Wallis Budge for the British Museum proved to include the lost treatise by Aristotle on the Constitution of Athens, the lost poems of Herodas, a portion of a speech by Hyperides, and an unknown medical treatise, besides known works of Homer, Demosthenes and Isocrates. This fairly aroused public interest, and search in Egypt was actively pursued, with the result that now many thousands of papyrus documents are to be found in the great libraries of Europe and America, and among them several hundreds of literary texts, large and small, known and unknown.

Biblical Papyri.

For a long time, however, very few of these papyri contained any portion of the Scriptures. When the first edition of the present work was published, there was just one known, thirty-two leaves of a late (seventh century) papyrus book, said to have been found among the rubbish of an ancient convent at Thebes. Since then several more have from time to time come to light, culminating (for the present) in the discovery, quite recently, of considerable portions of manuscripts far earlier than any hitherto known. These will be described in their proper place in subsequent chapters. For the subject of our present chapter, all that is relevant is to state that the discoveries of the last few years, besides adding an earlier section to the record of the transmission of the Bible text, have also revealed a new feature in the history of the use of papyrus.

The Papyrus Codex.

Until recently, it was supposed that the roll form of book continued in use up to the time of the supersession of papyrus by vellum in the fourth century. It has now become clear that this is true only (and even there not wholly) of pagan literature, and that at any rate from the early part of the second century the Christian community was using the material in a different way—that, namely, which is known as the *codex* form—which is in fact our modern form of book with leaves arranged in quires or gatherings. To produce these, a sheet of papyrus, twice the size of the leaf required, was taken and folded in the middle. This produced the simplest form of quire, composed of two leaves or four pages; and a codex could be formed of a number of such quires sewn together. Or a number of such sheets, calculated to be sufficient for the whole of the text to be written, could be laid one on top of another, and the whole folded so as to produce a codex consisting of a single enormous quire. Examples are extant composed of as many as fifty-nine such sheets, or 118 leaves. This form must have been very inconvenient, and ultimately it was found that quires of about ten or twelve leaves was the more convenient form. Bible codices of all these types have been found in recent years, and will be described in Chapters V and VII below (see Plates VII, XII, XIII). The advantage of the codex form was that a much greater amount of matter could be included than was possible in a roll of normal length. We now have, as will be told in greater detail below, substantial portions of a codex containing the four Gospels and the Acts, written in the first half of the third century, another of the Pauline Epistles of about A.D. 200, another of the books of Numbers and Deuteronomy from the first half of the second century, a tiny scrap of St. John of the same date, and even a fragment of Deuteronomy from a roll of the second century before Christ. A great gap in the history of the transmission of the Bible text has thus been filled by the discoveries of the last seven years.

Vellum.

Until the discovery of papyri in Egypt, it was supposed that no actual copies of the Scriptures had survived previous to the date when vellum came into use as the predominant material for book-production. Vellum (or parchment) is a material prepared from the skins of cattle, sheep, goats or occasionally deer, and preferably from the young of these animals, and forms an exceedingly durable and handsome receptacle for writing. It is, in fact, a development and improvement of the use of skins. According to Pliny, quoting the earlier Roman writer Varro (first century B.C.), it was invented by Eumenes of Pergamum, at a time when Ptolemy of Egypt, jealous of a rival book-collector, laid an embargo on the export of papyrus. This implies a date between 197 and 182 B.C., and probably does not mean that vellum had never been heard of before this date, but that it then temporarily came to the front as a material of book production. In point of fact, some documents on vellum were found in 1923 among the ruins of the Roman fortress of Dura on the Euphrates, which bear dates equivalent to 196-5 and 190-89 B.C., showing that the material was then already in use at a place far distant from Pergamum. Apart, however, from the temporary needs of the Pergamum library, the use of vellum seems at first to have been in the form of note-books, for which purpose it competed with the wax tablet. Gradually it appears to have come into use for books, but from the point of view of the book trade it remained an inferior article to papyrus for works of literature throughout the first three centuries of the Christian era.

Exactly how the change came about is not clear, but it is certain that in the course of the first half of the fourth century vellum definitely superseded papyrus as the material in use for the best books; and since this was also the time when the Emperor Constantine the Great adopted Christianity as the official religion of the Eastern Empire, the change had a decisive influence on the tradition of the Bible text. Eusebius records that when Constantine ordered fifty copies of the Scriptures for the churches in his new capital, Constantinople, they were to be on vellum; and a little later (about A.D. 350) we learn from Jerome that the papyrus volumes in the library at Cæsarea, which had become damaged by use, were replaced by vellum copies. The acceptance of Christianity must have led to a great demand for copies of the Bible throughout the Empire; and though papyrus continued in use in its native home, Egypt, the remains that have come down to us after this period are fewer in number and inferior in quality.

Uncial MSS.

From this point, therefore, we must regard the fortunes of the Scriptures as committed to vellum; and it is precisely to this period that the earliest vellum manuscripts now extant belong. The Codex Vaticanus and the Codex Sinaiticus are both assigned to the first half of the fourth century. Both, when complete, contained both Old and New Testaments, in Greek, with some books which were not finally accepted as canonical; and, in spite of the recent discoveries of earlier papyrus copies of parts of some of the books, they remain the principal foundation of our modern texts of the Greek Bible. Of their textual character much will have to be said in later chapters. In appearance, as may be judged even from the reduced reproductions in Plates XV and XVII, they are extremely handsome volumes (especially the Sinaiticus), written in three or four columns to the page respectively, in capital letters separately formed. Subsequently an arrangement in two columns to the page was generally adopted as more convenient (see Plate XVI), and this style of writing, technically known as "uncial,"[1] continued in use until the tenth century.

Minuscules.

It was, however, a style more adapted for use at a lectern than for private reading; and in the ninth century a new style, known as "minuscule" or "cursive," was developed, which in a short time drove the more cumbrous uncial out of use. It was evolved from the style of writing then in use for non-literary purposes (as we now know from late documents on papyrus found in Egypt, containing accounts and other papers of the period after the Arab conquest of Egypt), and at its best it is an exceedingly beautiful form of script (see Plate XXI). In this script, in its various modifications, the Scriptures continued to be written until the invention of printing. Many such manuscripts are described below, for they form the main part of the materials for the history of the Bible text.

The Extant Manuscripts of the Bible.

The visitor to the British Museum may still see manuscripts which reproduce in external form the books of the Bible as they were first written. In one of the exhibition-cases he will see the great synagogue rolls of the Hebrew Scriptures, written on large and heavy skins, and wound round great wooden rollers, a weight too heavy to lift with comfort in the hand. Elsewhere he may see the copies for common use, written on ordinary vellum in the familiar book form. Among the earliest Greek manuscripts he will find delicate papyrus rolls, now spread out under glass for their protection, with their narrow columns of small writing, which may well represent that in which the Gospels and Epistles were first written down. In a special case he will see two of the earliest extant copies of the Greek Bible written in uncial letters upon fine vellum, the monument of a time when the Church was becoming prosperous under a Christian Empire, and now among the most valuable witnesses to the original text of the Bible that have been spared to us by the ravages of time. Elsewhere he will see copies written in the minuscule script which was the vehicle of literature throughout the later Middle Ages; and also copies of the translations of the Bible into other languages —Syriac, Coptic, Latin, and ultimately English. A new room, for the special display of manuscripts and printed copies of the Bible, has recently (1938) been added to the Manuscript Department of the Museum.

[1] This term is derived from a phrase of Jerome's, in which he mentions (and condemns) books extravagantly written "in what they call uncial letters." The word probably means "inch-high"; but it is now universally used for all writing in what we call capital letters.

CHAPTER II

VARIATIONS IN THE BIBLE TEXT

Various Readings.

WE now have to consider what happened to the text of ancient writings during the period when they were transmitted by hand-written copies; and in so doing we shall have to explain what is meant by the phrase "various readings," which recurs frequently in the discussion of the text of the Bible, or indeed of any ancient book. No one can read our English Revised Version intelligently without seeing that in very many places there is considerable doubt as to the exact words used by the original writers. On nearly every page, especially of the New Testament, we see notes in the margin to the effect that "Some ancient authorities read" this, or "Many ancient authorities read" that—these readings being alternatives to the readings actually adopted in the text of the Revisers. The question inevitably follows, What are these "ancient authorities"? How comes it that they differ so frequently among themselves? How do we, or how does anyone, know which to follow among these divergent witnesses?

The Variorum Bible.

The difficulties suggested by the various readings in the Revised Version are made more prominent if we look at such an edition as the Variorum Bible.[1] Here we find the several "ancient authorities" quoted separately whenever there is any important conflict of evidence as to the exact reading of any passage. Thus at Matt. xix. 17, to the words "Why callest thou Me good?" there is the following note: "*So* C Δ, *Pesh. Theb. Mcl.* R *marg.*; Why askest thou me concerning the good? א B D L, *Al. La. Ti. Tr. We. WH.* R." The meaning of this note

[1] This is, I believe, the only critical edition of the Bible in English. It gives a digest, under the head of "Various Renderings," of the translations or interpretations proposed by the best commentators in doubtful passages, and, under the head of "Various Readings," of the more important variations of the principal manuscripts, versions, and editions. The names of the editors (Professor Driver and Professor Cheyne of the Old Testament, Professor Sanday and the Rev. R. L. Clarke of the New Testament, and the Rev. C. J. Ball of the Apocrypha) are guarantees for the excellence of the work. The surest results of Biblical criticism, up to a recent date, are thus made accessible to English readers in a clear and compact form, and since the present book is intended primarily for those who study the Bible in English, reference will generally be made to the notes of the Variorum Bible, rather than to the critical editions of the Hebrew or Greek text.

is that there are two divergent readings recorded in this passage. The manuscripts known as C and Δ (which will be found described in Chapter VII), two ancient translations of the New Testament into Syriac and Coptic, the editor McClellan, and the margin of the Revised Version, read "Why callest thou Me good?" On the other hand, the four manuscripts א, B, D, L, the editors Alford, Lachmann, Tischendorf, Tregelles, Weiss, Westcott and Hort, and the text of the Revised Version, have "Why askest thou Me concerning the good?" To the student acquainted with these critical symbols, this information is intelligible and important; but unless we have some previous knowledge of the subject we shall not understand the comparative value of the various authorities quoted. The indispensable information is given in the preface and introduction to the Variorum Bible; but, although stated with admirable completeness and conciseness, it is necessarily brief, and it may occur to many to wish to know more about the authorities on which our knowledge of the Bible rests. It is all very well to say that such-and-such manuscripts support one reading of a passage, while other manuscripts support another; but we are no better able than before to judge which reading is to be preferred unless we know which manuscripts are most likely to be right. The questions asked above recur with doubled force: How do there come to be differences in different records of the Bible text, and how do we know which reading to prefer when the authorities differ?

Examples of Important Variations.

That these questions are not idle nor unimportant may be seen by mentioning a few of the passages in which important variations are found. We will take, for the moment, the Gospels alone. The Doxology of the Lord's Prayer is omitted in the oldest copies of Matt. vi. 13; several copies omit Matt. xvi. 2, 3 altogether; a long additional passage is sometimes found after Matt. xx. 28; the last twelve verses of St. Mark are omitted altogether by the two oldest copies of the original Greek; one very ancient authority inserts an additional incident after Luke vi. 4, while it alters the account of the institution of the Lord's Supper in Luke xxii. 19, 20, and omits altogether Peter's visit to the sepulchre in xxiv. 12, and several other details of the Resurrection; the version of the Lord's Prayer in Luke xi. 2-4 is much abbreviated in many copies; the incident of the Bloody Sweat is omitted in xxii. 43, 44, as also is the word from the Cross, "Father, forgive them," in xxiii. 34; the mention of the descent of an angel to cause the moving of the waters of Bethesda is entirely absent from the oldest copies of John v. 4, and all the best authorities omit the incident of the woman taken in adultery in vii. 53-viii. 11.

Besides the larger discrepancies, such as these, there is scarcely a verse in which there is not some variation of phrase in some copies.[1] No one can say that these additions or omissions or alterations are matters of mere indifference. It is true (and it cannot be too emphatically stated) that none of the fundamental truths of Christianity rests on passages of which the genuineness is doubtful; but it still remains a matter of concern to us to know that our Bible, as we have it to-day, represents as closely as may be the actual words used by the writers of the sacred books. It is the object of this volume to present, within a moderate compass and as clearly as possible, the means we have for knowing that it does so; to trace the history of the sacred texts from the time of their original composition to the present day; to show the authorities on which they rest, and the comparative value to be put upon each. It is the special duty of scholars to weigh the evidence on each particular disputed passage, and to form editions and translations of the sacred books; but any intelligent reader, without any knowledge of either Greek or Hebrew, can learn enough to understand the processes of criticism and the grounds on which the judgments of scholars must be based. Nor is the subject dry or uninteresting. The history of the Bible text has a living interest for all those who care for its contents; and no Englishman should be altogether ignorant of the history of the English Bible.

The Origin of Variations in the Text.

How then do various readings of a passage come into existence? It is a question easily answered, so soon as the character of ancient books is understood. Nowadays, when an author writes a book, he sends his manuscript or typescript to the printer, from whom he receives proof-sheets; he corrects the proof-sheets until he is satisfied that it is printed accurately; and then hundreds or thousands of copies, as the case may be, are struck off from the same types and distributed to the world. Each one of these copies is exactly like all the rest, and there can be no varieties of readings. All the extant copies of, say, any one edition of Macaulay's History or Tennyson's Poems are identical. Tennyson may have himself altered his own verses from time to time, and so have other authors; but no one doubts that in each edition of a modern book we have (slips of editor or printer excepted) exactly what the author intended at the time, and that each

[1] In Appendix I at the end of this volume will be found a selection of one hundred of the more important various readings in the Gospels and Acts, in which books such variations are most numerous. This will give the reader some idea of the issues involved, and an outline of the evidence relating to them.

copy of it is exactly like every other copy. But before the invention of printing this was far from being the case. Each separate copy of a book had to be written by hand; and the human hand and brain have not yet been created which could copy the whole of a long work absolutely without error. Often (and this we may easily believe to have been especially the case in the early days of the Christian Church, when it was a poor, half-educated, and persecuted body) copies were made hurriedly and without opportunity for minute revision. Mistakes were certain to creep in; and when once in existence they were certain to increase, as fresh copies were made from manuscripts already faulty. If the original manuscripts of the sacred books were still preserved, the errors of later copies would be to us now a matter of indifference; but since the original manuscripts perished long ago, we have to try to arrive at their contents by a comparison of later copies, all of which are more or less faulty and all varying from one another. This is the problem of textual criticism, and it will be seen that its sphere is large. Printing was invented about 1450, less than five centuries ago; but for all the centuries before that date, books existed only in hand-written copies, which we call manuscripts (from the Latin *manu-scriptum* = "written by hand," often abbreviated as "MS."). Of the chief of these manuscripts we shall have to speak at greater length in the course of this book. Meanwhile it will be clear that the existence of differences of reading in many passages of the Bible as we have it to-day is due to the mistakes made in copying them by hand during the many centuries that elapsed between the composition of the books and the invention of printing.

The Mistakes of Copyists.

1. *Errors of Hand and Eye.*—The mistakes of scribes are of many kinds and of varying importance. Sometimes the copyist confuses words of similar sound, as in English we sometimes find our correspondents write *there* for *their* or *here* for *hear*. Sometimes he passes over a word by accident; and this is especially likely to happen when two adjoining words end with the same letters. Sometimes this cause of error operates more widely. Two successive lines of the manuscript from which he is copying end with the same or similar words; and the copyist's eye slips from the first to the second, and the intermediate line is omitted. Sometimes a whole verse, or a longer passage, may be omitted owing to the identity of the first or last words with those of an adjoining passage. Sometimes, again, the manuscript from which he is copying has been furnished with short explanatory notes in the margin, and he fails to see where the text ends and the note begins, and so copies the note into the text itself.

2. *Errors of Mind.*—These are all simple errors of hand and eye. Errors of the mind are more dangerous, because they are less easy to detect. The copyist's mind wanders a little from the book he is copying, and he writes down words which come mechanically into his head, just as we do nowadays if people talk while we are writing and distract our attention. Some words are familiar in certain phrases, and the familiar phrase runs off the pen of the copyist when the word should be written in some other combination. A form of this error is very common in manuscripts of the Gospels. The same event is often narrated in two or more of them, in slightly different language; and the copyist, either consciously or unconsciously, alters the words of the one version to make them the same as those of the other. A careful reader of the Variorum Bible or the Revised Version will note many instances where this has happened. Thus in Matt. xi. 19 the Authorised Version has "But wisdom is justified of her children," as in Luke vii. 35; but the Revised Version tells us that the original text had "works" instead of "children" here, the truth being that the copyists of all except the earliest extant manuscripts have altered it, so as to make it correspond with the account in St. Luke. Similarly in Matt. xvi. 13, our Lord's question runs (in the R.V.) "Who do men say that the Son of Man is?" and the margin tells us that "Many ancient authorities read *that I, the Son of Man, am*; see Mark viii. 27, Luke ix. 18." In Matt. xxiii. 14 a whole verse has probably been inserted from the parallel passages in Mark and Luke; and so with Mark xv. 28. In Luke vi. 48 the concluding words of the parable of the house built on the rock, "because it had been well builded," have been altered in "many ancient authorities" in accordance with the more striking and familiar phrase in St. Matthew, "for it had been founded upon the rock." Errors like these increase in the later copies, as the words of the sacred narrative are more and more familiar to the copyists; and when once made they do not admit of correction, unless we are able to examine copies written before the corruption took place. They do not betray themselves by injuring the sense of the passage, as is generally the case with errors of the first class.

3. *Errors of Deliberate Alteration.*—An untrue hand or eye or an over-true memory may do much harm in a copyist; but worst and most dangerous of all is it when the copyist begins to think for himself. The veneration in which the sacred books were held has generally protected them against intentional alterations of the text, but not entirely so. The *harmonisation* of the Gospel narratives, described in the last paragraph, has certainly been in some cases intentional; and that, no doubt, without the smallest wish to deceive, but simply with the idea of supple-

menting the one narrative from its equally authentic companion. Sometimes the alterations are more extensive. The earliest Greek translation of the Old Testament contains several passages in the books of Esther and Daniel which are not found in the Hebrew. The long passages, Mark xvi. 9-20 and John vii. 53–viii. 11, which are absent from the oldest manuscripts of the New Testament, must have been either omitted in these or inserted in the others intentionally. If, as is more probably the case, they have been inserted in the later copies, this was no doubt done in order to supplement the Gospel from some other good source, and the narratives are almost certainly authentic, though they may not have been written by the Evangelist in whose Gospel they now appear. There is, however, no reason at all to suppose that additions of this kind have been made in any except a very few cases. The evidence for our Bible text is too great and of too varied a description to allow us to suppose that passages have been interpolated without any sign of it being visible. The intentional alterations of scribes are, for the most part, verbal, not substantial, such as the modifications of a phrase in one Evangelist to suit the narrative of another, or the combination of two reports of some utterance into one; and errors of this kind can generally be detected on a comparison of several different manuscripts, in some of which the alteration will not have been made.

Early Manuscripts the Most Likely to be Free from Error.

From this short account of the different classes of mistakes into which the copyists of manuscripts were most liable to fall, it will be clear that the later a manuscript is in date the more likely it is to contain many errors. Each time a fresh copy is made, some new mistakes will probably be introduced, while only the most obvious blunders in the manuscript copied will be corrected. It may therefore be stated as a general rule that the earlier a manuscript is the better is its text likely to be. The rule is only a general one, and is liable to exceptions; for instance, a manuscript written in the year 1200, if copied direct from a manuscript of the year 350, will probably be more correct than a manuscript written in the year 1000, which was copied from one written in 850 or 900. Each manuscript must therefore be searched, to see if it shows signs of containing an early form of the text; but the general rule that the earliest manuscripts are the best will still usually hold good.

The Method of Recovering the True Text.

The problem which lies before the textual critic, as the student of the language of the Bible is technically called, is now becoming clear. The original manuscripts of the Bible, written by the authors of the various books, have long ago disappeared. The critic's object, consequently, is to reconstruct the text of these original manuscripts by a comparison of the later copies which have come down to us; and the difficulty of his task depends on the age and number of these copies which he is able to compare. A diagram will make the position clear.

Here A represents the original author's copy of a book; *b* and *c* are copies made from it; *d, e, f, g* are copies made from *b* and *c*; and so on. Some errors are sure to be made in *b* and *c*, but not the same in each; *d* will correct a few of those in *b*, but will copy the rest and add more; *e* will both correct and copy different ones, and so will *f* and *g* and all the subsequent copies. So, as time goes on, the number of errors will go on increasing, and the extreme copies diverge from one another more and more. Sometimes a copyist will use two manuscripts to copy from (for instance, we may suppose the writer of *p* to have copied from *n* as well as from *h*), and then the errors of two different lines of descent will become mixed. At some stage in the history of the text perhaps some scholar will compare several copies, correct what he thinks are mistakes in them, and cause copies to be made of his corrected text; and then all manuscripts which are taken, directly or indirectly, from these corrected copies will bear the stamp of this revision, and will differ from those of which the line of descent is different. Now suppose all the manuscripts denoted by the letters in the diagram to have disappeared (and it must be remembered that by far the greater number of copies of any ancient book have perished long ago), except *p*, *l*, and *y*. It is evident that none of these copies will contain exactly the true text of A; each will have diverged from it, but each will have diverged differently. Some mistakes they may have in common, but in most they will differ; and wherever they differ it is the business of textual criticism to determine which manuscript has the true reading, and so to try to re-establish by comparison the original text of A.

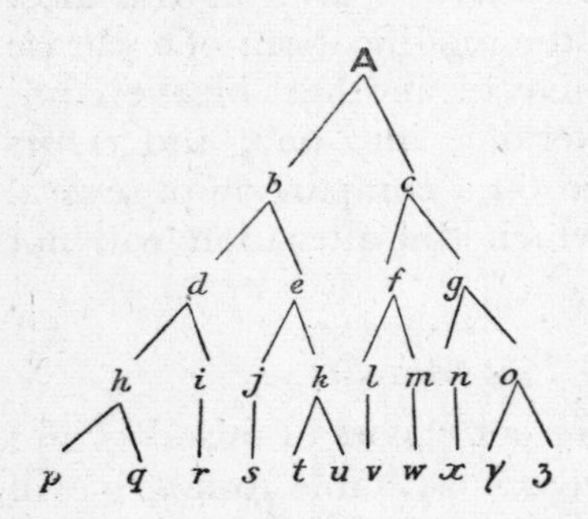

Such, but infinitely complicated by the number of manuscripts of the Bible which have come down to us, and by the long lapse of years since the originals were written, is the task of the scholars who try to restore to us the exact words of the sacred books. The object of the chapters which follow is to show in more detail the nature of the problem in respect to the Old

HEBREW MS.—9TH CENT.

(Original size, 16½ in. × 13 in.)

PLATE V.

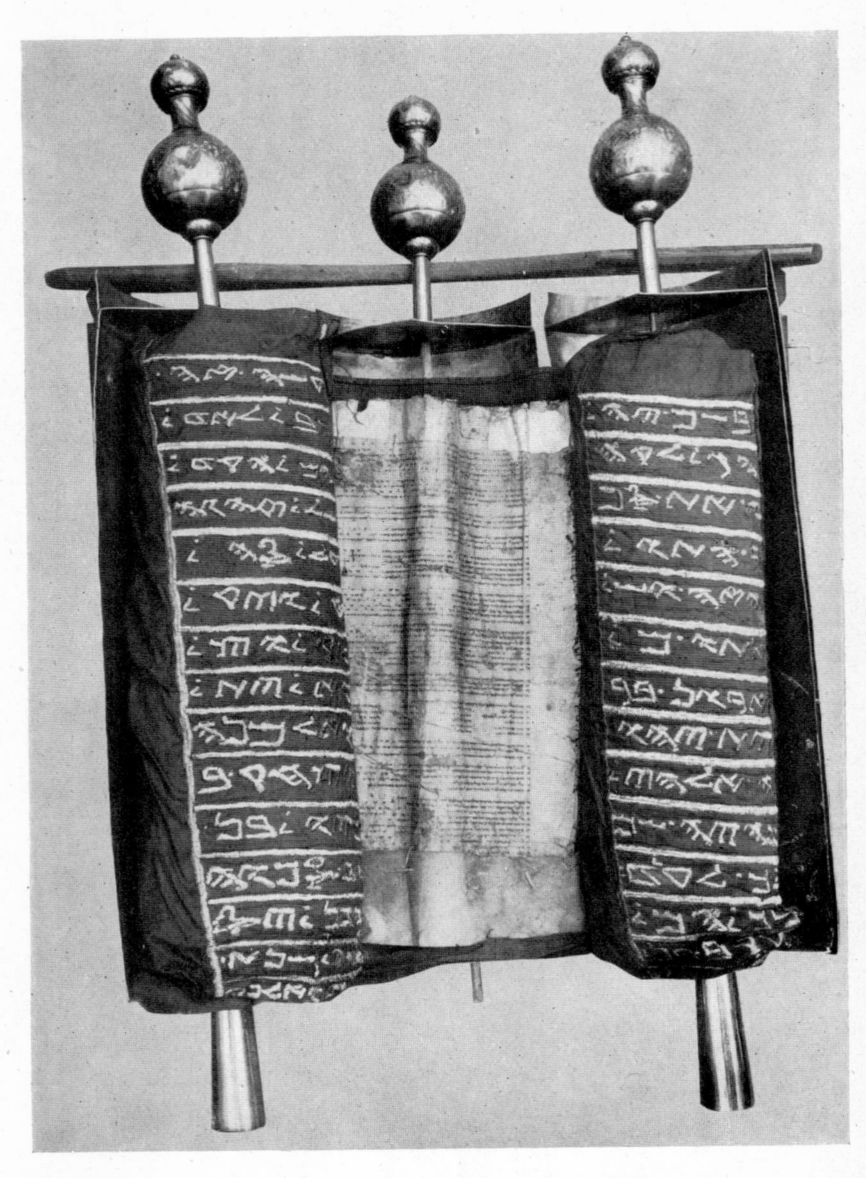

OLDEST SAMARITAN MS. FROM NABLUS.
(Original height, excluding rollers, about 19 in.)

Testament and New Testament respectively; to state what is known, or plausibly conjectured, concerning the history of their text; and to describe the principal manuscripts of each, and the other means available for the detection of mistakes and the restoration of the truth. The story is not so technical but that all may understand it, and all can appreciate the interest and value of the minutest study of the true Word of God.

Textual Errors do not Endanger Doctrine.

One word of warning, already referred to, must be emphasised in conclusion. No fundamental doctrine of the Christian faith rests on a disputed reading. Constant references to mistakes and divergences of reading, such as the plan of this book necessitates, might give rise to the doubt whether the substance, as well as the language, of the Bible is not open to question. It cannot be too strongly asserted that in substance the text of the Bible is certain. Especially is this the case with the New Testament.[1] The number of manuscripts of the New Testament, of early translations from it, and of quotations from it in the oldest writers of the Church, is so large that it is practically certain that the true reading of every doubtful passage is preserved in some one or other of these ancient authorities. This can be said of no other ancient book in the world. Scholars are satisfied that they possess substantially the true text of the principal Greek and Roman writers whose works have come down to us, of Sophocles, of Thucydides, of Cicero, of Virgil; yet our knowledge of their writings depends on a mere handful of manuscripts, whereas the manuscripts of the New Testament are counted by hundreds, and even thousands. In the case of the Old Testament we are not quite in such a good position, as will be shown presently. In some passages it seems certain that the true reading has not been preserved by any ancient authority, and we are driven to conjecture in order to supply it. But such passages are an infinitesimal portion of the whole and may be disregarded. The Christian can take the whole Bible in his hand and say without fear or hesitation that he holds in it the true Word of God, handed down without essential loss from generation to generation throughout the centuries.

[1] Dr. Hort, whose authority on the point is quite incontestable, estimates the proportion of words about which there is *some* doubt at about one-eighth of the whole; but by far the greater part of these consists merely of differences in order and other unimportant variations, and " the amount of what can in any sense be called substantial variation . . . can hardly form more than a thousandth part of the entire text " (Introduction to *The New Testament in the Original Greek*, p. 2).

CHAPTER III

THE AUTHORITIES FOR THE BIBLE TEXT

We have seen that the Bible has been preserved to us, for many centuries previous to the invention of printing, by means of copies written by hand; and we have seen that in such copies mistakes are certain to arise and multiply. Now if a scholar at this present day were to take in hand the task of correcting these mistakes and recovering the true text, how would he set about it? Of course, as a matter of fact, he would find that very much of the work had already been done for him by earlier scholars; but we will suppose that nothing has been done, and see how he must go to work. That will show us the way in which scholars for the last four centuries have laboured on the text of the Bible.

1. *Manuscripts.*

In the first place he will examine as many as possible of the manuscripts of the Bible in the original languages in which it was written, Hebrew and Greek. These are scattered about in all the great libraries of the world, and must be visited and carefully studied. He will note which are the oldest, he will use his judgment to determine which are the best. Where all the manuscripts are agreed, he has nothing more to do, and those parts of the text are put down at once as certain. Where there are differences between the manuscripts, he will have to decide which of the various readings is the more probable. In some cases the reading of a manuscript will be obviously wrong; in many it will be easy to see that the one reading is a perversion of the other—that the copyist has inadvertently dropped out a word or misread the word in the original from which he was copying, or has fallen into some other of the classes of error described in the preceding chapter. In this way a correct representation of the greater part of the text will be obtained. Still there will remain a considerable number of passages about which the manuscripts differ, but in which it is not possible to decide at once what reading is right. Then it will be necessary to discriminate between the manuscripts. Our scholar's earlier investigations will have shown him which manuscripts are generally trustworthy, and which are most full of mistakes. As a general rule he will prefer the reading which is supported by the oldest manuscripts, as being nearest to the time of the original work; and if all the oldest manuscripts are on one side, and all the later on the other, the reading of the former will certainly be adopted. Where the older manuscripts are divided, his task becomes harder; he has to consider whether either of the alternative readings is likely to have been derived from the other, or if one of them is more likely than the other to have been invented at a later time. For instance, there is a tendency among scribes, when they do not understand a phrase, to substitute one more easy of comprehension; and hence it is a rule of criticism that a harder reading is generally to be preferred to an easier one, since the latter is more likely to have been substituted for the former than *vice versa*. This rule must be applied with discretion, however, for the *unintentional* alterations of scribes will often produce a harder reading than the true one. Another principle is to try to classify the manuscripts in groups, those which habitually agree with one another being probably descended from some common ancestor; and a reading which is supported by two or more groups is more likely to be right than one which is supported by one only, even though that one may be a very large and numerous group. By the time our scholar has proceeded so far in his work, he will have formed a pretty confident opinion as to which manuscripts are the most worthy of trust; and then, when other methods fail to determine the true reading in a doubtful passage, he will be inclined to accept that reading which is supported by the manuscripts which he believes to be the best. He will, however, if he is wise, recognise that a margin of doubt remains. The best manuscript is not always right, and the balance of probability may be changed by the discovery of fresh evidence. The soundest scholar is not always the most dogmatic as to the certainty of his results.

2. *Versions.*

So far our scholar has confined himself entirely to the manuscripts of the sacred books in their original languages; but he will be making a great mistake if he stops there. He will remember that the Bible has been translated into many different languages, and he will bethink himself that a translation which has been made with any care and accuracy will generally show what was the Hebrew or Greek text which the translator had before him. Now several of the translations of the Bible—such as the Samaritan and Greek versions of the Old Testament, the Syriac and Latin versions of the New—were certainly made at a date much earlier than that at which any of the manuscripts which we now possess of the original Hebrew and Greek were written. The oldest manuscripts of the Greek New Testament now in existence (except one tiny fragment) can hardly be earlier than A.D. 200, and most of them are much later; but the earliest Syriac and Latin translations of the New Testament were made somewhere about A.D. 150. Hence, if we can gather from the existing copies of these translations what were the Greek words which their authors were translating, we know what was read in that particular passage in a Greek manuscript current about the year 150, when these translations were made; and this brings us back very near to the time when the originals of the New Testament books were themselves written. The versions are also valuable for telling us in what part of the world a particular type of text was current. As will be seen later, different types of text can be associated with different parts of the world—Syria, Egypt, Roman Africa, and so on; and the evidence for this is largely derived from the translations in these languages. It is true that we have not the original copies of the Latin and Syriac

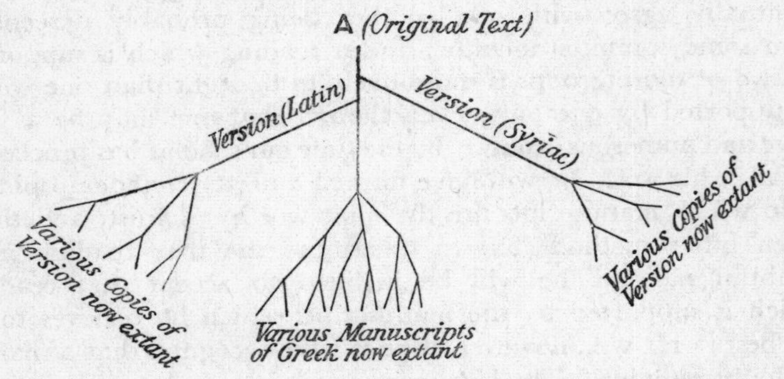

versions, any more than we have the originals of the Greek itself, and that a similar process of comparison of copies to that described in the last paragraph must be gone through if we are to discover the original readings of the translations; but in many cases this can be done with certainty, and then we have a very early testimony indeed to the original Greek text. We talk sometimes of the " stream of tradition " by which the text of the Bible has been borne down to us from the fountain-head in the original manuscripts; well, the service of the Versions (as the translations of the Bible into other languages are technically called) is that they tap the stream near the fountain-head. They are unaffected by any corruptions that may have crept into the Greek text *after* the translations were made; they may have corruptions of their own, but they will not generally be the same as the corruptions in the Greek text, and they will serve mutually to correct one another. To alter the comparison, we get several groups of evidence converging on the same spot, as the above diagram shows.

3. *The Early Fathers.*

Our scholar has yet one other source to which he may turn for evidence as to the original text—namely, the quotations of isolated passages in the writings of the early Fathers. Many of the first Christian writers whose works have been preserved—for instance, Irenæus, Origen, Athanasius, Jerome—must have used manuscripts of the Bible older than any that we now have, and many of them quoted largely from the Bible in their writings. If, therefore, we know in what form they quoted any particular passage, we may argue that they found that form of it in the manuscript which they used. But this argument must be used with much caution. In the first place, it is evident that they often quoted from memory. Copies of the Bible were not so common in those days as they are now, and, in the absence of the modern division into chapters and verses, it was less easy to turn up a passage when required to verify a quotation. A curious proof of the liability to error in quotations from memory is furnished by a modern divine. It is said that Jeremy Taylor quotes the well-known text, "Except a man be born again he cannot see the kingdom of God," no less than nine times, yet only twice in the same form, and in no single instance correctly. We must not assume that the ancient Fathers were infallible in their memories. Further, it is often difficult to be certain that we have the quotations as the Fathers themselves wrote them. If a scribe who was copying a manuscript of one of the early Fathers found a text quoted in a form unfamiliar to him, he would be not unlikely to alter it into the form then current. For these reasons it is dangerous to base an argument for a reading on the Fathers alone, except when the context in which it is found shows conclusively in what form the writer quoted it; but to confirm other evidence they may often be of very great value. They also contribute to show at what time and in what country particular readings or types of text were current. They will be of still more value when their own texts have themselves been critically edited, which is at present far from being the case with all of them.

Manuscripts, Versions, Fathers—such are the resources of our scholar in his task of recovering the true text of the Bible. Of the third of these we cannot speak at length within the compass of this book, though reference will occasionally be made to it; but in the history of the two first is the history of the Bible text. Our object will be to describe, first the principal manuscripts, and then the chief translations, of each Testament in turn, and so to carry down the history of the Bible from the earliest times to our own days—to show how our own English Bible is the lineal descendant of the volumes once written by Prophet, Apostle, and Evangelist.

CHAPTER IV

THE HEBREW OLD TESTAMENT

THE history of the Hebrew Old Testament falls into two parts, divided by the great national catastrophe of the destruction of Jerusalem. In the earlier part the history of the text is closely bound up with the history of the Canon—the history, that is, of how and when the several books came into existence, and how and when they were accepted by the Hebrews as the authoritative sacred books of their faith.

The Responsibility of Critical Examination.

The consideration of these questions is made more difficult and delicate because of beliefs and misconceptions which have at certain times and among many people assumed almost the character of dogmas of faith. The Bible is so intertwined with our inmost religion, is so rightly regarded as the immutable basis of our faith, that to many people it is hard to admit that any doubt can be allowed to attach to either the form or the substance of any of its statements. But this is to make an assumption with regard to God's methods which is not warranted by what we see of His methods elsewhere. Doubtless He might have imposed the true doctrines of religion on mankind in such a manner that no possible opening could have been left for doubt. He might have made it impossible for man to sin. He might have solved the mystery of pain. But that has not been His method. He has left to man the privilege of free will, and has imposed on him the responsibility of thought, of examination, of faith. There is therefore nothing that need disturb or unsettle us in the idea that He has also imposed on us the responsibility of using the intellectual faculties with which He has endowed us in the study of the records in which the history of the chosen Hebrew people and of the foundation of the Christian Church have come down to us. These intellectual faculties may lead us astray, just as we may go astray in far more important matters of faith and conduct; but it is a poor faith which does not believe that the Holy Spirit will, if we trust Him, ultimately lead us to the truth. It is incredible, to anyone who believes in God, that there should be an irreparable discrepancy between the truth and the results to which we can attain by the exercise of those faculties which God has given to us, and which He has imposed on us the responsibility of using.

This is not to say that every result which every new critic proclaims is to be accepted forthwith as truth. It is only to say that it is not to be condemned forthwith without examination because it offends our present opinions and beliefs. The history of Biblical criticism, as of the criticism of all ancient history and literature, is full of erroneous views, confidently proclaimed, eagerly accepted by those who wish to appear in the vanguard of advance, and then disproved or allowed gradually to sink into obscurity. The way to counter the results of research which are distasteful to us is more research; and it is surely a healthier faith to believe that truth is great and will prevail than to hide one's head, ostrich-like, in the sand.

The Principle of Free Inquiry.

This insistence on a stereotyped form of faith which must not be questioned is a relatively late development. It was not the attitude of the Fathers of the Christian Church. They readily admitted that there were doubts about the authorship of certain books. They knew, only too well, that there were differences of opinion about articles of faith, and were not disturbed by obscurities as to the history of the Hebrew people. We do not always accept their interpretations of doubtful passages, or their reading of the history of the past; but we can follow their acceptance of the principle of free inquiry, and can hope that with fuller knowledge we may gradually come nearer to the truth.

In these pages, therefore, an attempt will be made to set out the results which modern criticism is at present disposed to accept with regard to the history of the books composing our Bible; fully recognising that many of these results are still uncertain, but also deriving satisfaction from the belief, of which proofs will be given in the following pages, that the tendency of modern research has been, again and again, to confirm the substantial integrity and trustworthiness of the Bible record.

"Higher Criticism."

It seems advisable at this point to utter a warning against the misuse which is frequently made of the phrase "Higher Criticism," as if it implied an attitude of disbelief in the authenticity of the Bible. This is a complete misunderstanding of the real meaning of the words. "Higher Criticism" is criticism applied to the substance or contents of a book, while "Lower Criticism" is criticism applied to its form or text. And criticism is not necessarily hostile criticism. It is merely examination or judgment. It is just as much "Higher Criticism" to argue that

Moses personally wrote all the books of the Pentateuch as it is to maintain that they are of late date and consequently untrustworthy. The question of importance is not whether the criticism is "higher," but whether it is sound; and that is a question of evidence and argument, not of *a priori* assumptions or of impeaching the motives of those whose views we find unpalatable or consider to be unsound.

True History not necessarily Contemporary.

It seems sometimes to be thought that the credibility of the Old Testament history depends on the books in their present form being contemporary with the events that they describe. A little reflection will show that this is contrary to experience. For the most trustworthy histories of the reigns of Elizabeth or Charles I, and still more for those of Alfred or William the Conqueror, we do not look to the contemporary chroniclers, but to the modern historian. It is of course necessary for a satisfactory history that good contemporary evidence should be available, but this evidence can generally be best handled by a later writer, who is in a position to collate materials from several quarters, and to combine the evidence of different writers. So long as it was maintained that writing was unknown in the time of Moses and Joshua, and even in that of David, there was ground for questioning the trustworthiness of the narratives of the early history of the Hebrew people; but now that archæology has shown that writing was well known and commonly used from times far earlier than that of Abraham, we are free to examine the materials and structure of the historical books in the light of the ordinary principles of historical and literary criticism, without feeling that we are in the least impugning their general reliability.

Historical Books of O.T. Based on Earlier Material.

It is to be observed that there is nothing in the books themselves inconsistent with this way of looking at them. The books of the Pentateuch do not claim Moses as their author; they may be referred to in later times as "the books of Moses," but that is because four out of the five are books about him. His words or actions may be quoted from them, without implying that he himself recorded them. That older materials underlay them appears, for instance, in the reference to the book of the Wars of the Lord (Num. xxi. 14). The later historical books also repeatedly refer to the materials out of which they have been constructed: the book of Jasher, the book of the acts of Solomon, the book of the chronicles of the kings of Israel, or of Judah, and so on. They are avowedly works composed by a later writer or writers, based upon such materials as were available.

Composite Materials of O.T. Books.

This *a priori* probability is confirmed by the literary examination of the books themselves. This reveals to a Hebrew scholar differences in language and style, which are concealed from the English reader by the uniformity of the English translation. He can, however, easily understand it if he imagines what a history of England would be like which was compounded of extracts from Holinshed, Clarendon, Hume, Macaulay, Green and Trevelyan. The several elements would reveal themselves by the difference of their style and language. And this method of compiling history by putting together sections from different sources can be paralleled from our own medieval chroniclers. Their general practice was, not to rewrite the history of a past period in their own words, as a modern historian would do, but to take over whole slabs from an earlier chronicler, with insertions from other sources or of their own. Thus Matthew Paris, the great St. Albans historian of the thirteenth century, in his *Greater Chronicles* took over (with additions and corrections) the work of his predecessor Roger of Wendover, who himself adopted the chronicle of Abbot John de Cella, which was itself compiled from the Bible and various early historians and romancers. Similarly Roger of Hoveden wrote a history of England from 731 to 1201 which has been thus described:

"For the part from 731 to 1148 he simply copied an earlier chronicle, written at Durham, which was itself compounded from the histories of Simeon of Durham and Henry of Huntingdon; while, to go still further back, Simeon's history was largely derived from Florence of Worcester and an early Northumbrian chronicle. From 1148 to 1169 Hoveden's narrative appears to be original, though partly based on the Chronicle of the Abbey of Melrose and the lives and letters of Becket. From 1170 to 1192 his work is merely a revision of the chronicle assigned to Benedict of Peterborough. Finally from 1192 to 1201 he is an original and independent witness."

Dates of Final Composition.

This analysis of the methods of the medieval chroniclers of England may help us to understand the methods of the chroniclers of Judah and Israel, and may satisfy us that there is nothing unnatural or unreasonable in the differences which Hebrew scholars discern in the strata of which the historical books of the Old Testament are, according to their analysis, composed. When they were finally put together in their present form may never be definitely known, and it is not necessary to suppose that modern scholarship has yet said its last word. The Jews themselves attributed the definite fixing of the Canon of the Law to

Ezra, who promulgated it at the great assembly of the people recorded in Nehemiah (chapter viii.); but of course that does not mean that the books themselves were not of earlier date. The book of Deuteronomy is generally believed to be (at any rate in its main substance) the book found in the Temple by Hilkiah the high priest in the time of Josiah (2 Kings xxii. 8). Its discovery at this time (621 B.C.) was evidently a complete surprise, and the book itself may have been composed a century or so earlier, perhaps in the time of the early prophets. The earlier strata in the other books of the Pentateuch are variously assigned by scholars to dates between 900 and 750, with full recognition of the fact that they rest on materials of earlier date. The later (the so-called "priestly") elements, and the final redaction of the whole, are attributed to the time of Ezra (about 400 B.C.), or by some even later. There is still great divergence in the views of scholars, and none can claim decisive authority.

Of the other historical books, Joshua has strata similar to those of the Pentateuch. The books of Judges, Samuel and Kings are evidently and avowedly compiled from a large variety of materials of different dates, put together after the fall of the monarchy. Chronicles, Ezra and Nehemiah all hang together, and are of the fourth century. Job may be of the same date, but there is little evidence, and opinions vary greatly. The Psalms and Proverbs are composed of several collections, ranging from the eighth to the third, or possibly the second century. Esther, Ecclesiastes, Song of Solomon, and Daniel are the latest books of the Old Testament. The Prophets range from Amos, Hosea, Micah and Isaiah, in the eighth century, to Joel and Jonah, probably in the fourth; but in all cases there may be later additions or editorial revisions. On this point there is infinite scope for the ingenuity of scholars. Some are never tired of subdividing, and see the hands of editors everywhere. Some seem to have very little sense of the way in which it is reasonable to suppose that books were written and circulated.

Arrangement of the Books of the O.T.

We have therefore in the Old Testament a collection of books, the materials of which go back to an indefinite antiquity, and which were put together in their present forms, or approximately in their present forms, at various times between the ninth and the second centuries. The process of their adoption as having canonical authority appears to be indicated by the classification which the Jews themselves made of them. This classification is into three groups, known as the Law, the Prophets, and the Hagiographa, or sacred writings. The Law included the five books of Moses, which we now call the Pentateuch. The

Prophets comprised the historical books of Joshua, Judges, 1 and 2 Samuel, 1 and 2 Kings (these four being a continuous work, known as the four books of " Kingdoms " or " Reigns "),[1] which were known as " the Former Prophets "; and Isaiah, Jeremiah, Ezekiel, and the twelve Minor Prophets, known as " the Later Prophets." The Hagiographa consisted of the Psalms, Proverbs, Job, Song of Solomon, Ruth, Lamentations, Ecclesiastes, Daniel, Esther, 1 and 2 Chronicles, Ezra and Nehemiah. The origin of this classification and of the inclusion of several historical and prophetic books among the Hagiographa is unknown; but it almost certainly implies that those books were written later, and were among the last to be recognised as inspired. Divisions of the books themselves into reading-lessons, paragraphs, and verses (very nearly corresponding to our modern verses) were made in very early times; but they are not of much importance to us here. They are indicated in the manuscripts by blank spaces of greater or lesser size.

Its Stages.

1. *The Law.*—It seems tolerably certain that the three divisions of the books of the Old Testament, just mentioned, represent three stages in the process known as the formation of the Hebrew Canon of Scripture. Whenever the books of the Pentateuch were written, it is at least certain that they, constituting the Law, were the first group of writings to be thus accepted. In the days of the kings it was possible for the " book of the Law " (perhaps meaning our Deuteronomy) to be lost and forgotten, and to be recovered as it were by accident (2 Kings xxii. 8); but the Captivity taught the Jews to be careful of their Scriptures, and the Canon of the Law may be taken as fixed about the time of the return from exile, possibly under the guidance of Ezra, to whom Jewish tradition assigned a special prominence in the work of collecting the sacred books.[2] From this time forth the five books of Moses, as they were commonly called, were regarded as a thing

[1] The sequence of nomenclature appears to be as follows. These books originally formed a continuous work in two books, to the first of which the title of " Samuel " is given in Hebrew MSS., although Samuel himself disappears before the middle of it. The Septuagint divided it into four books (presumably to suit the length of a normal papyrus roll), with the title of 1-4 Kingdoms. Jerome followed the Septuagint division, only substituting " Kings " for " Kingdoms." The Hebrew printed Bibles, from 1517 onwards, also adopted the division into four books, but restored the title " Samuel " to the first two. The English translators accepted this, together with Jerome's " Kings " for " Kingdoms " in the second pair.

[2] The Jews themselves attributed the formation of the whole Canon to Ezra, with the help of elders composing a body known as " The Great Synagogue "; but it has been shown that this body is an imaginary one, and it is now generally recognised that the formation of the Canon must have been gradual, following the stages here indicated.

apart. They were sacred; and by degrees the greatest care came to be devoted to copying them with perfect accuracy and studying minutely every word that they contained. There is reason to suppose that this extreme accuracy was not at first required or obtained; but in the time of our Lord it is clear that the text of the Law was held in the utmost veneration, and the class of the "scribes," whose special duty was to copy the sacred books, was fully established and held in considerable esteem.

2. *The Prophets.*—The second group of books to obtain recognition as inspired, and to be adopted into the Canon, was that of the Prophets. This must have taken place between the date of Malachi, the last of the Prophets, about 430 B.C.,[1] and the reference to "the twelve prophets" in Ecclus. xlix. 10, written about 180 B.C.; but the date cannot be fixed precisely.

3. *The Hagiographa.*—The remaining group, known as the Hagiographa, is of a miscellaneous character, and for some time the books composing it evidently circulated on much the same footing as other books which were eventually excluded from the Canon, such as Judith, Tobit, and Ecclesiasticus.

It is certain that this was the case among the Greek-speaking Jews at Alexandria, for in the Septuagint translation made for them (see p. 54 below) the books which now constitute our Apocrypha appear intermingled among the canonical books. It would not appear, however, that they enjoyed the same acceptation elsewhere; for it is noticeable that while there are many quotations in the New Testament from each of the three divisions of the Old, there is not a single direct quotation from the Apocrypha. A similar distinction is found in Josephus and Philo.

The Synod of Jamnia.

A decisive point in the history of both the Canon and the text of the Old Testament seems to have been reached about the end of the first century of the Christian era. Throughout the period of the wars of the Maccabees, there may well have been little time to spare for the labours of scholarship;[2] but with the return

[1] Modern criticism would place Joel and Jonah later than this, and holds that a good deal of editorial work which gave the books their present form was done on some of the other prophets in the fourth century or later.

[2] In the description of the persecution of Antiochus in 1 Macc. i. 56, 57, it is said: "And they rent in pieces the books of the law which they found, and set them on fire. And wheresoever was found with any a book of the Covenant, and if any consented to the law, the king's sentence delivered him to death." But in 2 Macc. ii. 13, 14, after a reference to "the public archives and the records that concern Nehemiah, and how he, founding a library, gathered together the books about the kings and prophets, and the books of David, and letters of kings about sacred gifts," it is added: "And in like manner Judas also gathered together for us all those writings that had been scattered by reason of the war that befell, and they are still with us."

of peace came greater attention to study, and in the famous schools of Hillel and Shammai, about the beginning of the Christian era, we may find the origin of the long line of rabbis and scribes to whom is due the fixing of the Hebrew canon and text as we now have them. The destruction of Jerusalem in A.D. 70, and the annihilation of Judæa as a nation, compelled the Jews to find their centre in their sacred books; and somewhere between A.D. 90 and 100 a synod is recorded to have been held at Jamnia (near Jaffa), at which certain disputed questions with regard to the acceptability of some of the books were decided. It is from this point that we may regard both the Canon and the text of the Hebrew Scriptures as having been definitely fixed. The books accepted as canonical were those which now appear in our Old Testament; and there is good reason to think (as will appear below) that the text has suffered no material alteration since that date. The two great centres of Jewish scholarship were Palestine and Babylonia, the former having its headquarters successively at Jamnia and Tiberias, the latter in Babylon, where a Jewish colony had remained since the days of the Exile. It is from the records of these schools, each of which preserved to some extent distinct traditions of text and interpretation, that we derive our earliest direct knowledge of the Hebrew text as it existed among the Jews themselves. Indirect evidence for an earlier time may be derived, as we shall see, from the Samaritan and Greek translations which have come down to us from the pre-Christian period; but in the present chapter we are concerned with the Hebrew text alone.

History of the Hebrew Text.

1. *The Targums.*—The earliest direct evidence which we possess as to the text current among the Jews themselves is that provided by the TARGUMS, or paraphrases of the Scriptures into the Aramaic dialect. After their return from the Captivity the Jews gradually adopted this language (a tongue closely related to Hebrew, being a kindred branch of the same Semitic family of speech, sometimes called, as in the margins of our Bible, Chaldee); and it became thenceforth the current language of ordinary life. Thus, it may be remarked by the way, it was the language commonly spoken in Judæa at the time of our Lord's life on earth. Meanwhile the ancient Hebrew remained as the language in which the sacred books were written, being studied and preserved by the educated and literary class among the Jews, but becoming continually less familiar to the common folk. Hence arose the necessity of paraphrasing the Scriptures into the current Aramaic tongue. At first these paraphrases were simply given by word of mouth, as in the scene described in Neh. viii. 1-8, when Ezra

read the book of the Law before the people, "and Jeshua and Bani and Sherebiah . . . the Levites, caused the people to understand the Law"; but subsequently the method of interpretation was reduced to a system, and written down, and this practically became the popular Bible of the Jewish nation. These written paraphrases are known as "Targums," the word itself probably meaning "paraphrase." In the form in which we now have them, they probably represent accumulated layers of tradition, going back to a time before the foundation of Christianity, of which they show no knowledge; but they did not reach their present shape until a much later date. The Palestinian and Babylonian schools possessed distinct Targums of their own. The best of those that have come down to us is the Babylonian Targum on the Pentateuch, which is ascribed to a writer named Onkelos (and hence is cited in the Variorum Bible as *Onk.*). The date of this is rather uncertain. Onkelos is sometimes identified with Aquila, the author of a very literal translation of the Old Testament into Greek (see p. 56), who lived in the second century after Christ; but the best opinion seems to be that this Targum was produced in its present shape about the third century, on the basis of an earlier paraphrase. It is a very simple and literal translation of the Pentateuch, and is for that reason the more useful as evidence for the Hebrew text from which it was taken. Of the other Targums (cited collectively as *Targ.* in the Variorum Bible) much the best is that which bears the name of Jonathan ben Uzziel, on the Prophets (using that term in its technical sense, see p. 33). It was written about the fourth century, and is somewhat more free than that of Onkelos. There is also a Palestinian Targum on the Law which is ascribed, but falsely, to this same Jonathan (hence cited as *Ps.-Jon.*); but this, which was probably not written till the seventh century, and all the other Targums are of small critical value compared with those of Onkelos and Jonathan. It is not always possible to use the Targums as evidence for the Hebrew text of the sacred books on which they are based, since they at times paraphrase freely, inserting explanations, moderating strong expressions, and otherwise introducing alterations. It is, however, clear that the Hebrew text from which they are made (that is, the text current in Judæa about the end of the first century B.C., to which their tradition reaches back) was not identical with that which has come down to us. The student of the Variorum Bible will find many passages in which they are quoted as differing from the received text, sometimes for the better—*e.g.*, Deut. xxxiii. 13; Josh. ix. 4; Judg. v. 30; 2 Sam. xviii. 13; 1 Kings xiii. 12; Ps. c. 3; Isa. xlix. 5; etc. They have this advantage at least over most of the other versions, that whenever we can be sure of the Hebrew text which they represent we know that it was a text accepted by the leaders of criticism among the Jews themselves.

2. *The Talmud.*—The period of the Targums is overlapped by that of the TALMUD. While the Targumists paraphrased the Hebrew text, the scholars known as the Talmudists explained and commented on it. The fact that in ancient Hebrew writing the vowels were entirely omitted led, as explained below, to the occurrence of many words and phrases in which a different sense could be obtained according as different vowels were supplied. Hence plenty of scope was left to the ingenuity of the Talmudists, who gradually accumulated a mass of tradition concerning the proper reading and explanation of the text. It does not appear that they themselves did much towards fixing the actual text which appears in the manuscripts. On the contrary, even in the earliest among the writings of the Talmud, the quotations from Scripture generally agree with our received text; the existence of a settled text of the Scriptures seems to be implied, and the most minute rules are laid down to ensure the faithful copying of this text by the scribes. The Talmudist scholars did not by any means confine their attention to textual matters; on the contrary, the Talmud contains the essence of many generations of traditional commentary of all kinds on the sacred books, concentrated and approved by the judgment of the leading scholars of the period.

3. *The Massoretes.*—The Talmudist period extends from about A.D. 270 to 500, and is succeeded by that of the MASSORETES. This is the final and decisive stage in the history of the Hebrew text. From about the beginning of the seventh century the scholars whom we now call the Massoretes set themselves to sift out from the mass of the Talmud the traditions which bore on the actual text of the sacred books. Hitherto, although the Talmudists had accumulated a great quantity of tradition concerning the correct vowel-punctuation of the Hebrew, the vowel-points had not been introduced into the manuscripts in use, and the textual traditions of the Talmudists were not separated from the exegetical or explanatory. The work of the Massoretes was to edit the Old Testament books in accordance with the traditions preserved in the Talmud. The headquarters of the school of Jewish doctors which undertook this labour was at Tiberias; but it was not the work of a single generation or of a single place. The text was provided with points to indicate the vowels; and this in itself went far towards fixing the interpretation of doubtful passages. In addition, the body of traditional remarks handed down from previous generations was recorded, so far as it related to strictly textual matters, with additions by the Massoretes

themselves, and the whole of this textual commentary received the name of the "Massorah," which means "tradition." So far were the Massoretes from introducing alterations into the actual text of the sacred books, that, even where the traditional text was plainly wrong, they confined themselves to stating in the margin the reading which they held to be superior. Such variations were known by the names of Kri ("read") and Kthib ("written"), the latter being the reading of the text, the former that of the margin, which was to be substituted for the other when the passage was read. The Massorah is generally found in manuscripts in the margins of the pages, surrounding the text; and according as it is given in a fuller or a more abbreviated form it is called the Greater or the Lesser Massorah. Sometimes both are found together. Thus in our illustration of a Hebrew MS. (Plate IV) the Lesser Massorah is written in the margins to the left of the columns, and the Greater Massorah at the top and bottom of the page.

Besides recording varieties of reading, tradition, or conjecture, the Massoretes undertook a number of calculations which do not enter into the ordinary sphere of textual criticism. They numbered the verses, words, and letters of every book. They calculated the middle word and the middle letter of each. They enumerated verses which contained all the letters of the alphabet, or a certain number of them; and so on. These trivialities, as we may rightly consider them, had yet the effect of securing minute attention to the precise transmission of the text; and they are but an excessive manifestation of a respect for the sacred Scriptures which in itself deserves nothing but praise. The Massoretes were indeed anxious that not one jot nor tittle—not one smallest letter nor one tiny part of a letter—of the Law should pass away or be lost.

The Extant Hebrew Text entirely Massoretic.

The importance of the Massoretic edition to us lies in the fact that it is still the standard text of the Hebrew Bible. *All the extant manuscripts of the Hebrew Old Testament contain substantially a Massoretic text.*

The Copying of Hebrew Manuscripts.

When once that revision was completed, such precautions were taken to secure its preservation, to the exclusion of any other form of text, as to make it certain that the text has been handed down to us, not indeed without any errors or variations, but without essential corruption. Extraordinary care was taken to secure perfect accuracy in the transcription of the sacred books. Especially was this the case with the *synagogue rolls*, or copies of the Pentateuch intended for use in the synagogues. These were written on skins, fastened together so as to form a roll, never in modern book form. Minute regulations are laid down in the Talmud for their preparation. "A synagogue roll must be written on the skins of clean animals, prepared for the particular use of the synagogue by a Jew. These must be fastened together with strings taken from clean animals. Every skin must contain a certain number of columns, equal throughout the entire codex.[1] The length of each column must not extend over less than forty-eight, or more than sixty lines; and the breadth must consist of thirty letters. The whole copy must be first lined; and if three words be written in it without a line, it is worthless. The ink should be black, neither red, green, nor any other colour, and be prepared according to a definite receipt. An *authentic* copy must be the exemplar, from which the transcriber ought not in the least to deviate. No word or letter, not even a *yod*, must be written from memory, the scribe not having looked at the codex before him. . . . Between every consonant the space of a hair or thread must intervene; between every word the breadth of a narrow consonant; between every new *parshiah*, or section, the breadth of nine consonants; between every book, three lines. The fifth book of Moses must terminate exactly with a line; but the rest need not do so. Besides this, the copyist must sit in full Jewish dress, wash his whole body, not begin to write the name of God with a pen newly dipped in ink, and should a king address him while writing that name he must take no notice of him. . . . The rolls in which these regulations are not observed are condemned to be buried in the ground or burned; or they are banished to the schools, to be used as reading-books."[2]

Private or common copies were not subject to such precise regulations. They are written in book form, sometimes on vellum, sometimes on paper. Inks of various colours are used, and the size of the columns is not necessarily uniform. The Hebrew text is often accompanied by an Aramaic paraphrase, arranged either in a parallel column or between the lines of the Hebrew. In the upper and lower margins (generally speaking) the Great Massorah may be written; in the external side margins are notes, comments, corrections, and indications of the divisions of the text; between the columns is the Lesser Massorah. Vowel-points and accents, which are forbidden in synagogue rolls, are generally inserted in private copies; but they were always written separately, after the consonant text had been finished.

[1] "Codex" is a Latin word, meaning properly a manuscript arranged in modern book form (see p. 13). It is, however, often used simply as equivalent to "manuscript" generally, and especially of manuscripts of the Bible.

[2] Davidson, *Introduction to the Old Testament*, 1856, p. 89.

It is under conditions such as these that the Massoretic text has been handed down, from manuscript to manuscript, until the invention of printing. Now what of the actual manuscripts which are still in existence? What will the student see when he opens one of the old Hebrew volumes in one of our great libraries, and what will it tell him concerning the text which it contains?

In the first place he will see the page covered with characters which to most people are quite unfamiliar. It is writing such as that represented in Plate IV. The letters are generally of a square shape, and underneath them are little dots and strokes. The writing is usually arranged in columns, two or more going to the page if the manuscript is in book form; and the margins are filled with other writing of similar appearance. What, now, is the meaning of this? What is the history of the Hebrew writing?

The Hebrew Characters.

The characters in which modern Hebrew manuscripts are written are not the same as those which were in use when the books of the Hebrew Scriptures were composed, and to which reference was made above, when dealing with the origins of writing (p. 6). In the time of the Jewish kingdom, Hebrew was written in characters which were common to the Hebrews themselves, the Samaritans, and the Phœnicians; and these characters, having been preserved by the Samaritans when the Jews abandoned them, are known to us in the manuscripts of the Samaritan Pentateuch (see Plate V). As explained above, the origins of this writing can now, as the result of recent discoveries, be traced back to the inscriptions in the Sinai peninsula, of about 2000 B.C., and it is found approaching its recognised ancient form in the Lachish inscriptions of about 1300 B.C., and on the tomb of Ahiram at Byblos about 1200 B.C. Then come the famous Moabite Stone of about 890 B.C., and the Siloam Inscription (about B.C. 700), carved on the conduit leading to the Pool of Siloam in Jerusalem. After this date it appears on coins and later inscriptions, and, as just stated, in MSS. of the Samaritan Pentateuch. The Jewish story of the origin of the "square" writing, as the later Hebrew characters are called, is that Ezra brought it back with him from Babylon, and that it was forthwith adopted for general use. This is only an instance of the common habit of tradition, to assign to a single man and a single moment a change which must have been spread over several generations. The contemporary coins and inscriptions enable us to trace the process, though imperfectly. In the first place, the old stiff Hebrew characters were gradually modified, after the Exile, so as to make them more *cursive*—more easily written, that is, in running hand; a change partly due to the example of the contemporary Aramaic writing in Syria and Arabia. Then, by way of reaction from this, and with the intention, no doubt, of making the writing of the sacred books more beautiful, the square characters were developed, and were thenceforth adopted as the essential form for the manuscripts of the Scriptures. A similar phenomenon is seen in the case of the Greek Bible, where we find the handsomest uncial writing springing up, in the fourth century, for use in great copies of the Bible in the midst of a very debased and unornamental style of cursive characters, of which many examples have come down to us on papyrus. In the case of the Hebrew writing, the change must have taken place before the time of our Lord, for the proverbial use of "jot" (=*yod*, the tenth letter in the Hebrew alphabet) to indicate a very small object (as in Matt. v. 18) would only be possible after the adoption of the square characters, since in the earlier alphabet *yod* was by no means the smallest letter.

The Hebrew Language.

The *language* in which the manuscripts we are examining are written is, of course, Hebrew, a branch of the great Semitic family of languages, which includes the Babylonian, Assyrian, Chaldæan, Phœnician, and other tongues spoken in Western Asia. It was the spoken language of Palestine down to the time of the Exile; and even after that date, when Aramaic was adopted for ordinary use, Hebrew remained the literary language of the educated Jews. It is written from right to left, not from left to right as in our modern European books. But the special peculiarity of it is that in its original state *only the consonants were written*, the vowels being left to be filled up by the reader's mind. In the Hebrew manuscript which we have supposed ourselves to be examining, the great letters which form the lines of the writing are all consonants. The vowels are indicated by the dots or points beneath these letters, and these vowel-points are only a comparatively late invention, as described above (p. 37). This ancient practice of omitting the vowels is one fertile cause of varieties in the text, for it will readily be understood that doubts might often occur as to the proper vowels to be supplied to a group of consonants. To take a parallel from English, the consonants M R might be read either as m(a)r(e) or m(i)r(e), or m(o)r(e), and it is quite possible that in some cases the sense of the passage would not show for certain which way was right. A glance at the notes of the Variorum Bible will show that this danger is far from being imaginary; *e.g.*, in Deut. xxviii. 22, either "sword" or "drought" may be read, according to the vowels supplied; in Judg. xv. 16, "heaps upon heaps" or "I have flayed them"; in Isa. xxvii. 7, "them that are slain by him" or "those that slew him"; and see Gen. xlix. 5 and Judg. vii. 13 for more extensive variations due to the same cause. Besides the vowel-points, accents are also added, to indicate the rhythmical pronunciation of each word; but these, too, are a comparatively late invention.

Extant Hebrew MSS. late,—

Now with regard to the manuscripts themselves. How well are we provided with manuscripts of the Hebrew Old Testament? It is generally rather a shock when one first learns that the oldest extant MSS. are no earlier than the ninth century after Christ. Over a thousand years separate our earliest Hebrew manuscripts from the date at which the latest of the books contained in them was originally written. It is a disquieting thought, when one reflects how much a text may be corrupted or mutilated in the course of transmission by manuscript over a long period of time; but in the case of the Old Testament there are several considerations which greatly mitigate this disquietude, and which account for the disappearance of the earlier manuscripts.

but Faithful.

In the first place, the extreme care with which manuscripts were written, as described above, is a guarantee against serious errors having crept into all the copies which have come down to us. The comparison of existing manuscripts does indeed show that, in spite of all precautions, variations have arisen; but as a rule they are not of much importance. Scholars are generally agreed that from a comparison of manuscripts, especially of those from the ninth to the twelfth centuries, which are the oldest that we have, the Massoretic text can be ascertained with almost complete certainty. The Massoretic text, as we have seen, is substantially the same as that which was used by the writers of the Talmud, and the way in which the writers of the Talmud speak of it shows that it had been in existence for some time previously. There is good reason, therefore, to believe that we have in the Massoretic text substantially the text of the synod of Jamnia, or in round figures about A.D. 100. It is for the period before that date that the evidence of the Hebrew manuscripts fails us. They do not carry us back so far as the time of the actual composition of the several books of the Old Testament; but within their limits their evidence may be accepted as trustworthy.

Destruction of Older Copies.

The same extreme care which was devoted to the transcription of manuscripts is also at the bottom of the disappearance of the earlier copies. When a manuscript had been copied with the exactitude prescribed by the Talmud, and had been duly verified, it was accepted as authentic and regarded as being of equal value with any other copy. If all were equally correct, age gave no advantage to a manuscript; on the contrary, age was a positive disadvantage, since a manuscript was liable to become defaced or damaged in the lapse of time. A damaged or imperfect copy was at once condemned as unfit for use. Attached to each synagogue was a "Gheniza," or lumber cupboard, in which defective manuscripts were laid aside; and from these receptacles some of the oldest manuscripts now extant have in modern times been recovered. Thus, far from regarding an older copy of the Scriptures as more valuable, the Jewish habit has been to prefer the newer, as being the most perfect and free from damage. The older copies, once consigned to the "Gheniza," naturally perished, either from neglect or from being deliberately buried when the "Gheniza" became overcrowded.

The absence of very old copies of the Hebrew Bible need not, therefore, either surprise or disquiet us. If, to the causes already enumerated, we add the repeated persecutions (involving much destruction of property) to which the Jews have been subject, the disappearance of the ancient manuscripts is adequately accounted for, and those which remain may be accepted as preserving that which alone they profess to preserve—namely, the Massoretic text. There is consequently not much to be said in the way of description of individual manuscripts. When we come to speak of the Greek text, whether of the Old or of the New Testament, we shall find it both interesting and important to describe the chief manuscripts with some minuteness, in respect of their age, their comparative value, and the groups or families into which they fall. In none of these respects is it possible to distinguish effectually between Hebrew manuscripts. The reader of the Variorum Bible will easily see this for himself; for whereas in the New Testament the readings of a considerable number of manuscripts are cited individually, each manuscript being distinguished by its own letter, in the Old Testament no manuscript is named individually. Since all represent the same type of text, and none is conspicuously older than the rest, there is little opportunity for marked preeminence. Moreover, even the best authorities differ widely both as to the age and the relative value of different copies, so that we have no certain ground beneath our feet.

Classification of Hebrew MSS.

The points to be taken into consideration in examining a Hebrew manuscript are the following; but it will be seen that their importance is not very great. First, whether it was intended for public or private use; since those intended for the service of the synagogue, like the great leather rolls of the Law, are most likely to be accurately copied. Next, its age; but on this head it is difficult to arrive at any certainty. Many manuscripts contain a statement of their date; but these statements are extremely misleading and of doubtful authenticity. Sometimes we do not know by what era the date is calculated; sometimes the date is evidently that of the manuscript from which it was copied, not of the manuscript itself; sometimes, unfortunately, the date is simply fraudulent. And it is not possible always to test such statements by the handwriting of the manuscript, as can generally be done with Greek writings. The best authorities differ so widely (in the case of one well-known manuscript, one good authority assigns it to the tenth century, and another to the fourteenth, while another copy has been assigned to various dates between the sixth and the fifteenth centuries) as to prove that the science of dating Hebrew writing is very imperfect. It is more possible to distinguish the country in which a manuscript has been written. But even so our advantage is small; for while the Jews themselves have generally held manuscripts written in Spain to be the best, two most distinguished scholars (the Englishman Kennicott and the Italian De Rossi) prefer those which were made in Germany. Finally, manuscripts may be distinguished as containing an Eastern or a Western text, the former being derived from the school of Babylonia, the latter from that of Palestine. Each of these schools had its own Talmud, each had a different system of vowel punctuation, and each had a certain number of textual variations peculiar to itself, which are recorded in several manuscripts; but these very rarely affect the sense to any material extent.

The Chief Extant MSS.

Probably the oldest manuscript now in existence of any part of the Hebrew Bible is one acquired towards the end of the last century by the British Museum, of which a page is reproduced in Plate IV. It is not dated, but its writing is of an earlier type than that of the earliest copies of which the precise date is known, and it is consequently supposed to have been written not later than the ninth century. It contains the Pentateuch, written in book form (not as a roll), and is imperfect at the end. Both Greater and Lesser Massorah have been added in the margins, the former at the top and bottom, the latter at the side. The text is furnished with vowel-points and accents; the Massorah is without them in some places, but in others, contrary to the usual practice, it has them. The passage shown in the plate is the end of Genesis and the beginning of Exodus (Gen. l. 23–Exod. ii. 14).

The oldest manuscript containing a precise statement of its date which can be trusted is the Leningrad manuscript of the Prophets. This was written in the year 916, and contains the "Later Prophets," written on vellum, in double columns, with the Massorah between, below, and on the outer margin. The accents and vowel-points are written above the letters, instead of below, according to a system in use at Babylon. The text is correctly written, and furnishes a strong proof of the truth of the assertion that all extant Hebrew MSS. are descended from a single copy; for although it contains an Eastern text, while the commonly received text is based on Western MSS. (no Babylonian MSS. having been known to exist until within the last eighty years), and although it only came to light long after the formation of the received text, yet on a comparison of it with a standard edition of the latter in a single book, that of Ezekiel (in which the Massoretic text is certainly often corrupt), it was found to contain only *sixteen* real variations from it.[1] Similarly, the British Museum MS. of the Pentateuch is substantially in full agreement with the received text.

Although these two copies have been described as the oldest now in existence, there are many others which *claim* a considerably earlier date. There are quite a large number of such in Russia, one of which purports to have been *corrected* in the year 580, while others are dated 489, 639, 764, 781, 789, 798, besides many of the ninth and tenth centuries. Unfortunately these dates are universally discredited, and most of them are known to be due to the fraudulent enterprise of a Jew named Firkowitzsch. A manuscript in the Cambridge University Library bears the date of 856, and the correctness of this date has been maintained by at least one capable scholar; but it is not generally accepted. Of other manuscripts perhaps the most notable are—(1) the Codex Ben-Asher, now at Aleppo, supposed to have been written in the tenth century, and held to be one of the best authorities for the text of the Old Testament, though both its age and its value have been strongly questioned; (2) Codex Laudianus, at Oxford, containing the whole Old Testament except a large part of Genesis, numbered 1 by Kennicott, and held by him to have been written in the tenth century and to contain a very important text; (3) No. 634 in the list of De Rossi, containing the Pentateuch, assigned by him to the eighth century, by others to the tenth or later. It seems useless to extend the list, in view of the great doubts attaching to all dates, and to the general unimportance of the divergences.

[1] Cornill, *Das Buch des Propheten Ezechiel*, p. 9

MSS. now Lost.

One other source of knowledge for the Hebrew text should, however, be mentioned—namely, readings quoted in the Middle Ages from manuscripts since lost. The chief of these is a manuscript known as the Codex Hillelis, which was at one time supposed to date back to the great teacher Hillel, before the time of our Lord. It is, however, probable that it was really written after the sixth century. It was used by a Jewish scholar in Spain, and a considerable number of its readings have been preserved by references to it in various writers. Other lost manuscripts are sometimes quoted, but less often, and their testimony is less important.

The Printed Hebrew Text.

The first portion of the Hebrew Bible to appear in print was the Psalms, which issued from the press, probably at Bologna in Italy, in 1477. The first complete Old Testament followed in 1488, at Soncino. Both these editions were due to Jews. The first edition prepared by a Christian scholar was that which appeared in the great Bible printed by Cardinal Ximenes at Alcala (and hence known as the Complutensian Bible, from Complutum, the Latin name of Alcala), in Spain, during the years 1514-17. In this Bible the Hebrew, Greek, and Latin texts were printed side by side; and it forms, as will be seen more fully hereafter, a most important landmark in the story of the beginnings of Biblical study in modern Europe. It was not, however, until the end of the eighteenth century that scholars fairly took in hand the critical study of the Hebrew text. The first collection of the evidence was made by Bishop Kennicott, who published at Oxford in 1776-80 the readings of no less than 634 Hebrew manuscripts (giving, however, only the consonants, without vowel-points). He was followed, in 1784-8, by the Italian scholar De Rossi, who published collations of 825 more manuscripts. De Rossi used better MSS., on the whole, than Kennicott, but the general result of the labours of both is the same. It is to them that the proof is due of the fact that all Hebrew manuscripts represent the same text—namely, the Massoretic—and that without substantial variation. Other manuscripts have come to light since their time, notably in Russia, where a number of MSS. of the Babylonian type were discovered within our own day; but, as has been shown above in the case of the most important of these, the Leningrad MS. of the Prophets, the conclusion established by Kennicott and De Rossi remains undisturbed. A critical edition of the Hebrew Bible, "diligently revised according to the Massorah and the early editions, with the various readings from MSS. and the ancient versions," occupied Dr. C. D. Ginsburg for many years, and was ultimately published by the British and Foreign Bible Society in 1926. But this has now been superseded by the work of R. Kittel and P. Kahle, of which the third edition, completed by A. Alt and O. Eissfeldt, was published by the Württemberg Bibelanstalt at Stuttgart in 1937.

Summary of Results.

The result of our examination of the Hebrew text is, then, this. We have manuscripts which collectively give us a good representation of a text which reached its final shape about the seventh century. We also have evidence that the scholars who made this final revision did not substantially alter the text which had been in use for some five centuries previously. We may therefore be satisfied that the text of our Old Testament has been handed down without serious change from about A.D. 100. Further back we cannot go with the aid of the Hebrew manuscripts alone. The great, indeed all-important, question which now meets us is this—Does this Hebrew text, which we call Massoretic, and which we have shown to descend from a text drawn up about A.D. 100, faithfully represent the Hebrew text as originally written by the authors of the Old Testament books? To answer this question it is necessary to bring up our second line of authorities, described in Chapter III. We must refer to those translations of the Old Testament into other languages which were made before the date at which we have arrived. We must see what evidence they can give us as to the Hebrew text from which they were translated, and examine the extent and credibility of that evidence. In this way alone can we hope to bridge over the gap in our knowledge between the actual composition of the books of the Old Testament and the text whose descent from about the first century of the Christian era has been traced in this present chapter.

CHAPTER V

THE ANCIENT VERSIONS OF THE OLD TESTAMENT

In August, 1883, the world was startled by the announcement of a discovery which, if it were authentic, seemed to go far towards bridging the great gap in our knowledge of which we spoke at the end of the last chapter. This was no less than some fragments of a manuscript of the Old Testament purporting to have been written about eight hundred years before Christ, which their owner, a Jew of the name of Shapira, stated that he had obtained from some Arabs about five years before. The material was old leather, and the writing was similar to that of the Moabite Stone. The contents were striking enough. They purported to be portions of the Book of Deuteronomy, but with many remarkable variations. To the Ten Commandments was added an eleventh, and the language of the others was altered and amplified. In these strips of leather there was enough to cast doubt upon the whole of the received text of the Old Testament and to discredit the whole science of textual criticism. The sensation, however, lasted only a few days. Evidences of forgery soon began to pour in; and the final blow was given when it was shown that the strips of leather on which the characters were written had been cut from the margins of an ordinary synagogue roll.

There is, indeed, no probability that we shall ever find manuscripts of the Hebrew text going back to a period before the formation of the text which we know as Massoretic. We can only arrive at an idea of it by a study of the earliest translations made from it; and our task in the present chapter is to describe these translations in turn.

§ 1.—The Samaritan Pentateuch.

Its Origin.

The version of the Old Testament which possesses the longest pedigree is that which owes its existence to the Samaritans. Strictly speaking, it is not a version at all, as it is in the Hebrew tongue, though written in a different character from that of the extant Hebrew MSS. It is written in the *old* Hebrew character, such as it was before the adoption by the Jews of the square characters, as described in the last chapter (p. 40). The precise origin of this separate Samaritan Bible has been a subject of dispute; but the most probable account is that it takes its rise in the events described in Neh. xiii. 23-30—namely, the expulsion by Nehemiah of those Jews who had contracted marriages with the heathen. Among those expelled was a grandson of the high-priest Eliashib, whose name, as we learn from Josephus, was Manasseh. This Manasseh, in indignation at his expulsion, took refuge among the Samaritans, and set up among them a rival worship to that at Jerusalem. The Samaritans, whom we know from 2 Kings xvii. 24-41 to have been foreigners imported into the country of the Ten Tribes by the king of Assyria, and there, presumably, to have mingled with the scanty remnant of Israelites, had at first incorporated the worship of Jehovah, as the God of the land, into the worship of their own gods; and later, on the return of the Jews from captivity, had been willing to join in the rebuilding of the Temple at Jerusalem, but had been refused permission. Since this repulse they had been bitterly hostile to the Jews, and the schism of Manasseh gave them a head and a rival worship, which embittered and perpetuated the quarrel. Manasseh obtained leave from Darius Nothus, king of Persia, to set up a temple on Mount Gerizim, which became the centre of the new religion and the rival of Jerusalem. He had brought with him, it is believed, the Hebrew Pentateuch, and this, with certain alterations (notably the substitution of Gerizim for Ebal in Deut. xxvii. 4 as the hill on which the memorial altar should be placed), became the sacred book of the Samaritans. As we have seen in the last chapter, probably this was the only part of the Old Testament which had at that time been definitely recognised as inspired Scripture by the Jews themselves; and when the Prophets and Hagiographa were subsequently added to the Canon, the Samaritans refused to accept them. They refused also to accept the square Hebrew characters adopted by the Jews; and we may be quite certain that they would pay little respect to any alterations in the text, if such there were, which were made by Jewish scribes and scholars after the date of the original secession.

Its Discovery.

So far, then, it appears as if we had, in the Samaritan Pentateuch, an invaluable means of testing the extent of the variation which the Hebrew text has undergone since the days of Nehemiah. We have an independent tradition, coming down from about B.C. 408 (the date of Manasseh's secession), without any contact with the Hebrew text, preserving the original form of writing, and thereby avoiding one considerable source of possible error and corruption. No wonder that when, in 1616, the first copy of the Samaritan Bible came to light many scholars thought that they had obtained evidence for the original text of the Old Testament far preferable to that of the Hebrew manuscripts. The Samaritan community had existed from the days of its first settlement by Sargon of Assyria until then, and it exists still, a little community now of less than a hundred persons, settled at Nablus, the ancient Shechem, still observing the Mosaic Law, and still celebrating the Passover on Mount Gerizim; but none of their sacred books had come to light until, in that year, a copy was obtained by Pietro della Valle. Several other copies have since been secured by travellers and are now in European libraries. The first printed edition was issued in the Paris Polyglot Bible in 1632, and for generations a hot controversy raged among Biblical scholars as to the comparative value of the Samaritan and Hebrew texts. At length, in 1815, it was settled, for the time, by an elaborate examination of all the variations by the great Hebrew scholar Gesenius, whose verdict was wholly against the Samaritan version. He divided the variations into groups, according to their character, and argued that in hardly a single instance was a Samaritan reading to be preferred to that of the Hebrew. This opinion has held the field until recently; but there seems to be a disposition now to question its justice.

Its Character.

The Samaritan version has been estimated to differ from the Hebrew in about 6,000 places. The great majority of these are of very trifling importance, consisting of grammatical alterations or the substitution of Samaritan idioms for Hebrew. Others (as in Deut. xxvii. 4, quoted above) are alterations of substance, so as to suit Samaritan ideas of ritual or religion. Others contain supplements of apparent deficiencies by the help of similar passages in other books, repetitions of speeches and the like from parallel passages, the removal of obscurities or insertion of explanatory words or sentences, or distinct differences of reading. In all these latter cases there may evidently be two opinions as to whether the Samaritan or the Hebrew reading is preferable. The apparent deficiencies in the Hebrew may be real, the obscurities may be due to error, and the Samaritan text may be nearer to the original language. This probability is greatly increased when we find that in many passages where the Samaritan version differs from the Hebrew, the Greek Septuagint version (of which we shall speak presently) agrees with the former. For example, the Samaritan and Hebrew texts differ very frequently as to the ages of the patriarchs mentioned in the early chapters of Genesis. Gesenius classified these variations as alterations introduced on grounds of suitability; but it is at least possible that they are not alterations at all, but the original text, and that the numbers have become corrupt in the Hebrew text; and this possibility is turned into a probability when we find the Septuagint supporting the Samaritan readings. There is no satisfactory proof of either the Septuagint or the Samaritan text having been corrected from the other, nor is it in itself likely; and their independent evidence is extremely difficult to explain away. Hence scholars are now becoming more disposed to think favourably of the Samaritan readings. Many of them may be errors, many more may be unimportant, but there remain several which are of real value. The editors of the Variorum Bible give thirty-five variations of the Samaritan text in the five books of the Pentateuch as being either equal or superior to the Hebrew readings. Among these may be mentioned, for the sake of example, Gen. iv. 8, where the Samaritan has "Cain said to Abel his brother, Let us go into the field"; xlvii. 21, "As for the people he made slaves of them," instead of "he removed them to cities"; Exod. xii. 40, the 430 years of the sojourning of the children of Israel are said to have been in Egypt *and in Canaan* (thus agreeing with Gal. iii. 17), instead of in Egypt only; Num. iv. 14, the following words are added at the end of the verse, "And they shall take a cloth of purple, and cover the laver and his foot, and put it into a covering of seals' skins, and shall put them upon a frame"; and in Deut. xxxii. 35 the first half of the verse runs "against the day of vengeance and recompence; against the time when their foot shall slip." These are perhaps the most notable of the Samaritan variants, and it is observable that in every case the Septuagint confirms them. The general result of the comparison of this and the other versions with the Hebrew text must be reserved to the end of the chapter; meanwhile it will be sufficient to observe that these variations, though sufficient to arouse our interest, are not serious enough to cause any disquietude as to the substantial integrity of the text of our Old Testament.

Its Manuscripts.

No manuscript of the Samaritan Bible (so far as is known) is older than the tenth century. It is true that the Samaritan community at Nablus cherishes a precious roll, which it maintains to have been written by Abisha, the great-grandson of Moses, in the thirteenth year after the conquest of Canaan; but this story, which rests on the authority of an inscription said to be found in the MS. itself, may very safely be dismissed.[1] All the

[1] There is much mystery about this MS. It has never been examined by any competent authority, nor have the columns containing the inscription been photographed. An ancient roll used to be shown to visitors, but it was said that this was not the real roll of Abisha, which was kept secret. In

existing manuscripts of the Samaritan version are written on either vellum or paper, in the shape of books, not rolls, with the exception of three rolls at Nablus, without any vowel-points or accents, but with punctuation to divide words and sentences. The whole of the Pentateuch is divided into 964 paragraphs.

§ 2.—The Septuagint and other Greek Versions.

Two considerations make the Samaritan version of the Old Testament less important than it would otherwise be. In the first place, it contains only the Pentateuch, and it is just this part of the Old Testament which is best preserved in the Hebrew text, and consequently needs least correction. Secondly, none of the extant copies of it is older than the tenth century, so that they are as far removed from the fountain head as the Hebrew manuscripts themselves. Neither of these drawbacks applies to the Greek version, of which we have now to speak. It is a complete translation of the Old Testament, containing, indeed, not only the books which now compose our Old Testament, but also those which, after a considerable period of uncertainty, were finally excluded from the Hebrew Canon and now constitute our Apocrypha. Further, it is preserved in several manuscripts of very great age, the earliest, as we shall see presently, going back to the second century after Christ, not to mention a scrap which is even earlier. In every respect, both textually and historically, the Greek version of the Old Testament is by far the most important of all the ancient translations. On the one hand, it is our chief means of testing the accuracy of the Massoretic

---

1926, however, all antiquities in Palestine had to be registered with the Department of Antiquities, to secure ownership. At that time I happened to visit Nablus with the Director of Antiquities, and was shown what purported to be the original roll (as well as others), and even the inscription was pointed out to me. This is not written at the beginning or end of the MS., but (according to a special Samaritan practice) was inserted, acrostic-wise, in the middle of several consecutive columns of the text, by isolating selected letters about the middle of each line. Such an inscription could not be inserted later, though it might be possible to alter letters. The roll was of thin vellum (not leather, as one would expect in the case of the age suggested), rather tattered, and had a distinctly medieval appearance to my eye. Subsequently some photographs were sent to me, which were certified by Dr. L. A. Mayer, of the Jerusalem Department of Antiquities, as being taken from the oldest MS. One of these is reproduced as Plate V. Unfortunately they did not include the columns with the inscription. In the expert opinion of Sir A. Cowley, the hand shown in these photographs is of a thirteenth-century type, certainly not materially older. The knobs on the rollers are not relevant, since they are removed when the roll is put away, and can be attached to other rolls. The photographs have been presented to the Department of Oriental Printed Books and Manuscripts in the British Museum. According to Sir A. Cowley, the Samaritan historian Abulfath says that the roll of Abisha was "discovered" in 1355 by the High Priest Phinehas b. Joseph. Probably its real date is not much earlier than that.

Hebrew text, and of correcting it when it is wrong; and, on the other, it has been the Bible of Greek Christendom from the earliest age of Christianity down to this present day. It will consequently require and deserve a somewhat extended notice at our hands.

Origin of the Septuagint.

The first questions to be answered are those that relate to its origin. When was it made? Why was it made? For whom was it made? Curious as it may seem at first sight, this Greek translation of the Hebrew Bible was made in a land which was neither Greek nor Hebrew—namely, Egypt. After the submission of Egypt to Alexander the Great, and the introduction of Greek settlers under Ptolemy, his lieutenant, Alexandria became the headquarters alike of the commerce and the literature of the East. Its population, mainly Greek, included also a large colony of Jews. Greek became the common language of intercourse between people of different nationalities in the East, and the Jews in Egypt learnt, before long, to use it as their native tongue. Hence there arose the necessity of having their Scriptures accessible in Greek; and the answer to this demand was the version known as the Septuagint. The story which was long current as to its origin is largely mythical, but it contains a kernel of truth. In a letter purporting to be written by one Aristeas to his brother Philocrates, in the reign of Ptolemy Philadelphus (B.C. 285-246), it is said that King Ptolemy, hearing of the Jewish Scriptures, and being urged by his librarian to obtain a copy of them for his great library at Alexandria, sent an embassy (of which the writer of the letter was one) to the high priest at Jerusalem with magnificent presents, begging him to send a copy of the sacred books, with a body of men capable of translating them. Thereupon six translators were selected from each of the twelve tribes and despatched to Alexandria, bearing with them a copy of the Law, written in letters of gold. They were splendidly received by the king, and, after a banquet and public display of their wisdom, set about their task of translation, working separately in the first instance, but afterwards comparing their results, and finally producing the version which was thenceforth known as the Septuagint, or the Version of the Seventy. Later generations improved upon this story, until the legend ran that each of the seventy-two translators was shut up in a separate cell (or by pairs in thirty-six cells) and each produced a translation of the whole Old Testament in exactly seventy-two days; and when their translations were compared it was found that they all agreed precisely with one another, in every word and every phrase, thus proving that their version was directly inspired by God. This, however, is merely an exaggeration of the original story, which itself is now generally believed to be an exaggeration of the real facts, at least in respect of the special and magnificent patronage of Ptolemy. What is true is that the Septuagint version was begun in or about his reign, in Alexandria, and that the Pentateuch was probably translated first. Of this there is confirmation in the fact that the version of Genesis is quoted by a writer in the last quarter of the third century B.C. The other books were added later, by different translators and at different times. The style of translation differs so markedly in different books as to prove that the whole Testament cannot have been the work of a single group of translators, while some of the later books, such as Ecclesiasticus, were not even written at the time of which the story speaks.

Its Contents.

The Septuagint version, as finally completed, contains not merely the books which now form our Old Testament, but also those which, since the Reformation, have been placed apart in the Apocrypha.[1] Some of these books (2 Esdras, the additions of Esther, Wisdom, part of Baruch, the Song of the Three Children, 2-4 Maccabees) never existed in Hebrew at all; but the others were originally written in Hebrew and circulated among the Jews (chiefly, it would seem, in their Greek form) for some time on very much the same footing as some of the books which form the section of the Hagiographa (p. 33). They never, however, attained the same position of authority, and when the Canon of the Old Testament was finally closed they were left outside. From this point dates their disappearance in their Hebrew form; they ceased to be copied in Hebrew; and so they have come down to us only in the Greek, or in translations made from the Greek. Jerome rejected them from his Latin Bible because they were not extant in Hebrew; but the older Latin translations of them were subsequently incorporated into the Vulgate, and they have remained in the Latin Bible of the Roman Church to the present day. The Septuagint is, however, their real home, and there they take their proper places among the books of the Old Testament. The First Book of Esdras takes pre-

[1] It is unfortunate that the Apocrypha is generally omitted from copies of the English Bible. No doubt a little explanation of the nature of the books contained in it is needed by most people, but that information is now easily accessible in many popular handbooks—*e.g.*, in the Rev. C. H. H. Wright's article in the *Variorum Aids to the Bible Student*. The *Variorum Apocrypha*, also, by the Rev. C. J. Ball, can be confidently recommended as containing excellent critical and (in the form of " various renderings ") explanatory notes. In addition there is the Revised Version of the Apocrypha, which was published in 1895.

PLATE VI.

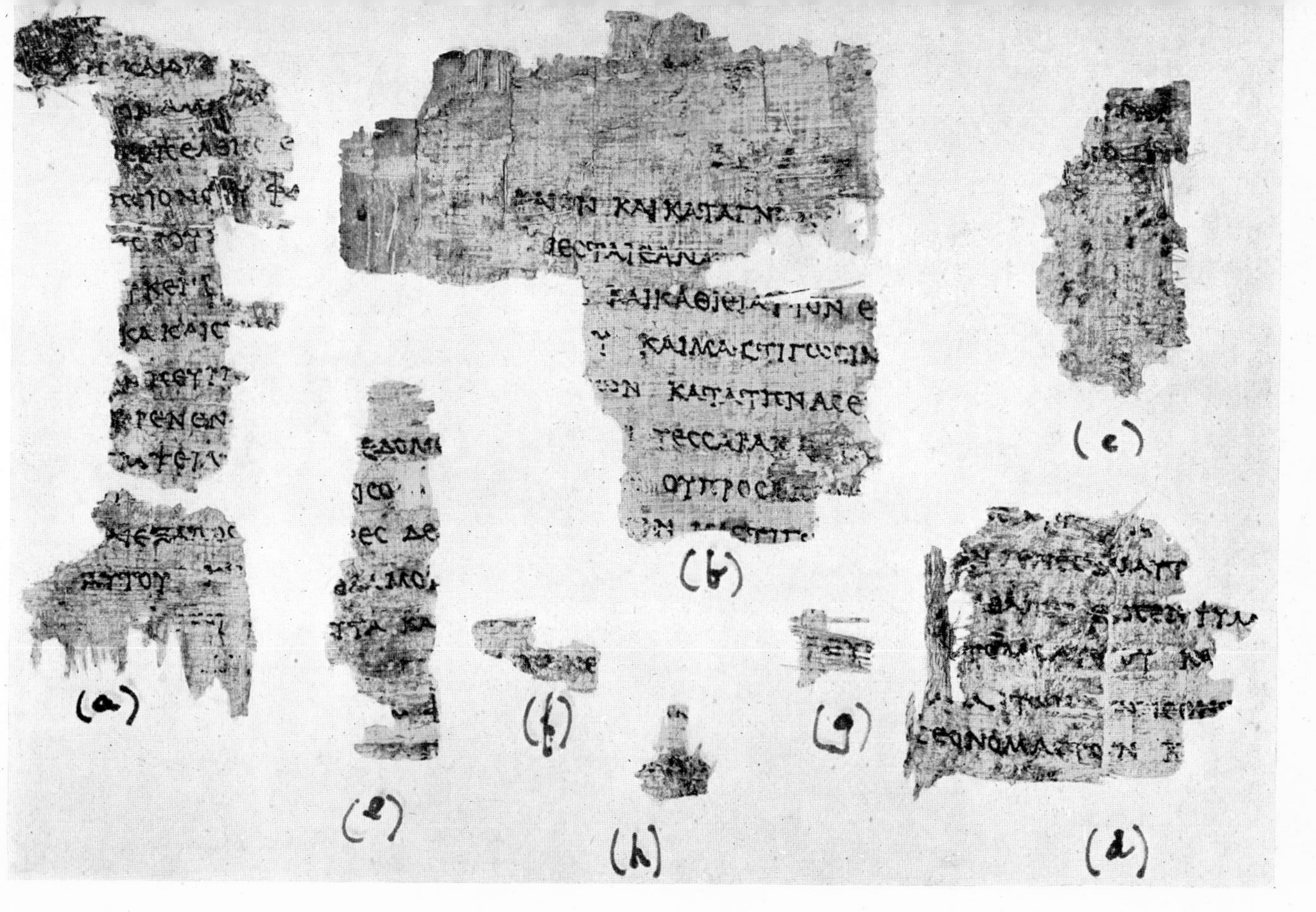

RYLANDS LIBRARY DEUTERONOMY FRAGMENT—2ND CENT. B.C.

(*Original size of b*, $3\frac{1}{4}$ *in.* × $3\frac{3}{8}$ *in.*)

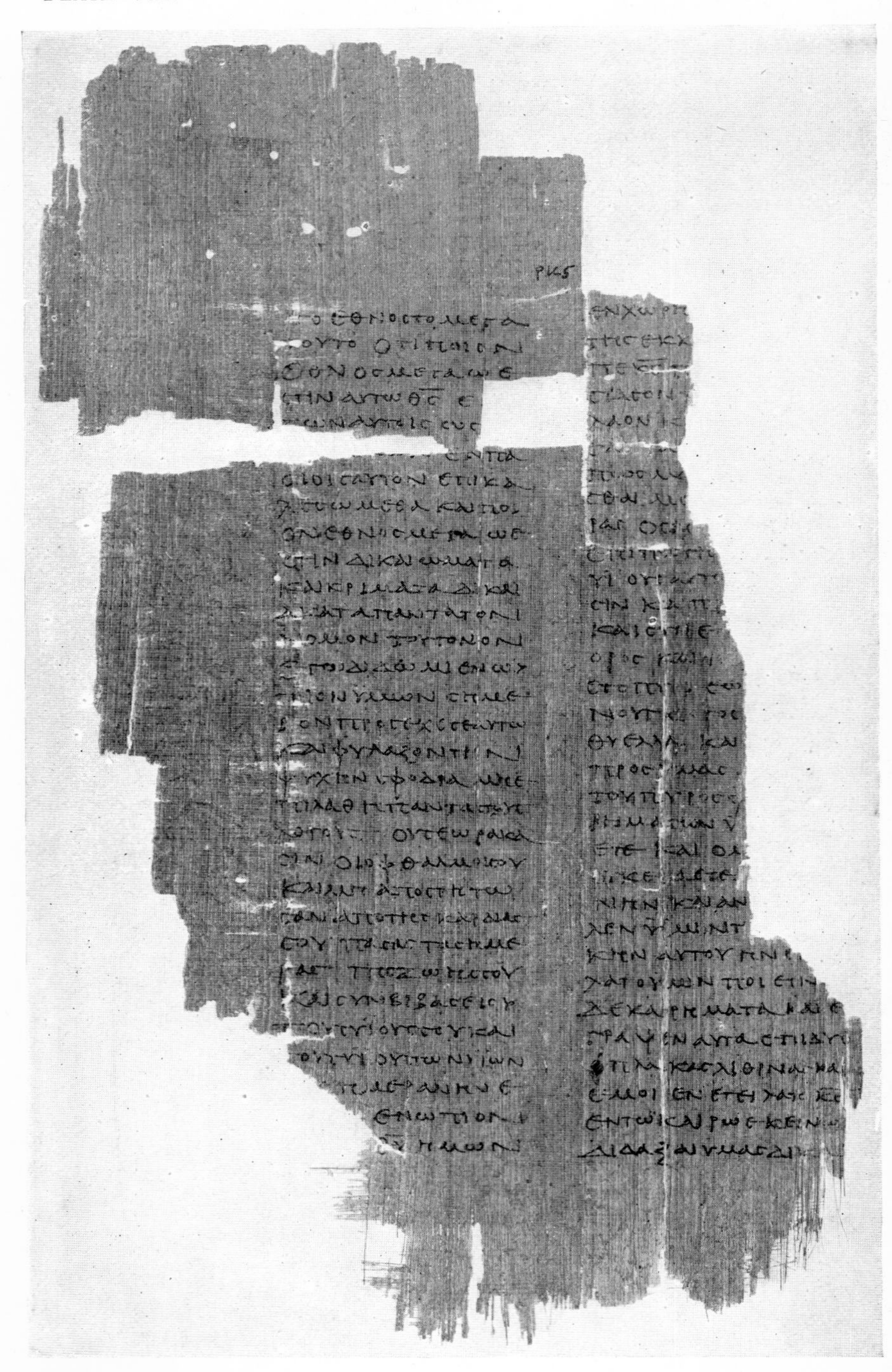

CHESTER BEATTY CODEX OF NUMBERS-DEUTERONOMY—2ND CENT.

(Original size of page, as reproduced, 11 in. × 5 in.)

cedence of the Book of Ezra, of which it is an alternative version with some additions. After the Book of Nehemiah (which, in conjunction with the canonical Ezra, is called the Second Book of Esdras) come, in the principal manuscript of the Septuagint, the Psalms, Proverbs, Ecclesiastes, Song of Solomon, Job, Wisdom, Ecclesiasticus (or the Wisdom of Sirach), Esther (including the parts now banished to the Apocrypha), Judith, Tobit. Then follow the Prophets; but Jeremiah is succeeded by Baruch, Lamentations, and the Epistle of Jeremiah (=Baruch, chapter vi.), and Daniel is preceded by Susanna and followed by Bel and the Dragon. Finally the Old Testament is concluded by the books of the Maccabees, of which there are, in some of the earliest copies, four instead of only two.[1]

Adopted by Greek-speaking Jews and the Christian Church.

When the Septuagint translation was completed, it became at once the Bible of the Greek-speaking Jews, and circulated in Palestine and Asia as well as in Egypt, the home of its birth. At the time of our Lord's life on earth, Greek was the literary language of Palestine, as Aramaic was the spoken language of the common people. Hebrew was known only to the small class of students, headed by the rabbis and the scribes. All the books of the New Testament (with the possible exception of the Gospel of St. Matthew in its original form) were written in Greek; and most of the quotations from the Old Testament which appear in them are taken from the Septuagint version, not from the

[1] Luther followed Jerome in rejecting the books which did not form part of the Hebrew Canon, and the English translators followed Luther. The sixth of the Thirty-nine Articles confirms this. The English Apocrypha includes, in addition to the books named above, 2 Esdras (an apocalyptic work, originally written in Greek, or just possibly in Hebrew, but now only known in Latin and other versions, which was included, though not accepted as canonical, in the Latin Vulgate, and thence passed into the English Genevan Bible, and so to the Authorised Version), and the Prayer of Manasses, a work of unknown origin, which is included among hymns attached to the Psalter in the Codex Alexandrinus (see p. 67). On the other hand, it does not include 3 and 4 Maccabees. The Song of the Three Children, Susanna, and Bel and the Dragon are parts of the Greek version of Daniel; and "the rest of the book of Esther" is similarly made up of parts of the Greek Esther which do not appear in the Hebrew. The numeration of the books of Esdras is rather confusing. In the Greek Bible 1 and 2 Esdras are alternative versions of Ezra-Nehemiah, 1 Esdras being an expanded version, including part of Chronicles and some other matter, which is now by many believed to represent the original Septuagint, while 2 Esdras is a close representation of the Hebrew text. In the Latin Vulgate 1 Esdras=Ezra, 2 Esdras=Nehemiah, 3 Esdras= the Greek 1 Esdras, and 4 Esdras=the apocalyptic work. In our sixth Article, 3 and 4 Esdras are the same as in the Latin; but in the Authorised and Revised Versions these are called 1 and 2 Esdras, Ezra and Nehemiah appearing under their own names among the canonical books. To avoid confusion, however, the apocalyptic book is generally referred to by scholars as Fourth Esdras rather than Second Esdras.

original Hebrew. As Christianity spread beyond the borders of Palestine, Greek was necessarily the language in which it appealed alike to the Jew and to the Gentile; and when, in speaking to the former, it based its claim on the fulfilment of prophecy, it was in the language of the Septuagint version that the prophecies were quoted. The Christian Church adopted the Septuagint as its own Book of the Old Covenant, and looked to that as its Bible long before it had come to realise that its own writings would take a place beside it as equally sacred Scripture.

Rival Translations in the Second Century.

The result of this appropriation of the Septuagint by the Christian Church was that the Jews cast it off. When the Christians in controversy pressed them with quotations from the Prophets, of which the fulfilment had been found in Jesus Christ, the Jews took refuge in a denial of the accuracy of the Septuagint translation. In the second century of our era this repudiation took form in the production of rival versions. The Hebrew text had been fixed, in the form in which it has come down to us, in the preceding century, and what was now needed was a faithful translation of this into Greek for the use of Greek-speaking Jews.

1. *Aquila.*—The production of such a translation was the work of AQUILA, who may be identical with the Onkelos to whom is ascribed the principal Targum on the Pentateuch (see p. 36). The name is the same, in a Latin dress, and the spirit in which the translation was executed is the same. The version of Aquila is an exceedingly bald and literal rendering of the Hebrew, adhering to the original so closely as to lose most of the Greek idiom, and often falling into obscurity and even nonsense. Aquila is said to have been a disciple of the celebrated Rabbi Akiba, the chief and leader of the extremest anti-Christian Jews at the end of the first century, and his version, which must have been made somewhere about the year 150, became the official Greek translation of the Scriptures in use among the non-Christian Jews.

2. *Theodotion.*—Later in the same century another translation was made, upon the opposite side, by THEODOTION (diversely described as a Jewish proselyte or an Ebionite Christian), said to have been a native of Ephesus. Theodotion's translation resembled Aquila's in being based upon the authorised Jewish text of the Old Testament (though retaining the apocryphal additions to the book of Daniel), but was exactly contrary in its treatment of it, being very free in its rendering of the original. It does not seem to have been adopted by the Jews, but it obtained much popularity among Christians, and exercised a considerable influence upon the subsequent history of the Septuagint. Notably

was this the case in respect of the books of Daniel and Job. Theodotion's version of Daniel was so much preferred to that of the Septuagint, that it actually took its place in the manuscripts of the Septuagint itself, and the original Septuagint version was until quite recently known only from a single Greek manuscript and a Syriac translation. Within the last few years, however, an early papyrus manuscript of a considerable part of it has been discovered (see p. 65). In the case of Job, the Septuagint version did not contain many passages (amounting to about one-sixth of the book in all) which appear in the received or Massoretic text of the Hebrew; and these were supplied in the Septuagint from the version of Theodotion. It is believed by some also that the version of Ezra-Nehemiah known as 2 Esdras is the work of Theodotion, the looser and expanded version of 1 Esdras being the original Septuagint;[1] but this cannot yet be said to be established.

3. *Symmachus.*—Yet one other Greek version of the Old Testament remains to be mentioned, that of SYMMACHUS, which was made about the year 200. The special feature of this translation is the literary skill and taste with which the Hebrew phrases of the original are rendered into good and idiomatic Greek. In this respect Symmachus approaches nearer than any of his rivals to the modern conception of a translator's duty; but he had less influence than any of them on the history of the Greek Bible. Curiously enough, he had more influence upon the Latin Bible; for Jerome made considerable use of him in the preparation of the Vulgate.

Revisions of the Septuagint.

1. *Origen's Hexapla.*—At the beginning of the third century there were thus three Greek versions of the Old Testament in existence, besides the Septuagint itself. The next step, and one of much importance in the history of the Greek text, was taken by the great Alexandrian scholar, ORIGEN, whose life occupies the first half of the third century (A.D. 186-253). Finding all these various, and often conflicting, versions of the Scriptures existing side by side, he determined to draw them together, and to try to use them for the production of one more perfect version than them all. Accordingly, with that stupendous energy which earned for him the admiration of his contemporaries and of posterity, he set about the colossal work to which was given the name of the *Hexapla,* or " sixfold " version of the Old Testament Scriptures. In six parallel columns, at each opening of his book, were arrayed the following six different versions: (1) the Hebrew text then current (substantially identical with the

[1] Josephus certainly used 1 Esdras.

Massoretic text); (2) the Hebrew text in Greek letters; (3) the Greek translation of Aquila (placed here as being the nearest to the Hebrew in fidelity); (4) the translation of Symmachus; (5) the Septuagint, as revised by Origen himself; (6) the translation of Theodotion, coming last in the series as being the furthest removed in style from the original.[1] The last four columns seem to have existed in a separate form, known as the *Tetrapla*, or fourfold version, which was probably a later reproduction in handier size of the more important part of Origen's work; but in any case the Hexapla, whether earlier or later, is the complete and authoritative form of it. So huge a work as this (the Old Testament is rarely contained entire in any manuscript in a single version, and this contained it in six) was not likely to be copied as a whole. The original manuscript still existed at Cæsarea at the beginning of the seventh century, but it perished shortly afterwards, and of all its columns, except the fifth, no complete representation has come down to us. In 1896, however, a young Italian scholar, now well known as Cardinal Mercati, found a palimpsest fragment at Milan containing the text of eleven Psalms in five of the six columns of the Hexapla, written about the tenth century. The Hebrew column is omitted, but another is added containing isolated various readings, presumably from the other versions referred to above. This gives us a concrete example of what the Hexapla would have looked like, and adds something to our knowledge of the several versions. There is also a fragment at Cambridge, discovered in a "gheniza" (see p. 43) at Cairo, containing part of Psalm xxii. in all six columns.

It is with the fifth column, however, that we are principally concerned, since it contained Origen's edition of the Septuagint, and this edition had a considerable influence on the text of the version in subsequent ages. Unfortunately, Origen's efforts were not directed towards the recovery of the original form of the Septuagint, but at bringing it into harmony with the Hebrew text then current, and to do this he introduced alterations into it with the utmost freedom. At the same time he tried to indicate all such alterations by the use of certain symbols. Passages occurring in the Septuagint which were not found in the Hebrew were marked by an *obelus* (—); passages occurring in the Hebrew but not in the Septuagint were inserted in the latter from the version of Theodotion, such insertions being marked by an *asterisk* (※ or ⁜); a *metobelus* (✓) in each case marking the end

[1] In some books (chiefly the poetical ones, it would seem) three other Greek versions were appended. These were obscure translations which Origen had discovered, and their importance seems to have been small. Very little of them has been preserved, and their authors do not seem to have been known to Origen himself. They are simply called the Fifth, Sixth, and Seventh versions.

of the passage in question. For Origen's purpose, which was the production of a Greek version corresponding as closely as possible with the Hebrew text as then settled, this procedure was well enough; but for ours, which is the recovery of the original Septuagint text as evidence for what the Hebrew was before the formation of the Massoretic text, it was most unfortunate, since there was a natural tendency for his edition to be copied without the critical symbols, and thus for the additions made by him from Theodotion to appear as part of the genuine and original Septuagint. This has certainly happened in some cases; it is difficult to say with certainty in how many. Fortunately we are not left without some means of discovering these insertions, for in the year 617, shortly before the disappearance of the original manuscript of the Hexapla, Bishop Paulus, of Tella in Mesopotamia, made a Syriac translation of the column containing the Septuagint, copying faithfully into it the critical symbols of Origen; and a copy of part of this, written in the eighth century, is still extant in the Ambrosian library at Milan, containing the Prophets and most of the Hagiographa.[1] For the Pentateuch the chief authority is a Greek manuscript at Leiden, written in the fifth century, and known as the Codex Sarravianus (see p. 69); and a few other manuscripts exist, likewise containing an Origenian text, some of which will be described below. There are thus fair means for recovering the Septuagint column of Origen's great work.

The versions of Aquila, Theodotion, and Symmachus have, however, for the most part perished. In 1897, among a quantity of fragments brought to Cambridge from the Cairo "gheniza" mentioned on the previous page, were found three palimpsest leaves which were identified by Dr. F. C. Burkitt as containing the Aquila text of 3 Kingdoms xx. 7-17 and 4 Kingdoms xxiii. 11-27, in a hand of the sixth century. One curious feature is that the Divine Name is written in the *old* Hebrew characters, which for ordinary purposes had gone out of use 600 years before. This confirms an express statement of Origen, which modern scholars had causelessly doubted. Another fragment, containing Ps. xc. (xci.) 6[b]-13[a] and xci. (xcii.) 3[b]-9, apparently from the same MS., was separately edited by Dr. C. Taylor; and a tiny papyrus scrap, containing Gen. i. 1-5, is described below (p. 66). Otherwise no continuous manuscripts of any of these versions have survived, except those parts of Theodotion which were incor-

[1] The Ambrosian MS. contains Job, Psalms, Proverbs, Ecclesiastes, Song of Solomon, and the Prophets. The first volume of this MS. was in existence in 1574, but has since disappeared. On the other hand, fragments of other MSS. have been discovered, and are now in the British Museum, containing Exodus and Ruth complete, and portions of Genesis, Numbers, Deuteronomy, Joshua, Judgse, and 3 Kingdoms, while 4 Kingdoms is preserved in a MS. at Paris.

porated in the received text of the Septuagint; but a very large number of individual readings have been preserved in the margin of Septuagint MSS. (especially the Codex Marchalianus, see p. 71), and these have been collected and arranged with great skill and care in the two portly volumes of Dr. Field's edition of the Hexapla, published by the Oxford University Press in 1875.

Origen's own colossal work went to the ground, but the part of it which was most important in his eyes, and the ultimate object of the whole—the revised text of the Septuagint—survived, and had a most noteworthy influence on the subsequent history of the version. At the beginning of the fourth century we find a sudden crop of new editions of the Septuagint, all more or less affected by his work. Three such are known to us, and they are of great importance for our present purpose, as we shall see when we come to describe the form in which the Septuagint has come down to us. These three editions are those of (1) Eusebius, (2) Lucian, (3) Hesychius.

New Editions of the Septuagint.—1. EUSEBIUS of Cæsarea, the first great historian of Christianity, with the assistance of his friend Pamphilus, produced Origen's text of the Septuagint (the fifth column of the Hexapla) as an independent edition, with alternative readings from the other versions in the margin.

2. *Lucian.*—LUCIAN of Samosata, a leading scholar at Antioch, produced another edition, of which the most marked characteristic was his habit, when he found different words or phrases in different copies, to combine them into a composite phrase, and so to preserve both. In the next chapter we shall see reason to believe that a similar course has been followed in the case of the New Testament at some period of its history.

3. *Hesychius.*—Lucian suffered martyrdom during the persecution of Maximinus, in A.D. 311; and the same fate is believed to have befallen HESYCHIUS, the author of the third edition of the Septuagint during the period of which we are speaking. Of the identification of this version, and of the manuscripts in which it is probably to be found, more will be said below.

These three editions were practically contemporary, and must all have been produced about the year 300. Each circulated in a different region. The edition of Eusebius and Pamphilus was generally used in Palestine; that of Lucian had its home in Antioch, and was also accepted in Constantinople and Asia Minor; while Hesychius was a scholar of Alexandria, and his edition circulated in Egypt.

The Present State of the Septuagint.

After the beginning of the fourth century the Septuagint, so far as we know, underwent no further revision, and it is unnecessary to trace its history beyond this point. In one form or another, and gradually becoming corrupted in all by the errors of copyists, it continued to be, as it is to this day, the Old Testament of the Greek or Eastern Church. We have now to begin at the other end, and ask in what form it has come down to us, and what means we have of ascertaining its origina text. And the method of this inquiry must be exactly the same as we have already applied in the case of the Hebrew text, and as we shall again have to apply when we come to the Greek text of the New Testament. We have to ask, primarily, in what manuscripts it has come down to us, what are their age and character, and into what groups they can be divided; and then it will be necessary to ask further whether any light can be thrown upon its history by the translations which have been made from it in ancient times, and by the quotations made from it by the early Christian Fathers.

MSS. of the Septuagint.

We have seen in the last chapter that no copy of the Hebrew Bible now extant was written earlier than the ninth century, while those of the Samaritan Pentateuch only go back to the tenth. The oldest copies of the Greek Bible are, however, of far greater antiquity than this, and take rank as the most venerable, as well as the most valuable, authorities for the Bible text which now survive. The oldest and best of them contain the New Testament as well as the Old, and will have to be described again in greater detail (since the New Testament portion has generally been more minutely studied than the Old) in a subsequent chapter. But a short account of them must be given here.

Classification of MSS.: Papyri, Uncials, Minuscules.

It has already been explained in Chapter I that Greek manuscripts fall into three classes: Papyri, Uncials, and Minuscules. The papyri (a class which for practical purposes has only come into existence since the first edition of this book was published) extend from the date at which the books of the Septuagint were first produced to the seventh century of the Christian era, when the Arab conquest of Egypt (in 640) put an end to the export of papyrus from Egypt; though Græco-Coptic copies of the Scriptures continued to be produced after that date. The vellum uncials cover the period from the fourth to the tenth century, while the minuscules begin in the ninth and go on until the end of the fifteenth century. In the earliest list of Septuagint manuscripts (that of Holmes and Parsons, see p. 73) all were comprised in a single numerical series, but the uncials were distinguished by Roman numerals I to XII, and the minuscules by Arabic numerals from 13 onwards. Modern editors, however, have usually followed the New Testament custom of denoting the uncials by capital letters, and this practice will be followed here. The papyri and minuscules will be given the numbers under which they appear in the list of Rahlfs (now continued by Dr. W. Kappler of Göttingen). It will be convenient, however, to describe the papyri separately, as forming a class by themselves of much earlier date than the vellum minuscules, and, indeed, than most of the vellum uncials.

1. *Papyri.*

The total number of papyrus fragments, great and small, is now considerable. A list compiled in 1933 by the Rev. P. L. Hedley contained 174 Old Testament items, including vellum fragments from Egypt, and ostraka (inscribed potsherds) as well as papyri; but most of these are small and of very little importance. The few that are of substantial value will now be described. The first two are indicated in the official list by capital letters, the others by Arabic numerals.

U. British Museum Papyrus 37. This was the first Biblical papyrus to be discovered, having been acquired by the Museum in 1836 from Dr. Edward Hogg, who stated that it had been discovered among the rubbish of an ancient convent at Thebes. It consists of thirty-two leaves of a papyrus codex of the Psalms, containing the text of Ps. x. (xi.) 2—xviii. (xix.) 6; xx. (xxi.) 14—xxxiv. (xxxv.) 6.[1] Written in a sloping hand, probably of the seventh century. Edited by Tischendorf (*Monumenta Sacra Inedita*, nov. coll. i., 1855), and used by Swete and Rahlfs in their editions. The text belongs to the Upper Egyptian family, with the Sahidic version.

X. Freer Greek MS. V at Washington. Acquired by Mr. C. L. Freer in 1916 as a mass of cohering fragments, which after skilled treatment and mounting in the library of the University of Michigan were added to the Freer Collection at Washington (see pp. 73, 151). The fragments form portions of thirty-three leaves, out of a probable total of forty-eight, of a codex of the Minor Prophets, probably of the later part of the third century. Of Hosea and the first verses of Amos (which follow) only a few letters are preserved; but from Amos i. 10 it is continuous (with some local mutilations) to the end of Malachi. Edited by Professor H. A. Sanders of Michigan, with 911.

[1] The Hebrew and Greek numerations of the Psalms differ. Psalms ix. and x. of the Hebrew are combined into one Psalm in the Greek; consequently the Greek numbers are one less than the Hebrew numbers (which are those used in our Bible and Prayer Book) as far as Ps. cxlvi. (Hebrew cxlvii.). Psalms cxlvi. and cxlvii. in the Greek are, however, combined into one Psalm in the Hebrew, so that the numeration agrees before the end.

905. Oxyrhynchus Papyrus 656, now in the Bodleian. Parts of four leaves of a codex, containing Gen. xiv. 21-23, xv. 5-9, xix. 32—xx. 11, xxiv. 28-47, xxvii. 32, 33, 40, 41, in a text rather different from any other MS. Early third century.

911. Berlin, Staatsbibliothek Gr. fol. 66, I, II. A codex of thirty-two leaves, of which the first and last (the latter being blank) are lost, and the others more or less mutilated. The hand is not a literary one, but such as is found in documents of the early part of the fourth century. The writing is very irregular, and the first nine leaves are in double columns, while the remainder is in single columns with long lines. It contains (with many mutilations) a great part of Genesis as far as xxxv. 8, where it breaks off, the title (" Creation of the World ") being appended, which shows that the rest of the book must have been contained in another volume. (The codex was no doubt copied from a roll, and Gen. i.-xxxv. is about as much as a single roll would hold.) The text shows many agreements with the two papyri of Genesis described below (**961** and **962**). Edited by H. A. Sanders and C. Schmidt, with X.

919. Heidelberg Septuagint Papyrus 1. Twenty-seven leaves, all more or less mutilated, of a codex of the Minor Prophets, written in a large, rough hand of the seventh century, by which time papyrus MSS. were generally poor examples of book production. Contains portions of Zechariah (iv. 6—v. 1, v. 3—vi. 2, vi. 4-15, vii. 10—x. 7, xi. 5—end) and nearly all Malachi, in a text akin to that of the vellum uncials A and Q. Edited by A. Deissmann.

952. British Museum Papyrus 2486. Acquired in 1922. Two conjoint leaves of a codex of which one leaf contains Song of Solomon v. 12—vi. 10, and the other the Apology of Aristides, chapter xv. The latter is important as confirming the Syriac version of the Apology, as against the rather shortened Greek text preserved in *Barlaam and Josaphat*. Early fourth century.

957. John Rylands Library, Papyrus Greek 458. The earliest extant fragment of a Bible MS., consisting of portions of four columns of a roll of papyrus extracted from the cartonnage of a mummy acquired in 1917 by Dr. Rendel Harris. It is written in a fine book-hand, which can be assigned with confidence to the second century B.C., and contains Deut. xxiii. 24—xxiv. 3, xxv. 1-3, xxvi. 12, 17-19, xxviii. 31-33. Small though these fragments are, their great age gives them a special interest, and it is noteworthy that they concur with the next earliest extant Septuagint MS. (**963**, described below) in agreeing with the vellum uncials Θ and A rather than with B. Identified and edited by C. H. Roberts only two years ago (*Two Biblical Papyri in the John Rylands Library, Manchester*, 1936). See Plate VI.

961. Chester Beatty Papyrus IV. The most remarkable discovery of Biblical manuscripts since Tischendorf's finding of the Codex Sinaiticus (see below, p. 128) was made about 1930, when Mr. A. Chester Beatty, an American collector of manuscripts resident in London, acquired from a dealer in Egypt a group of papyrus leaves, which on examination proved to be portions of codices of various books of the Greek Bible, ranging from the second to the fourth centuries. Several leaves from the same find were disposed of to other owners, as will be described in their place below. It is these manuscripts that have contributed most to our knowledge alike of book production and of the history of the text of the Greek Bible for the previously obscure period before the great vellum MSS. of the fourth century. The find, which is said to have come from the region of Aphroditopolis, on the right bank of the Nile, about thirty miles above Memphis, and presumably represents the library of some early Christian church, comprised portions of seven MSS. of the Old Testament, three of the New, and one which contained part of the lost Greek original of the book of Enoch and a homily on the Passion by Melito, Bishop of Sardis in the third quarter of the second century. The texts of all the Biblical texts have been edited by the present writer (*The Chester Beatty Biblical Papyri*, fasc. i.-vii., 1933-37), and full photographic facsimiles by Messrs. Emery Walker are in course of publication. The Enoch text has been edited by Professor Campbell Bonner, of Michigan University, who also has in hand the homily of Melito, which he was the first to identify. The New Testament portion of the collection is described below (pp. 125-127). Of the Old Testament MSS. the two first contain large portions of the book of Genesis, which are particularly welcome because the two oldest vellum MSS., the Vaticanus and the Sinaiticus, lack all except a few verses of this book. **961** consists of fifty leaves, all more or less mutilated, out of an original total of sixty-six, written in double columns in a rather large and thick uncial hand of the fourth century. Subject to many mutilations, it contains the text of Gen. ix. 1—xliv. 22.

962. Chester Beatty Papyrus V. Twenty-seven leaves (seventeen of which are nearly perfect) out of an original total of eighty-four, written in a document hand of the second half of the third century, with a single column to the page. Contains (with mutilations) Gen. viii. 13—ix. 1, xxiv. 13—xxv. 21, xxx. 24—xlvi. 33. From the three papyrus MSS. **911, 961,** and **962,** which show many affinities with one another, we now have substantial evidence for the text of Genesis circulating in Egypt about the end of the third century.

963. Chester Beatty Papyrus VI. Portions of fifty leaves (of which twenty-eight are substantially preserved) out of an original total of 108, of a codex containing the books of Numbers and Deuteronomy, written in a small and good hand which cannot be later than the middle of the second century, with two columns to the page (Plate VII). It is thus the earliest extant MS. of the Greek Bible with the exception of the fragment **957**, and the earliest example of a papyrus codex at present known. It contains portions of Numbers from v. 12 onwards (principally xxv.-xxxvi.) and of Deut. i. 20—xii. 17, xviii. 22—end. A few fragments of this MS. are in the possession of the University of Michigan. It is noteworthy that while the text of Numbers is most akin to that of B, in Deuteronomy it is conspicuously not in agreement with B, but rather with G and Θ.

964. Chester Beatty Papyrus XI. One complete leaf and one incomplete of a codex of Ecclesiasticus containing Ecclus. xxxvi. 28—xxxvii. 22, xlvi. 6-11, 16—xlvii. 2. Written in a large rough hand, probably of the fourth century.

965. Chester Beatty Papyrus VII. Fragments of thirty-three leaves, out of an estimated total of 112, of which the last eight were blank, of a codex of Isaiah, written in a beautiful hand, apparently of the first half of the third century. Two of the leaves are the property of Mr. W. Merton, and several fragments were originally acquired by the University of Michigan, but were courteously ceded to Mr. Chester Beatty. The text of all has been edited together. It contains scattered fragments between Isa. viii. 18—xix. 13, xxxviii. 14—xlv. 5, liv. 1—lx. 22, with a few marginal notes in Coptic (a very early example of this writing, without the additional letters which were eventually adopted).

966. Chester Beatty Papyrus VIII. Small portions of two leaves of a codex of Jeremiah, containing Jer. iv. 30—v. 1, 9-14, 23, 24, written probably about the end of the second century.

967, 968. Chester Beatty Papyri IX, X. Twenty-nine imperfect leaves of a codex containing the books of Ezekiel, Daniel and Esther. The Daniel leaves were originally described as a separate MS., hence the double numeration. Subsequently an American collector, Mr. John H. Scheide, acquired twenty-one perfect leaves of the Ezekiel portion of the MS., with the page numeration preserved intact. When complete, the manuscript seems to have consisted of 118 leaves, Ezekiel occupying the first half of the codex, and Daniel (including probably Susanna and Bel) and Esther the second, which was written by a different scribe. The date is probably in the first half of the third century. The Chester Beatty leaves (which have lost nearly half their height) contain portions of Ezek. xi. 25—xvii. 21, Dan. iii. 72—viii. 27 (chapters v. and vi. follow vii. and viii., and the preserved portion ends at vi. 18), Esther ii. 20—viii. 6; while the Scheide leaves contain Ezek. xix. 12—xxxix. 29, with gaps of five leaves. The Ezekiel and Esther texts agree markedly with B rather than with A. In Daniel the MS. is remarkable for containing the original Septuagint text, hitherto known only in a single late Greek copy and in a Syriac translation, instead of the version of Theodotion (see p. 57 above). The Scheide leaves have been deposited by their owner at the University of Princeton, and have been edited by Professor A. C. Johnson, with the assistance of Dr. H. S. Gehman and Dr. E. H. Kase.

2013. Leipzig Papyrus 39. Portions of a roll, about 13 feet 6 inches long, with the Bible text written on the back of a document bearing a date equivalent to A.D. 338. It may therefore be safely assigned to the later part of the fourth century. Contains Ps. xxx.-lv., but the first five Psalms are much mutilated. The text is akin to that of U. Edited by C. F. Heinrici (1903).

2019. British Museum Papyrus 230. Acquired in 1893 with a parcel of papyri from the Fayum. Two columns, apparently of a roll, written about the end of the third century. Contains Ps. xi. (xii.) 7—xiv. (xv.) 4. A second hand has marked off the syllables by dots, presumably for singing or reading. On the back is a portion of a speech by Isocrates, similarly marked, which seems to show that the book was used for school instruction. The Psalter text was edited by the present writer in *Biblical MSS. in the British Museum* (1900.)

2055. Papyrus Societa Italiana 980. Two leaves of a codex, containing Ps. cxliii. (cxliv.) 14—cxlviii. 3. Late third or fourth century. Its text agrees in several instances with that of the corrector of the Codex Sinaiticus known as $\aleph^{ca}$. Edited by G. Vitelli (1927).

Several other small fragments appear to be assignable to the third or fourth century, but they are too small to be of much importance. Among them, however, may be mentioned as a curiosity Amherst Papyrus III, on the back of which are written, in a hand of the first half of the fourth century, the first five verses of Genesis, first in the Septuagint version and then in that of Aquila (see p. 56 above), our knowledge of which is thus slightly increased.

2. *Vellum Uncials.*

Next follow the vellum uncial manuscripts, in the alphabetical order of the letters by which they are commonly indicated, with fuller descriptions of the most important.

א (*Aleph*, the first letter of the Hebrew alphabet) stands for the famous *Codex Sinaiticus* (sometimes designated by the letter S), one of the two oldest copies, apart from the papyri just described, of the Greek Bible. The story of the romantic discovery of this manuscript in the last century, when part of it was in the very act of being consumed as fuel, must be reserved for Chapter VIII. For the present it must suffice to say that it was first seen by the great German Biblical scholar, Constantine Tischendorf, in 1844, in the monastery of St. Catherine, at Mount Sinai. At his first visit he secured forty-three leaves belonging to the Old Testament, and presented them to his patron, King Frederick Augustus of Saxony, who placed them in the Court Library at Leipzig, where they still remain, with the name of the Codex Friderico-Augustanus. A subsequent visit brought to light 199 more leaves of the Old Testament and the whole of the New Testament; and these ultimately found a home in the Imperial Library at St. Petersburg, until in 1933 the whole MS. was sold by the Soviet Government to the British Museum, where it is now Add. MS. 43725. Parts of three more leaves were subsequently discovered in the bindings of other manuscripts in the library of Mount Sinai; these were also acquired for St. Petersburg, where they still remain. The manuscript was written in the fourth century, in a beautiful uncial hand; and it is extremely unfortunate that so much of the Old Testament has been lost. The parts which survive include fragments of Gen. xxiii., xxiv., and of Num. v., vi., vii.; 1 Chron. ix. 27—xix. 17; 2 Esdras [*i.e.*, canonical Ezra-Nehemiah] ix. 9 to end; Esther, Tobit, Judith, 1 Macc., 4 Macc., Isaiah, Jeremiah, Lament. i. 1—ii. 20, Joel, Obadiah, Jonah, Nahum to Malachi, Psalms, Proverbs, Ecclesiastes, Song of Solomon, Wisdom, Ecclesiasticus, Job. Three different scribes were employed on the writing of it, besides several correctors, the most important of whom were some scholars (indicated by the symbol $\aleph^{ca}$ or $\aleph^{c, b}$) who seem to have worked on the MS. at Cæsarea at the end of the sixth or beginning of the seventh century. In notes in this hand at the end of Esdras and Esther it is stated that the MS. was collated with an exceedingly ancient MS. which itself had been corrected by the martyr Pamphilus and had an autograph note by him, saying that he had corrected it in prison from Origen's own copy of the Hexapla. A facsimile of a page of this beautiful and most valuable manuscript is given in Plate XV.

A. *Codex Alexandrinus*, in the British Museum. This was probably written in the first half of the fifth century, and contains the whole Bible, except Gen. xiv. 14-17; xv. 1-5, 16-19; xvi. 6-9; 1 Kingdoms [=1 Sam.] xii. 18—xiv. 9; Ps. xlix. (l.) 20—lxxix. (lxxx.) 11, and some parts of the New Testament, which have been lost through accidental mutilation. It includes all four books of the Maccabees, for which it is the principal authority. Before the Psalms are placed the Epistle of Athanasius to Marcellinus on the Psalter, and the summary of the contents of the Psalms by Eusebius. At the end of the Psalms is an additional psalm (the 151st), which is found in some other early manuscripts, and a number of canticles, or chants, extracted from other parts of the Bible (for instance, the songs of Moses, in Deut. xxxii., of Hannah, in 1 Kingdoms ii. 1-10, and the Magnificat), which were used in the services of the Church. The apocryphal Psalms of Solomon were originally added at the end of the New Testament, but the leaves containing them have been lost. Two scribes were employed on the Old Testament portion of the MS., one of whom wrote the Octateuch (*i.e.*, Genesis-Ruth), Prophets, Maccabees, and the poetical books Job, Proverbs, Ecclesiastes, Song of Solomon, Wisdom and Ecclesiasticus, and the other the historical books (1-4 Kingdoms, 1-2 Chronicles, Esther, Tobit, Judith, 1-2 Esdras) and Psalms. For the history of the manuscript and a specimen of its writing, see pp. 135-138 and Plate XVI.

B. *Codex Vaticanus*, in the Vatican Library at Rome. It contains the whole Bible, written in the fourth century, and is (apart from the papyri) the oldest and generally the best extant copy of the Septuagint. It is nearly perfect, wanting only Gen. i. 1—xlvi. 28; 2 Kingdoms [=2 Sam.] ii. 5-7, 10-13; Ps. cv. (cvi.) 27—cxxxvii. (cxxxviii.) 6 of its original contents, so far as the Old Testament is concerned; but the Prayer of Manasses and the books of Maccabees were never included in it. The text of the current editions of the Septuagint are mainly derived from this manuscript. Its quality differs in different books. In Deuteronomy, Isaiah, Chronicles and 1-2 Esdras, it seems to be inferior to A, but elsewhere on the whole superior. In Judges it has quite a different text, which is found also in the Sahidic version and in Cyril of Alexandria (both, it will be observed, from Egypt, where B was probably written); but in Job it differs from the Sahidic in having the additions from Theodotion made by Origen in his Hexapla. In several books, on the other hand, its text is believed to be pre-Hexaplar. (See pp. 138-142 and Plate XVII.)

C. *Codex Ephraemi*, in the National Library at Paris. (See pp. 142, 143 and Plate XVIII.) This is a *palimpsest*; that is, the original writing has been partially washed or scraped out in order that the vellum might be used again to hold some other work—in this case a theological treatise. The result is that only parts of the original writing can now be read; and, in addition, most of the leaves containing the Old Testament have been lost. The sixty-four leaves which remain contain parts of Job, Proverbs, Ecclesiastes, Wisdom, Ecclesiasticus, and the Song of Solomon, written in the fifth century.

The manuscripts hitherto mentioned were originally complete Greek Bibles, containing both the Old and the New Testaments. Those which follow do not appear ever to have included the New Testament, and many of them only a portion of the Old.

D. *The Cotton Genesis.* One of the most lamentable sights in the Manuscript Department of the British Museum is that of the charred remains of many manuscripts of the greatest value which were burnt in the fire among Sir R. Cotton's books in 1731. Perhaps the most valuable of all the volumes then destroyed was this copy of the book of Genesis, written in a fine uncial hand of the fifth century, and adorned with 250 illustrations in a manner evidently derived directly from the ancient Greek style of painting. The remains of this once beautiful manuscript still show the general character of the writing and the miniatures, but in a lamentably shrunken and defaced condition. Fortunately the manuscript had been examined and its text carefully collated by Grabe before the fire; and from this collation its evidence for the text of Genesis is now known.

E. *The Bodleian Genesis,* at Oxford. Written in the tenth century, but, though thus considerably later than the copies hitherto mentioned, it contains a good text. The following passages are wanting, owing to mutilation of the manuscript: Gen. xiv. 7—xviii. 24, xx. 14—xxiv. 54. The manuscript at Oxford, which is commonly known as the Bodleian Genesis, ends at xlii. 18, but a leaf at Cambridge contains xlii. 18—xliv. 13, one side of the leaf being written in uncials, like the Oxford leaves, while the other is in minuscules, which shows that it is part of a volume which carries on the text as far as 3 Kingdoms xvi. 28. Most of this is at Leningrad, but some portions are lacking, of which the largest (Josh. xxiv. 27—end of Ruth) is in the British Museum. It was Tischendorf who disposed of the Oxford, London and Leningrad portions to their respective owners; but the tell-tale leaf which connected the uncial and minuscule portions was kept in his own possession till his death, when it was acquired by Cambridge University and identified by Dr. H. B. Swete and Mr. H. A. Redpath. The minuscule portion has the number 509 (a_2 in the large Cambridge Septuagint).

F. *Codex Ambrosianus,* at Milan. Written in the fifth century, with three columns to the page, and having (what is very unusual in early manuscripts) punctuation, accents, and breathings by the original scribe. It contains Gen. xxxi. 15—Josh. xii. 12, with many losses, however, from mutilation, and small fragments of Isaiah and Malachi. Its evidence is valuable, and where A and B differ it generally agrees with A.

G. *Codex Sarravianus*: 130 leaves at Leiden, twenty-two at Paris, and one at Leningrad. A very fine manuscript, probably of the fifth century, though it has sometimes been attributed to the fourth. It is written with two columns to the page, and (like the Vatican and Sinaitic MSS. above) has no enlarged initials. It contains portions of the Pentateuch, Joshua and Judges, and its special characteristic is that it contains a *Hexaplar* text. It is provided with Origen's asterisks and obeli; but, unfortunately, as in all other MSS. of this class, these symbols have been very imperfectly reproduced, so that we cannot depend absolutely on it to recover the text as it was before Origen's additions and alterations. Plate VIII shows (in reduced form) the page containing Deut. xvi. 22—xvii. 8. Asterisks will be seen in the margins of both columns. That near the bottom of the first column indicates that words corresponding to "and thou hast heard of it" in xvii. 4 were not found in the original Greek of the Septuagint, but were inserted by Origen to make it correspond with the Hebrew. Similarly the asterisks in the second column show that in xvii. 5 the words "which have committed that wicked thing unto thy gates, even that man or that woman" were not in the original Septuagint, but were inserted by Origen from the Hebrew. Both passages occur in our Authorised Version, which of course follows the Hebrew; but they are not in the best MSS. of the Septuagint, though A and F have the second passage, which is a sign that they have been affected by Hexaplaric influences.

H. *Codex Petropolitanus*, a palimpsest at Leningrad, of the sixth century; contains portions of the book of Numbers.

I. A Bodleian MS. of the Psalms (including, like A, the canticles), of the ninth century. It was wrongly included by Holmes and Parsons among the cursive MSS., and numbered 13. In its margin many readings are given from Aquila, Symmachus, and Theodotion, and from the "fifth" and "seventh" versions (see p. 58).

K. Twenty-two palimpsest leaves at Leipzig, of the seventh century, containing fragments of Numbers, Deuteronomy, Joshua, and Judges.

L. *The Vienna Genesis*: a splendid MS. at Vienna, written in silver letters upon purple vellum, and adorned with illustrations, which, like those of D, recall the classical style of painting. It is of the fifth or sixth century, and contains portions of the book of Genesis on twenty-four leaves.

M. *Codex Coislinianus*, at Paris: a handsome MS. of the seventh century, containing the earlier books of the Old Testament, from Genesis to 3 Kingdoms viii. 40, though mutilated in places. This MS. belongs to the same class as G, containing a Hexaplar text.

N. *Codex Basiliano-Vaticanus*, at Rome and Venice; written in sloping uncials of the eighth or ninth century. It consists of

PLATE VIII.

93

ΛΕΜΕΙϹΙΗϹΕΝΚϹΟΘϹΟΥ
ΟΥΘΥϹΕΙϹΚΩΤΩΘΩ — CAPVT XVII.
ϹΟΥΜΟϹΧΟΝΗΠΡΟΒΑ
ΤΟΝΕΝΩΕϹΤΙΝΕΝΑΥ
ΤΩΜΩΜΟϹΠΑΝΡΗΜΑ
ΠΟΝΗΡΟΝΒΔΕΛΥΓΜΑ
ΚΥΤΟΥΘΥϹΟΥΕϹΤΙΝ
ΕΑΝΔΕΕΥΡΕΘΗΕΝϹΟΙ
ΕΝΜΙΑΤΩΝΠΟΛΕΩΝ
ϹΟΥΩΝΚϹΟΘϹϹΟΥΔΙ
ΔΩϹΙΝϹΟΙΑΝΗΡΗΓΥ
ΝΗΟϹΤΙϹΠΟΙΗϹΕΙΤΟ
ΠΟΝΗΡΟΝΕΝΑΝΤΙΚΥ
ΤΟΥΘΥϹΟΥΠΑΡΕΛΘΕΙΝ
ΤΗΝΔΙΑΘΗΚΗΝΑΥΤΟΥ
ΚΑΙΕΛΘΟΝΤΕϹΛΑΤΡΕΥ
ϹΩϹΙΝΘΕΟΙϹΕΤΕΡΟΙϹ
ΚΑΙΠΡΟϹΚΥΝΗϹΩϹΙΝ
ΑΥΤΟΙϹΤΩΗΛΙΩΗΤΗ
ϹΕΛΗΝΗΗΠΑΝΤΙΤΩ
ΕΚΤΟΥΚΟϹΜΟΥΤΟΥΟΥ
ΡΑΝΟΥΑΟΥΠΡΟϹΕΤΑ
ΞΕΝΚΑΙΑΝΑΓΓΕΛΗϹΟΙ
※ ΚΑΙΑΚΟΥϹΗϹ· ΚΑΙΕΚ
ΖΗΤΗϹΗϹΕϹΦΟΔΡΑΚΑΙ
ΙΔΟΥΑΛΗΘΩϹΓΕΓΟ
ΝΕΝΤΟΡΗΜΑΓΕΓΕΝΗ

ΤΑΙΤΟΒΔΕΛΥΓΜΑΤΟΥ
ΤΟΕΝΙΗΛ·ΚΑΙΕΞΑΡΕΙϹ
ΤΟΝΑΝΟΝΕΚΕΙΝΟΝ
ΗΤΗΝΓΥΝΑΙΚΑΕΚΕΙ
ΝΗΝ ※ ΟΙΕΠΟΙΗϹΑΝ
※ ΤΟΡΗΜΑΤΟΠΟΝΗΡΟΝ
※ ΤΟΥΤΟΠΡΟϹΠΥΛΑΙϹ
※ ϹΟΥΤΟΝΑΝΔΡΑΗΤΗΝ
※ ΓΥΝΑΙΚΑ·ΚΑΙΛΙΘΟΒΟ
ΛΗϹΕΤΕΑΥΤΟΥϹΕΝΛΙ
ΘΟΙϹΚΑΙΤΕΛΕΥΤΗϹΟΥ
ϹΙΝΕΠΙΔΥΟΜΑΡΤΥϹΙΝ
ΗΕΠΙΤΡΙϹΙΝΜΑΡΤΥϹΙΝ
ΑΠΟΘΑΝΕΙΤΑΙΟΑΠΟ
ΘΝΗϹΚΩΝΟΥΚΑΠΟ
ΘΑΝΕΙΤΑΙΕΠΙΜΑΡΤΥ
ΡΙΕΝΙΚΑΙΗΧΕΙΡΤΩΝ
ΜΑΡΤΥΡΩΝΕϹΤΑΙΕΠ
ΑΥΤΩΕΝΠΡΩΤΟΙϹ
ΘΑΝΑΤΩϹΑΙΑΥΤΟΝΚ
ΗΧΕΙΡΠΑΝΤΟϹΤΟΥΛΑ
ΟΥΕΠΕϹΧΑΤΩΚΑΙΕ
ΞΑΡΕΙϹΤΟΝΠΟΝΗΡΟΝ
ΕΞΥΜΩΝΑΥΤΩΝΕΑΝ
ΔΕΑΔΥΝΑΤΗϹΗΑΠΟ
ϹΟΥΡΗΜΑΕΝΚΡΙϹΕΙ
ΑΝΑΜΕϹΟΝΑΙΜΑΤΟϹΑΙΜΑ

CODEX SARRAVIANUS—5TH CENT.

(*Original size*, 9½ *in.* × 9 *in.*)

PLATE IX.

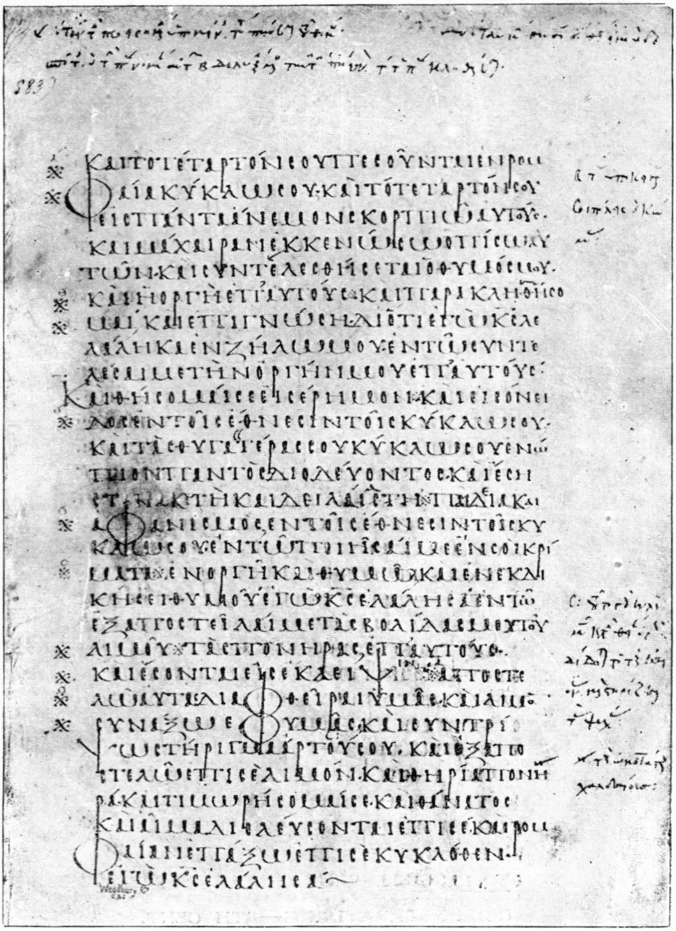

CODEX MARCHALIANUS—6TH CENT.

(*Original size,* 11½ *in.* × 7 *in.*)

two volumes, both of which have, unfortunately, been much mutilated. In their present condition, the first (at Rome) contains from Lev. xiii. 59 to the end of Chronicles (with some lacunæ), 1 Esdras i. 1—ix. 1, 2 Esdras (*i.e.*, the canonical Ezra-Nehemiah) v. 10—xvii. 3, and Esther; the second (at Venice) begins with Job xxx. 8, and contains the rest of Job, Proverbs, Ecclesiastes, Song of Solomon, Wisdom, Ecclesiasticus, Minor Prophets, Major Prophets, Tobit, Judith, and the four books of the Maccabees. Until quite recently the two volumes were regarded as different MSS., and the second had assigned to it a distinct letter, V, and was entitled *Codex Venetus*. In conjunction with B, this was used for the Roman edition of the Septuagint, published in 1587, which has been the edition in common use until the appearance of Swete's edition in 1887-94. The person who examined it for Holmes and Parsons omitted to tell the editors that it was written in uncials, and it consequently appears in their list among the cursives, with the number 23, while its first volume takes its proper place among the uncials.

O. *Codex Dublinensis Rescriptus*, at Trinity College, Dublin. This is a *palimpsest*, like C, but consists of only eight leaves, containing portions of Isaiah, written early in the sixth century. Its special value is due to the fact that it was written in Egypt and apparently provides us with information as to the text of the edition by Hesychius, which circulated in that country.

P. Fragments of Psalms, at Emmanuel College, Cambridge; originally reckoned by Holmes and Parsons among the cursives, as No. 294, but subsequently placed among the uncials (No. IX).

Q. *Codex Marchalianus*, in the Vatican Library at Rome. This is a most valuable copy of the Prophets, written in Egypt in the sixth century, in a fine bold uncial hand. The editor of this manuscript, Dr. Ceriani, has shown that the text, as originally written, is that of Hesychius; and its value is still further increased by the fact that an almost contemporary hand has added a great number of various readings in the margin from a copy of the Hexaplar text. These marginal readings include the additions made by Origen, generally accompanied by the proper critical marks (the obelus or asterisk), together with readings from Aquila, Symmachus, and Theodotion. Plate IX gives a representation of a page of this manuscript (the whole of which has been published in a photographic facsimile) containing Ezek. v. 12-17.[1] In the margin will be seen several asterisks, which are repeated in the line itself at the point at which the insertion

[1] A papyrus fragment of this same passage, also containing the Hexaplar text and symbols, was acquired in Egypt by Mr. B. P. Grenfell in 1894-5, and is now in the Bodleian Library at Oxford. It was apparently written about the fourth century.

begins (*e.g.*, lines 6, 10), and before the beginning of each line of the passage affected, while the *metobelus*, indicating the close of the inserted passage, is represented by a sort of semicolon (*e.g.*, lines 2, 7). In most cases the name of the version from which the inserted passage was taken is indicated by an initial in the margin, α standing for Aquila (*e.g.*, line 1), θ for Theodotion (lines 6, 11, 15, 17, 22), and σ or συ for Symmachus. Where Hesychius has introduced words on his own account which were not in the original Septuagint, the asterisk indicating such words has been written by the original scribe, and has ample space allowed it in the writing; but the great majority of the critical signs have been added by the reviser, and show that the insertion had already been made by Origen in his Hexaplar text, which Hesychius often followed. The small writing in the margin consists of notes added in the thirteenth century, of no textual importance.

R. *Verona Psalter*, containing both Greek and Latin versions of the Psalms, written in the sixth century. Several canticles are added, as in A, and the 151st Psalm has been supplied by a later hand. The Greek is written in Latin letters.

T. *Zurich Psalter*, in its original state a splendid manuscript, written in silver letters with gold initials upon purple vellum. Several leaves are now missing. The canticles are included. Written in the seventh century, and often agrees with the readings of A in doubtful passages.

U. See above, p. 62.

V. *Codex Venetus*; see N, above.

W. Fragments of Psalms, at Paris, of the ninth century. Included by Holmes and Parsons among the cursives, as No. 43.

X. A MS. in the Vatican at Rome, containing most of Job, of the ninth century. Included by Holmes and Parsons among the cursives, as No. 258.

Y. *Codex Taurinensis*, at Turin, of the ninth century, containing the Minor Prophets.

Z^a, Z^b, Z^c, Z^d, Z^e, are small fragments of various books, of slight importance.

Γ (*Gamma*, the third letter of the Greek alphabet, those of the Latin alphabet being now exhausted). *Codex Cryptoferratensis*, at Grotta Ferrata, in Italy; *palimpsest* fragments of the Prophets, written in the eighth or ninth century. Much of the original writing has been hopelessly obliterated. It is remarkable that most of the Greek manuscripts in the monastery of Grotta Ferrata are palimpsests, showing how scarce vellum was there, and how the literary activity of the monks caused them to use the same sheets twice over, and sometimes even thrice.

Δ (*Delta*, the fourth letter of the Greek alphabet). Fragments of Bel and the Dragon, according to the version of Theodotion, written in the fifth century, if not earlier; in the Bodleian Library at Oxford.

Θ (*Theta*, the eighth letter of the Greek alphabet). *Codex Washingtonianus* I, in the Freer Collection at Washington, containing the books of Deuteronomy and Joshua, of the sixth century. The quire-numeration shows that it originally included the previous books of the Pentateuch, and Judges and Ruth may have been appended. In text it agrees more with A than with B. The manuscript was acquired in Egypt by Mr. C. L. Freer in 1906, together with **1219** and two New Testament MSS. (see below, pp. 149, 151).

Π (*Pi*, the sixteenth letter of the Greek alphabet). Fragments of 4 Maccabees, of the ninth century, at St. Petersburg.

1219. *Codex Washingtonianus* II, in the Freer Collection; 107 fragmentary leaves of a Psalter, of the sixth or seventh century. The last quire, from Ps. cxlii. 5 to cli. 6, is a later addition, of the ninth century. The earlier part of the codex is particularly incomplete. The text is akin to that of A.

The catalogue above given shows the material now available in the shape of uncial manuscripts. The most important of them are, no doubt, B, A, and (where it is available) ℵ, and, in their own special departments, G and Q.

3. *Minuscules.*

The cursive manuscripts of the Septuagint are far too numerous to be described in detail. In the great edition of Holmes and Parsons no less than 280[1] such manuscripts are described, and their various readings quoted. It may be of some interest, however, as showing the amount of evidence available for each part of the Old Testament to indicate which manuscripts contain, in full or in part, each of the chief groups of books. The following 63 MSS. contain the Pentateuch, or part of it: Nos. 14-10, 25, 28-32, 37, 38, 44-47, 52-59, 61, 64, 68, 71-79, 82-85, 105-108, 118, 120-122, 125-136. Fifty-five contain the historical books: 15, 16, 18, 19, 29, 30, 44, 52-59, 63, 64, 68, 70-72, 74-77, 82, 84, 85, 92, 93, 98, 106-108, 118-121, 123, 128, 131, 134, 144,

[1] Nominally 313, but at least 20 of them (1-13, 27, 43, 156, 188, 190, 258, 294) are really uncials, and several manuscripts are described more than once under different numbers. Thus 33=97=238, 41=42, 56=64, 63=129, 73=237, 89=239, 94=131, 109=302, 130=144, 186=220, 221=276, 234=311. This reduces the total to 280. Since Holmes and Parsons, however, great additions have been made to the list. The official catalogue, kept formerly by Rahlfs and now by Kappler, includes all MSS. (papyri, uncials, and minuscules) in a single numerical list (incorporating the H. and P. numbers with the necessary revisions). This now extends to 2055, but with some intentional gaps to receive additions. The actual total is about 1560.

158, 209, 236, 237, 241-249, besides one (No. 62) which contains only the books of Maccabees. The Psalms are preserved in no less than 122 copies—viz.: 21, 39, 55, 65-67, 69, 70, 80, 81, 99-102, 104, 106, 111-115, 140-146, 150-152, 154, 162-187, 189-197, 199-206, 208, 210-219, 222, 223, 225-227, 262-293. The Prophets appear, more or less perfectly, in 62 manuscripts—viz.: 22-24, 26, 33-36, 40-42, 45, 48, 49, 51, 61, 62, 68, 70, 86-88, 90, 91, 93, 95-97, 104-106, 109, 114, 130, 132, 144, 147-149, 153, 185, 198, 228-233, 238-240, 301-311. Finally there are 39 manuscripts containing the books of the Hagiographa: 55, 68, 70, 103, 106, 109, 110, 137-139, 147, 149, 155, 157, 159-161, 248-261, 295-300, 307[a], 308[a]. This classification, it will be observed, applies only to MSS. in the Holmes and Parsons list; but it does not seem worth while to carry it further. The value of the cursives only appears when they can be divided into groups, showing common descent from one or other of the ancient editions of the Septuagint which have been described above. How far this is at present feasible will be shown presently.

Printed Editions.

Such are the manuscripts on which scholars must depend for recovering the genuine text of the Greek Old Testament. It will be useful to describe briefly what has been done in this direction, as showing the kind and the amount of labour which scholars have bestowed on the task of making the text of the Bible as accurate as possible in every point. The first printed edition of the Septuagint was made by the Spaniard Cardinal Ximenes, who combined the Hebrew, Greek, and Latin versions of the Bible in the four volumes known as the Complutensian Polyglot (dated 1514-17, but not actually issued until 1522). His Greek text was mainly based on two late MSS. in the Vatican, now known as 108 and 248. Meanwhile in 1518 the great printer Aldus had issued an edition based on MSS. then at Venice, which accordingly has the honour of being the first printed Septuagint in order of publication. But the most important edition in early times is the Roman, published under the patronage of Pope Sixtus in 1587. This edition, which rests mainly on the great Codex Vaticanus (B), though with many errors and divergences,[1] remained the standard text of the Septuagint until the appearance of Swete's edition, mentioned below. In 1707-28 a very good edition of the Codex Alexandrinus (A), supplemented from other MSS. where A is deficient, was published by the Anglo-Prussian scholar Grabe. But the greatest work on the Septuagint up to

[1] It has been estimated that the Roman text differs from that of B in over 4000 places.

quite recent years was that which R. Holmes and J. Parsons produced at Oxford in 1798-1827. In this colossal work the Roman text of 1587 is reprinted without variation, but in the critical notes are given the various readings of no less than 300 manuscripts, as above described. Unfortunately many of these MSS. were very imperfectly examined by the persons employed for the task by the editors, so that much of the work has had to be done over again; but the edition of Holmes and Parsons remains the only complete one which gives a general view of the manuscript evidence, and has been the basis of all study of the Septuagint text since their day. Of later editors it is only necessary to mention Tischendorf, who between 1850 and 1869 produced four editions based on the Roman text, with variants from א, A, and C (seventh edition in 1887, by Dr. Nestle); Field, who edited the remains of the Hexapla in 1875; Lagarde, who in 1883 published an attempt to recover the edition of Lucian, besides many other valuable contributions to the criticism of the Septuagint; and Dr. Swete, of Cambridge, who in 1887-94 produced an edition giving the text of the Septuagint according to the best MS. extant in each part (B, wherever it is available, elsewhere א or A), with all the variants in three or four of the next best manuscripts. This was the first stage in a project envisaging eventual production of a full critical edition, which would replace Holmes and Parsons in the light of all the information accumulated since their day. The editorship of this larger Cambridge edition was entrusted to Dr. A. E. Brooke and Dr. N. McLean, who since 1906 have produced eight parts, containing the Octateuch and the later historical books (1-4 Kingdoms, 1-2 Chronicles, 1-2 Esdras). In this edition the text is the same as that of Swete, but the critical apparatus includes the readings of all the papyri and uncials and a large selection of minuscules, together with all the principal versions and the quotations in the Fathers.

Another large critical edition was planned by the Septuaginta-Kommission of Göttingen, but has been seriously delayed by adverse conditions arising out of the war. The German scholars have wisely devoted their attention primarily to books which are not likely to be reached by the Cambridge editors for some time. The Psalter was published by Rahlfs in 1930-1, and 1 Maccabees by Kappler in 1936; and 2 Maccabees and Isaiah are in preparation. Further, an edition of Genesis, on a reduced scale, was published in 1926; and in 1935 Rahlfs produced a handy edition of the whole Septuagint in two volumes, with a revised text based upon א A B and a short apparatus with variants from these and a few other MSS. As compared with the smaller Cambridge edition, this gives a revised text (instead of merely reprinting the text of a selected MS., right or wrong), but a smaller critical apparatus.

How to Recover the Original Text.

Much has thus been done, yet the work which remains to be done in connection with the text of the Septuagint is still very considerable. One would wish, first of all, to disengage the editions of Eusebius, Lucian, and Hesychius, and thereby to see what was the state of the Septuagint text at the end of the third century. Then we want to go further back, and discover, if possible, what the original text was like when it left the hands of the translators themselves. And when that is done we still have to ask the question which is the ultimate cause of all our interest in the Septuagint—What does this original text tell us as to the character of the Hebrew text from which it was taken ?

Reconstruction of the Three Editions.

For the first part of this inquiry scholars have already collected considerable materials. The manuscripts of the Septuagint, when closely examined, are found to fall into certain groups which point to several different centres of origin; and, chiefly by the evidence afforded by quotations in the writings of the early Fathers whose places of residence we know, it is possible to localise these centres, and thereby to say that one group represents the Antiochian edition of Lucian, and another the Alexandrian edition of Hesychius.

1. *Eusebius.*—The most recognisable of the three editions is that of Eusebius and Pamphilus, which in fact reproduced the text fixed by Origen. For this the leading authorities are the Syriac translation by Bishop Paulus of Tella, which contains the Prophets and Hagiographa, with Origen's apparatus of asterisks and obeli; the Codex Sarravianus (G), containing large parts of the Pentateuch, Joshua and Judges; the Codex Coislinianus (M), containing the same books, together with those of Samuel and Kings; the cursive MSS. known as 54 and 75 in the Octateuch, and 86 and 88 in the Prophets; and the copious marginal notes in the Codex Marchalianus (Q), which give Hexaplar readings with an indication of the author (Aquila, Symmachus, or Theodotion) from whom they were taken.

2. *Lucian.*—Of the other two editions, the most recognisable is that of Lucian. Certain direct references to it in early writers, and the statement that it was the standard text in Antioch and Constantinople, have enabled modern editors to recognise it in certain extant manuscripts and in the copious Biblical quotations of Chrysostom and Theodoret. The first suggestion to this effect seems to have been made by Dr. Ceriani, of Milan, and it was

simultaneously worked out by Field, in the Prolegomena to his *Hexapla*, and by Lagarde, who produced a text of half the Old Testament (Genesis-Esther) according to this edition, the completion of it being prevented by his lamented death. No uncial MS. contains a Lucianic text, with the exception of the Codex Venetus (V or N). In the books Genesis-Judges it appears in the cursives 19, 108, 118; in the historical books, 19, 36, 62, 82, 93, 108, 118; in the Prophets, 22, 36, 48, 51, 93, 144, 231, 308. The text of the Hagiographa has not yet been investigated. A Lucianic text also appears in the Gothic and old Slavonic versions, and in the first printed edition of the Septuagint—the Complutensian, which was mainly taken from the MS. known as 108.

3. *Hesychius.*—The edition of Hesychius remains, and the identification of this is still involved in some uncertainty. As the edition which circulated in Egypt, it seems likely that it would be found in MSS. written in that country, in the Coptic versions, which were made from the Septuagint for the use of the native Egyptians, and in the writings of the Alexandrian Fathers, such as Cyril. Good authorities differ, however, as to the Greek manuscripts in which this edition is to be looked for. Ceriani assigns to it the Codex Alexandrinus (A), the original text of the Codex Marchalianus (Q), the Dublin fragments of Isaiah (O), and the cursives 26, 106, 198, 306 (all of the Prophets). The able German professor, Cornill, however, also dealing with MSS. containing the Prophets, finds the Hesychian version in 49, 68, 87, 90, 91, 228, 238, with the Coptic, Ethiopic, Arabic, and Old Latin versions. These are akin to the above-mentioned group represented by A, 26, etc., but have (in his opinion) more of the appearance of an authorised edition, in which marked peculiarities of text, such as there are in A, are not to be expected. The question cannot be solved without further investigation, to which it may be hoped that the large Cambridge edition will considerably contribute.

It will be observed that only a comparatively small number of manuscripts can be definitely assigned to one or other of the ancient editions, and even as to these it has to be remembered that any manuscript may have texts of different character in different books. All manuscripts eventually go back to a period when each book was contained in a separate roll or rolls; and when they were combined into single codices, there could be no guarantee that all the rolls copied into a single codex were of the same textual type. Thus **75**, which is Origenian in Deuteronomy, is said to be Lucianic in Genesis; and the papyrus **963** has quite different textual affinities in Numbers and Deuteronomy.

Texts of the Great Uncials.

The majority of the minuscules are later copies containing mixed and corrupt texts, which will be of little use towards the recovery of the original form of the Septuagint. There remain, however, some of the early uncial manuscripts, including the oldest of all, the great Codex Vaticanus (B). Cornill at one time suggested that B was based on the edition of Eusebius, with the omission of all the passages therein marked by asterisks as insertions from the Hebrew; but this view has been abandoned, and it is more probable (as stated by Dr. Hort) that it is akin to the manuscripts which Origen used as the foundation of his Hexapla. Origen would, no doubt, have taken as his basis of operations the best copies of the Septuagint then available; and if B is found to contain a text like that used by Origen, it is a strong testimony in its favour. Hence it is commonly held to be, on the whole, the best and most neutral of all the manuscripts of the Septuagint; and it is a happy accident that it has formed the foundation of the commonly received text—that, namely, of the Roman edition of 1587. It is becoming clear, however, that the character of B is not uniform throughout (see above, p. 68). Between B and A the differences of reading are sometimes very strongly marked, and the divergences have not yet by any means been explained. All conclusions are at present tentative and provisional, and the best scholars are the least positive as to the certainty of their results. Of the other great manuscripts, א seems to contain a text intermediate between A and B, though in the book of Tobit it has a form of the text completely different from both. Ceriani considers that it shows some traces of Hesychian influence. He makes the same claim for C; but of this the fragments are so scanty that it is difficult to arrive at any positive conclusion.

Comparison of Septuagint with Massoretic Text.

But although many points of detail still remain obscure, we yet know quite enough about the Septuagint to be able to state broadly the relation in which it stands to the Massoretic Hebrew text. And here it is that the great interest and importance of the Septuagint becomes evident. Rightly or wrongly, it is certain that the Septuagint differs from the Massoretic text to a very marked extent. Words and phrases constantly differ; details which depend upon figures and numbers, such as the ages of the patriarchs in the early chapters of Genesis, show great discrepancies; whole verses, and even longer passages, appear in the one text and not in the other; the arrangement of the contents of several books varies very largely. The discrepancies are least in the Pentateuch, the words of which were no doubt held most sacred by all Jews, and so would be less likely to suffer change either in the Hebrew or in the Greek. But in the books of Kingdoms, the Septuagint departs frequently from the Massoretic text; the student of the Variorum Bible may be referred for examples to 1 Kingd. iv. 1; v. 6; x. 1; xiii. 1, 15; xiv. 24, 41; xv. 13; 2 Kingd. iv. 6-7; xi. 23; xvii. 3; xx. 18, 19; 3 Kingd. ii. 29; viii. 1; xii. 2, 3, 4-24. In the narrative of David and Goliath the variations are especially striking; for the best MSS. of the Septuagint omit 1 Kingd. xvii. 12-31, 41, 50, 55-58, together with xviii. 1-5, 9-11, 17-19, and the rest of the references to Merab. In the book of Job there is good reason to believe that the original text of the Septuagint omitted nearly one-sixth of the whole (see p. 82). In Jeremiah the order of the prophecies differs greatly, chapters xlvi.-li. being inserted (in a different order) after chapter xxv. 13, while the following passages are altogether omitted: x. 6-8, 10; xvii. 1-4; xxvii. 1, 7, 13, and a great part of 17-22; xxix. 16-20; xxxiii. 14-26; xxxix. 4-13. Even if we reduce the number of minor variations as much as possible (and very many of them may be due to mistakes on the part of the Septuagint translators, to different methods of supplying the vowels in the Hebrew text, to different divisions of the words of the Hebrew, or to a freedom of translation which amounts to paraphrase), yet these larger discrepancies, the list of which the reader of the Variorum Bible may easily increase for himself, are sufficient to show that the Hebrew text which lay before the authors of the Septuagint differed very considerably from that which the Massoretes have handed down to us. What the explanation of this difference may be, or which of the two texts is generally to be preferred, are questions to which it would be rash, in the present state of our knowledge, to pretend to give a decided answer. Some statement of the case is, however, necessary for those who wish to understand what the evidence for our present Old Testament text really is; but it will be better to postpone the discussion of it until we have completed the list of the versions from which some light upon the question may be expected. Some of them help us to reconstruct the text of the Septuagint; others tell us of the condition of the Hebrew text at dates later than those at which the Samaritan and the Greek versions were made; all in some degree help forward our main purpose—the history of the Hebrew text of the Old Testament.

§ 3.—Other Eastern Versions.

The Syriac Version.—The two versions of which we have hitherto spoken, the Samaritan and the Greek, were made before the institution of Christianity. It is otherwise with all the remaining versions of the Old Testament. Outside the Jewish and Samaritan communities there was no desire to know the Hebrew Scriptures until Christianity came, preaching the fulfilment of those Scriptures and the extension of their promises to all nations. As the Christian missionaries spread abroad from Judæa into the surrounding countries, fulfilling their Master's last command to preach the Gospel to every people, they necessarily referred much to the history of the nation among which He wrought His ministry, and to the prophets who had prepared His way before Him. Hence there arose a demand for translations of the Hebrew Scriptures into the languages of every country in which Christianity was preached; and the versions of which we have now to speak were all the offspring of that demand. The first of these in geographical nearness to Judæa was the Syriac. Syriac is the language of Syria and Mesopotamia, which lie north and north-east of Palestine, and, with some slight differences of dialect, it was the actual language commonly spoken in Palestine (and there known as Aramaic) at the time of our Lord's life on earth. In the case of the New Testament, as we shall see, several translations into Syriac were made; but of the Old Testament there was (apart from the version of Origen's Hexaplar text, mentioned above, p. 59, and some other late translations from the Septuagint, of which only fragments remain) only one, and that the one which is and always has been the standard version of all the Syriac Churches. It is known as the Peshitta, or " Simple " version, but the exact explanation of the name is unknown. It was probably made in the second or third century after Christ; certainly not later, since in the fourth century we find it quoted and referred to as an authority of long standing. A considerable number of copies of it are known, most of them forming part of a splendid collection of Syriac manuscripts which were secured for the British Museum in 1842 from the monastery of St. Mary Deipara, situated in the Nitrian desert in Egypt. Among these is a manuscript dated in the year A.D. 464, which has the distinction of being the oldest copy of the Bible in any language of which the exact date is known. We thus have direct evidence of the text of this version in the fifth century, and in the century before that we find copious quotations from it in the writings of two Syrian Fathers, Ephraem and Aphraates.

The Peshitta version originally omitted the books of the Apocrypha, and hence was evidently taken from Hebrew MSS. after the Canon of the Hebrew Scriptures had been finally fixed. It also was originally without the Chronicles, which were added to it (from a Jewish Targum) at a later time. The cause of the omission is not known, and it may have been due simply to a belief that the Jewish history was sufficiently represented by the books of Kings. The whole translation is from the Hebrew, but the translators have been rather free in their renderings, and seem also to have been acquainted with the Septuagint. The books of the Apocrypha (except 1 Esdras and perhaps Tobit) were added at an early date, and they now appear in all the earlier Syriac MSS. which make any pretence to contain a complete Old Testament. The Syriac version of these books is often useful in correcting errors which have found their way into the Greek text.[1] At a later date the whole version was revised by comparison with the Septuagint; and hence it is not very trustworthy as evidence for the Hebrew text, and its agreements with the Septuagint cannot be taken with any certainty as independent confirmations of its reading.

The Coptic Versions (see Plate XXIII).—Coptic is the language which was used by the natives of Egypt at the time when the Bible was first translated for their use. It is, indeed, a modified form of the language which had been spoken in the country from time immemorial; but about the end of the first century after Christ it began, owing to the influence of the great number of Greeks settled in Egypt, to be written in Greek characters, with six additional letters, and with a considerable admixture of Greek words. It is to this form of the language that the name of Coptic was given, and it continues to the present day to be used in the services of the Christian Church in Egypt. There were, however, differences in the dialects spoken in different parts of the country, and consequently more than one translation of the Scriptures was required. The number of these dialects is still a matter of uncertainty, for the papyri discovered in Egypt of late years have been, and still are, adding considerably to our knowledge of them; but it appears that four or five different versions of the New Testament have been identified, and three of the Old. Two of these stand out as of real importance, the others being mere fragments.

The Coptic versions of the Bible are more important for the New Testament than for the Old, and it will consequently be convenient to treat of them at greater length in the chapter dealing with the versions of the New Testament. In the Old Testament they were made from the Septuagint, and consequently their evidence is mainly valuable for the purpose of restoring the Greek text, and only indirectly for the Hebrew text which lies behind the Greek. For the student of the Septuagint, however, they should be of considerable service. As it is probable that they were taken from the edition of the Septuagint current in

[1] Especially in the book of Ecclesiasticus, in which the Syriac version must have been made from the Hebrew original; see the Variorum Apocrypha and the editor's preface. On the Hebrew original of this book, see below, p. 93.

Egypt, which was that of Hesychius, they should give valuable assistance in identifying and recovering the text of that edition. The two most important of the Coptic versions are—(*a*) the *Memphitic* or *Bohairic Version*, current in Lower or Northern Egypt, and (*b*) the *Thebaic* or *Sahidic Version*, current in Upper or Southern Egypt. Neither version is complete. Of the Bohairic, the Pentateuch, Psalms and Prophets have been published, and other fragments are known. The Sahidic exists in very considerable fragments, which have been much increased by recent discoveries. The British Museum alone has acquired a complete MS. of Deuteronomy and Jonah (with Acts), of the fourth century, a seventh-century palimpsest of Joshua, Judges, Ruth, Judith and Esther, sixty-two leaves of Proverbs, Ecclesiastes, Song of Solomon, Wisdom and Ecclesiasticus, of the same date, and a complete Psalter, also of the seventh century. Mr. Pierpont Morgan has MSS. of 1 and 2 Kingdoms, Leviticus-Deuteronomy, and Isaiah; and there are other valuable fragments elsewhere. One portion of the Sahidic version is of especial interest; for copies of the book of Job in this version have been discovered containing a text which bears every mark of being its original form. It is shorter than the received text by about one-sixth, omitting in all about 376 verses; but the passages which disappear are in many cases inconsistent with the general argument of the book, and appear to have been inserted by Jewish scholars who did not understand, or did not approve of, the plan of the poem as it was originally written. Indeed the whole Sahidic Old Testament seems to have been at first free from Hexaplar additions, but to have been subsequently revised from MSS. containing these additions, presumably copies of the Hesychian text which was current in Egypt. The Sahidic version was probably made before the end of the second century, the Bohairic somewhat later. Of the third version, (*c*) the *Middle Egyptian*, only a few fragments have as yet been discovered.

The Ethiopic Version.—With the versions of Egypt may naturally go the version of Ethiopia; but it will require only a brief notice. The Ethiopian manuscripts (most of which were acquired by the British Museum at the time of the Abyssinian war in 1867) are of very late date, but the original translation was probably made in the fourth century after Christ. This version was, no doubt, made from the Septuagint; but it has been questioned whether the extant MSS. really represent this translation, or a much later one, made in the fourteenth century from the Arabic or Coptic. The fact is that at present little can be said to be known about the version at all. Both Old and New Testament are preserved to us entire, though in very late manuscripts, but they have never been properly edited. One special feature, however, of the Ethiopic Old Testament deserves to be noticed. Besides the ordinary books contained in the Septuagint, it includes also two apocryphal books which have no place in either our Old Testament or our Apocrypha—namely, the book of Jubilees and the book of Enoch. The latter book is of special interest, from its having been quoted in the Epistle of Jude; but it was wholly lost, except for some extracts in Syncellus, until James Bruce brought back some manuscripts of it from Abyssinia in 1773, from one of which it was edited by Archbishop Laurence in 1821. The original Greek remained unknown until 1886, when a little vellum volume was discovered at Akhmim in Egypt, containing the first thirty-six chapters, along with portions of the Gospel and Apocalypse of Peter. Still more recently, the last eleven chapters have been recovered from one of the papyri in Mr. Chester Beatty's collection. A new edition of the Ethiopic Bible, with the modern Amharic text in parallel columns, has just been produced by the native Abyssinian Church; but this is not a critical edition.

The remaining Oriental versions may be dismissed in a few words. A few fragments remain of the *Gothic* version, made for the Goths in the fourth century by their bishop, Ulfilas, while they were still settled in Mœsia, the modern Serbia and Bulgaria. Its chief interest lies in the fact that it was taken from a copy of the Lucianic edition of the Septuagint.

The *Armenian*, *Arabic*, *Georgian*, and *Slavonic* versions were all made from the Septuagint, but they have been little studied.

§ 4.—The Latin Versions.

(*a*) *The Old Latin Version.*—When Christianity reached Rome, the Church which was founded there was at first more Greek than Latin. St. Paul wrote to it in Greek, the names of most of its members, so far as we know them, are Greek, and its earliest bishops were Greek: one of them, Clement, wrote an epistle to the Corinthians in Greek which is found along with the books of the New Testament in one of the earliest Greek Bibles, the Codex Alexandrinus. There was therefore at first no necessity for a Latin version of the Scriptures; and the necessity, when it arose, was felt less in Rome itself than in the Roman province of Africa. It is in this province, consisting of the habitable part of northern Africa, lying along the southern coast of the Mediterranean, that a Latin Bible first makes its appearance.

The importance of the Old Latin version, as it is called, to distinguish it from the later version of St. Jerome, is much greater in the New Testament than in the Old. In the former, it is one of the earliest translations of the original Greek which we possess, and is an important evidence for the state of the text in the second century. In the latter it is only a version of a version, being made from the Septuagint, not from the original Hebrew. Historically, moreover, it is of less importance; for it was almost entirely superseded by the version of Jerome, and it exists to-day only in fragments. No entire manuscript survives of the Old Testament in this version; a few books only, and those chiefly of the Apocrypha, exist complete; for the rest we are indebted for most of our knowledge of this version to the quotations in the early Latin Fathers.

The Old Latin version of the New Testament was extant in Africa in the second century after Christ, and it is probable that the translation of the Old Testament was made at the same time, since it is almost certain that a complete Latin Bible was known to Tertullian (about A.D. 200). Whether the first translation was actually made in Africa it is impossible to say, for want of positive evidence; but this view is commonly held and is at least probable. What is certain is that the version exists in two different forms, known, from the regions in which they circulated, as the *African* and the *European*. How far they are independent is uncertain. The original translation was rough and somewhat free; in the European edition the roughnesses are toned down and the translation revised with reference to the Greek. As the translation was originally made before the time of the various editions of Origen, Lucian, and Hesychius, its evidence, wherever we possess it, is useful as a means to the recovery of the earlier form of the Septuagint; and it is observable that its text is akin to that which appears in the Codex Alexandrinus, which seems to indicate an Egyptian origin. Unfortunately it is available only to a limited extent. The apocryphal books of Esdras, Wisdom, Ecclesiasticus, Baruch, and 1 and 2 Maccabees, together with the additions to Daniel and Esther, were not translated or revised by Jerome, and consequently the Old Latin versions of these books were incorporated in the later Latin Bible and remain there to this day.[1] The Psalter survives in a very slightly altered form, as explained below; but the historical and prophetical books have disappeared almost completely. The Octateuch is in better case. There has long been a fine manuscript of the fifth century at Lyons, containing portions of Genesis, Exodus and Leviticus, the whole of Numbers, and the first ten chapters of Deuteronomy. To this M. Delisle, Director of the Bibliothèque Nationale in Paris, was able to add

[1] The Old Latin version of Ecclesiasticus enables us to correct a disarrangement which has taken place in the text of the Septuagint. In the Greek version, chap. xxx. 25—xxxiii. 13*a* is placed after chap. xxxvi. 16*a*, which is plainly wrong. The Latin version has preserved the true order, which has been followed in our Authorised Version.

in 1895 the rest of Deuteronomy, the whole of Joshua, and Judges as far as xi. 21. Probably Ruth was originally included, so that the whole MS. would have been an Octateuch. Ruth has come down in another MS. at Madrid; and Esther, Judith and Tobit are also preserved in that MS. and in others. For the rest we are dependent on a few fragments and quotations in the Fathers.

(*b*) *The Vulgate.*—It is very different when we come to the great work of St. Jerome, which, in the main, continues to be the Bible of the Roman Church to this day. Its origin is known to us from the letters and prefaces of its author; its evidence is preserved to us in hundreds and even thousands of manuscripts of all ages from the fourth century to the fifteenth. Its historical importance is enormous, especially for the Churches of Western Europe; for, as we shall see in the progress of our story, it was the Bible of these Churches, including our own Church of England, until the time of the Reformation. We shall have to trace its history in the later chapters of this book; for the present we are concerned with the story of its birth.

By the end of the fourth century the imperfections of the Old Latin version had become evident to the leaders of the Roman Church. Not only was the translation taken from the Greek of the Septuagint, instead of the original Hebrew, but the current copies of it were grossly disfigured by corruptions. The inevitable mistakes of copyists, the omissions and interpolations of accident or design, the freedom with which early translators handled the text of their original, the alterations of revisers, and the different origin of the African and European forms of the version, all contributed to produce a state of confusion and distortion intolerable to an educated Churchman.

Jerome.

Hence about the year 382 Pope Damasus appealed to the most capable Biblical scholar then living, Eusebius Hieronymus, whom we know better under the abbreviated form of his name, Jerome, to undertake a revision of the Latin Bible. Jerome was born in 346, a native of Stridon in Pannonia, not far from the modern Trieste. Throughout his life he was devoted to Biblical studies. In 374 he set himself to learn Hebrew, then a very rare accomplishment in the West, taking as his teacher a converted Jew. His first Biblical undertaking, however, was not connected with his Hebrew studies. The existing Latin Bible was a translation from the Greek throughout, in the Old Testament as well as in the New, and all that Pope Damasus now invited Jerome to do was to revise this translation with reference to the Greek. He began with the Gospels, of which we shall have to speak later; but about the same time he also made his first revision of the Psalter.

His Three Psalters.

He produced eventually no less than three versions of the Psalms, all of which are still extant. The first was this very slight revision of the Old Latin version, with reference to the Septuagint, and is known as the *Roman* Psalter; it was officially adopted by Pope Damasus, and still remains in use in the cathedral of St. Peter at Rome. The second, made between 387 and 390, was a more thorough revision, still with reference to the Septuagint; but Jerome attempted to bring it into closer conformity with the Hebrew by using Origen's Hexaplar text and reproducing his asterisks and obeli; this version was first adopted in Gaul, whence it is known as the *Gallican* Psalter, and it has held its place as the Psalter in general use in the Roman Church and in the Roman Bible from that day to this, in spite of the superior accuracy of the third version which Jerome subsequently published. This is known as the *Hebrew* Psalter, being an entirely fresh translation from the original Hebrew. It is found in a fair number of manuscripts of the Vulgate, often in parallel columns with the Gallican version, but it never attained to general usage or popularity.

His Old Testament.

About the time when Jerome produced his Gallican Psalter, he also revised some of the other books of the Old Testament, such as Job (which alone now survives in this form), with reference to the Hexaplar text; but it would appear that this undertaking was not carried to completion. It is probable that Jerome, as his knowledge of Hebrew increased, grew dissatisfied with the task of merely revising the Old Latin translation with reference to a text which itself was only a translation. He had completed the revision of the New Testament on these lines; but with the Old Testament he resolved to take in hand an altogether new translation from the Hebrew. He appears to have felt no doubt as to the superiority of the Hebrew text over the Greek, and in all cases of divergence regarded the Hebrew as alone correct. This great work occupied him from about the year 390 to 404; and separate books or groups of books were published as they were completed. The first to appear were the books of Samuel and Kings, next the Prophets, then Ezra, Nehemiah and Genesis, then (after an interval) the books of Solomon, and finally the rest of the Octateuch and Esther.

Reception of His Version.

In the prefatory letters prefixed to these books, Jerome tells us much of his work and its reception. In spite of much individual support which he received, the general attitude towards it was one of great hostility. The sweeping nature of the changes introduced, the marked difference in the text translated, alienated those who had been brought up to know and to love the old version, and who could not understand the critical reasons for the alteration. Jerome felt this opposition keenly, and raged against what he regarded as its unreasonableness; and his sensitiveness, not to say irritability, finds vigorous expression in his prefaces. We who have seen the introduction of a Revised Bible in our own country, intended to supersede the version to which England has been devotedly attached for centuries, can understand the difficulties which surrounded the work of Jerome. Gradually, as we shall see in a later chapter, the superior accuracy and scholarship of his version gave it the victory, though not in a perfect or complete form. The Gallican Psalter continued to hold its own, and was never replaced by the version from the Hebrew. The apocryphal books he wished to reject entirely, because they found no place in the current Hebrew Bible. He did indeed consent reluctantly to make a very hurried translation of the books of Judith and Tobit; but the remaining books he left untouched. In spite of this, they continued to find a place in the Latin Bible; and the Vulgate, as finally adopted by the Roman Church, contains these books in the form in which they had stood, before the days of Jerome, in the Old Latin version. In the rest of the Old Testament, Jerome's version ultimately superseded the Old Latin, and in the New Testament his revision of the Old Latin held its ground. To this composite Bible, consisting partly of unrevised translations from the Greek, partly of revised translations from the same, and partly of translations from the Hebrew, was given in later days, when it had been generally accepted in Western Europe, the name of the "Vulgate," or commonly received translation; and of this, the Bible of our own country until the Reformation, and of the Roman Church until to-day, we shall have much to say hereafter as we trace its history through the centuries. We shall also reserve for later chapters an account of the chief manuscripts in which it is now preserved. In the present chapter we have to do with it only as it affords evidence which may help us to recover the original Hebrew text of the Old Testament.

Its Character.

In this respect its importance is not to be compared with that of the Septuagint. The Hebrew text accessible to Jerome was practically identical with that which is accessible to ourselves; for although the Massoretes themselves are later in date than Jerome by several centuries, yet, as we have seen, the text which they stereotyped had come down practically unchanged since the beginning of the second century after Christ. Hence the version of Jerome is of little help to us in our attempt to recover the Hebrew text as it existed in the centuries before the Christian era; on the other hand, if the Massoretic text is in itself superior to the Greek version as a whole, then the Vulgate is a more satisfactory national Bible than the Septuagint. The translation itself is of unequal merit; some parts are free to the verge of paraphrase, others are so literal as to be nearly unintelligible; but on the whole the work is one of very great merit, and justifies the commanding position which Jerome holds among the Fathers of the Roman Church. Jerome was, indeed, for the West what Origen was for the East—the greatest Biblical scholar which the Church produced before the revival of learning at the end of the Middle Ages.

§ 5.—Condition of the Old Testament Text.

The Vulgate is the last of the versions of the Old Testament which need be mentioned here; and now we come back to the question with which we ended the preceding chapter. What light, after all, do these versions throw on the text of the Old Testament? Do they help us to get behind the Massoretic text, and see what the words of the Scriptures were when they were first written down? And, if so, does this earlier evidence confirm the accuracy of the Massoretic text, or does it throw doubt upon it? With the answer to this question we can close our examination of the Old Testament text.

A diagram may serve to summarise, in broad outline, the information which has been given above.

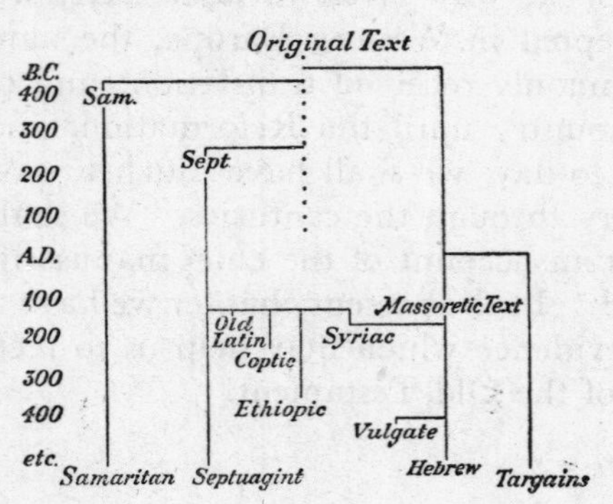

Most of the Versions too Late to Help Us.

In the first place it will be clear that some of the versions we have described must be excluded on the ground that they are not translations of the Hebrew at all. Thus the Coptic, Ethiopic, Gothic, Armenian, Arabic, Georgian, Slavonic, and Old Latin versions were made from the Greek of the Septuagint; and they can only indirectly help us to recover the original Hebrew. Their value is that they help us to restore the original text of the Septuagint; and from the Septuagint we may get on to the Hebrew. In the next place, the Peshitta Syriac and the Latin Vulgate, though translated from the Hebrew, were translated at a time when the Hebrew text was practically fixed in the form in which we now have it. The Peshitta was made in the second or third century, the Vulgate at the end of the fourth; but we have already seen that we can trace back the Massoretic text to about the beginning of the second century. In some cases, when the Hebrew has been corrupted at a comparatively late date, these versions may show us the mistake; but their main value arises from the fact that, at the time when they were made, the Hebrew vowel-points were not yet written down, but were supplied in reading the Scriptures according to the tradition current among the Jews. Hence the Peshitta and the Vulgate show us in what way the absent vowels were supplied at a date very much earlier than any of our existing manuscripts. The same is the case with the Greek versions of Aquila, Theodotion, and Symmachus. They were made from the Hebrew, but from a Hebrew text too late to be of much service to us in our present inquiry.

Evidence of the Samaritan Pentateuch.

There remain the Samaritan and the Septuagint versions. Of these the Samaritan is the oldest; and as it is not really a translation into a different language, but a direct descendant of the original Scriptures in the same language and written in the same characters, its evidence might be expected to be of exceptional value. Unfortunately, however, it relates only to the Pentateuch; and we have seen (p. 51) that it is exactly here that help is least required, and that the variations of the Samaritan text, even where they appear to be right, are not of very great or striking importance. With the Septuagint it is quite otherwise. It contains all the books of the Old Testament, including those which the Jews finally refused to accept as inspired; and its variations are, in many of the books, both numerous and important. The real question to be debated, then, is this: Does the Septuagint or the Massoretic text represent most accurately the words and form of the Old Testament Scriptures as they were originally written?

Septuagint v. *Massoretic.*

So far as the weight of authority goes, the preponderance is decidedly in favour of the Hebrew. Origen and Jerome, the two greatest Biblical scholars of antiquity, deliberately abandoned the original Septuagint and its descendants, the translations made from it, in order to produce versions which should correspond as nearly as possible with the Hebrew. So, too, in the modern world, all the translators of the Bible whose scholarship was equal to it went to the Hebrew for their text of the Old Testament, while those who could not read Hebrew fell back upon the Vulgate, which was itself translated from the Hebrew. Our own Authorised and Revised Bibles, as well as nearly all the translations which preceded them, rest almost entirely upon the Massoretic text, and only very rarely follow the versions in preference to it. And this is very natural; for the Old Testament books were written in Hebrew, and it seems reasonable to suppose that they would be best represented in the Hebrew manuscripts. In the case of no other book in the world should we look to a translation rather than to copies in the original language for the best representation of the contents of the work. Since the last century, however, there have been scholars who have maintained that the Septuagint, the origin of which goes back to a date far earlier than that to which the Massoretic text can be traced, comes nearer to the original Hebrew than do the Hebrew manuscripts of the Massoretic family. It would be absurd to attempt to decide the point authoritatively in such a work as this; but the conditions of the problem can be stated, and the apparent course of the controversy indicated in brief.

The Hebrew Text sure to be Corrupted.

In the first place it is only natural that the Hebrew text should have suffered considerable corruption. If we take the year 100 after Christ as representing the date to which we can trace back the existence of the Massoretic text, there is still a gap of many centuries before we reach the dates at which most of the books were composed. Nearly a thousand years separate us from the earliest of the Prophets, and even if we accept the latest date which modern criticism assigns to the composition of the Pentateuch in its present form, there are still more than five hundred years to be accounted for. It would be contrary to reason to suppose that the text had been handed down through all these centuries without suffering damage from the errors of scribes, the alterations of correctors, or the revision of editors, especially when we remember that in the course of that period the whole style of writing had been changed by the introduction of the square Hebrew characters, that the words were not divided from one another, and that the vowels were not yet indicated by any marks. It is thus natural in itself that the Hebrew text as we have it now should need some correction. It is also natural that the Septuagint version, which we can trace back to an origin more than 350 years earlier than the Massoretic text, should in some cases enable us to supply the needed correction. The text of the Septuagint may itself have suffered much corruption between the time of its composition and the time to which our direct knowledge of it goes back; but it is contrary to reason to suppose that it has always been corrupted in those places where the Hebrew has been corrupted, and that it does not sometimes preserve the right reading where the Hebrew is wrong.

And certainly Corrupt in Some Places.

A partial confirmation of this conclusion is provided by the Targums, the earliest portions of which go back a century or more before the formation of the Massoretic text. In these there are indications that the text on which they are based, though very like the Massoretic text, was not identical with it. We can, however, go further, and show that there is a much larger number of passages in which corruption has almost certainly taken place between the date at which the Septuagint was written and that at which the Massoretic text was formed. It would need an entire treatise to do this thoroughly, but the reader of the Variorum Bible will find a considerable number of places noted in which the reading of the Septuagint makes better sense than that of the Hebrew. In not a few passages the Hebrew gives no natural meaning at all; for instance, Ex. xiv. 20; 1 Sam. xiii. 21; xxvii. 10 (where even the Authorised Version departs from the Massoretic text); much of 1 Kings vi. and vii.; Job iii. 14; xxxv. 15, and many other passages indicated in the Variorum Bible. In other places verses are supplied by the Septuagint which are not in the Hebrew; in these it will be a matter for critics to decide in each case whether the Hebrew has wrongly omitted words, or the Septuagint wrongly inserted them, but it is not likely that the answer will always be the same. A list of some such passages has already been given on p. 79. Again, take the larger variations there mentioned in the books of Jeremiah and Job. In the former the arrangement found in the Septuagint is by many scholars considered preferable to that of the Hebrew. and its text in many doubtful passages appears to be superior. In Job the proof is even more complete; for a large number of passages in it, which had already been believed, on the ground of their style, to be later additions to the Hebrew, have recently been shown to have been absent from the original text of the Septuagint, and to have been added by Origen in his Hexapla, with the usual marks indicating that they had been introduced by him from the Hebrew. Once more, in the Pentateuch we find the Septuagint and the Samaritan version often agreeing in opposition to the Hebrew; and since there is no reasonable ground for asserting that either of these translations was influenced by the other, we can only suppose that in such passages they represent the original reading of the Hebrew, and that the Massoretic text is corrupt. To this it may be added that the "Book of Jubilees," a Jewish work written not long before the fall of Jerusalem (A.D. 70) and containing a modified version of the story of Genesis, frequently supports the Septuagint and Samaritan readings in preference to those of the Hebrew.

But the Septuagint not always Trustworthy.

It seems, then, reasonable to conclude that in many cases the Septuagint contains a better text than the Hebrew; and if this is so, it is likely that it is often right in passages where we are not able to decide with certainty between alternative readings. Can we go further and say that it is *generally* so, and that wherever the two differ, the presumption is in favour of the Septuagint? Certainly not, without considerable qualifications. There can be no doubt, first, that the Septuagint as originally written contained many mistakes; and, secondly, that the text of it has been much corrupted in the earlier course of its history. It must be remembered that the Septuagint was translated from a Hebrew text in which the words were not separated from one another and were unprovided with vowel-points. Hence some of the differences between the Septuagint and the Hebrew do not imply a difference of reading at all, but simply a difference in the division of the letters into words or in the vowel points supplied. Sometimes the one may be right and sometimes the other; but in any case the difference is one of *interpretation*, not of *text*. Then, again, there can be no doubt that the authors of the Septuagint made many actual mistakes of translation. Hebrew, it must be remembered, was not their habitual language of conversation; it was a matter of study, as old English is to scholars to-day, and it was quite possible for them to mistake the meaning of a word, or to confuse words which were written or spoken nearly alike. The possibility of such mistakes must be borne in mind, and only a good Hebrew scholar can warn us of them.[1]

Additions in Septuagint.

It is a more difficult point to decide whether the authors of the Septuagint made deliberate additions to the text. Translators held a different view of their rights and duties from that which would be accepted to-day. They thought themselves at

[1] Some interesting examples of errors caused by the Greek translator having misunderstood the Hebrew, or having supplied the wrong vowel-points, are given in the preface to the *Variorum Apocrypha*.

liberty to add explanatory words and phrases, to paraphrase instead of adhering closely to their original, to supplement what they believed to be omissions (often by incorporating words from other passages where the same or similar events were recorded, as from Kings into Chronicles, and *vice versa*), even to omit passages which they regarded as unnecessary or unedifying, or insert incidents which they believed to be true and edifying. This would seem to be the case with the additions to the books of Daniel and Esther, which the Jews refused to accept as part of the inspired Scriptures, and which have been banished to the Apocrypha in the English Bible. In smaller details, the authors of the Septuagint seem at times to have softened down strong expressions of the Hebrew, no doubt from a feeling that the more refined literary taste of Alexandria would be offended by them.

The Hebrew Text of Ecclesiasticus.

A welcome and valuable contribution to our comprehension of the relation between the Septuagint and the Massoretic Hebrew was made in 1897 by the publication of a portion of the Hebrew original of the book of Ecclesiasticus, previously believed to be wholly lost. The Hebrew text was known to Jerome, and there is evidence that it was still in existence early in the tenth century; but thenceforward, for a space of more than 950 years, no traces of it could be met with. In 1896, however, Mrs. Lewis, the fortunate discoverer of the Sinaitic Syriac manuscript of the Gospels, brought back from the East a single leaf, which, on being examined at Cambridge, was found to contain part of the original Hebrew text of Ecclesiasticus; and almost simultaneously Dr. Ad. Neubauer at Oxford, in examining a mass of fragments sent to England by Professor Sayce, discovered nine more leaves of the same MS., following immediately after the Cambridge leaf. The total amount of text thus recovered includes chapters xxxix. 15–xlix. 11; and the whole was edited by Mr. Cowley and Dr. Neubauer, of the Bodleian Library, Oxford.[1] The manuscript is on paper, and was written about the end of the eleventh or beginning of the twelfth century.

The most striking feature about the discovery is the extent of the divergence between the Hebrew and the Greek versions; and the character of the divergence shows that it is generally due to the mistakes or omissions of the Greek translator. It is a most instructive exercise to read the newly recovered original side by side with the notes in the *Variorum Apocrypha*, which indicate

[1] A very convenient small edition was issued in 1898 for those who are not Hebrew scholars, giving a translation of the Hebrew side by side with the Revised Version of the same portion of the book. A short introduction supplies all the necessary information.

the passages previously suspected of error in the Greek, the variations found in the other versions, and the conjectures of editors. Sometimes the suspicions of scholars are confirmed; often it is seen that they could not go far enough, nor divine the extent to which the Greek departed from the original. A small instance may be given here, from Ecclus. xl. 18-20:

GREEK TRANSLATION (FROM THE REVISED VERSION OF 1895)	HEBREW ORIGINAL
18 The life of one that laboureth, and is contented, shall be made sweet;	A life of wine and strong drink is sweet,
And he that findeth a treasure is above both.	But he that findeth a treasure is above them both.
19 Children and the building of a city establish a man's name;	A child and a city establish a name,
	But he that findeth wisdom is above them both.
	Offspring (of cattle) and planting make a name to flourish,
And a blameless wife is counted above both.	But a woman beloved is above them both.
20 Wine and music rejoice the heart;	Wine and strong drink cause the heart to exult,
And the love of wisdom is above both.	But the love of lovers is above them both.

The divergences in verses 18 and 20 are evidently due to a desire to improve the sentiments of the original by removing the laudatory mention of "strong drink," and the substitution of "the love of wisdom" for "the love of lovers"; while the omission in verse 19, whether it be accidental or intentional, distorts the sense of the passage. That the Hebrew text is the more authentic cannot be questioned; and this is but a sample of what is found throughout the book. It is clear, both that the translator took considerable liberty of paraphrase, and that he sometimes did not understand the Hebrew before him. This latter fact might seem strange, since we know (from the translator's preface) that the original was probably written about 200-170 B.C., and the translation (by the author's grandson) in 132 B.C., so that the interval of time between them was short; but it is accounted for both by the fact that the translator was no scholar, and by the transition through which the Hebrew language passed during this period. Classical Hebrew, the language of nearly all the canonical books of the Old Testament, was passing into modern or Rabbinical Hebrew, a change quite sufficient to disconcert a moderate scholar. The Rabbinical element appears already in the book of Ecclesiastes; and hitherto it has been supposed that in Ecclesiasticus, which is probably of somewhat later date, it would be more strongly developed. The newly discovered manuscript, however, shows that Jesus Ben-Sira wrote in pure classical Hebrew, equal to that of the Psalms; and no doubt it is partly to this cause that the errors of the translator are due. The moral to be drawn from this discovery is consequently one of caution in assuming that variations (even considerable ones) in the Septuagint from the Massoretic Hebrew necessarily imply a different original text. They *may* do so, no doubt; but we must be prepared to make considerable allowances for liberty of paraphrase and for actual mistakes, especially in the case of the books which are likely to have been the latest to be translated. When the earliest parts of the Septuagint were translated, a competent knowledge of classical Hebrew must have been much commoner, and a higher standard of accuracy, though not necessarily of literalness, may be expected.

Minor Corruptions.

As to the minor corruptions of the Septuagint text, the history of it in the preceding pages explains these sufficiently. It is no easy task, in many places, to be sure what the true reading of the Septuagint is. Some manuscripts represent the text of Origen, in which everything has been brought into conformity with the Hebrew as it was in his day; many are more or less influenced by his text, or by the versions of Aquila and Theodotion. Some represent the edition of Lucian; others that of Hesychius. Even those which belong to none of these classes do not agree among themselves. The great manuscripts known as A and B frequently differ very markedly from one another, and א sometimes stands quite apart from both. It is clear that in many cases it is impossible to correct the Hebrew from the Greek until we have first made sure what the Greek reading really is.

Deliberate Falsification of Hebrew not Proven.

One further possibility remains to be considered, that of deliberate falsification of either Greek or Hebrew for party purposes. Such accusations were made, both by Christians and by Jews, in the early centuries of the Church's history, when the Jews held to the Hebrew text as it was fixed about A.D. 100, and the Christians to the Septuagint. They have been renewed from time to time; and a modern controversialist, Sir H. Howorth, in his contention for the superiority of the Septuagint, has declared the Massoretic text to have been deliberately altered by the Jews with an anti-Christian purpose. But the proof for so serious a charge is wholly lacking. It is true that the Hebrew Bible as we know it assumed its present form at a time when the antagonism between Jew and Christian was strongly marked, and probably under the direction of the Rabbi Akiba, the great leader of the extreme party of the Jews at the end of the first century. At such a time and under such a leader it might seem not impossible that an attempt would be made to remove from the Old Testament those passages and expressions to which the Christians referred most triumphantly as prophecies of Christ. The best answer to such a charge is that these passages have not been removed, and that the differences between the Massoretic text and the Septuagint are by no means of this character. Nothing can have been gained, from the party point of view, by altering the order of the prophecies of Jeremiah, or by expanding the book of Job. The books of Wisdom and Ecclesiasticus, which were ejected from the Hebrew text and retained in the Greek, do not testify of Christ more than the undisputed books which remain in both. The Christians had less reason to feel special interest in the books of the Maccabees than the patriotic Jews. Indeed, it is untrue to say that the books of the Apocrypha were at this time ejected from the Hebrew Bible; the fact being that they had never formed part of it, and were never quoted or used on the same level as the books recognised as inspired. It is true that one verse has dropped out of a long list of towns (after Josh. xv. 59), in which was contained (as the Septuagint shows; see Variorum footnote) the name of "Ephratah, which is Bethlehem," by the help of which the reference to Ephratah in Psalm cxxxii. 6 might be interpreted as a prophecy of our Lord's birth at Bethlehem; but seeing that the same identification is repeated in four other places, including the much more strongly Messianic passage in Micah v. 2, the omission in Joshua alone would be perfectly useless for party purposes, and may much more fairly be explained as an accident. It is needless to add that the greater prophecies of the Messiah, such as the fifty-third chapter of Isaiah, stand quite untouched in the Hebrew, and that the vast majority of the differences between the Hebrew and the Greek throughout the Old Testament could have no possible partisan motive whatever.

Summing-up.

The authors of our Revised Version of the Old Testament, while recognising the probable existence of earlier editions of the Hebrew differing from the Massoretic text, yet declare that "the state of knowledge on the subject is not at present such as to justify any attempt at an entire reconstruction of the text on the authority of the versions," and have consequently "thought it most prudent to adopt the Massoretic Text as the basis of their work, and to depart from it, as the Authorised Translators had done, only in exceptional cases." There can be no doubt that they did rightly. The versions have as yet been too insufficiently studied to justify a general use or a rash reliance upon them. When the text of the Septuagint, in particular, has been placed on a satisfactory footing (to which it is to be hoped the large Cambridge edition will greatly contribute) it will be time enough to consider how far its readings may be taken in preference to those of the Hebrew. It is probable that eventually a much fuller use will be made of the Septuagint than has hitherto been the case, and those have done good work who have called attention, even in exaggerated tones, to the claims of the ancient Greek version; but no general substitution of the Greek for the Hebrew as the prime authority for the text of the Old Testament will be possible unless the universal assent of students be won to the change. It will not be enough for one section of specialists to take up the cry, and, proclaiming themselves to be the only advanced and unprejudiced school, look down upon all others as unenlightened laggards. Such schools and such cries, stimulative as they are of thought and of work, are for the moment only. If the Massoretic text is ever to be driven from the assured position of supremacy which it has held since the days of Origen and of Jerome, it will only be when the great bulk of sober criticism and the general intelligence of Biblical students have been convinced that the change is necessary. It is very doubtful whether such a conviction will ever be reached; but it is probable that increasing use will be made of the Septuagint evidence, and students will do well to keep an eye on it in their work on the Old Testament.

CHAPTER VI

THE TEXT OF THE NEW TESTAMENT

WHEN we pass from the Old Testament to the New, we pass from obscurity into a region of comparative light. Light, indeed, is plentiful on most of its history; our danger is rather lest we should be confused by a multiplicity of illumination from different quarters, as the electric searchlights of a fleet often bewilder those who use them. We know, within narrow limits, the dates at which the various books of the New Testament were written; we have a multitude of manuscripts, some of them reaching back to the century following the date of the composition of the books; we have evidence from versions and the early Christian writers which carry us almost into the apostolic age itself. We shall find many more disputes as to *minor* points concerning the text of the New Testament than we do in the Old, just because the evidence is so plentiful and comes from so many different quarters; but we shall find fewer doubts affecting its general integrity.

The Original MSS.

The books of the New Testament were written between the years 50 and 100 after Christ. If anyone demurs to this lower limit as being stated too dogmatically, we would only say that it is not laid down in ignorance that it has been contested, but in the belief that it has been contested without success.[1] But this is not the place for a discussion on the date of the Gospels or Epistles, and if anyone prefers a later date, he only shortens the period that elapsed between the composition of the books in question and the date at which the earliest manuscripts now extant were written. The originals of the several books have long ago disappeared. They must have perished in the very infancy of the Church; for no allusion is ever made to them by any Christian writer.[2] We have, however, in recent years, learnt much as to the manner of production of books during this

[1] Since the publication of Harnack's *Chronologie der altchristlichen Litteratur* in 1897 it has been generally admitted that, with very few exceptions, the traditional dates of the New Testament books may be accepted as approximately correct. The doctrines of the school of Baur, which regarded the earliest Christian books as a tissue of falsifications of the second century, have been exploded. "That time," says Harnack, "is over. It was an episode, during which science learnt much, and after which it must forget much." Recent discoveries have only confirmed this conclusion

[2] A very rhetorical passage in Tertullian may be ignored.

period, and can form a good idea of what they must have looked like. Each book, we must remember, was written separately, and there can have been no thought at first of combining them into a single collection corresponding in importance and sacredness to the Law, the Prophets, and the Hagiographa. St. Luke merely wrote down, as many had taken in hand to do before, a memoir of our Lord's life; St. Paul wrote letters to the congregation at Rome or at Corinth, just as we write to our friends in Canada or India. The material used was, no doubt, papyrus (see p. 10); for this was the common material for writing, whether for literary or for private texts, though parchment was used at times for special purposes. Thus, when St. Paul directs Timothy to bring with him "the books, but especially the parchments," the latter may possibly have been copies of parts of the Old Testament, but it is more probable that they were notebooks. His own letters would certainly have been written on papyrus; and the discoveries of the last fifty years have given us back quantities of books and letters written on this material by inhabitants of the neighbouring country of Egypt at this very time. The elder of the church in Western Asia who arose in his congregation to read the letter of St. Paul which we know as the Epistle to the Ephesians must have held in his hand a roll of whitish or light yellow material about 4 feet in length and some 10 inches in height. The Acts of the Apostles or the Gospel of St. Luke would have formed a portly roll of some 30 feet. Even had the idea been entertained of making a collection of all the books which now form our New Testament, it would have been quite impossible to have combined them in a single volume, so long as the papyrus roll was the form of book in use.

Complete New Testaments Impossible at First.

But in fact the formation of a single "New Testament" was impossible, so long as no decision had been reached by the Church to distinguish between the inspired and the uninspired books. The four Gospels had indeed been marked off as a single authoritative group early in the second century; and the Epistles of St. Paul formed a group by themselves, easily recognisable and generally accepted. But in the second and third and even in the fourth century the claims of such books as 2 and 3 John, 2 Peter, Jude, and the Apocalypse were not admitted by all; the authorship of Hebrews, and consequently its place among the Epistles, was a matter of doubt, as to which East and West took different views; while other early Christian writings, such as the Epistle of Clement, the epistle which passed by the name of Barnabas, and the "Shepherd" of Hermas, ranked almost, if not quite, on the same footing as the canonical books.

All this time it is highly improbable that the sacred books were written otherwise than singly or in small groups. Only when the minds of men were being led to mark off with some unanimity the books held to be authoritative, are collected editions, as we should now call them, likely to have been made. Only gradually did men arrive at the conception of a Canon, or authoritative collection, of the New Testament which should rank beside the Canon of the Old.

We now have concrete evidence of the stages of this process. The adoption by the Christian community, early in the second century, of the codex form of book (see above, p. 12) made the inclusion of groups of books in a single volume possible; and we have actual examples, which will be described in the next chapter, of papyrus codices containing the four Gospels and the Acts, or the collected Epistles of St. Paul, which can be assigned to the first half of the third century. But for complete New Testaments we must, so far as our present evidence goes, wait for the official recognition of Christianity and the great vellum codices of the time of Constantine in the fourth century.

We need, then, feel no surprise at the great quantity of various readings which we find to have come into existence by the time our earliest extant manuscripts were written. The earliest Christians, a poor, scattered, often illiterate body, looking for the return of their Lord at no distant date, were not likely either to care sedulously for minute accuracy of transcription or to preserve their books religiously for the benefit of posterity. Salvation was not to be secured by exactness in copying the precise order of words; it was the substance of the teaching that mattered, and the scribe might even incorporate into the narrative some incident which he believed to be equally authentic, and think no harm in so doing. So divergent readings would spring up, and different texts would become current in different regions, each manuscript being a centre from which other copies would be taken in its own neighbourhood. Persecution, too, had a potent influence on the fortunes of the Bible text. On the one hand, an edict such as that of Diocletian in 303, ordering all the sacred books of the Christians to be burnt, would lead men to distinguish between the sacred and non-sacred books, and so assist the formation of an authoritative Canon. On the other hand, numberless copies must have been destroyed by the Roman officials during these times of persecution, the comparison of copies with a view to removing their divergences must have been difficult, and the formation of large and carefully written manuscripts must have been discouraged.

Careful Copying of Texts Begins in Fourth Century.

The change comes with the acceptance of Christianity by the Emperor Constantine. After the Edict of Milan (or the instructions to which this name has generally been given), in A.D. 313, Christianity ceased to be persecuted, and before long became the religion of the Empire. Its books needed no longer to be concealed; on the contrary, a great demand for additional copies must have been created to supply the new churches and the new converts. The Emperor himself instructed Eusebius of Cæsarea, the great historian of the early Church, to provide fifty copies of the Scriptures for the churches of Constantinople; and the other great towns of the Empire must have required many more for their own wants. Here then, and possibly not before, we may find the origin of the first collected New Testaments; and here we are already in touch with actual manuscripts which have come down to us, from which point the chain of tradition is complete as far as our own days.

Transmission from First to Fifteenth Century.

The forms of ancient books, in the period of which we are treating, have been described in Chapter I. First there is the papyrus period, extending from the date of the composition of the books of the New Testament to about the first quarter of the fourth century. When the first edition of this book appeared, it was supposed that all copies belonging to this period had disappeared, on account of the perishable nature of the material. Now we have a small fragment which goes back to the first half of the second century, and some substantial manuscripts and a considerable number of fragments which can be assigned to the third. The earliest complete, or approximately complete, New Testaments belong, however, to the opening of the vellum period in the fourth century. Two splendid volumes are assigned by all competent critics to this period. One, the Codex Vaticanus, has long been in the Vatican Library at Rome. The other, the Codex Sinaiticus, has lately migrated from Leningrad to the British Museum. To the next century belongs that other glory of the British Museum, the Codex Alexandrinus; also the mutilated Codex Ephraemi in the National Library at Paris, the highly remarkable Codex Bezæ at Cambridge, and the Freer Gospels at Washington. In addition to these there are perhaps twelve very fragmentary manuscripts of the same century which contain only some small portions of the New Testament. From the sixth century twenty-seven documents have come down to us, but only five of these contain so much as a single book complete. From the seventh we have eight small fragments; from the eighth six manuscripts of some importance and eight fragments.[1] So far the stream of tradition has run in a narrow bed. Time has, no doubt, caused the destruction of many copies; but it is also probable that during these centuries not so many copies were made as was the case subsequently. The style of writing then in use for works of literature was slow and laborious. Each letter was a capital, and had to be written separately; and the copying of a manuscript must have been a long and toilsome task. In the ninth century, however, as already described in Chapter I, a change was made of great importance in the history of the Bible, and indeed of all ancient Greek literature. In place of the large capitals hitherto employed, a smaller style of letter came into use, modified in shape so as to admit of being written continuously, without lifting the pen after every letter. Writing became easier and quicker; and to this fact we may attribute the marked increase in the number of manuscripts of the Bible which have come down to us from the ninth and tenth centuries. From this point numeration becomes useless. Instead of counting our copies by units we number them by tens and scores and hundreds, until by the time that printing was invented the total mounts up to a mass of several thousands. And these, it must be remembered, are but the remnant which has escaped the ravages of time and survived to the present day. When we remember that the great authors of Greek and Latin literature are preserved to us in a mere handful of copies, in some cases indeed only in one single manuscript, we may feel confident that in this great mass of Bible manuscripts we have much security that the true text of the Bible has not been lost on the way.

The Earliest Printed Texts.

With the invention of printing in the fifteenth century a new era opens in the history of the Greek text. The earliest printed document (so far as Europe is concerned) was issued about the year 1450; and the first complete book produced by the printing press was, rightly enough, the Bible, in 1456. This, however, was a Latin Bible; for Latin was, in the fifteenth century, the language of literature in Western Europe. Greek itself was little known at this date. It was only gradually that the study of it spread from Italy (especially after the arrival there of fugitives from the East, when the Turkish capture of Constantinople overthrew the Greek Empire) over the adjoining countries to the other nations of the West. It was not until the sixteenth century

[1] It must be understood that the dates here given are not absolutely certain. Early manuscripts on vellum are never dated, and their age can only be judged from their handwriting. But the dates as here stated are those which have been assigned by competent judges, and may be taken as approximately correct.

οἱ μαθηταὶ αὐτοῦ λέγοντες, τίς εἴη ἡ παρα/
βολὴ αὕτη. ὁ δὲ εἶπεν, ὑμῖν δέδοται γνῶναι
τὰ μυστήρια τῆς βασιλείας τοῦ θεοῦ, τοῖς δὲ
λοιποῖς ἐν παραβολαῖς, ἵνα βλέποντες μὴ
βλέπωσιν, καὶ ἀκούοντες μὴ συνιῶσιν. ἔστιν
δὲ αὕτη ἡ παραβολή. ὁ σπόρος ἐστὶν ὁ λόγος
τοῦ θεοῦ. οἱ δὲ παρὰ τὴν ὁδὸν εἰσὶν, οἱ ἀκού/
οντες, εἶτα ἔρχεται ὁ διάβολος, καὶ αἴρει τὸν
λόγον ἀπὸ τῆς καρδίας αὐτῶν, ἵνα μὴ πιστεύ/
σαντες σωθῶσιν. οἱ δὲ ἐπὶ τῆς πέτρας, οἳ ὅτ'
ἂν ἀκούσωσιν μετὰ χαρᾶς δέχονται τὸν
λόγον, καὶ οὗτοι ῥίζαν οὐκ ἔχουσιν, οἳ πρὸς
καιρὸν πιστεύουσιν, καὶ ἐν καιρῷ πειρασμοῦ
ἀφίσανται. τὸ δὲ εἰς τὰς ἀκάνθας πεσὸν,
οὗτοί εἰσιν οἱ ἀκούοντες, καὶ ὑπὸ μεριμνῶν
καὶ πλούτου, καὶ ἡδονῶν τοῦ βίου πορευό/
μενοι συμπνίγονται, καὶ οὐ τελεσφοροῦσιν.
τὸ δὲ ἐν τῇ καλῇ γῇ, οὗτοί εἰσιν οἵτινες ἐν καρ/
δίᾳ καλῇ καὶ ἀγαθῇ ἀκούσαντες τὸν λόγον
κατέχουσιν καὶ καρποφοροῦσιν ἐν ὑπο/
μονῇ. οὐδεὶς δὲ λύχνον ἅψας καλύπτει αὐ/
τὸν σκεύει, ἢ ὑποκάτω κλίνης τίθησιν, ἀλλ'
ἐπὶ τὴν λυχνίαν ἐπιτίθησιν, ἵνα οἱ εἰσπορευ/
όμενοι βλέπωσιν τὸ φῶς. οὐ γάρ ἐστιν κρυ/
πτὸν ὃ οὐ φανερὸν γενήσεται. οὐδὲ ἀπόκρυ/
φον, ὃ οὐ γνωσθήσεται, καὶ εἰς φανερὸν ἔλ/
θῃ. βλέπετε οὖν πῶς ἀκούετε. ὃς γὰρ ἐὰν ἔχῃ
δοθήσεται αὐτῷ. καὶ ὃς ἐὰν μὴ ἔχῃ, καὶ ὃ
δοκεῖ ἔχειν, ἀρθήσεται ἀπ' αὐτοῦ. παρεγένον/
το δὲ πρὸς αὐτὸν ἡ μήτηρ, καὶ οἱ ἀδελφοὶ
αὐτοῦ, καὶ οὐκ ἠδύναντο συντυχεῖν αὐτῷ
διὰ τὸν ὄχλον. καὶ ἀπηγγέλη αὐτῷ. ἡ
μήτηρ σου καὶ οἱ ἀδελφοί σου ἑστήκασιν
ἔξω ἰδεῖν σε θέλοντες, ὁ δὲ ἀποκριθεὶς εἶ/
πεν πρὸς αὐτούς. μήτηρ μου καὶ ἀδελφοί
μου οὗτοί εἰσιν, οἱ τὸν λόγον τοῦ θεοῦ ἀ/
κούοντες καὶ ποιοῦντες. καὶ ἐγένετο ἐν
μιᾷ τῶν ἡμερῶν, καὶ αὐτὸς ἀνέβη εἰς πλοῖ/
ον, καὶ οἱ μαθηταὶ αὐτοῦ. καὶ εἶπεν πρὸς
αὐτούς.

discipuli eius, dicẽtes, q̃ esset hæc para/
bola. At ipse dixit. Vobis datum est
nosse mysteria regni dei, cæteris autem
in parabolis, ut uidentes non uideant,
& audientes nõ intelligant. Est autem
hæc parabola. Semen est uerbum dei.
Qui autem secus uiam, hi sunt qui au/
diunt, deinde uenit diabolus, & tollit
uerbum de corde eorum, ne credentes
salui fiant. Nam qui supra petram, qui
cum audierint, cum gaudio suscipiunt
uerbum. Et hi radices nõ habent, qui
ad tempus credunt, & in tempore ten/
tationis recedunt. Quod autem in spi/
nas cecidit, hi sunt qui audierunt, & a
sollicitudinibus & diuitijs & uoluptati
bus uitæ euntes suffocantur, & non re/
ferunt fructum. Quod autem in bonã
terram, hi sunt qui in corde honesto &
bono audiẽtes uerbum retinent, & fru
ctum afferunt in patientia. Nemo au/
tem lucernam accẽdens operit eam ua/
se, aut subter lectum ponit, sed super
candelabrũ ponit, ut intrantes uideãt
lumen. Non est enim occultum quod
nõ manifestetur, nec abscõditum quod
nõ cognoscat' & in ꝓpatulũ ueniat. Vi
dete ergo quomodo audiatis. Quisqs
enim habet dabitur illi, & quicumq; nõ
habet, etiam quod putat se habere au/
feretur ab illo. Venerunt autem ad il/
lum mater & fratres eius, & non pote/
rant adire eũ præ turba. Et nũciatũ est
illi. Mater tua & fratres tui stant foris,
uolẽtes te uidere. Qui rñdens dixit ad
eos. Mater mea & fratres mei hi sunt, q
uerbũ dei audiunt, & faciunt. Factum
est autem in una dierũ, & ipse ascendit
in nauiculam, & discipuli eius, & ait ad
illos.

ERASMUS' NEW TESTAMENT—A.D. 1516.

(Original size as reproduced, omitting margins, 9½ in. × 6½ in.)

ἐν τῷ ὀνόματι τῷ ἰδίῳ, ἐκεῖνον λήψεσ-
θε. πῶς δύνασθε ὑμεῖς πιστεῦσαι δόξαν
παρά ἀλλήλων λαμβάνοντες, καὶ τὴν δόξαν τὴν παρά τοῦ μόνου θεοῦ οὐ ζητεῖτε.
μὴ δοκεῖτε ὅτι ἐγώ κατηγορήσω ὑμῶν
πρὸς τὸν πατέρα. ἐστίν ὁ κατηγορῶν ὑμῶν
μωσῆς εἰς ὃν ὑμεῖς ἠλπίκατε. εἰ γὰρ ἐπιστεύετε μωσεῖ, ἐπιστεύετε ἂν ἐμοί, περί γὰρ
ἐμοῦ ἐκεῖνος ἔγραψεν. εἰ δὲ τοῖς ἐκείνου
γράμμασιν οὐ πιστεύετε πῶς τοῖς ἐμοῖς
ῥήμασι πιστεύσετε. Cap. 6.

Μετά ταῦτα ἀπῆλθεν ὁ ἰησοῦς πέραν
τῆς θαλάσσης τῆς γαλιλαίας τῆς τιβε-
ριάδος. καὶ ἠκολούθει αὐτῷ ὄχλος πολύς,
ὅτι ἑώρων αὐτοῦ τὰ σημεῖα ἃ ἐποίει ἐπί
τῶν ἀσθενούντων. ἀνῆλθε δὲ εἰς τὸ ὄρος ὁ
ἰησοῦς, καὶ ἐκεῖ ἐκάθητο μετά τῶν μαθητῶν
αὐτοῦ. ἦν δὲ ἐγγύς τὸ πάσχα ἡ ἑορτή τῶν
ἰουδαίων. ἐπάρας οὖν ὁ ἰησοῦς τοὺς ὀφ-
θαλμούς καὶ θεασάμενος ὅτι πολύς ὄχλος
ἔρχεται πρὸς αὐτόν, λέγει πρὸς τὸν φί-
λιππον. πόθεν ἀγοράσομεν ἄρτους, ἵνα φά-
γωσιν οὗτοι. τοῦτο δὲ ἔλεγε πειράζων αὐτόν. αὐτός γὰρ ἤδει τί ἤμελλε ποιεῖν. ἀπε-
κρίθη αὐτῷ φίλιππος. διακοσίων δηναρίων
ἄρτοι οὐκ ἀρκοῦσιν αὐτοῖς, ἵνα ἕκαστος αὐτῶν βραχύ τι λάβῃ. λέγει αὐτῷ εἷς ἐκ τῶν
μαθητῶν αὐτοῦ ἀνδρέας ἀδελφός σίμω-
νος πέτρου. ἔστι παιδάριον ἓν ὧδε ὃ ἔχει
πέντε ἄρτους κριθίνους καὶ δύο ὀψάρια.
ἀλλά ταῦτα τί ἐστίν εἰς τοσούτους. εἶπε
δὲ ὁ ἰησοῦς. ποιήσατε τοὺς ἀνθρώπους ἀ-
ναπεσεῖν. ἦν δὲ χόρτος πολύς ἐν τῷ τόπῳ.
ἀνέπεσον οὖν οἱ ἄνδρες τὸν ἀριθμόν ὡσεί
πεντακισχίλιοι. ἔλαβε δὲ τοὺς ἄρτους ὁ ἰησοῦς, καὶ εὐχαριστήσας διέδωκε τοῖς μαθηταῖς, οἱ δὲ μαθηταί τοῖς ἀνακειμένοις. ὁ-
μοίως καὶ ἐκ τῶν ὀψαρίων ὅσον ἤθελον.
ὡς δὲ ἐνεπλήσθησαν, λέγει τοῖς μαθηταῖς
αὐτοῦ. συναγάγετε τὰ περισσεύσαντα κλά-
σματα, ἵνα μή τι ἀπόληται. συνήγαγον οὖν
καὶ ἐγέμισαν δώδεκα κοφίνους κλασμάτων
ἐκ τῶν πέντε ἄρτων τῶν κριθίνων, ἃ ἐπερίσ-
σευσε τοῖς βεβρωκόσιν. οἱ οὖν ἄνθρωποι ἰ-
δόντες ὃ ἐποίησε σημεῖον ὁ ἰησοῦς, ἔλεγον.
ὅτι οὗτος ἐστίν ἀληθῶς ὁ προφήτης ὁ ἐρ-
χόμενος εἰς τὸν κόσμον. ἰησοῦς οὖν γνοὺς
ὅτι μέλλουσιν ἔρχεσθαι καὶ ἁρπάζειν αὐτόν
ἵνα ποιήσωσιν αὐτόν βασιλέα, πάλιν ἀνε-
χώρησεν εἰς τὸ ὄρος αὐτός μόνος. ὡς δὲ
ὀψία ἐγένετο κατέβησαν οἱ μαθηταί αὐτοῦ ἐπί τὴν θάλασσαν. καὶ ἐμβάντες

in nomine suo illum accipietis.
Quō vos potestis credere qui gloriam
ab inuicem accipitis: ⁊ gloriam que
a solo deo est non queritis.
Nolite putare qr ego accusaturus sum
apō patrē. Est qui accusat vos
moyses i quo vos speratis. Si eni cre
deretis moysi crederetis forsitā ⁊ mihi. De
me eni ille scripsit. Si autem illius
litteris non creditis: quō verbis meis
credetis? Cap. 6.

Post hec abijt iesus trans
mare galilee qḋ est tiberiadis.
Et sequebatur eum multitudo magna:
quia videbant signa que faciebat super
his qui ifirmabant. Subijt ergo i mō
tem iesus: et ibi sedebat cum discipulis
suis. Erat aūt proximū pascha dies fe
stus iudeorū. Cū sublevasset ergo oculos
iesus ⁊ vidisset quia multitudo maxima
venit ad eum: dicit ad philippum.
Unde ememus panes vt manducent
hi? Hoc aūt dicebat temptans eum.
Ipse ei sciebat qḋ esset facturus. Rndit
ei philippus. Ducentorum denariorum
panes non sufficiunt eis: vt vnusquisq
modicū quid accipiat. Dicit ei vnus ex
discipulis eius andreas frater simonis
petri. Est puer vnus hic qui habet
qnq panes hordeaceos ⁊ duos pisces.
Sed hec quid sunt inter tantos? Dicit
ergo iesus. Facite homines discūbere.
Erat autem fenum multum in loco
Discubuerunt ergo viri numero quasi
qnq milia. Accepit ergo iesus panes
et cum gratias egisset distribuit
discumbentibus. Similiter
et ex piscibus quantum volebant.
Ut autem impleti sūt: dixit discipulis
suis. Colligite q̄ superauerūt fragmēta
ne pereant. Collegerunt ergo
⁊ ipleuerūt duodeci cophinos fragmētorū
ex qnq panibus hordeaceis ⁊ duobus pisci
bus: q̄ supfuerūt his q̄ mādūcauerāt. Illi
ergo hoies cū vidissēt qḋ iesus fecerat si
gnū dicebāt. Quia hic est vere ppheta q̄
vēturus ē in mūdū. Jesus ergo cū cogno
uisset quia venturi essent vt raperent eū
et facerent eū regem: fugit iterum
in montem ipse solus. Ut autem
sero factum est: descenderūt discipuli eius
ad mare. Et cum ascendissent

A
Mat. 4. g.
Mar. 3. b.
Luce. 4. b.
Mat. 14. c
Luce. 9. b.
Mat. 14. c.
Mar. 6. c.
Luce. 9. b.
Mat. 14. d
Mar. 6. e.
Luce. 9. b
B
Mat. 14. d
⁊ 15. g
Mar. 6. f. ⁊
8. a.
Luce. 9. b.
sup. 4. c.
Luce. 7. c.
Mat. 14. c.
Mar. 6. g.
Luce. 6. b.

COMPLUTENSIAN POLYGLOT—A.D. 1522.
(*Original size*, 12 *in.* × 9 *in.*)

had begun that there was any demand for a printed Greek Bible; and the honour of leading the way belongs to Spain. In 1502, Cardinal Ximenes formed a scheme for a printed Bible containing the Hebrew, Greek, and Latin texts in parallel columns. Many years were spent in collecting and comparing manuscripts, with the assistance of several scholars. It was not until 1514 that the New Testament was printed, and the Old Testament was only completed in 1517 (see Plate XI). Even then various delays occurred, including the death of Ximenes himself, and the actual publication of this edition of the Greek Bible (known as the Complutensian, from the Latin name of Alcala, where it was printed) only took place in 1522; and by that time it had lost the honour of being the first Greek Bible to be given to the world.

Erasmus' Greek Testament, 1516.

That distinction belongs to the New Testament of the great Dutch scholar Erasmus. He had been long making collections for an edition of the Bible in Latin, when in 1515 a proposal was made to him by a Swiss printer, named Froben, to prepare an edition in Greek, probably with the intention of anticipating that which Ximenes had in hand. Erasmus consented: the work was rapidly executed and as rapidly passed through the press; and in 1516 the first printed copy of the New Testament in the original Greek was given to the world (Plate X). The first edition was full of errors of the press, due to the failure of a subordinate who had been entrusted with the duty of revising the sheets; but a second edition quickly followed, and a third, and a fourth, each representing an advance in the direction of a more accurate text. Erasmus' first edition was based on not more than six manuscripts at the most, and of these only one was even moderately ancient or valuable, and none was complete, so that some verses of the Apocalypse were actually re-translated by Erasmus himself into Greek from the Latin; and, what is more remarkable, some words of this translation, which occur in no Greek manuscript whatever, still hold their place in our received Greek text. That text is, indeed, largely based on the edition of Erasmus. The work of Ximenes was much more careful and elaborate; but it was contained in six large folio volumes, and only 600 copies were printed, so that it had a far smaller circulation than that of Erasmus.

The Received Text.

The great printer-editor, Robert Estienne, or Stephanus, of Paris (sometimes anglicised as Stephens, without ground), issued

8

several editions of the Greek New Testament, based mainly on Erasmus, but corrected from the Complutensian and from fifteen manuscripts, most of them comparatively late; and of these editions the third, printed in 1550, is substantially the "received text" which has appeared in all our ordinary copies of the Greek Bible in England down to the present day. On the Continent the "received text" has been that of the Elzevir edition of 1624, which differs very slightly from that of Stephanus, being in fact a revision of the latter with the assistance of the texts published in 1565-1605 by the great French Protestant scholar Beza.

Its Deficiencies.

Such is the history of our received text of the Greek New Testament; and it will be obvious from it how little likelihood there was that it would be a really accurate representation of the original language. For fourteen hundred years the New Testament had been handed down in manuscript, copy being taken from copy in a long succession through the centuries, each copy multiplying and spreading errors (slight, indeed, but not unimportant in the mass) after the manner described in our second chapter. Yet when the great invention of printing took place, and the words of the Bible could at last be stereotyped, as it were, beyond the reach of human error, the first printed text was made from a mere handful of manuscripts, and those some of the latest and least trustworthy that existed. There was no thought of searching out the oldest manuscripts and trusting chiefly to them. The best manuscripts were still unknown to scholars or inaccessible, and the editors had to content themselves with using such later copies as were within their reach, generally those in their native town alone. Even these were not always copied with such accuracy as we should now consider necessary. The result is that the text accepted in the sixteenth and seventeenth centuries, to which we have clung from a natural reluctance to change the words which we have learnt as those of the Word of God, is in truth full of inaccuracies, many of which can be corrected with absolute certainty from the vastly wider information which is at our disposal to-day. The difference between the Authorised Version and the Revised Version shows in great measure the difference between the text accepted at the time of the first printed editions and that which commends itself to the best modern scholars. We do not find the fundamentals of our faith altered, but we find many variations in words and sentences, and are brought so much nearer to the true Word of God, as it was written down in the first century by Evangelist and Apostle.

Means for Amending It.

What, then, are the means which we have for correcting the "received text," and for recovering the original words of the New Testament? This question will be answered more fully in the next two chapters; but it will be useful to take a brief survey of the ground before us first, and to arrange in their proper groups the materials with which we have to deal. As was explained in Chapter III, the evidence by which the Bible text is examined and restored is threefold. It consists of (1) MANUSCRIPTS, (2) VERSIONS, (3) Quotations in the FATHERS.

1. *Manuscripts.*

In the first edition of this work it was stated that "the early papyrus manuscripts of the New Testament have all perished (unless indeed some are still lying buried in the soil of Egypt, which is far from improbable)." This possibility has happily been realised, and, as has already been indicated, we now have a slender thread of tradition extending back to a point barely a generation later than the date of the Apocalypse or the Fourth Gospel. A few years ago a list compiled by the Rev. P. L. Hedley enumerated 157 New Testament fragments on papyrus (including vellum fragments found with papyri, and ostraka), and to these may now be added the Chester Beatty manuscripts and other recent discoveries, which may bring the total up to 170 or more. Not by any means all of these, however, are earlier than the earliest vellum manuscripts, and many of them are small and of slight importance. A few of them, on the other hand, are of very great value, both as early links in the chain of tradition, and for the light which they throw on the state of the text in the earliest centuries.

The vellum manuscripts, which comprise by far the greater number of our authorities, are divided into two great classes, according to the style in which they are written—namely, UNCIALS and CURSIVES. Uncials are those written throughout in capital letters, each formed separately (see Plates VIII, IX, XV-XX). Cursives are those written in smaller letters and in a more or less running hand (see Plate XXI). As explained above (p. 14), uncial manuscripts are the earliest, running from the fourth century to the tenth, while cursives range from the ninth to the fifteenth, and even later, wherever manuscripts were still written after the invention of printing.[1]

[1] This sharp distinction in time between uncial and cursive writing does not apply to papyri. Here we find cursive writing side by side with uncial from the earliest times at which Greek writing is known to us (the third century B.C.). The reason for the difference in the case of vellum MSS. is simply that vellum was only employed for books intended for general use, and for such books

Uncial MSS.—Uncial manuscripts, being the oldest, are also the rarest and the most important. Including even the smallest fragments, little more than two hundred uncial manuscripts of the Greek New Testament are known to exist,[1] and of these only two contain all the books of it, though two more are nearly perfect. The books of the New Testament, throughout the manuscript period, were generally formed into four groups—viz., Gospels, Acts and Catholic Epistles, Pauline Epistles, Apocalypse—and most manuscripts contain only one, or at most two, of these groups. Uncial manuscripts are distinguished for purposes of reference by capital letters of the Latin, Greek, or Hebrew alphabets, such as A, B, Δ, א, etc., as the reader may see by looking at the notes on any page of the New Testament in the Variorum Bible. Reserving a full description of these manuscripts for the next chapter, it will be sufficient for the present to say that the most important of them are those known as B (Codex Vaticanus) and א (Codex Sinaiticus), which are assigned to the fourth century; A (Codex Alexandrinus), C (Codex Ephraemi), D (of the Gospels and Acts, Codex Bezæ), and W (of the Gospels, Codex Washingtonianus), of the fifth century; D_2 (Pauline Epistles), and E_2 (Acts), of the sixth century. These are the main authorities upon which the text of the New Testament is based, though they need to be supplemented and reinforced by the testimony of the later copies, both uncial and cursive.

Cursive MSS.—Cursive manuscripts are enormously more common than uncials. The earliest of them date from the ninth century, and from the tenth century to the fifteenth the cursives were the Bible of Eastern Europe. Multitudes have no doubt perished; but from the fact of their having been written nearer to the times of the revival of learning many have been preserved. Every great library possesses several of them, and many are no doubt still lurking in unexamined corners, especially in out-of-the-way monasteries in the East. The latest enumeration of those whose existence is known gives the total as 2,429, besides 1,678 Lectionaries, or volumes containing the lessons from the New Testament prescribed to be read during the Church's year. The numeration of them by Arabic numerals goes back to a list compiled in 1751-2 by J. J. Wetstein (a pupil of Bentley), who made a separate numeration for each of the four groups mentioned above, and additional lists for the Lectionaries. Thus Evan. 100

uncial writing was regularly used until the ninth century, because it was the most handsome style. In the ninth century an ornamental style of running-hand was invented, and this superseded uncials as the style usual in books. A cursive hand must always have existed for use in private documents, where publication was not intended; and on papyrus we have many examples of it.

[1] The official catalogue, completed by Gregory in 1908, and carried on by von Dobschütz and Lietzmann, now reaches 212.

meant cursive manuscript No. 100 of the Gospels, Act. 100 meant cursive No. 100 of the Acts and Catholic Epistles, and similarly with Paul. 100 and Apoc. 100; while lectionaries of the Gospels were classed as Evst., and those of the Acts and Epistles as Apost. This economised numbers, but had the inconvenience that if a manuscript contained more than one of these groups, it had a different number in each of them. Thus one of the best of all the minuscules, which contains three of the groups, was variously known as Evan. 33, Act. 13, Paul. 17; while another, which has the complete New Testament, was known as Evan. 584, Act. 228, Paul. 269, Apoc. 97. Accordingly in 1908 C. R. Gregory, with the assent of nearly all Biblical scholars, compiled a continuous list of all the minuscules, and it is this list (continued by Professor H. Lietzmann) which has now reached the above-mentioned total of 2,429.[1] The vast majority of them are of very slight textual importance; but something will be said below of their collective evidence, and of the few which possess special value.

2. *Versions.*

The most important versions, or translations of the New Testament into other languages, are the Syriac, Egyptian, and Latin. They will be described in detail in the next chapter but one, but a short statement of their respective dates is necessary here, in order that we may understand the history of the New Testament text. As soon as Christianity spread beyond the borders of Palestine there was a necessity for translations of the Scriptures into all these languages. Syria was the nearest neighbour of Palestine, Egypt a prominent literary centre and the home of many Jews, while Latin was the language of Africa and Italy and the West of Europe generally. At first, no doubt, Christian instruction was given by word of mouth, but in the course of the second century written translations of most, at any rate, of the New Testament books had been made in these languages; and these versions are of great value to us now, since from them we can often gather what reading of a disputed passage was found in the very early copies of the Greek Testament from which the original translations were made. In SYRIAC four versions are known to have been made: (1) the *Old Syriac*, of the Gospels only; (2) the *Peshitta*, the standard translation of the whole Bible into Syriac; (3) the *Harkleian*, a revision made by Thomas of Harkel in A.D. 616 of an earlier version made in A.D. 508; (4) the *Palestinian*, an independent version from the Greek, extant in

[1] The occasion of Gregory's revision was the publication of a wholly new numeration by H. von Soden, in connection with his new edition of the Greek text (see p. 121). This numeration was unsatisfactory in itself, and inconvenient as blurring the whole textual record; and since it has not been generally adopted, it is not necessary to trouble the reader with it.

fragments only, and of doubtful date. Of these the Old Syriac and the Peshitta are much the most important. In Egypt no less than five versions were current in different dialects of the COPTIC or native tongue, but only two of these are at present known to be important for critical purposes: (1) the *Memphitic* or *Bohairic*, belonging to Lower Egypt; (2) the *Thebaic* or *Sahidic*, of Upper Egypt. Both of these appear to have been made about the beginning of the third century, or perhaps earlier; but the Sahidic is the earlier and the more valuable. The LATIN versions are two in number, both of great importance: (1) the *Old Latin*, made early in the second century, and extant (though only in fragments) in three somewhat varying shapes, known respectively as African, European, and Italian; (2) the *Vulgate*, which is the revision of the Old Latin by St. Jerome at the end of the fourth century. Other early translations of the Scriptures exist in various languages—Armenian, Georgian, Ethiopian, Arabic, and Gothic; but these are neither so early nor so important as those we have mentioned. The Old Syriac, Peshitta, Memphitic, Thebaic, Old Latin, and Vulgate versions are referred to in the notes of the Variorum Bible, and they are unquestionably the most important of the versions for the purposes of textual criticism.

3. *Fathers.*

The evidence of early Christian writers for the text of the New Testament begins to be available about the middle of the second century. The most important are Justin Martyr (died A.D. 164); Tatian, the author of a famous Harmony of the Gospels, known as the Diatessaron (died about A.D. 180); Irenæus, bishop of Lyons, who wrote about A.D. 185; Clement of Alexandria, at the end of the century; Hippolytus of Rome and Origen of Alexandria, in the first half of the third century; and the two great Latin writers of Africa, Tertullian and Cyprian, the former at the beginning of the third century, and the latter about the middle of it. Later still we have the great scholars, Eusebius of Cæsarea in the first half of the fourth century, and Jerome in the second. The evidence of the Fathers has, however, to be used with care. As has been already explained (p. 27), copyists were liable to alter the words of a Scriptural quotation in the Fathers into the shape most familiar to themselves, so that the evidence of a Father is less trustworthy when it is in favour of a commonly accepted reading than when it is against it; and further, the early writers were apt to quote from memory, and so to make verbal errors. When, however, we can be sure that we have a quotation in the form in which the Father actually wrote it (and the context sometimes makes this certain), the evidence is of great value, because the Father must have been copying from a manuscript of the Bible much older than any that we now possess. There is also this further advantage, that we generally know in what part of the world each of the Fathers was writing, and so can tell in what country certain corruptions of the text began or were most common. This is a very important consideration in the part of the inquiry to which we are now coming.

Now when we have got all this formidable array of authorities, —our four thousand Greek manuscripts, our versions in half a dozen languages, and all the writings of the Fathers—what more can be done? Are we simply to take their evidence on each disputed passage, tabulate the authorities for each various reading, and then decide according to the best of our judgment which reading is to be preferred in each several case? Well, very much can be, and very much has been, done by this method. Allowing proper weight for the superior age of the leading uncial manuscripts, so that the evidence of the uncials shall not be overborne by the numerical preponderance of late cursives, a mere statement of the authorities on either side will often be decisive. Thus, if we find in Mark vii. 19 that eight of the later uncials and hundreds of cursives have the received reading, "purging all meats," while ℵ, A, B, E, F, G, H, L, S, X, Δ, and three Fathers have a slight variety which gives the sense, "This he said, making all meats clean," no one will doubt that the superiority, both fo authority and of sense, is on the side of the latter, even though the numerical preponderance of MSS. is with the former; and consequently we find that all editors and the Revised Version have rejected the received reading. This is only one instance out of a great many, which the reader of the Variorum Bible or of any critical edition can easily pick out for himself, in which a simple inspection of the authorities on either side and of the intrinsic merit of the alternative readings is sufficient to determine the judgment of editors without hesitation.

Grouping of Authorities.

But is it possible to go beyond this? Can we, instead of simply estimating our authorities in order of their age, arrange them into groups which have descended from common ancestors, and determine the age and character of each group? It is obvious that no manuscript can have greater authority than that from which it is copied, and that if a hundred copies have been taken, directly or indirectly, from one manuscript, while five have been taken from another which is older and better, the reading of the five will carry more weight than that of the hundred. In other words, the number of manuscripts in a group which has a common parentage proves nothing, except that the form of text represented by that group was preferred in former times; which may or may not be an important factor of the evidence. It does not in itself prove superiority in either age or merit. The question then arises, Is it possible to arrange the authorities for the text of the New Testament in groups of this kind? The general answer of critics in the past was, No. It has been very rare, in the history of Biblical criticism, to find an editor forming his manuscripts into groups. They have generally been content to use the best manuscripts that were available to them, and to judge each on its own merits, or even, at times, to decide every question according to numerical preponderance among a small number of selected manuscripts.

A few scholars in the past, however, realised the importance of classifying and weighing manuscripts, instead of merely counting them. The first was J. A. Bengel (1734), who made a division into two groups, African and Asiatic; and this was developed into a division into three groups by J. S. Semler (1767) and J. J. Griesbach (1775-7). The common feature of all these classifications was the recognition that the great mass of later authorities was of much less value than a small number of earlier authorities. This, which is a commonplace of the textual criticism of classical literature, was for a long time received with little favour by Biblical students. It was, however, taken up, elaborated, and definitely established as the basis of the textual criticism of the New Testament by the two great Cambridge scholars of the latter part of the nineteenth century, Bishop B. F. Westcott and Professor F. J. A. Hort; and since their classification (expounded by Hort in the *Introduction* to their joint text of the New Testament in 1881) has been the basis of all subsequent study, it is necessary to give a brief summary of it.

Westcott and Hort's Classification of Authorities.

An examination of passages in which two or more different readings exist shows that one small group of authorities, consisting of the uncial manuscripts B, א, L, a few cursives such as 33 and 81, and the Bohairic and Sahidic versions, is generally found in agreement; another equally clearly marked group consists of D, the Old Latin and Old Syriac versions, and cursives 13, 69, 431, 565, 614, 876, and Evst. 39, with a few others more intermittently; while A (in the Gospels), C (generally), the later uncials, and the great mass of cursives and the later versions form another group, numerically overwhelming. Sometimes each of these groups will have a distinct reading of its own; sometimes two of them will be combined against the third; sometimes an authority which usually supports one group will be found with one of the others. But the general division into groups remains constant and is the basis of the present theory.

Combined or "Conflate" Readings.

Next, it is possible to distinguish the origins and relative priority of the groups. In the first place, passages occur in which the first group described above has one reading, the second has another, and the third combines the two. Thus in the last words of St. Luke's Gospel (as the Variorum Bible shows), א, B, C, L, with the Bohairic and one Syriac version, have "blessing God"; D and the Old Latin have "praising God"; but A and twelve other uncials, all the cursives, the Vulgate and other versions, have "praising and blessing God." Instances like this occur, not once nor twice, but repeatedly. Now it is in itself more probable that the combined reading in such cases is later than, and is the result of, two separate readings. It is more likely that a copyist, finding two different words in two or more manuscripts before him, would put down both in his copy, than that two scribes, finding a combined phrase in their originals, would each select one part of it alone to copy, and would each select a different one. The motive for combining would be praiseworthy—the desire to make sure of keeping the right word by retaining both; but the motive for separating would be vicious, since it involves the deliberate rejection of some words of the sacred text. Moreover, we know that such combination was actually practised; for, as has been stated above, it is a marked characteristic of Lucian's edition of the Septuagint.

Localisation of Groups by Aid of the Fathers.

At this point the evidence of the Fathers becomes important as to both the time and the place of origin of these combined (or as Dr. Hort technically calls them "conflate") readings, and of the other readings characteristic of the third group. They are found to be characteristic of the Scripture quotations in the works of Chrysostom, who was bishop of Antioch in Syria at the end of the fourth century, and of other writers in or about Antioch at the same time; and thenceforward it is the predominant text in manuscripts, versions, and quotations. Hence this type of text, the text of our later uncials, cursives, early printed editions, and Authorised Version, is believed to have taken its rise in or near Antioch, and is known as the "Syrian" text. The type found in the second of the groups above described, that headed by D, the Old Latin and Old Syriac, is called the "Western" text, as being especially found in Latin manuscripts and in those which (like D) have both Greek and Latin texts, though it probably had its origin in the East. There is another small group, earlier than the Syrian, but not represented continuously by any one MS. (mainly by C in the Gospels, A, C, in Acts and Epistles, with certain cursives and occasionally א and L), to which Dr. Hort gives the name of "Alexandrian." The remaining group, headed by B, may be best described as the "Neutral" text.

The "Syrian" Readings Latest.

Now among all the Fathers whose writings are left to us from before the middle of the third century (notably Irenæus, Hippolytus, Clement, Origen, Tertullian, and Cyprian), we find readings belonging to the groups described as Western, Alexandrian, and Neutral, but *no distinctly Syrian readings*. On the other hand we have seen that in the latter part of the fourth century, especially in the region of Antioch, Syrian readings are found plentifully. Add to this the fact that, as stated above, the Syrian readings often show signs of having been derived from a combination of non-Syrian readings, and we have strong confirmation of the belief, which is the corner-stone of Dr. Hort's theory, that the Syrian type of text originated in a revision of the then existing texts, made about the end of the third century in or near Antioch. The result of accepting this conclusion obviously is that, where the Syrian text differs from that of the other groups, it must be rejected as being of later origin, and therefore less authentic; and when it is remembered that by far the greater number of our authorities contain a Syrian text, the importance of this conclusion is manifest. In spite of their numerical preponderance, the Syrian authorities must be relegated to the lowest place.

The "Western" Group.

Of the remaining groups, the Western text is characterised by considerable freedom of addition, and sometimes of omission. Whole verses, or even longer passages, are found in manuscripts of this family, which are entirely absent from all other copies. Some of them will be found enumerated in the following chapter in the description of D, the leading manuscript of this class, and a fuller survey of them is given in Appendix I. It is evident that this type of text must have had its origin in a time when strict exactitude in copying the books of the New Testament was not regarded as a necessary virtue. In early days the copies of the New Testament books were made for immediate edification, without any idea that they would be links in a chain for the transmission of the sacred texts to a distant future; and a scribe might innocently insert in the narrative additional details which he believed to be true and valuable. Fortunately the literary conscience of Antioch and Alexandria was more sensitive, and so this tendency did not spread very far, and was checked before it had greatly contaminated the Bible text. Western manuscripts often contain old and valuable readings, but any variety which shows traces of the characteristic Western vice of amplification or explanatory addition must be rejected, unless it has strong support outside the purely Western group of authorities.

The "Alexandrian" Group.

There remain the Alexandrian and the Neutral groups. The Alexandrian text is represented, not so much by any individual MS. or version, as by certain readings found scattered about in manuscripts which elsewhere belong to one of the other groups. They are readings which have neither Western nor Syrian characteristics, and yet differ from what appears to be the earliest form of the text; and being found most regularly in the quotations of Origen, Cyril of Alexandria, and other Alexandrian Fathers, as well as in the Memphitic version, they are reasonably named Alexandrian. Their characteristics are such as might naturally be due to such a centre of Greek scholarship, since they affect the style rather than the matter, and appear to rise mainly from a desire for correctness of language. They are consequently of minor importance, and are not always distinctly recognisable.

The "Neutral" Group.

The Neutral text, which Westcott and Hort believe to represent most nearly the original text of the New Testament, is chiefly recognisable by the absence of the various forms of aberration noticed in the other groups. Its main centre is at Alexandria, but it also appears in places widely removed from that centre. Sometimes single authorities of the Western group will part company with the rest of their family and exhibit readings which are plainly both ancient and non-Western, showing the existence of a text preceding the Western, and on which the Western variations have been grafted. This text must therefore not be assigned to any local centre. It belonged originally to all the Eastern world. In many parts of the East, notably in Asia Minor, it was superseded by the text which, from its transference to the Latin churches, we call Western. It remained pure longest in Alexandria, and is found in the writings of the Alexandrian Fathers, though even here slight changes of language were introduced, to which the name of Alexandrian has been given. Our main authority for it at the present day is the great Vatican manuscript known as B, and this is often supported by the equally ancient Sinaitic manuscript (א), and by the other manuscripts and versions named above (p. 110). Where the readings of this Neutral text can be plainly discerned, as by the concurrence of all or most of these authorities, they may be accepted with confidence in the face of all the numerical preponderance of other texts; and in so doing lies our best hope of recovering the true words of the New Testament.

Importance of Westcott and Hort's Theory.

Such is, in brief, the theory of Dr. Hort. Its importance in the history of the Bible text, especially in England, is evident when it is seen that it largely influenced the Revisers of our English Bible. The text underlying the Revised Version does not indeed go so far as that of Westcott and Hort in its departure from the received text and from the mass of manuscripts other than B, ℵ, and their fellows; but it is unquestionable that the cogent arguments of the Cambridge Professors had a great effect on the Revisers, and most of the leading scholars of the country have given in their allegiance to the theory. It is indeed on these lines alone that progress in Biblical criticism is possible. The mere enumeration of authorities for and against a disputed reading—the acceptance of the verdict of a majority—is plainly impossible, since it would amount to constructing our text from the latest and least original MSS. To select a certain number of the earliest MSS. and count their votes alone (as was done by Lachmann) is better; but this too is uncritical, and involves the shutting of our eyes to much light which is at our service. To estimate the intrinsic merit of each reading in a disputed passage, taking into account the *general* predominance of good authorities on one side or the other, is better still, and good critics have gone far by this method; but it still leaves much to the personal taste and judgment of the critic, which in the last resort can never be convincing. Only if our authorities can be divided into groups—if their genealogical tree, so to speak, can be traced with some approach to certainty, so that the earlier branches may be distinguished from the later—only so is there any chance of our criticism advancing on a sound basis and being able to command a general assent.

Objections to It.

The theory of Westcott and Hort has not, however, been universally accepted. On its first promulgation it was vehemently opposed by the advocates of the "received" (or, as Hort calls it, the Syrian) text, such as Dean Burgon and Dr. Scrivener. Much was made of the well-nigh absolute predominance of the received text in the later Middle Ages, and the vast numerical majority of the manuscripts containing it. But the weakness of this argument became evident when it was pointed out that exactly the same sort of preponderance of later and inferior witnesses was found, on a smaller scale, in classical literature generally. A greater difficulty (and it is a real one) in the theory is that there is absolutely no historical confirmation of the Syrian revision of the text, which is its corner-stone. It is rightly urged that it is very strange to find no reference among the Fathers to so important an event as an official revision of the Bible text and its adoption as the standard text throughout the Greek world. We know the names of the scholars who made revisions of the Septuagint and of the Syriac version; but there is no trace of those who carried out the far more important work of fixing the shape of the Greek New Testament. Is not the whole theory artificial and illusory, the vain imagining of an ingenious mind, like so many of the products of modern criticism, which spins endless webs out of its own interior, to be swept away to-morrow by the ruthless broom of common sense?

Considerations of Objections.

Against this indictment may be placed the consideration that even if we can find no historical reference to a revision, yet the critical reasons which indicated the separation of the Syrian text from the rest, and its inferiority in date, remain untouched. We still have the groups of authorities habitually found in conjunction; we still have the fact that the readings of the group we have called Syrian are shown by their intrinsic character to be probably later than the non-Syrian; and we still have the fact that readings of the Syrian type are not found in any authorities earlier than about A.D. 300. Unless these facts can be controverted, the division into groups and the relative inferiority of the Syrian group must be considered to be established. At the same time, it does seem possible that the formal revision of the text at a set time in or about Antioch may be a myth. Dr. Hort himself divides the revision into two stages, separated by some interval of time, and thus doubles the difficulty of accounting for the total absence of any mention of a revision. It seems possible that the Syrian text is the result rather of a process continued over a considerable period of time than of a set revision by constituted authorities. In the comparatively prosperous days of the third, and still more of the fourth, century the Church had leisure to collect and compare different copies of the Scriptures hitherto passing without critical examination. At a great centre of Christianity, such as Antioch, the principle may have been established by general consent that the best way to deal with divergences of readings was to combine them, wherever possible, to smooth away difficulties and harshnesses, and to produce an even and harmonious text. Such a principle might easily be adopted by the copyists of a single neighbourhood, and so lead in time to the creation of a local type of text, just as the Western text must be supposed to have been produced, not by a formal revision, but by the development of a certain way of dealing with the text in a certain region. The subsequent acceptance of the Antiochian or Syrian type as the received text of the Greek New Testament must have been due to the predominant influence of Constantinople. The Antiochian revision aimed at producing a smooth, intelligible text, suitable for popular use. Such a text, if once approved by metropolitan churches so influential as Constantinople and Antioch, would naturally become the received text of the whole Byzantine Church. Such, whatever its origin, it certainly eventually became; and it is only the discovery of more ancient authorities which has convinced practically all scholars that it is in fact a secondary text, the result of a long process of revision, and that we must get behind it if we wish to recover, as nearly as may be, the original form of the sacred text.

But this is not to say that the "Neutral" text of Westcott and Hort must be accepted forthwith as final. On the contrary, it has been sharply assailed from another side. It was early pointed out that the argument which the Cambridge scholars used against the "Syrian" text might be turned against their "Neutral" text; for in the earliest Christian writers the form of text found in their quotations was much more "Western" than "Neutral." A disposition accordingly manifested itself among the less conservative critics to advocate the claims of the "Western" text, and to maintain that it was the original form, from which the "Neutral" had been derived by a process of revision. This view was reinforced by the discovery of the Sinaitic MS. of the Old Syriac version, as described below (p. 161); for here was an authority, unquestionably of early date, with a number of readings which were certainly not "Neutral," but had affinities rather with the Old Latin and other truly Western witnesses. For a time, therefore, there was a tendency to exalt the "Western" text and to question the "Neutral."

But this view too is hardly standing up to criticism and the increasing evidence; for the more that instances multiplied of readings which were pre-Syrian and yet were not "Neutral," the more difficult it became to define what the term "Western" meant. If it were asked what the "Neutral" text is, it was easy to answer that it was the text found in the Codex Vaticanus and its allies. But if it were asked what the "Western" text is, no such easy answer lay at hand, because the habit had grown up of giving the title of "Western" to any and every early reading which was not "Neutral." The Western text was therefore a congeries of readings, some with Latin attestation, some with

Syrian, some even with Egyptian, although Egypt was accepted as the home of the "Neutraltext. This loose use of the term "Western" as equivalent to "non-Neutral pre-Syrian" is not yet extinct, but the truth is that in this sense the "Western" text is not a text at all. The general trend of modern discoveries is to show that a distinction must be drawn between the truly Western text, to be found mainly in Græco-Latin MSS. such as the Codex Bezæ and the Codex Claromontanus, and in the Old Latin Version, and the remaining early non-Neutral readings, for which other classifications may still be found, and some of which will probably remain unclassified.

One such classification has emerged within the last few years, as the result of researches in which many scholars have had a hand, but in which the greater and more decisive part has been played by the late Dr. B. H. Streeter and Professor Kirsopp Lake. So long ago as 1877 W. H. Ferrar and T. K. Abbott indicated a group of four minuscule MSS. (13, 69, 124, 346) as having many peculiar readings which showed that they had a common parentage. Then, in 1902, Lake isolated another group of four (1, 118, 131, 209) which similarly formed a single family. In 1906 attention was called to a late uncial (now known as the Codex Koridethianus, or Θ), and it was shown that it had connections with both of these groups and with some other minuscules (28, 565, 700 and others). Finally, Dr. Streeter proved that this type of text, which stood midway between Neutral and Western, was used by Origen in certain commentaries and other works of his, written during the later part of his life, when he was resident at Cæsarea. Streeter accordingly felt justified in dubbing it the "Cæsarean" text, and claiming for it a right to recognition as a definite family. Lake subsequently showed that there is reason to believe that Origen may have used this type of text before he left Alexandria for Cæsarea; and the possibility that it may have been of Egyptian origin was strengthened when the Chester Beatty Gospels papyrus (see below, p. 125) was found to have a text of "Cæsarean" character. But whatever its character, the "Cæsarean" text has been placed "on the map," and the scope of the "Western" by so much reduced.

The truth would seem to be (and every new discovery of early fragments seems to confirm it) that in the second and third centuries the text of the New Testament, and especially of the Gospels, was under very little control. There was no one centre issuing authoritative copies of the Scriptures, and for some time no need was felt for it. It was the substance of the Christian story that mattered, not the exact words. One community would borrow a copy of a Gospel or Epistle from its neighbour and copy it, and the copyist would not always be a skilled scribe. Means of controlling and correcting mistakes were lacking; and in such conditions various readings would multiply greatly. We know that a similar state of confusion existed among the manuscripts of the Old Latin Version when, towards the end of the fourth century, Pope Damasus commissioned Jerome to restore them to order. So, no doubt, in the Greek world, efforts at reform would be made by bishops and scholars, but their effect would be mainly local; and the result would be the formation of local types of text. Such, it would appear, was the origin of the several families which we now know as Neutral (or Alexandrian), Western (in the proper restricted sense), Syriac (the text of the Old Syriac Version), Cæsarean, and Byzantine (a title for Hort's "Syrian" text, which seems preferable, as avoiding confusion with "Syriac," and indicating the important fact that it became the received text of the Byzantine Church). And if the text which Hort called "Neutral" is on the whole to be regarded as the best, it is not because (as Hort thought) it has come down substantially intact without having undergone editorial revision, but rather because it is the result of more scholarly and scientific revision than the others, while the Western, on the contrary, is the result of a lax treatment of the text. But on these points, as to which agreement has not been reached among scholars, more may be said after the list of manuscripts and versions has been surveyed.[1] With this preliminary outline of textual theory, the reader will be able to appreciate the position in relation to it held by the several manuscripts and versions which we now proceed to describe.

[1] A classification of authorities, somewhat different from that of Westcott and Hort, was put forward in 1906 by H. von Soden in the very elaborate *prolegomena* to his critical edition of the Greek text. He formed three classes, indicated by the letters K, H, and I. K (from the Greek word Κοινή) is identical with Hort's "Syrian," H (so called because he attributes it to the Alexandrian scholar, Hesychius, whose edition of the Septuagint has been described above, p. 60) is equivalent to Hort's "Neutral," and I (Jerusalem) includes the Western authorities and a number of others. Von Soden claimed this family as his special discovery, and regarded it as the best; but in truth it is difficult to identify, and consists of a number of incongruous groups. The identification of the Cæsarean family, which forms part of it, has further discredited it, and von Soden's principal service would appear to be his classification of a number of subgroups of his K family, which throws light on the evolution of the Received Text.

CHESTER BEATTY GOSPELS PAPYRUS—EARLY 3RD CENT.
(*John* x. 7-25. *Original size*, 6¼ *in.* × 5¾ *in.*)

CHESTER BEATTY PAPYRUS OF PAULINE EPISTLES—EARLY 3RD CENT.

(*Gal.* vi. 10-*Phil.* i. 1. *Original size,* 8½ *in.* × 6 *in.*)

APPENDIX TO CHAPTER VI

THE CHIEF EDITIONS OF THE NEW TESTAMENT

THE earliest printed editions of the New Testament—those of Erasmus, Ximenes, Stephanus, and Beza—have been mentioned in the preceding chapter (pp. 102-4), and there would be little profit or interest in a list of all the editions which have followed these down to the present day. But since certain editors stand out above their fellows by reason of their exceptional services towards the improvement of the text, and their opinions are often quoted among the authorities presented to the student in critical editions, it may be useful to give (mainly from the more detailed histories of Tregelles and Scrivener) some slight record of their labours, and of the principles adopted by them. It will not be inappropriate, in a history of the Bible text, to record the names of those who have especially devoted their lives to the task of freeing it from the errors of past ages, and the restoration of it, as near as may be, to its original truth.

There are two steps in this operation; first, the collection of evidence, and, secondly, the using of it. The "received text," as shown above, was based on the comparison of a few manuscripts, mostly of late date, and for more than a century the most pressing need was the examination of more and better manuscripts. BRIAN WALTON, afterwards Bishop of Chester, led the way in 1657, by publishing in his Polyglot Bible the readings of fourteen hitherto unexamined MSS., including the newly acquired Codex Alexandrinus (A) and the two important Græco-Latin MSS. D and D_2; but the real father of this department of textual criticism is JOHN MILL (1645-1710), of Queen's College, Oxford. Mill, in 1707, reprinted Stephanus' text of 1550, with only accidental divergences, but added the various readings of nearly 100 manuscripts, and thereby provided all subsequent scholars with a broad basis of established evidence. RICHARD BENTLEY (1662-1742), the most famous of all English classical scholars, planned a critical edition of the New Testament in both Greek and Latin, and to that end procured collations of a large number of good manuscripts in both languages; but an increasing sense of the complexity of the task, and the distraction of other occupations, prevented the completion of his work, and his masses of materials proved of little use. He had, however, stimulated others to carry on the task he left unfinished, and J. J. WETSTEIN (1693-1754), of Basle, who had originally worked for Bentley, made very large additions to the stores of manuscript evidence. His New Testament, published in 1751-2, quotes the readings of more than 300 MSS., including nearly all those which are now recognised as being of the greatest value. As mentioned above (p. 106) he also drew up the first list of manuscript authorities, which has served as the basis of all subsequent lists. To this list some seventy more were added by C. F. MATTHÆI (1744-1811).

Meanwhile other scholars had begun to turn their attention to the use of the materials thus collected; and the pioneer of critical method was J. A. BENGEL, of Tübingen (1687-1752). To this scholar belongs the honour of having been the first to divide the manuscripts of the New Testament into groups. The great majority of MSS. he assigned to a group which he called the *Asiatic*, though its headquarters were at Constantinople, while the few better ones were classed as *African*. Bengel did not, however, advance far with this principle, and the first working out of it must be assigned to J. J. GRIESBACH (1745-1812), who made a careful classification of MSS. into three groups—the Alexandrian, the Western, and the Byzantine. These groups roughly correspond to the Neutral, Western, and Syrian groups of Dr. Hort, of whom Griesbach is the true forerunner. On the basis of this classification Griesbach drew up lists of readings which he regarded as, in greater or less degree, preferable to those of the received text, and so paved the way for the formal construction of a revised Greek Testament.

So far all editors had been content to reprint the received text of the New Testament, merely adding their collections of various readings in footnotes; but with the nineteenth century a new departure was made, and we reach the region of modern textual criticism, of which the principle is, setting aside the "received text," to construct a new text with the help of the best authorities now available. The author of this new departure was C. LACHMANN (1793-1851), who published in 1831, and with a fuller exposition in 1842-50, a text constructed according to principles of his own devising. Out of all the mass of manuscripts collected by Mill, Wetstein, and their colleagues, he selected a few of the best (A, B, C, and sometimes D, with the fragments P, Q, T, Z, in the Gospels; D, E_2, in the Acts; D_2, G_3, H_3, in the Pauline Epistles; together with some of the best MSS. of the Latin Vulgate, and a few of the Fathers), and from these he endeavoured to recover the text of the New Testament as it was current in the fourth century (when the earliest of these authorities were written) by the simple method of counting the authorities in favour of each reading, and always following the majority. Lachmann's method was too mechanical in its rigidity, and the list of his authorities was too small; at the same time his use of the best authorities led him to many unquestionable improvements on the received text. Lachmann was followed by the two great Biblical critics of the last generation, Tischendorf and

Tregelles, who unite in themselves the two distinct streams of textual criticism, being eminent alike in the collection and the use of evidence. A. F. C. TISCHENDORF (1815-1874) published no fewer than eight editions of the Greek New Testament, with an increasing quantity of critical material in each; and the last of these (1869-72, with prolegomena on the MSS., versions, etc., by Gregory in 1884-94) remains still the standard collection of evidence for the Greek text. Besides this, he published trustworthy editions of a large number of the best individual manuscripts, crowning the whole with his great discovery and publication of the Codex Sinaiticus, as described in the next chapter. Tischendorf's services in the publication of texts (including א, B, C, D_2, E_2, L, and many more of the Greek New Testament, with the Codex Amiatinus of the Latin) are perfectly inestimable, and have done more than anything else to establish textual criticism on a sound basis. His use of his materials, in his revisions of the New Testament text, is less satisfactory, owing to the considerable fluctuations in his judgments between one edition and the next; but here, too, his work has been very useful. S. P. TREGELLES (1813-75) published only two MSS. in full, but collated very many with great accuracy, and used his materials with judgment in the preparation of a revised text. Like Lachmann, he based his text exclusively on the ancient authorities; but he used a larger number of them, paid much attention to the versions and Fathers, and did not tie himself down to obedience to a numerical majority among his witnesses. Like Tischendorf, he followed no principle of grouping in his use of his authorities, so that his choice of readings is liable to depend on personal preference among the best attested variants; but his experience and judgment were such as to entitle his opinion to very great weight.

Of WESTCOTT and HORT we have spoken at length in the preceding chapter, showing how they revived Griesbach's principle, and worked it out with greater elaboration and with a far fuller command of material.

Since Westcott and Hort there has been much publication of new discoveries, which will be described in their proper place below, but only one large-scale critical edition of the whole New Testament. This is the work of Hermann VON SODEN, who in 1902-10 published elaborate Prolegomena, including the catalogue and classification of MSS. referred to above (pp. 107, 118), followed in 1913 by the text and critical apparatus. It is a work of immense labour, but difficult to use and unsatisfactory in results by reason of defects of plan. His text is prepared largely according to his own judgment, and does not differ materially from that of most other critical editions.

Apart from actual editions of the text, most valuable work was done by C. R. Gregory, an American scholar domiciled in Germany, who, in spite of his advanced age, insisted on fighting for his adopted country, and died in the field in 1915. As editor of the Prolegomena to Tischendorf's last edition, and of several subsequent volumes, he provided the chief magazine of textual materials on which scholars still depend; and his catalogue of manuscripts, with the renumbering referred to above (p. 107), is, with the continuations of von Dobschütz and Lietzmann, the universally accepted official list. In England a similar service was rendered by F. H. A. Scrivener (1813-91), whose *Introduction to the Criticism of the New Testament*, first published in 1861 (fourth edition, 1894, by E. Miller, with chapters by other scholars) is still the fullest description, up to its date, of the textual materials for English readers. His list of MSS., partly coincident with and partly parallel to that of Gregory, is now superseded by the latter, which alone has been kept up-to-date. Other scholars who may be mentioned are J. W. Burgon, conspicuous for his vehement and even intemperate defence of the Received Text against the doctrines of Westcott and Hort; and Bernard Weiss, whose textual studies of successive portions of the New Testament (1892-9) led him along quite independent lines of argument to support Westcott and Hort's high opinion of the Vatican MS.

Von Soden's edition having proved a disappointment, an attempt has recently been set on foot by an English committee to produce a new critical edition on the same lines as Tischendorf —that is, a plain statement of the evidence of manuscripts, versions, and Fathers, without any attempt to classify or group it according to any textual theory. The first part of this, containing the Gospel of St. Mark, in the text of Westcott and Hort, with full apparatus, appeared from the Oxford University Press in 1935, under the editorship of the Rev. S. C. E. Legg. St. Matthew is now ready for the press. If this enterprise can be carried through, scholars will have a full statement of the textual material, embodying all the most recent discoveries.

The foregoing list includes all the editors whom the reader may expect to find often quoted in any textual commentary on the Bible which he is likely to use, and may, it is hoped, help him to understand the principles on which their opinions are given. To the reader who wishes to find a statement of the evidence on all important passages in the New Testament, without wading through such a mass of material as that provided by Tischendorf, von Soden, or Legg, the following hints may be useful. The Cambridge School Greek Testament, edited by Scrivener, gives the received text, with notes stating the readings adopted by Lachmann, Tischendorf, Tregelles, Westcott and Hort, and the Revised Version of 1881. The Oxford Greek Testament, which contains the received text as edited by Bishop Lloyd in 1828, was provided in 1899 by Professor Sanday with an appendix containing an admirable selection of various read-, ings, and a statement of the principal manuscripts, versions-Fathers, and editors in favour of each, and, in addition, a come plete collation of the text of Westcott and Hort. This may by confidently recommended to students who wish for a hande critical edition of the Greek text, though of course it lacks the most recent discoveries. The student who prefers to use the English Bible will find a similar collection of evidence, amply sufficient for all practical purposes, and excellently selected by Professor Sanday and Mr. R. L. Clarke, in the notes to the Variorum Bible; where he will likewise find notes which summarize the best opinions on the translation, as well as the text, of the most important passages about which there is any doubt.

Since 1881, however, there have been several handy editions containing revised texts instead of the "received text" of 1550. The one that will probably be found most useful by students it the Oxford edition of 1910, which contains the Greek text followed in the English Revised Version, with a select textual apparatus by Professor A. Souter. Another very handy text with select apparatus is that produced by Dr. E. Nestle in 1898 and published by the Bible Society of Stuttgart, which reached its twelfth edition in 1937. An edition on somewhat similar lines has been produced by H. J. Vogels (1920). The student therefore now has an ample supply of editions of the New Testament with modern texts and sufficient textual apparatus for most purposes.

CHAPTER VII

THE MANUSCRIPTS OF THE NEW TESTAMENT

It is now time to describe the more important of the individual manuscripts of the New Testament in the original Greek, and to show how they take their several places in the textual theories which have been outlined in the preceding chapter. Each manuscript has its own individual character, which reveals itself only to the student who examines it in detail; and some of them have had stories to which an element of romance attaches. It will of course be understood that only the most important can be individually described here; but it will be possible to include all those which the reader is likely to find mentioned in the Variorum Bible or in the smaller critical editions of the Greek text, or in works dealing with textual criticism.

1. *Papyri.*

It has already been explained (p. 12) that to the two categories of vellum manuscripts, Uncials and Minuscules, there has now to be prefixed a third, which has only come into existence within the last fifty years, and indeed has only acquired much importance within the last seven. That is the category of Papyri, which has added a new chapter to textual history, and has gone far to bridge the gap between the autographs of the New Testament books and the great vellum uncials. Of these, fifty-three[1] are now included in the official lists, where they have a section to themselves, being indicated by a letter P and a number. Most of them, however, are quite small fragments, which have little individual importance, though those which are earlier than the fourth century have some collective value, as indicating what types of text were current in Egypt in the early years of the Christian Church.

P⁵. British Museum Papyrus 782. This is a conjoint pair of leaves (*i.e.*, two leaves from a single quire, still joined together as when the sheet of which they are composed was originally folded), found by Grenfell and Hunt at Oxyrhynchus in 1896-7, and published as Oxyrhynchus Papyrus 208. Since one leaf of it contains John i. 23-31, 33-41, and the other John xx. 11-17, 19-25, it is evident that the whole Gospel was included in a single quire,

[1] The 157 items comprised in the list compiled by the Rev. P. L. Hedley in 1933 include ostraka, vellum fragments, amulets, etc.

probably of twenty-five folded sheets, of which this is the outermost but one; it was thus the first example to be discovered of this form of codex, of which several other specimens are now known. In date it is of the third century, and its text agrees generally with that of the Sinaiticus.

P[13]. British Museum Papyrus 1532. Published by Grenfell and Hunt in 1904 as Oxyrhynchus Papyrus 657. It contains Heb. ii. 14–v. 5, x. 8-22, 29–xi. 13, xi. 28–xii. 17. It is an example of the re-use of a papyrus which had already been used for another text. Originally it was a roll, containing an epitome of Livy, written in the third century. Late in that century, or early in the fourth, the back of it was used to receive the Epistle to the Hebrews, of which these portions survive. Its text is akin to that of the Vaticanus, and it is valuable as containing part of the Epistle which is lost in that manuscript. Now, however, we have an earlier and more perfect copy of the Epistle in *P*[46].

P[38]. Michigan Papyrus 1571. Probably fourth century, though its first editor would put it earlier. Contains Acts xviii. 27–xix. 6, xix. 12-16. Its importance lies in the fact that its text is markedly of the " Western " type, concurring often with Codex Bezæ. Another example is found in *P*[48]. It is interesting to know that texts of this type (a type specially strongly marked in Acts) were in use even in Egypt. Edited by H. A. Sanders (*Harvard Theological Review*, 1927).

We now come to the great Chester Beatty find, the Old Testa ment part of which has been described above (p. 64). The New Testament part comprises portions of three codices, which when complete would have covered the whole of the New Testament, except the Pastoral and Catholic Epistles; and since all are of the third century or earlier, it will be seen what an important addition they make to our textual material.

P[45]. Chester Beatty Papyrus I (see Plate XII). This consists of portions of thirty leaves of a codex which originally consisted of about 220 leaves, and contained all four Gospels and the Acts. In direct contrast with *P*[5] and *P*[46] it is formed of a succession of quires of only two leaves. It seems that these two methods of forming papyrus codices represent early experiments, which were eventually abandoned in favour of quires of eight, ten, or twelve leaves, such as we find in late papyrus codices, and universally in vellum and paper books. The leaves are wide, and the writing is small, in a single broad column. Consequently a full page contains a large amount of text, and even small fragments may have enough to be of value. The extant remains consist of portions of two leaves of Matthew, six of Mark, seven of Luke, two of John and thirteen of Acts. Those of Luke and John consist of the major part of leaves, those of Mark and Acts are smaller but sufficient for the character of the text and the readings of many important passages to be clear, those of Matthew so small as to be negligible. For the details of the passages preserved, reference must be made to the publication of the papyrus by the present writer (*Chester Beatty Biblical Papyri*, fasc. ii., 1933), or *The Text of the Greek Bible* (1937). The interest of the papyrus lies in the fact that it cannot be assigned wholly to any of the families of text described in the previous chapter. In Mark it is nearer to the Cæsarean family than to either Neutral or Western. In Luke and John (where the Cæsarean text has not yet been determined) all that can be said is that it is intermediate between Neutral and Western; in Acts it is distinctly nearer to the Neutral and has *none* of the major variants characteristic of the Western text in this book, though it has some of the minor ones. It therefore adds to the proof that the Neutral text has no exclusive predominance in Egypt, but that rather there was, by the beginning of the third century, a welter of various readings which were only gradually crystallising into distinct families, and that the Cæsarean text may well have had its growth in Egypt, before Origen took it to Cæsarea.

P ^{46}. Chester Beatty Papyrus II (Plate XIII). The fortunes of this MS. are an illustration of the chances of discovery. In Mr. Beatty's original acquisition there were ten leaves, in conjoint pairs, containing portions of Romans on the first halves, and portions of Philippians, Colossians, and 1 Thessalonians on the second—evidently, therefore, part of a single-quire codex of the Pauline Epistles—and calculations of space made it probable that Hebrews had been included in the missing intermediate portion. This calculation was confirmed when, shortly after the ten leaves had been published by the present writer, it was announced that the University of Michigan had acquired thirty more leaves of the same codex, in excellent condition, which showed that Hebrews was indeed included, and was placed immediately after Romans. Scarcely had these been published by Professor H. A. Sanders, of Michigan, together with the ten Beatty leaves, when they were capped by the acquisition by Mr. Beatty of forty-six leaves more. The entire manuscript therefore consists, in its present state, of eighty-six nearly perfect leaves out of a total of 104, of which the last five were probably blank; at least they are not needed for the completion of Thessalonians, and would not be enough for the Pastorals, which seem to have been omitted.[1] The order of the Epistles is: Romans,

[1] It is theoretically possible that the scribe, when he got to the end of 2 Thessalonians, realising that he had only five leaves left when he wanted ten for the Pastorals, may have taken five more sheets and folded them on

PLATE XIV.

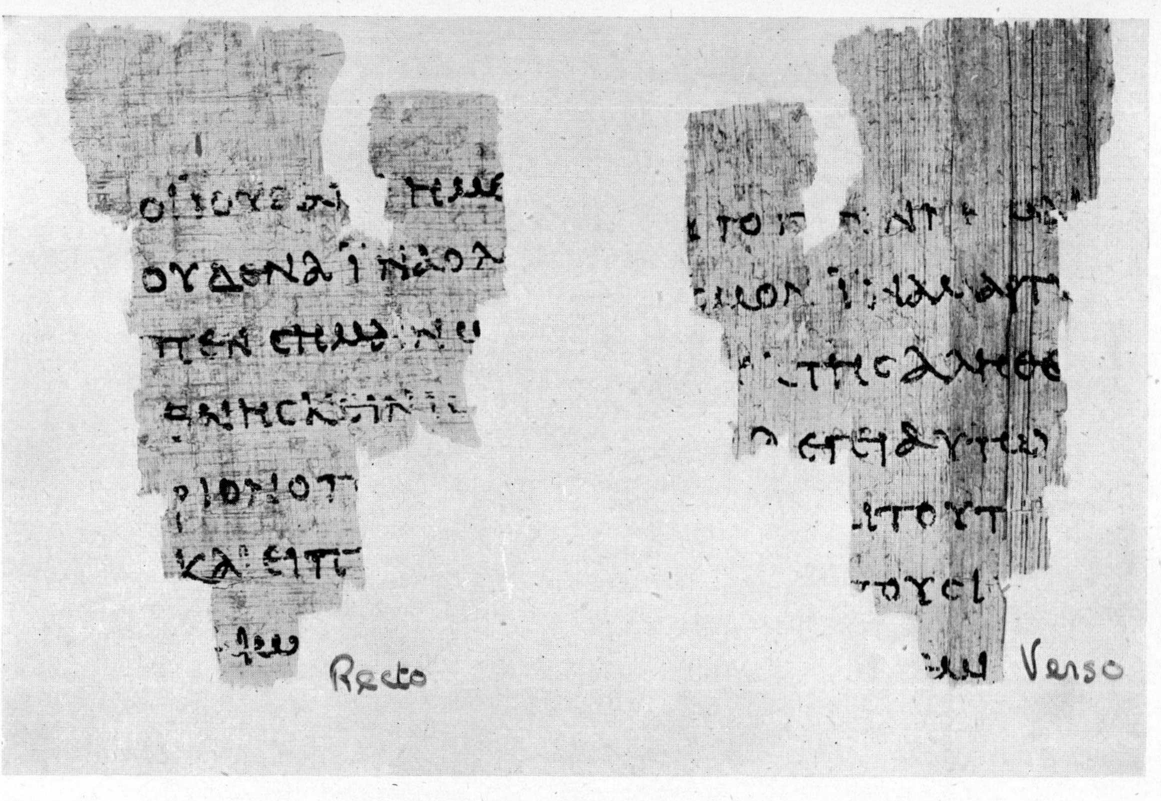

RYLANDS LIBRARY FRAGMENT OF ST. JOHN—2ND CENT.

(Unreduced.)

Plate XV.

ΤΗϹΤΡΑΠΕΖΗϹΟΤΙ
ΟΥϹΤΟΥΑΝΘΡΩΠΟΥ
ΚΑΤΑΤΟΩΡΙϹΜΕ
ΝΟΝΠΟΡΕΥΕΤΑΙ
ΠΛΗΝΟΥΑΙΤΩΑΝ
ΘΡΩΠΩΕΚΕΙΝΩ
ΔΙΟΥΠΑΡΑΔΙΔΟΤΑΙ
ΚΑΙΑΥΤΟΙΗΡΞΑΝΤΟ
ϹΥΝΖΗΤΕΙΝΠΡΟϹ
ΕΑΥΤΟΥϹΤΟΤΙϹΑΡΑ
ΕΙΗΕΞΑΥΤΩΝΕΙΗ
ΟΤΟΥΤΟΜΕΛΛΩΝ
ΠΡΑϹϹΕΙΝ
ΕΓΕΝΕΤΟΔΕΦΙΛΟΝΙ
ΚΙΑΕΙϹΕΑΥΤΟΥϹ
ΤΟΤΙϹΑΥΤΩΝΔΟ
ΚΕΙΕΙΝΑΙΜΙΖΩΝ
ΟΔΕΕΙΠΕΝΑΥΤΟΙϹ
ΟΙΒΑϹΙΛΕΙϹΤΩΝ
ΕΘΝΩΝΚΥΡΙΕΥΟΥ
ϹΙΝΑΥΤΩΝΚΑΙΟΙ
ΑΡΧΟΝΤΕϹΤΩΝΕ
ΞΟΥϹΙΑΖΟΥϹΙΝΑΥ
ΤΩΝΚΑΙΕΥΕΡΓΕ
ΤΑΙΚΑΛΟΥΝΤΑΙΥ
ΜΕΙϹΔΕΟΥΧΟΥΤΩϹ
ΑΛΛΟΜΕΙΖΩΝΕΝΥ
ΜΙΝΓΕΙΝΕϹΘΩ
ΩϹΟΝΕΩΤΕΡΟϹ
ΚΑΙΟΗΓΟΥΜΕΝΟϹ
ΩϹΟΔΙΑΚΟΝΩΝ
ΤΙϹΓΑΡΟΜΕΙΖΩΝ
ΟΑΝΑΚΕΙΜΕΝΟϹ
ΗΟΔΙΑΚΟΝΩΝΟΥ
ΧΙΟΑΝΑΚΕΙΜΕΝΟϹ
ΕΓΩΔΕΕΝΜΕϹΩ
ΥΜΩΝΕΙΜΙΩϹΟ
ΔΙΑΚΟΝΩΝΥΜΕΙϹ
ΔΕΕϹΤΕΟΙΔΙΑΜΕ
ΜΕΝΗΚΟΤΕϹΜΕ

ΤΗϹΤΡΑΠΕΖΗϹΜΟΥ
ΕΝΤΗΒΑϹΙΛΕΙΑΜΟΥ
ΚΑΙΚΑΘΗϹΕϹΘΕ
ΕΠΙΘΡΟΝΩΝΚΡΙΝΟΝ
ΤΕϹΤΑϹΔΩΔΕΚΑ
ΦΥΛΑϹΤΟΥΙΗΛ
ΕΙΠΕΝΔΕΟΚϹϹΙ
ΜΩΝΙΔΟΥΟϹΑΤΑ
ΝΑϹΕΞΗΤΗϹΑΤΟ
ΥΜΑϹΤΟΥϹΙΝΙΑϹΑΙ
ΩϹΤΟΝϹΙΤΟΝΕΓΩ
ΔΕΕΔΕΗΘΗΝΠΕΡΙ
ϹΟΥΙΝΑΜΗΕΚΛΙ
ΠΗΗΠΙϹΤΙϹϹΟΥ
ΚΑΙϹΥΠΟΤΕΕΠΙϹΤΡΕ
ΨΑϹϹΤΗΡΙϹΟΝΤΟΥϹ
ΑΔΕΛΦΟΥϹϹΟΥ
ΟΔΕΕΙΠΕΝΑΥΤΩ
ΚΕΜΕΤΑϹΟΥΕΤΟΙ
ΜΟϹΕΙΜΙΚΑΙΕΙϹ
ΦΥΛΑΚΗΝΚΑΙΕΙϹ
ΘΑΝΑΤΟΝΠΟΡΕΥ
ΕϹΘΑΙ
ΟΔΕΕΙΠΕΝΛΕΓΩϹΟΙ
ΠΕΤΡΕΟΥΦΩΝΗ
ϹΕΙϹΗΜΕΡΟΝΑΛΕ
ΚΤΩΡΕΩϹΤΡΕΙϹΜΕ
ΑΠΑΡΝΗϹΗΕΙΔΕ
ΝΑΙ
ΚΑΙΕΙΠΕΝΑΥΤΟΙϹ
ΟΤΕΑΠΕϹΤΙΛΑΥΜΑϹ
ΑΤΕΡΒΑΛΛΑΝΤΙΟΥ
ΚΑΙΠΗΡΑϹΚΑΙΥΠΟ
ΔΗΜΑΤΩΝΜΗΤΙΝΟϹ
ΥϹΤΕΡΗϹΑΤΑΙΟΙΔΕ
ΕΙΠΟΝΟΥΔΕΝΟϹ
ΟΔΕΕΙΠΕΝΑΥΤΟΙϹ
ΑΛΛΑΝΥΝΟΕΧΩΝ
ΒΑΛΛΑΝΤΙΟΝΑΡΑ
ΤΩΟΜΟΙΩϹΚΑΙΠΗ

ΝΑΙΕΝΕΜΟΙΤΟΚΑΙ
ΜΕΤΑΑΝΟΜΩΝΕ
ΛΟΓΙϹΘΗΚΑΙΓΑΡΤΟ
ΠΕΡΙΕΜΟΥΤΕΛΟϹΕΧΕΙ
ΟΙΔΕΕΙΠΑΝΙΔΟΥ
ΜΑΧΑΙΡΑΙΩΔΕΔΥΟ
ΟΔΕΕΙΠΕΝΑΥΤΟΙϹ
ΙΚΑΝΟΝΕϹΤΙΝ
ΚΑΙΕΞΕΛΘΩΝΕΠΟ
ΡΕΥΘΗΚΑΤΑΤΟΕΘΟϹ
ΕΙϹΤΟΟΡΟϹΤΩΝΕ
ΛΑΙΩΝΗΚΟΛΟΥ
ΘΗϹΑΝΔΕΑΥΤΩΚΑΙ
ΟΙΜΑΘΗΤΑΙ
ΓΕΝΟΜΕΝΟϹΔΕΕΠΙ
ΤΟΥΤΟΠΟΥΕΙΠΕΝΑΥ
ΤΟΙϹΠΡΟϹΕΥΧΕϹΘΕ
ΜΗΕΙϹΕΛΘΕΙΝΕΙϹ
ΠΙΡΑϹΜΟΝ
ΚΑΙΑΥΤΟϹΑΠΕϹΠΑ
ϹΘΗΑΠΑΥΤΩΝΩϹΕΙ
ΛΙΘΟΥΒΟΛΗΝΚΑΙ
ΘΕΙϹΤΑΓΟΝΑΤΑΠΡΟ
ϹΗΥΞΑΤΟΛΕΓΩΝ
ΠΑΤΕΡΕΙΒΟΥΛΗΠΑΡΕ
ΝΕΓΚΑΙΤΟΥΤΟΤΟ
ΠΟΤΗΡΙΟΝΤΟΥΤΟ
ΑΠΕΜΟΥΠΛΗΝΜΗ
ΤΟΘΕΛΗΜΑΜΟΥΑΛ
ΛΑΤΟϹΟΝΓΕΙΝΕϹΘΩ
ΩΦΘΗΔΕΑΥΤΩΑΓ
ΓΕΛΟϹΑΠΟΥΡΑΝΟΥ
ΕΝΙϹΧΥΩΝΑΥΤΟΝ
ΚΑΙΓΕΝΑΜΕΝΟϹΕ
ΝΑΓΩΝΙΑΕΚΤΕΝΕ
ϹΤΕΡΟΝΠΡΟϹΗΥ
ΧΕΤΟΚΑΙΕΓΕΝΕΤΟ
ΙΔΡΩϹΑΥΤΟΥΩϹΕΙ
ΘΡΟΜΒΟΙΑΙΜΑΤΟϹ
ΚΑΤΑΒΑΙΝΟΝΤΟϹ

ΤΟΙϹΤΙΚΑΘΕΥΔΕΤΕ
ΑΝΑϹΤΑΝΤΕϹΠΡΟϹ
ΕΥΧΕϹΘΕΙΝΑΜΗ
ΕΙϹΕΛΘΗΤΑΙΕΙϹΠΙ
ΡΑϹΜΟΝ
ΕΤΙΑΥΤΟΥΛΑΛΟΥΝ
ΤΟϹΙΔΟΥΟΧΛΟϹΚΑΙ
ΟΛΕΓΟΜΕΝΟϹΙΟΥ
ΔΑϹΕΙϹΤΩΝΔΩΔΕ
ΚΑΠΡΟΗΡΧΕΤΟΑΥ
ΤΟΥϹ
ΚΑΙΗΓΓΙϹΕΝΤΩΙΥ
ΦΙΛΗϹΑΙΑΥΤΟΝΙϹ
ΔΕΕΙΠΕΝΑΥΤΩΙΟΥΔΑ
ΦΙΛΗΜΑΤΙΤΟΝΥΝ
ΤΟΥΑΝΘΡΩΠΟΥΠΑ
ΡΑΔΙΔΩϹ
ΕΙΔΟΝΤΕϹΔΕΟΙΠΕ
ΡΙΑΥΤΟΝΤΟΕϹΟΜΕ
ΝΟΝΕΙΠΑΝΚΕΕΙ
ΠΑΤΑΞΟΜΕΝΕΝ
ΜΑΧΑΙΡΗΚΑΙΕΠΑ
ΤΑΞΕΝΕΙϹΤΙϹΕΞΑΥ
ΤΩΝΤΟΥΑΡΧΙΕΡΕ
ΩϹΤΟΝΔΟΥΛΟΝ
ΚΑΙΑΦΙΛΕΝΤΟΟΥϹ
ΑΥΤΟΥΤΟΔΕΞΙΟΝ
ΑΠΟΚΡΙΘΕΙϹΔΕΟΙϹ
ΕΙΠΕΝΕΑΤΕΕΩϹ
ΤΟΥΤΟΥ
ΚΑΙΑΨΑΜΕΝΟϹΤΟΥ
ΩΤΙΟΥΙΑϹΑΤΟΝ
ΤΟΝ
ΕΙΠΕΝΔΕΙϹΠΡΟϹ
ΤΟΥϹΠΑΡΑΓΕΝΟ
ΜΕΝΟΥϹΠΡΟϹΑΥ
ΤΟΝΑΡΧΙΕΡΕΙϹΚΑΙ
ϹΤΡΑΤΗΓΟΥϹΤΟΥΙΕ
ΡΟΥΚΑΙΠΡΕϹΒΥΤΕ
ΡΟΥϹΩϹΕΠΙΛΗϹΤΗΝ

Woodbury

CODEX SINAITICUS—4TH CENT.

(Original size of page, 15 in. × 13½ in.; of part reproduced, 9 in. × 10¼ in.)

PLATE XVI.

69

ΤΗΤΕΓΥΝΑΙΚΙΕΛΕΓΟΝΟΤΙ
ΟΥΚΕΤΙΔΙΑΤΗΝΣΗΝΛΑΛΙΑΝ
ΠΙΣΤΕΥΟΜΕΝΑΥΤΟΙΓΑΡΑΚΗ
ΚΟΑΜΕΝΚΑΙΟΙΔΑΜΕΝΟΤΙ
ΟΥΤΟΣΕΣΤΙΝΑΛΗΘΩΣΟΣΩΤΗΡ
ΤΟΥΚΟΣΜΟΥΟΧΣ
ΜΕΤΑΔΕΤΑΣΔΥΟΗΜΕΡΑΣΕΞΗΛ
ΘΕΝΕΚΕΙΘΕΝΚΑΙΑΠΗΛΘΕΝ
ΕΙΣΤΗΝΓΑΛΙΛΑΙΑΝ ΑΥΤΟΣ
ΓΑΡΙΣΕΜΑΡΤΥΡΗΣΕΝΟΤΙΠΡΟ
ΦΗΤΗΣΕΝΤΗΙΔΙΑΠΑΤΡΙΔΙ
ΤΙΜΗΝΟΥΚΕΧΕΙ ΟΤΕΟΥΝ
ΗΛΘΕΝΕΙΣ[illegible]ΤΗΝΓΑΛΙΛΑΙΑΝ
ΕΔΕΞΑΝΤΟΑΥΤΟΝΟΙΓΑΛΙΛΑΙΟΙ
ΠΑΝΤΑΕΩΡΑΚΟΤΕΣΟΣΑ
ΕΠΟΙΗΣΕΝΕΝΙΕΡΟΣΟΛΥΜΟΙΣ
ΕΝΤΗΕΟΡΤΗΚΑΙΑΥΤΟΙΓΑΡ
ΗΛΘΟΝΕΙΣΤΗΝΕΟΡΤΗΝ
ΗΛΘΕΝΟΥΝΠΑΛΙΝΟΙΣΕΙΣΤΗΝ
ΚΑΝΑΤΗΣΓΑΛΙΛΑΙΑΣΟΠΟΥ
ΕΠΟΙΗΣΕΝΤΟΥΔΩΡΟΙΝΟΝ
ΚΑΙΗΝΤΙΣΒΑΣΙΛΙΚΟΣΟΥΟΥΙΟΣ
ΗΣΘΕΝΕΙΕΝΚΑΠΕΡΝΑΟΥΜ
ΟΥΤΟΣΑΚΟΥΣΑΣΟΤΙΙΣΗΚΕΙ
ΕΚΤΗΣΙΟΥΔΑΙΑΣΕΙΣΤΗΝΓΑ
ΛΙΛΑΙΑΝ·ΑΠΗΛΘΕΝΠΡΟΣΑΥ
ΤΟΝΚΑΙΗΡΩΤΑΑΥΤΟΝΙΝΑΚΑ
ΤΑΒΗΚΑΙΙΑΣΗΤΑΙΑΥΤΟΥΤΟΝ
ΥΙΟΝΗΜΕΛΛΕΝΓΑΡΑΠΟΘΝΗΣΚΕΙΝ
ΕΙΠΕΝΟΥΝΟΙΣΠΡΟΣΑΥΤΟΝ
ΕΑΝΜΗΣΗΜΕΙΑΚΑΙΤΕΡΑΤΑ
ΙΔΗΤΕΟΥΜΗΠΙΣΤΕΥΣΗΤΕ

ΣΕΝΑΥΤΟΣΚΑΙΗΟΙΚΙΑΑΥΤΟΥΟΛΗ
ΤΟΥΤΟΠΑΛΙΝΔΕΥΤΕΡΟΝ[illegible]
ΕΠΟΙΗΣΕΝΟΙΣΕΛΘΩΝΕΚΤΗΣ
ΙΟΥΔΑΙΑΣΕΙΣΤΗΝΓΑΛΙΛΑΙΑΝ
ΜΕΤΑΤΑΥΤΑΗΝΗΕΟΡΤΗΤΩΝΙΟΥ
ΔΑΙΩΝΚΑΙΑΝΕΒΗΟΙΣΕΙΣΙΕΡΟ
ΣΟΛΥΜΑΕΣΤΙΝΔΕΕΝΤΟΙΣΙΕΡΟ
ΣΟΛΥΜΟΙΣΕΝΤΗΠΡΟΒΑΤΙΚΗ
ΚΟΛΥΜΒΗΘΡΑΗΕΠΙΛΕΓΟΜΕ
ΝΗΕΒΡΑΙΣΤΙΒΗΘΕΣΔΑ ΠΕΝΤΕ
ΣΤΟΑΣΕΧΟΥΣΑΕΝΤΑΥΤΑΙΣΚΑΤ
ΕΚΕΙΤΟΠΛΗΘΟΣΠΟΛΥΤΩΝ
ΑΣΘΕΝΟΥΝΤΩΝΤΥΦΛΩΝΧΩΛΩΝΞΗΡΩΝ
ΕΚΔΕΧΟΜΕΝΩΝΤΗΝΤΟΥΥΔΑΤΟΣΚΙΝΗΣΙΝ [illegible]
ΚΑΤΑΚΑΙΡΟΝΕΛΟΥΕΤΟΕΝΤΗ
ΚΟΛΥΜΒΗΘΡΑΚΑΙΕΤΑΡΑΣΣΕ
ΤΟΥΔΩΡΟΟΥΝΠΡΩΤΟΣΕΜΒΑΣ
ΜΕΤΑΤΗΝΤΑΡΑΧΗΝΤΟΥΥΔΑΤΟΣ
ΥΓΙΗΣΕΓΕΙΝΕΤΟΟΙΩΔΗΠΟΤΟΥΝ
ΚΑΤΕΙΧΕΤΟΝΟΣΗΜΑΤΙ
ΗΝΔΕΤΙΣΑΝΟΣΕΚΕΙΤΡΙΑΚΟΝΤΑ
ΚΑΙΟΚΤΩΕΤΗΕΧΩΝΕΝΤΗΑΣΘΕ
ΝΙΑΤΟΥΤΟΝΙΔΩΝΟΙΣΚΑΤΑ
ΚΕΙΜΕΝΟΝΚΑΙΓΝΟΥΣΟΤΙΠΟ
ΛΥΝΗΔΗΧΡΟΝΟΝΕΧΕΙ ΛΕΓΕΙ
ΑΥΤΩΘΕΛΕΙΣΥΓΙΗΣ[illegible]
ΓΕΝΕΣΘΑΙ[illegible]
[illegible]ΑΥΤΩ[illegible]
ΟΑΣΘΕΝΩΝΚΕΑΝΟΝΟΥΚΕΧΩ
ΙΝΑΟΤΑΝΤΑΡΑΧΘΗΤΟΥΔΩΡ
ΒΑΛΗΜΕΕΙΣΤΗΝΚΟΛΥΜΒΗΘΡΑ
ΕΝΩΔΕΕΡΧΟΜΑΙΕΓΩΑΛΛΟΣ

CODEX ALEXANDRINUS—5TH CENT.

(Original size of page, 13 in. × 10 in.; of part reproduced, 6½ in. × 8 in.)

ΠΡΟΣΤΟΝΠΑΤΕΡΑΛΕΓΟΥ
ΣΙΝΟΙΜΑΘΗΤΑΙΑΥΤΟΥ
ΙΔΕΝΥΝΕΝΠΑΡΡΗΣΙΑΛΑ
ΛΕΙΣΚΑΙΠΑΡΟΙΜΙΑΝΟΥ
ΔΕΜΙΑΝΛΕΓΕΙΣΝΥΝΟΙ
ΔΑΜΕΝΟΤΙΟΙΔΑΣΠΑΝ
ΤΑΚΑΙΟΥΧΡΕΙΑΝΕΧΕΙΣ
ΙΝΑΤΙΣΣΕΕΡΩΤΑΕΝΤΟΥ
ΤΩΠΙΣΤΕΥΟΜΕΝΟΤΙ
ΑΠΟΘΥΕΞΗΛΘΕΣ ΑΠΕ
ΚΡΙΘΗΑΥΤΟΙΣΙΣΑΡΤΙΠΙ
ΣΤΕΥΕΤΕΙΔΟΥΕΡΧΕΤΑΙ
ΩΡΑΚΑΙΕΛΗΛΥΘΕΝΙΝΑ
ΣΚΟΡΠΙΣΘΗΤΕΕΚΑΣΤΟΣ
ΕΙΣΤΑΙΔΙΑΚΑΜΕΜΟΝΟΝ
ΑΦΗΤΕΚΑΙΟΥΚΕΙΜΙΜΟ
ΝΟΣΟΤΙΟΠΑΤΗΡΜΕΤΕ
ΜΟΥΕΣΤΙΝ ΤΑΥΤΑΛΕ
ΛΑΛΗΚΑΥΜΙΝΙΝΑΕΝΕ
ΜΟΙΕΙΡΗΝΗΝΕΧΗΤΕ
ΕΝΤΩΚΟΣΜΩΘΛΕΙΨΙΝ
ΕΧΕΤΕΑΛΛΑΘΑΡΣΕΙΤΕ
ΕΓΩΝΕΝΙΚΗΚΑΤΟΝΚΟ
ΣΜΟΝ ΤΑΥΤΑΕΛΑΛΗ 47.
ΣΕΝΙΣΚΑΙΕΠΑΡΑΣΤΟΥΣ
ΟΦΘΑΛΜΟΥΣΑΥΤΟΥΕΙΣ
ΤΟΝΟΥΡΑΝΟΝΕΙΠΕΝΠΑ
ΤΕΡΕΛΗΛΥΘΕΝΗΩΡΑΔΟ
ΞΑΣΟΝΣΟΥΤΟΝΥΙΟΝ
ΙΝΑΟΥΙΟΣΔΟΞΑΣΗΣΕΚΑ
ΘΩΣΕΔΩΚΑΣΑΥΤΩΕΞΟΥ
ΣΙΑΝΠΑΣΗΣΣΑΡΚΟΣΙΝΑ
ΠΑΝΟΔΕΔΩΚΑΣΑΥΤΩ
ΔΩΣΕΙΑΥΤΟΙΣΖΩΗΝΑΙ
ΩΝΙΟΝΑΥΤΗΔΕΕΣΤΙΝ
ΗΑΙΩΝΙΟΣΖΩΗΙΝΑΓΙ

ΠΟΙΗΣΩΚΑΙΝΥΝΔΟΞΑ
ΣΟΝΜΕΣΥΠΑΤΕΡΠΑΡΑ
ΣΕΑΥΤΩΤΗΔΟΞΗΗΕΙ
ΧΟΝΠΡΟΤΟΥΤΟΝΚΟΣΜΟΝ
ΕΙΝΑΙΠΑΡΑΣΟΙΕΦΑΝΕ
ΡΩΣΑΣΟΥΤΟΟΝΟΜΑΤΟΙΣ
ΑΝΘΡΩΠΟΙΣΟΥΣΕΔΩ
ΚΑΣΜΟΙΕΚΤΟΥΚΟΣΜΟΥ
ΣΟΙΗΣΑΝΚΑΜΟΙΑΥΤΟΥΣ
ΕΔΩΚΑΣΚΑΙΤΟΝΛΟΓΟΝ
ΣΟΥΤΕΤΗΡΗΚΑΝΝΥΝ
ΕΓΝΩΚΑΝΟΤΙΠΑΝΤΑ
ΟΣΑΔΕΔΩΚΕΣΜΟΙΠΑΡΑ
ΣΟΥΕΙΣΙΝΟΤΙΤΑΡΗΜΑ
ΤΑΑΕΔΩΚΕΣΜΟΙΔΕΔΩ
ΚΑΑΥΤΟΙΣΚΑΙΑΥΤΟΙΕ
ΛΑΒΟΝΚΑΙΕΓΝΩΣΑΝΑ
ΛΗΘΩΣΟΤΙΠΑΡΑΣΟΥ
ΕΞΗΛΘΟΝΚΑΙΕΠΙΣΤΕΥ
ΣΑΝΟΤΙΣΥΜΕΑΠΕΣΤΕΙ
ΛΑΣΕΓΩΠΕΡΙΑΥΤΩΝ
ΕΡΩΤΩΟΥΠΕΡΙΤΟΥΚΟ
ΣΜΟΥΕΡΩΤΩΑΛΛΑΠΕΡΙ
ΩΝΔΕΔΩΚΑΣΜΟΙΟΤΙΣΟΙ
ΕΙΣΙΝΚΑΙΤΑΕΜΑΠΑΝΤΑ
ΣΑΕΣΤΙΝΚΑΙΤΑΣΑΕΜΑ
ΚΑΙΔΕΔΟΞΑΣΜΑΙΕΝΑΥ
ΤΟΙΣΚΑΙΟΥΚΕΤΙΕΙΜΙΕΝ
ΤΩΚΟΣΜΩΚΑΙΑΥΤΟΙΕΝ
ΤΩΚΟΣΜΩΕΙΣΙΝΚΑΓΩ
ΠΡΟΣΣΕΕΡΧΟΜΑΙΠΑΤΗΡ
ΑΓΙΕΤΗΡΗΣΟΝΑΥΤΟΥΣ
ΕΝΤΩΟΝΟΜΑΤΙΣΟΥΩ
ΔΕΔΩΚΑΣΜΟΙΙΝΑΩΣΙΝ
ΕΝΚΑΘΩΣΚΑΙΗΜΕΙΣΟ
ΤΕΗΜΗΝΜΕΤΑΥΤΩΝΕ

ΦΗ ΠΛΗΡΩΘΗΝΥΝΔΕΠΡΟΣ
ΣΕΕΡΧΟΜΑΙΚΑΙΤΑΥΤΑ
ΛΑΛΩΕΝΤΩΚΟΣΜΩΙΝΑ
ΕΧΩΣΙΤΗΝΧΑΡΑΝΤΗΝ
ΕΜΗΝΠΕΠΛΗΡΩΜΕΝΗΝ
ΕΝΕΑΥΤΟΙΣΕΓΩΔΕΔΩΚΑ
ΑΥΤΟΙΣΤΟΝΛΟΓΟΝΣΟΥ
ΚΑΙΟΚΟΣΜΟΣΕΜΙΣΗΣΕΝ
ΑΥΤΟΥΣΟΤΙΟΥΚΕΙΣΙΝ
ΕΚΤΟΥΚΟΣΜΟΥΚΑΘΩΣ
ΕΓΩΟΥΚΕΙΜΙΕΚΤΟΥΚΟ
ΣΜΟΥΟΥΚΕΡΩΤΩΙΝΑΑ
ΡΗΣΑΥΤΟΥΣΕΚΤΟΥΠΟ [margin: ΚΟΣΜΟΥ ΑΛΛ ΙΝΑ ΤΗΡΗΣΗΣ ΑΥΤΟΥΣ ΕΚ ΤΟΥ ΚΟΣΜΟΥ]
ΝΗΡΟΥΕΚΤΟΥΚΟΣΜΟΥ
ΟΥΚΕΙΣΙΝΚΑΘΩΣΕΓΩ
ΟΥΚΕΙΜΙΕΚΤΟΥΚΟΣΜΟΥ
ΑΓΙΑΣΟΝΑΥΤΟΥΣΕΝΑ
ΛΗΘΕΙΑΟΛΟΓΟΣΟΣΟΣΗ
ΑΛΗΘΕΙΑΕΣΤΙΝΚΑΘΩΣ
ΕΜΕΑΠΕΣΤΕΙΛΑΣΕΙΣΤΟ
ΚΟΣΜΟΝΚΑΓΩΑΠΕΣΤΕΙ
ΛΑΑΥΤΟΥΣΕΙΣΤΟΝΚΟ
ΣΜΟΝΚΑΓΩΑΠΕΣΤΕΙΛΑ
ΑΥΤΟΥΣΕΙΣΤΟΝΚΟΣΜΟΝ
ΚΑΙΥΠΕΡΑΥΤΩΝΕΓΩ
ΑΓΙΑΖΩΕΜΑΥΤΟΝΙΝΑ
ΩΣΙΝΚΑΙΑΥΤΟΙΗΓΙΑ
ΣΜΕΝΟΙΕΝΑΛΗΘΕΙΑΟΥ
ΠΕΡΙΤΟΥΤΩΝΔΕΕΡΩΤΩ
ΜΟΝΟΝΑΛΛΑΚΑΙΠΕΡΙΤΩΝ
ΠΙΣΤΕΥΟΝΤΩΝΔΙΑΤΟΥ
ΛΟΓΟΥΑΥΤΩΝΕΙΣΕΜΕ
ΙΝΑΠΑΝΤΕΣΕΝΩΣΙΝ
ΚΑΘΩΣΣΥΠΑΤΗΡΕΝΕ
ΜΟΙΚΑΓΩΕΝΣΟΙΙΝΑΚΑΙ
ΑΥΤΟΙΕΝΗΜΙΝΩΣΙΝ

CODEX VATICANUS—4TH CENT.

(Original size of page, 10½ in. × 10 in.; of part reproduced, 6 in. × 9½ in.)

Hebrews, 1 and 2 Corinthians, Ephesians, Galatians, Philippians, Colossians, 1 and 2 Thessalonians; and the only portions missing (apart from a line or two at the bottom of each page) are Rom. i. 1–v. 17, vi. 14–viii. 15, and 1 Thess. ii. 3–v. 4 and 2 Thess. By the courtesy of the authorities of the U iversity of Michigan, the entire text has now been printed in a single volume in the series of the *Chester Beatty Biblical Papyri*, and a complete photographic facsimile has also been published.

Here, then, we have a nearly complete manuscript of the Pauline Epistles, written apparently about the beginning of the third century—that is to say, more than a century before the Vaticanus and Sinaiticus. It emphatically confirms the general soundness of the text, while as between the Neutral and Western families it leans strongly to the former. There is a larger sprinkling of minor Western readings in Romans than elsewhere, but even there the Neutral preponderance is as nine to five, while in the other Epistles it varies between four to one and eight to one. One remarkable variant is the placing of the doxology in Romans (xvi. 25-27) at the end of chapter xv. Most of the minuscules place it at the end of xiv., most of the uncials have it at the end of xvi., while the Alexandrinus has it in both places. The position in *P*[46] would seem to confirm the views of those who regard chapter xvi. as not belonging to the Epistle at all, but as a letter of introduction for "our sister Phœbe" to a church (such as Ephesus) where Paul had many friends, which has accidentally become attached to the great letter to the Romans; but it would be dangerous to adopt this conjecture without confirmation, and it is possible that the variable position is due to its being treated like a doxology to a hymn, and being read at the end of xiv. or xv., when xvi., which is mainly a string of personal names, was omitted.

P[47]. Chester Beatty Papyrus III. Ten leaves out of the middle of a codex of Revelation, being either the central portion of a single-quire codex of thirty-two leaves or the middle quire of a three-quire codex. It contains Rev. ix. 10–xvii. 2, with the loss of from one to four lines at the top of each page. Written in rather a rough hand, probably of the third century. The manuscripts of Revelation fall into three groups: (1) the four uncials ℵ A C P, (2) a group headed by 046, (3) the great mass of minuscules. *P*[47] allies itself more with the first group than with either of the others; but these five MSS. show a good deal of divergence among themselves.

---

outside the ,est. He would then have had five blank leaves before the beginning of Romans. But it would be illegitimate to assume this. There are other papyrus codices which seem (from calculations) to have had blank leaves at the end.

P[48]. Società Italiana (PSI), Papyrus 1165. A fragment, apparently of the third century, containing Acts xxiii. 11-16, 24-29, important because its text, like that of *P*[38], is distinctly Western. Published by Vitelli (1932.)

P[52]. Rylands Papyrus 457. This scrap, measuring about 3½ by 2½ inches, was among some papyri acquired in 1920 by Dr. B. P. Grenfell for the John Rylands Library at Manchester, but remained unnoticed until Mr. C. H. Roberts identified it as the oldest existing manuscript of any part of the New Testament. It contains John xviii. 31-33, 37, 38 in a hand which can be confidently assigned to the first half of the second century. In the middle fifty years of the nineteenth century, if this scrap could have been produced and its date established, it would have created a profound sensation; for it would have convincingly refuted those who contended that the Fourth Gospel was not written until the second century was far advanced. Now we see that it was not only written, but had spread to a provincial town in Egypt, by the middle of the second century, which goes far towards confirming the traditional date of composition, in the last years of the first century. Published by Mr. Roberts in 1935. See Plate XIV.

2. *Uncials.*

We shall now proceed to describe the best of the vellum uncials in the order of their alphabetical precedence. In addition to their alphabetical designations, which are those commonly used, Gregory's official list provides a numeration in Arabic numerals with a **0** prefixed (*e.g.* **046**), so that additions can easily be made in the event of future discoveries. The total up to date is 212. Some of the more important we have met already in our catalogue of the manuscripts of the Septuagint.

א. *Codex Sinaiticus*; one of the latest found of all the flock, yet one of the most important, and therefore (since the letters of the Latin and Greek alphabets had been already appropriated for other manuscripts) designated by its discoverer by the first letter of the Hebrew alphabet, *Aleph*. The discovery of this manuscript, now nearly a century ago, was the supreme triumph of the great Biblical scholar Constantine Tischendorf. In the year 1844 he was travelling in the East in search of manuscripts, and in the course of his travels he visited the monastery of St. Catherine at Mount Sinai. While working in the library he noticed a basket containing a large number of stray pages of manuscripts, among which he was astounded to behold several leaves of the oldest Greek writing he had ever set eyes on, and, as a short inspection proved, containing parts of the Greek Bible. No less than forty-three such leaves did he extract, and the librarian casually observed that two basket loads of similar waste paper had already been consumed in the furnace of the monastery. It is therefore not surprising that he easily obtained permission to keep the leaves which he had picked up; but when he discovered that some eighty more leaves of the Old Testament from the same manuscript were also in existence, difficulties were made about letting him see them; and he had to content himself with informing the monks of their value, and entreating them to stoke their fires with something less precious. He then returned to Europe, and having presented his treasure to his sovereign, King Frederick Augustus of Saxony, published its contents under the name of the Codex Friderico-Augustanus. These forty-three leaves belonged, like all that Tischendorf had yet seen or heard of, to the Old Testament, containing portions of 1 Chronicles, 2 Esdras, Tobit, and Jeremiah, with Esther complete; they are now, as we have seen (p. 67), at Leipzig, separated from the rest of the volume to which they once belonged. In 1853 he returned to Sinai; but his former warning, and perhaps the interest aroused in Europe by the discovery, had made the monks cautious, and he could hear nothing more concerning the manuscript. In 1859 he visited the monastery once again, this time under the patronage of the Tsar Alexander II, the patron of the Greek Church; but still his inquiries were met with blank negation, until one evening, only a few days before he was to depart, in the course of conversation with the steward of the monastery, he showed him a copy of his recently published edition of the Septuagint. Thereupon the steward remarked that he too had a copy of the Septuagint, which he would like to show to his visitor. Accordingly he took him to his room, and produced a heap of loose leaves wrapped in a cloth; and there before the astonished scholar's eyes lay the identical manuscript for which he had been longing. Not only was part of the Old Testament there, but the New Testament, complete from beginning to end. Concealing his feelings, he asked to be allowed to keep it in his room that evening to examine it; leave was given, "and that night it seemed sacrilege to sleep." He tried to buy the manuscript, without success. Then he asked to be allowed to take it to Cairo to study; but since the monk in charge of the library objected, he had to leave it behind. The Superior of the monastery, however, was at Cairo; and he, at Tischendorf's request, sent for the manuscript, and placed it in his hands, a few sheets at a time, for copying. Then Tischendorf suggested that it would be a graceful act to present it to the Tsar of Russia, as the protector of the Greek Church; and since the monks desired the influence of the Tsar in connection with the election of a new Archbishop, they consented to this, and after dilatory negotiations Tischendorf was allowed to take the precious manuscript to Russia for presentation to the Tsar. In view of stories put about subsequently by later generations of monks at St. Catherine's, it should be emphasised that Tischendorf's behaviour was quite correct throughout. He acted all through in agreement with the monks, and when there was some delay in the arrival of the counter-gift which, in accordance with Oriental usage, was expected from the Tsar, he intervened and secured the transmission of a sum of 9000 roubles and some decorations. To the end of his life he remained on good terms with the Sinai community, as contemporary documents show.[1]

The romance of the Codex Sinaiticus was not yet over, however. Since the year 1856 an ingenious Greek, named Constantine Simonides, had been creating a considerable sensation by producing quantities of Greek manuscripts professing to be of fabulous antiquity—such as a Homer in an almost prehistoric style of writing, a lost Egyptian historian, a copy of St. Matthew's Gospel on papyrus, written fifteen years after the Ascension (!), and other portions of the New Testament dating from the first century. These productions enjoyed a short period of notoriety, and were then exposed as forgeries. Among the scholars concerned in the exposure was Tischendorf; and the revenge taken by Simonides was distinctly humorous. While stoutly maintaining the genuineness of his own wares, he admitted that he had written *one* manuscript which passed as being very ancient, and that was the Codex Sinaiticus, the discovery of which had been so triumphantly proclaimed by Tischendorf! The idea was ingenious, but it would not bear investigation. Apart from the internal evidence of the text itself, the variations in which no forger, however clever, could have invented, it was shown that Simonides could not have completed the task in the time which he professed to have taken, and that there was no such edition of the Greek Bible as that from which he professed to have copied it. This little cloud on the credit of the newly-discovered manuscript therefore rapidly passed away, and the manuscript reposed, still unbound and in the cloth which had wrapped it at Sinai, in what was presumed to be its final home. It had, however, one more transmigration to undergo. In 1933 it became known that the Soviet Government was not unwilling to sell it, having little use for Bibles and much for money. Indeed, negotiations had previously been opened with an American syndicate; but the financial crisis supervened, and America's difficulty gave England an unhoped-for opportunity. After prolonged negotiations a bargain was concluded by which it passed into the possession

[1] The full story may be found in a pamphlet issued by the Trustees of the British Museum in 1934 (*The Mount Sinai Manuscript of the Bible*).

of the Trustees of the British Museum for the sum of £100,000 (much less than the sum contemplated in the American negotiations), of which half was guaranteed by the British Government. Accordingly, just before Christmas, 1933, the great Bible entered the British Museum, amid scenes of much popular excitement. There were, of course, those who criticised the purchase. Some used the argument of Judas Iscariot in John xii. 5, but found that its parentage made it unpopular; some revived the legends of Tischendorf's misconduct and the claim of Simonides, but these also had little success. Others, more plausibly, argued that since an excellent photographic facsimile had been published by the Oxford University Press (New Testament, 1911; Old Testament, 1922) from photographs taken by Professor Kirsopp Lake, the original was of no further importance; but even this (which never commended itself to those who had experience of MSS. and photographs) has been disproved by a study of the scribes and correctors of the MS. by Messrs. H. J. M. Milne and T. C. Skeat of the British Museum (published 1938), which never could have been carried through without access to the MS. itself. The manuscript has now been beautifully and securely bound by Mr. Douglas Cockerell, and one may hope that it has now reached its final resting-place.

Plate XV gives a general idea of the appearance of the manuscript. The original size of the page is 15 inches by 13½ inches. There are four narrow columns to each page (except in the poetical books, where there are only two), and the eight columns thus presented to the reader when the volume is opened have much of the appearance of the succession of columns in a papyrus roll; it is not at all impossible that it was actually copied from such rolls. The vellum is made from fine skins, and is of excellent quality; the writing is large, clear, and good, without any attempt at ornamentation. The MS. originally contained the whole Greek Bible, but, as has been stated above (p. 129), only a part of the Old Testament escaped the waste-paper basket of the Sinai monastery. The New Testament is complete, and at the end are added two apocryphal works, which for a long time enjoyed almost equal credit with the New Testament books, but finally failed to obtain a position in the Canon—namely, the Epistle of Barnabas and the "Shepherd" of Hermas. The original text has been corrected in many places, the various correctors being indicated in critical editions as $\aleph^a$, $\aleph^b$, $\aleph^c$, etc. The date of the manuscript is in the fourth century, probably about the middle of it. It can hardly be much earlier than A.D. 340, since the divisions of the text known as the Eusebian sections are indicated in the margin of the Gospels, in a hand evidently contemporaneous with the text; and these sections, which are a device for forming a sort of Harmony of the Gospels, by showing which sections in each Gospel have parallel sections in any of the others, were due to the scholar Eusebius, who died about A.D. 340. On the other hand, comparison with other hands of the fourth century, of which more are now available than was formerly the case, seems to show that it cannot be appreciably later than the middle of the century. The oldest correctors, ℵ[a] and ℵ[b], are not much later than the manuscript itself, even if they are not, as Messrs. Milne and Skeat think, the original scribes themselves. ℵ[c], a very active group of correctors, is of the seventh century; the others, later and of small importance.

A study of the facsimile page will show something of the way in which manuscripts were written and corrected, besides providing a specimen of the readings of ℵ in an important passage. The page contains Luke xxii. 20-52, though it has been necessary to omit eight lines from the top of each column in the plate. In verse 22 (the first line of the plate), ℵ has "for" (ὅτι) in place of the received text "and"; and, as the note in the Variorum Bible shows, ℵ is supported by B, D, and L among the principal MSS., while A heads the mass of later uncials and cursives which contain the "received" reading. Of the editors, Tischendorf, Tregelles, McClellan, Westcott and Hort, and the Revised Version follow ℵ, while Lachmann and Weiss are on the other side. In line 2 the scribe has accidentally omitted the little word μεν, and has added it above the line. At line 14, which begins verse 24, will be seen an example of the usual procedure of ℵ in marking the beginning of a fresh paragraph by allowing the first letter to project into the margin, but without any enlargement. In line 15 the original scribe had written εις εαυτους, which is found in no other MS., but it has been corrected to the usual εν αυτοις: there is practically no difference in sense. In lines 22, 23 (verse 25) there is a more extensive alteration. The scribe began by writing και οι αρχοντες των εξουσιαζουςιν αυτων και ευεργεται καλουνται (="and their rulers exercise authority over them and are called benefactors"), which makes nonsense; accordingly he (or a corrector) has cancelled the erroneous letters αρχοντες των by putting dots above them (a common method in Greek MSS.), has altered the verb into a participle by writing the letters ντες over the erroneous υσιν, and has cancelled και ("and") by dots above each letter, thus restoring the text to its proper form. In verse 31 (column 2, line 7) there is a disputed reading, some authorities having the words "And the Lord said," as in our Authorised Version, while others omit them. The evidence is evenly balanced. Not only A and the mass of later MSS., but also ℵ, as our plate shows, and D give the disputed words (ειπεν δε ο κυριος), while B and L, with the two chief Coptic versions, omit them. Lachmann, Tregelles, and McClellan retain the words (see the Variorum note); Alford, Tischendorf, and Westcott and Hort reject them; and the Revisers have followed the latter, though the division of the best evidence must have made a decision difficult, ℵ and D being a fair set-off against B and L, even if the "Syrian" MSS. be disregarded.

Small alterations in the MS. must be passed over briefly; they will be seen in column 2, line 37; column 3, lines 5, 6; column 4, line 36. The reader may also note the common practice of writing the last letters of a line very small, so as to get more into a line. But in verses 43, 44, a very important textual question arises. These verses contain the mention of the Bloody Sweat, and of the Angel who appeared to strengthen our Lord in His agony—an incident, it is hardly necessary to say, of the deepest interest and value. Now these verses are omitted by the two great manuscripts A and B (so seldom found on the same side that their agreement is the more striking), and also by R and T, the valuable cursives 13 and 69, some MSS. of the Bohairic and Sahidic versions, and by some of the Fathers. Against these there were, before the discovery of ℵ, to be set only D and L among the better uncials, the Old Latin and Vulgate, the Peshitta Syriac, other MSS. of the Coptic versions, many Fathers, and the mass of later MSS. The better authorities might fairly be said to be against the genuineness of the verses; but the balance might be held to be redressed by the two modern discoveries, ℵ and the Curetonian Syriac.[1] They will be seen in the last ten lines of column 3 on our plate. The reader who looks closely at it, however, will see that a faint row of dots has been placed above the first line of the passage, and equally faint hooks or commas at the beginning and end of each of these lines. This shows that some corrector did not find the verses in the copy with which he was comparing the MS. and accordingly marked them as doubtful. Tischendorf believed the marks to be due to the first corrector of the MS., who certainly used a good and ancient copy, and accordingly in the Variorum note we find ℵ[a] enumerated among the authorities against the verses; but it is obviously difficult to be sure to what hand such simple marks are to be attributed. Careful scrutiny of the original, since its arrival in the British Museum, has shown (what no photograph could reveal) that an attempt has been made to erase the dots; so the conflict of evidence is made more plain. It is clear that the verses were absent from some very early copies; but it is also clear that some equally early ones contained them; and the

[1] A still later discovery, however, the Sinaitic MS. of the Old Syriac, omits them.

majority of editors have shown a wise discretion in preferring the evidence in favour of their authenticity.

Our analysis of this single page of the Codex Sinaiticus will have shown the reader something of the task of the textual critic, and something of the variations which he meets in every MS.—some of them being mere slips of the pen on the part of the scribe, while others testify to a real peculiarity of reading in the MS. from which this was copied. It remains to say something as to the general character of this ancient authority, and of the rank which critics assign it among the array of witnesses to the text of the New Testament.

Besides being one of the most ancient, the Codex Sinaiticus is also one of the most valuable texts of the New Testament. In many passages it is found in company with B, preserving obviously superior readings where the great mass of later manuscripts is in error. According to the analysis of Westcott and Hort, its text is almost entirely pre-Syrian; but it is not equally free from Western and Alexandrian elements. Especially in the Gospels, readings from these two sources are not unfrequent, Western readings being most prominent in St. John and in parts of St. Luke. One most noticeable case in which this manuscript is found in agreement with B is in the omission of the last twelve verses of St. Mark, in which א and B stand alone against all the other extant manuscripts (with the partial exception of L), though with some important support from three versions and some of the Fathers. Agreements between א and B are so frequent that it is evident that they belong to the same family of text; Westcott and Hort regard them as the two main representatives of the Neutral text; and whether the text be called Neutral, or Hesychian (as by von Soden), or Egyptian, or Alexandrian (as perhaps seems preferable now that it is clear that it was by no means the only text in Egypt), it is certain that it is one of the most important groups of witnesses to the New Testament text. As to their place of origin, much difference of opinion has prevailed. Dr. Hort was "inclined to surmise," from certain very slight indications of orthography, that they were written in the West, probably at Rome; and that the ancestors of B were also written in the West, while those of א were written in Alexandria. On the other hand, forms of letters are occasionally found in B which are certainly Egyptian, though it is impossible to be certain that they are exclusively so; and the writing of א bears a quite discernible resemblance to a hand which is found (at a considerably earlier date) in papyri from Egypt. Another eminent scholar, Professor Rendel Harris, suggested that both manuscripts came from the library of Pamphilus at Cæsarea, of which Eusebius made use, and it is almost certain that א was there when the corrector א^{c}

worked on it; but this would not necessarily be inconsistent with their having been written in Egypt. On the whole, however, this is one of the cases where the only fair course is to admit ignorance, and to hope that future discoveries may in time bring fuller knowledge.

A. *Codex Alexandrinus*.—This has been one of the chief treasures of the British Museum since its foundation, and a volume of it may be seen, side by side with the Sinaiticus, by every visitor in one of the showcases in the Department of Manuscripts. Its history, at least in later years, is much less obscure than that of the Sinaiticus. In 1624 it was offered by Cyril Lucar, Patriarch of Constantinople, to Sir Thomas Roe, our ambassador in Turkey, for presentation to King James I. King James died before the manuscript started for England, and the offer was transferred to Charles I. In 1627 the gift was actually accomplished, and the MS. remained in the possession of our sovereigns until the Royal Library was presented to the nation by George II, when it entered its present home. Its earlier history is also partially traceable. Cyril Lucar (according to contemporary statements) brought it to Constantinople from Alexandria, of which see he had previously been Patriarch; and an Arabic note at the beginning of the MS., signed by "Athanasius the humble" (possibly Athanasius III, Patriarch of Alexandria, who died about 1308), states that it was a gift to the Patriarchal cell in that town. A later Latin note adds that the gift was made in A.D. 1098, but the authority for this statement is unknown. Another Arabic note, written in the thirteenth or fourteenth century, states that the MS. was written by Thecla the martyr; and Cyril Lucar himself repeats this statement, with the additions that Thecla was a noble lady of Egypt, that she wrote it shortly after the Council of Nicæa (A.D. 325), and that her name was originally written at the end of the manuscript. This, however, was only tradition, since the end of the MS. had been lost long before Cyril's time. The authority for the tradition is quite unknown, and so early a date is hardly possible. The occurrence in the manuscript of treatises (see p. 67) by Eusebius (d. A.D. 340) and Athanasius (d. A.D. 373) makes it almost certain that it cannot be earlier than the middle of the fourth century, and competent authorities agree that the style of writing probably shows it to be somewhat later, in the first half of the fifth century. It is certain that the writing of this MS. appears to be somewhat more advanced than that of the Vaticanus or Sinaiticus, especially in the enlargement of initial letters and similar elementary ornamentation; but it must be remembered that these characteristics are already found in earlier MSS., and that similar differences between contemporary MSS. may be found at all periods. The dating of early Greek uncials on vellum is still very doubtful for want of materials to judge from, and it is possible that the tradition mentioned above is truer than is generally supposed; but for the present it is safer to acquiesce in the general judgment which assigns the manuscript to the fifth century.

Like the Codex Sinaiticus, it contained originally the whole Greek Bible, with the addition of the two Epistles of Clement of Rome, which in very early days ranked almost with the inspired books; and, in addition, the table of contents shows that it originally included the Psalms of Solomon, the title of which, however, is so separated from the rest of the books as to indicate that they were regarded as standing on a different footing.

The Old Testament has suffered some slight mutilations, which have been described already; the New Testament more seriously, since the whole of St. Matthew's Gospel, as far as chapter xxv. 6, is lost, together with leaves containing John vi. 50–viii. 52 (where, however, the number of pages missing shows that the doubtful passage, vii. 53–viii. 11, cannot have been present when the MS. was perfect), and 2 Cor. iv. 13–xii. 6, one leaf of the first Epistle of Clement and the greater part of the second. The leaves measure 12¾ by 10¼ inches, having two columns to each page, written in large and well-formed hands of round shape, apparently by two scribes in the Old Testament and three in the New,[1] with initial letters enlarged and projecting into the margin. The text has been corrected throughout by several different hands, the first being nearly or quite contemporary with the original scribe. The facsimile given in Plate XVI shows the upper part of the page containing John iv. 42–v. 14. In column 1, line 6, it will be seen that this MS. contains the words "the Christ"; and a reference to the Variorum Bible footnote shows that it is supported by C^3 (*i.e.*, the third corrector of C), D, L (with the later MSS.), while ℵ, B, C (with the Old Latin, Vulgate, Bohairic, and Curetonian Syriac versions) omit the words, and are followed by all the editors except McClellan. Though D and L represent pre-Syrian testimony, the balance of that testimony, as contained in ℵ, B, and the versions, overweighs them.

More important readings will be seen in the second column, which contains the story of the cure of the impotent man at the pool of Bethesda. It will be seen (lines 13, 14) that an alteration has been made in the MS., and that certain letters have been rewritten over an erasure, while others are added in the margin. The words which are thus due to the corrector, and not to the

[1] Messrs. Milne and Skeat, in an appendix to their study of the Sinaiticus, identify the scribes of the New Testament with the first scribe of the Old Testament, chiefly on the ground of the forms of the flourishes at the ends of the several books; but this seems to ignore certain marked differences of script.

original scribe, are those which are translated "halt, withered, *waiting for the moving of the water.* For an angel of the Lord." A close examination shows that the first and last parts of the passage originally occupied line 14, before the erasure; but the words in italics are an addition which was not in the original text. They are also omitted (see the Variorum Bible footnote) by ℵ, B, C, L, with the Curetonian Syriac and the Sahidic versions. They are found only in D, the corrections of A and C, and later MSS., and are thus inevitably omitted by nearly all the editors. With regard to verse 4 the distribution of evidence is different. It is omitted, like the former words, by ℵ, B, C, the Curetonian Syriac, most MSS. of the Bohairic and the Sahidic versions; and these are now joined by D, which in the previous case was on the other side. On the other hand, A and L have changed in the contrary direction, and are found to support the verse, in company with C^3, the later uncials, and all cursives but three, the Old Latin and Vulgate, and the Peshitto Syriac. Thus the versions are fairly equally divided; but ℵ, B, C, D form a very strong group of early authority, as against A and the mass of later MSS. L and the Old Latin are, in fact, the only witnesses to the verse which can be considered as pre-Syrian, and consequently we find the Revised Version omits the verse, in common with Tischendorf, Tregelles, and Westcott and Hort; Lachmann and McClellan alone appearing on the other side.

Specimens of scribes' errors and their corrections may be seen in lines 1, 2, 26-28. In the former the words first written have been erased, and the correct reading written above them; in the latter, some words had been written twice over by mistake (λεγει αυτω θελεις υγιης γενεσθαι λεγει αυτω θελεις υγιης γενεσθαι απεκριθη αυτω). The whole passage (from the first γενεσθαι) has been erased, and then correctly rewritten, with a slight variation (λεγει for απεκριθη); but as the correct reading was much shorter than that originally written, a considerable space is left blank, as the facsimile shows.

As regards the quality of the text preserved in the Codex Alexandrinus, it must be admitted that it does not stand quite so high as its two predecessors in age, ℵ and B. Different parts of the New Testament have evidently been copied from different originals; but in the Gospels, at any rate, A is the oldest and most pre-eminent example of that revised "Syrian" text which (to judge from the quotations in the Fathers) had become the predominant text as early as the fourth century. It will often be found at the head of the great mass of later uncials and cursives which support the received text; and although it is much superior to the late cursives from which the "received text" was in fact derived, it yet belongs to the same class, and will be found oftener in agreement with the Authorised Version than with the Revised. In the Acts and Epistles it ranks definitely with B and ℵ, and is perhaps an even better example of that class than they. In the Apocalypse also it belongs to the Neutral type, and is probably the best extant MS. of that book, with the possible exception of P^{47}. The Epistles of Clement, which are very valuable for the history of the early Church, the first having been written about the end of the first century and the other before the middle of the second, were until quite recently not known to exist in any other manuscript. The Eusebian sections and canons, referred to above (p. 132), are indicated in the margins of the Gospels, which also exhibit the earliest example of a division into chapters. A similar division of the Acts and Epistles, ascribed to Euthalius of Alexandria, who wrote about A.D. 458, is not found in this manuscript; and this is an additional reason for believing it not to have been written later than the middle of the fifth century.

The Codex Alexandrinus was the first of the greater manuscripts to be made accessible to scholars. The Epistles of Clement were published from it by Patrick Young in 1633, a collation of the New Testament and notes on the Pentateuch were published in Walton's Polyglot (1657), the Old Testament was printed by Grabe in 1707-20, and the New Testament by Woide in 1786. In 1816-28 the Rev. H. H. Baber published the Old Testament in type resembling as closely as possible the writing of the original. Finally a photographic reproduction of the whole MS. was published in 1879-83, under the editorship of E. Maunde Thompson, then Principal Librarian of the British Museum. A reduced facsimile of the New Testament, and of the Old Testament as far as Judith, has since appeared (1909-36).

B. *Codex Vaticanus*, the most valuable of all the manuscripts of the Greek Bible. As its name shows, it is in the great Vatican Library at Rome, which has been its home since some date before 1481. There is, therefore, no story to tell of the discovery of this MS.; the interest which attaches to its history is of a different kind, and relates to the long struggle that was necessary before its contents were made accessible to scholars. For some reason which does not clearly appear, the authorities of the Vatican Library put continual obstacles in the way of all who wished to study it in detail. A correspondent of Erasmus in 1533 sent that scholar a number of selected readings from it, as proof of its superiority to the received Greek text. In 1669 a collation (or statement of its various readings) was made by Bartolocci, but it was never published, and remained unknown until 1819. Other imperfect collations were made about 1720 and 1780. Napoleon carried the manuscript off as a prize of victory to Paris, where it remained till 1815, when the many treasures of which he had despoiled the libraries of the Continent were returned to their respective owners. While at Paris it was studied by Hug, and its great age and supreme importance were first fully made known; but after its return to Rome a period of seclusion set in. In 1843 Tischendorf, after waiting for several months, was allowed to see it for six hours. Next year De Muralt was permitted to study it for nine hours. In 1845 the great English scholar Tregelles was allowed indeed to see it but not to copy a word. His pockets were searched before he might open it, and all writing materials were taken away. Two clerics stood beside him and snatched away the volume if he looked too long at any passage! However, the Roman authorities now took the task in hand themselves, and in 1857 and 1859 editions by Cardinal Mai were published, which, however, differed so much from one another and were both so inaccurate as to be almost useless. In 1866 Tischendorf once more applied for permission to edit the MS., but with difficulty obtained leave to examine it for the purpose of collating difficult passages. Unfortunately the great scholar so far forgot himself as to copy out twenty pages in full, contrary to the conditions under which he had been allowed access to the MS., and his permission was naturally withdrawn. Renewed entreaty procured him six days' longer study, making in all fourteen days of three hours each; and by making the very most of his time Tischendorf was able in 1867 to publish the most perfect edition of the manuscript which had yet appeared. An improved Roman edition appeared in 1868-81; but the final and decisive publication was reserved for the years 1889-90, when a complete photographic facsimile of the whole MS. made its contents once and for all the common property of all scholars.

The Codex Vaticanus originally contained the entire Greek Bible, but it has suffered not a little from the ravages of time. The beginning has been lost, as far as Gen. xlvi. 28; in the middle Psalms cvi.-cxxxviii. have dropped out; at the end, the latter part of Hebrews (from chapter ix. 14), the Pastoral Epistles, and the whole of the Apocalypse have disappeared.[1] It is written on 759 leaves (out of an original total of about 820) of very fine vellum, each leaf measuring 10½ by 10 inches, with three columns to the page. The writing (see Plate XVII) is in small and delicate

[1] The Codex Vaticanus being deficient in the Apocalypse, the letter B is in the case of that book transferred to another MS., also in the Vatican, but much later in date, being of the eighth century. It is of some importance, as uncial MSS. of the Apocalypse are scarce; but it must be remembered that its authority is by no means equal to that of the great manuscript to which the letter B is elsewhere appropriated. It is better to refer to it by its alternative description as **046**.

uncials, perfectly simple and unadorned. There are no enlarged initials, no stops or accents, no divisions into chapters or sections such as are found in later MSS., but a different system of division peculiar to this manuscript. Unfortunately, the beauty of the original writing has been spoilt by a later corrector, who, thinking perhaps that the original ink was becoming faint, traced over every letter afresh, omitting only those letters and words which he believed to be incorrect. Thus it is only in the case of such words that we see the original writing untouched and uninjured. An example may be seen in the thirteenth and fourteenth lines from the bottom of the third column in our plate, where the corrector has not retouched the words καγω απεστειλα αυτους εις τον κοσμον, which have been written twice over by mistake. One scribe wrote the whole of the New Testament, but there is no sufficient ground for Tischendorf's assertion that he is identical with one of the scribes of the Sinaiticus, though there are certain resemblances which suggest that both may have come from the same scriptorium. There are corrections by various hands, one of them (indicated as B^2) being ancient and valuable. With regard to the date of the manuscript, critics are agreed in assigning it to the fourth century, about contemporary with א, though the more complete absence of ornamentation from B has generally caused it to be regarded as slightly the older.

Over the character of the text contained in B a most embittered controversy has raged. It will have been noticed that it is only within quite recent years that א and B have emerged from their obscurity and have become generally known; and it so happens that these two most ancient manuscripts differ markedly from the class of text represented by A, which up to the time of their appearance was held to be the oldest and best authority in existence. Hence there was a natural reluctance to abandon the ancient readings at the bidding of these two newcomers, imposing though their appearance might be; and this was especially the case after the publication of Dr. Hort's theory, which assigned to these two manuscripts, and especially to B, a pre-eminence which is almost overwhelming. Dean Burgon tilted desperately against the text of Westcott and Hort, and even went so far as to argue that these two documents owed their preservation, not to the goodness of their text, but to its depravity, having been, so to speak, pilloried as examples of what a copy of the Scriptures ought not to be! In spite of the learning with which the Dean maintained his arguments, and of the support which equally eminent but more moderate scholars such as Dr. Scrivener gave to his conclusions, they have failed to hold their ground. Scholars in general believe B to be the chief evidence for the most ancient form of the New Testament text, and it is clear that the Revisers of our English Bible attached the greatest weight to its authority. Even where it stands alone, or almost alone, its evidence must be treated with respect; and such readings not unfrequently find a place in the margin of the Revised Version. One notable instance, the omission of the last twelve verses of St. Mark, has been mentioned in speaking of the Codex Sinaiticus; others will be found recorded in the notes to the Variorum Bible or in any critical edition of the Greek New Testament.

The page exhibited in our facsimile contains John xvi. 27–xvii. 21. Six lines have been omitted from the top of the plate. It was chosen especially as showing a good example of the untouched writing of the MS., as described above; but it also contains several interesting readings. In xvi. 27 it has "the Father" instead of "God"; and the note in the Variorum Bible informs us that B is here supported by the original text of C and by D and L. On the other hand, it is opposed by the original text of א (both א and C have been altered by later correctors) and by A and Δ. Most of the later MSS. follow the latter group; the versions and Fathers are divided. The evidence is thus very evenly divided, and so, consequently, are the editors; Tischendorf, McClellan, and Weiss retaining the "received" reading, "God," while Lachmann, Tregelles, and Westcott and Hort follow B. The Revisers have done the same, being probably influenced by the fact that the evidence in support of the word "Father" comes from more than one group of authorities, B and L being Neutral, D Western, and C mixed, while the Coptic versions, which also support it, are predominantly Neutral. This is a good instance of an evenly balanced choice of readings. In xvi. 33 the received reading "shall have" is supported only by D and the Latin versions, while א, A, B, C, and nearly all the other uncials and versions read "have"; so that practically all editors adopt the latter reading. In xvii. 11 another instance occurs of an overwhelming majority in favour of a change, the received reading being supported only by a correction in D and by the Vulgate, while א, A, B, C, L, and all editors read "keep them in thy name which thou hast given me." In the next verse, א, B, C, D, L (all the best MSS. except A, and most of the versions) omit the words "in the world," which are found in A and the mass of cursives. Of the editors, only McClellan, preferring what he regards as internal probability to external evidence, retains the "received" reading. In the words which follow, a more complicated difference of opinion exists, for which reference may be made to the Variorum Bible note. One reading is supported by A and D; another by $א^{c}$ (the third corrector of א) and the two Coptic versions; a third by B, C, and L. Of the editors, Lachmann adopts the first reading, McClellan the second, and the others, including the Revisers, the third. None of the variations here mentioned as occurring on this page of B is of first-rate importance, but they furnish a fair example of the sort of problems with which the textual critic has to deal and of the conflicting evidence of MSS. and the divergent opinions of editors. Finally, in verse 15 (column 3, lines 13, 14 in the plate) there is a good example of a class of error to which, as mentioned above (p. 19), scribes were especially liable. The words to be copied were "I pray not that thou shouldest take them out of the world, but that thou shouldest keep them out of the evil"; but when the scribe had written the first "out of the," his eye wandered on to the second occurrence of these words, and he proceeded to write "evil" instead of "world," thus omitting several words, and producing nonsense. The correction of the blunder has involved the cancelling of some words in line 14 and the writing of others in the margin. Sometimes the omission of words in this way does not produce obvious nonsense, and then the error may escape notice and be perpetuated by being copied into other manuscripts.

C. *Codex Ephraemi*, now in the National Library of Paris, having been brought from the East to Italy early in the sixteenth century, and taken from Italy to Paris by Queen Catherine de' Medici. This manuscript is a prominent instance of a fate which befell many ancient books in the Middle Ages, before the introduction of paper into Europe. When vellum became scarce, a scribe who was unable to procure a sufficiency of it was apt to take some manuscript to which he attached little value, wash or scrape off the ink as well as he could, and then write his book on the vellum thus partially cleaned. Manuscripts so treated are called *palimpsests*, from a Greek word implying the removal of the original writing. The Codex Ephraemi is a palimpsest, and derives its name from the fact that the later writing inscribed upon its vellum (probably in the twelfth century) consists of the works of St. Ephraem of Syria. Naturally to us the earlier writing in such a case is almost always the more valuable, as it certainly is in this case; but it requires much labour and ingenuity, and often the application of chemicals (to which ultra-red or ultra-violet photography may now be added), in order to discern the faded traces of the original ink. Attention was first called to the Biblical text underlying the works of St. Ephraem at the end of the seventeenth century. In 1716 a collation of the New Testament was made, at the instance of the great English scholar Richard Bentley; but the first complete edition of it was due to the zeal and industry of Tischendorf, who published all that was decipherable, both of the Old and of the New Testament, in 1843-5.

The original manuscript contained the whole Greek Bible, but only scattered leaves of it were used by the scribe of St. Ephraem's works, and the rest was probably destroyed. Only sixty-four leaves are left of the Old Testament; of the New Testament there are 145 (out of 238), containing portions of every book except 2 Thessalonians and 2 John. It is written in a medium-sized uncial hand, in pages measuring 12½ by 9½ inches, and with only one column to the page. The Eusebian sections and the division into chapters appear in the Gospels, but there are no traces of divisions in the other books. The writing is generally agreed to be of the fifth century, perhaps a little later than the Codex Alexandrinus; and two correctors have left their mark upon the text, the first in the sixth century, and the other in the ninth. Of course it will be understood, in reference to other manuscripts as well as this, that the readings of an early corrector may be as valuable as those of the manuscript itself, since they must have been taken from other copies, perhaps no less old, then in existence.

The great age of C makes it extremely valuable for the textual criticism of the New Testament; but it is less important than those which we have hitherto described, owing to the fact that it represents no one family of text, but is rather compounded from them all. Its scribe, or the scribe of one of its immediate ancestors, must have had before him manuscripts representing all the different families which have been described above. Sometimes it agrees with the Neutral group of manuscripts, sometimes with the Western, not unfrequently with the Alexandrian, and perhaps oftenest with the Syrian. The page exhibited in Plate XVIII contains Matt. xx. 16-34 (eight lines being omitted from the bottom of the page), and a reference to the notes in the Variorum Bible will show that its readings here are of some interest. In verse 16 it is the chief authority for the words, "for many be called but few chosen"; in this case it is supported by D, but opposed by ℵ and B, which omit the sentence (A is defective here). Similarly in verses 22 and 23 the words, "and to be baptized with the baptism that I am baptized with," are found in C, E, and a multitude of later uncials and cursives, but are omitted by ℵ, B, D, L, Z, and most of the versions. In all these cases the Revised Version sides with ℵ and B against C, and there can be little doubt that the Revisers are right, and that these readings of C are due to the habit (very common in the Syrian type of text) of introducing into the narrative of one Evangelist words and clauses which occur in the description of the same or similar events in the others.

D. *Codex Bezæ*; in the University Library at Cambridge. This is undoubtedly the most curious, though certainly not the most trustworthy, manuscript of the New Testament at present known to us. Its place of origin is doubtful. Egypt, Rome, southern Italy, Sicily, Sardinia, northern Africa have all been advocated, the last having perhaps a slight balance of probability. It was at Lyons in the year 1562, when Theodore Beza, the disciple of Calvin and editor of the New Testament (see p. 104), procured it, probably after the sack of the city by the Huguenots in that year; and by Beza, from whom it derives its name, it was presented in 1581 to the University of Cambridge. It is remarkable as the first example of a copy of the Bible in two languages, for it contains both Greek and Latin texts. It is also remarkable, as will be shown directly, on account of the many curious additions to and variations from the common text which it contains; and no manuscript has been the subject of so many speculations or the basis of so many conflicting theories. It was partially used by Stephanus in his edition of 1550 and by Beza in his various editions. After its acquisition by Cambridge it was collated, more or less imperfectly, by various scholars in the seventeenth and eighteenth centuries, and published in full by Kipling in 1793. A new edition, with full annotations, was issued by Dr. Scrivener in 1864; and since that date two other Cambridge scholars, Professor Rendel Harris and Mr. Chase, have made careful studies of its text from rather different points of view. A complete photographic facsimile was published in 1889.

In size the Codex Bezæ is smaller than the manuscripts hitherto described, its pages measuring 10 by 8 inches. The Greek and Latin texts face one another on opposite pages, the Greek being on the left hand, the Latin on the right. Each page contains a single column, not written continuously, as in the MSS. hitherto described, but in lines of varying length, the object (imperfectly attained, it is true) being to make the pauses of sense come at the end of a line. It is written in uncials of rather large size, the Latin and Greek characters being made curiously alike, so that both pages have a similar general appearance at first sight. The writing is of unusual form, which suggests that it was not written in one of the principal centres of production, such as Alexandria or Rome, and which also caused it formerly to be assigned to a rather later date than now seems probable; it is now generally regarded as not later than the fifth century. The manuscript has been corrected by many hands, including the original scribe himself; some of the correctors are nearly contemporary with the original writing, others are much later.

The existence of a Latin text is sufficient proof by itself that the manuscript was written in the West of Europe, where Latin was the language of literature and daily life. In the East there would be no occasion for a Latin translation; but in the West Latin was the language which would be the most generally intelligible, while the Greek was added because it was the original language of the sacred books. Also the volume seems to have been used somewhere where the Scriptures were publicly read in Greek, for the liturgical directions are all on the Greek pages. But Latin copies of the Scriptures existed long before this manuscript was written; and the question arises, whether the scribe has simply copied a Greek manuscript for his Greek pages and a Latin manuscript for his Latin, or whether he has taken pains to make the two versions correspond and represent the same readings of the original. On this point a rather curious division of opinion has arisen. It is tolerably clear that in the first instance independent Greek and Latin texts were used as the authorities to be copied, but it is also clear that the texts have been to some extent assimilated to one another; and while Dr. Scrivener (and most scholars until recently) argues that the Latin has been altered to suit the Greek (and therefore ceases to be very valuable evidence for the text of the Old Latin version), Professor Rendel Harris and several later scholars maintain that the Greek has been altered to suit the Latin, and that therefore it is the Greek that is comparatively unimportant as evidence for the original Greek text. The latest editor of Acts, Professor A. C. Clark, regards the Latin text as having no independent value. Striking evidence can be produced on both sides; so that there seems to be nothing left but to conclude that *both* texts have been modified, which is in itself not an unreasonable conclusion. Some scholars also have maintained that it has been influenced by the Syriac version. The general result is that the evidence of D, whether for the Greek or Latin text, must be used with some caution; and care must be taken to make sure that any apparent variation is not due to some modification introduced by the scribe.

But the special interest of Codex Bezæ is not to be found so much in verbal variations as in wider departures from the normal text, in which there is no question of mere accommodations of language, but which can only be due to a different tradition. Codex Bezæ, unlike the MSS. hitherto described, which are copies of the entire Bible, contains only the Gospels and Acts, with a few verses of the Catholic Epistles, which originally preceded the Acts; but in these portions of the New Testament it exhibits a very remarkable series of variations from the usual text. It is the chief representative of the Western type of text, finding its nearest ally in the African type of the Old Latin version. Its special characteristic, as explained above (p. 112), is the free addition, and occasionally omission, of words, sentences, and even incidents. One of these will be found in the page of the MS. reproduced in our Plate XIX, containing Luke v. 38–vi. 9. The first word on the page shows that this manuscript contains the last words of verse 38, " and both are preserved," which are omitted by א, B, and L, and after them by Tischendorf, Westcott and Hort, and the Revised Version; while A, C, and the mass of later MSS. agree with D, and are followed by Lachmann, Tregelles, and McClellan. Verse 39 is omitted altogether, both by D and by the Old Latin version (see note in Variorum Bible). At the end of vi. 9 the words οἱ δὲ ἐσιώπων (" but they were silent ") are added by D alone; and in place of verse 5 D alone inserts the following curious passage (lines 16-20 in the plate): " On the same day, seeing one working on the sabbath day, he said unto him, Man, if thou knowest what thou doest, blessed art thou; but if thou knowest not, thou art accursed and a transgressor of the law." This striking incident, which is contained in no other manuscript or version, cannot be held to be part of the original text of St. Luke; but it may well be that it is a genuine tradition, one of the " many other things which Jesus did " which were not written in the Gospels. If this be so, one would forgive all the liberties taken by this manuscript with the sacred text, for the sake of this addition to the recorded words of the Lord.

It will be of interest to note some of the principal additions and omissions found elsewhere in this remarkable manuscript. After Matt. xx. 28, D is the principal authority (being supported by one uncial, Φ, the Old Latin and Curetonian Syriac versions, and a few copies of the Vulgate) for inserting another long passage: " But seek ye to increase from that which is small, and to become less from that which is greater. When ye enter into a house and are summoned to dine, sit not down in the highest places, lest perchance a more honourable man than thou shall come in afterwards, and he that bade thee come and say to thee, Go down lower; and thou shalt be ashamed. But if thou sittest down in the worse place, and one worse than thee come in afterwards, then he that bade thee will say to thee, Go up higher; and this shall be advantageous for thee." Matt. xxi. 44 (" and whosoever shall fall on this stone," etc.) is omitted by D, one cursive (33), and the best copies of the Old Latin. In Luke x. 42, D and the Old Latin omit the words, " one thing is needful, and." In Luke xxii. 19, 20 the same authorities and the Old Syriac omit the second mention of the cup in the institution of the Sacrament of the Lord's Supper, but differ markedly with one another in their arrangement of the text. In Luke xxiv. 6,

D and the Old Latin omit the words "He is not here, but is risen"; they omit the whole of verse 12, with Peter's entry into the sepulchre; they omit in verse 36 "and saith unto them, Peace be unto you"; the whole of verse 40, "And when he had thus spoken, he showed them his hands and his feet"; in verse 51 the words "and was carried up into heaven"; and in verse 52 the words "worshipped him and." In John iv. 9 the same authorities omit "for the Jews have no dealings with the Samaritans"; this time with the support of ℵ. In Acts xv. 20, D omits "and from things strangled," and adds at the end of the verse "and that they should not do to others what they would not have done to themselves." In the narrative of St. Paul's missionary journeys in Asia, this manuscript and its allies have so many variations as to have suggested the idea that they represent a separate edition of the Acts, equally authentic but different in date; or else that they (or rather the source from which they are descended) embody touches of local detail added by a scribe who must have been a resident in the country and acquainted with the local traditions. Little changes of phrase, which the greatest living authority on the history and geography of Asia Minor declares to be more true and vivid than the ordinary text, are added to the narratives of St. Paul's visits to Lycaonia and Ephesus. Thus in chapter xix. 9, D adds the detail that St. Paul preached daily in the school of Tyrannus "from the fifth hour to the tenth." In chapter xix. 1 the text runs thus, quite differently from the verse which stands in our Bibles: "Now when Paul desired in his own mind to journey to Jerusalem, the Spirit spake unto him that he should turn back to Ephesus; and passing through the upper parts he cometh to Ephesus, and finding certain disciples he said unto them." And when the evidence of D comes to an end, as it does at xxii. 29, the other authorities usually associated with it continue to record a text differing equally remarkably from that which is recorded in the vast majority of manuscripts and versions.

The instances which have been given are sufficient to show at once the interest and the freedom characteristic of the Western text, of which the Codex Bezæ is the chief representative. It is not, however, to be supposed that it is always so striking and so independent. In many cases it is found in agreement with the Neutral text of Band ℵ, when it no doubt represents the authentic words of the original. But space will not allow us to dwell too long on any single manuscript, however interesting, and further information as to its readings can always be found by a study of any critical edition or of the notes to the Variorum Bible. A selection will be found in Appendix I.

D_2. *Codex Claromontanus*; in the National Library at Paris. It has been said that the Codex Bezæ contains only the Gospels and Acts; and consequently when we come to the Pauline Epistles the letter D is given to another manuscript, which contains only this part of the New Testament. Like the Codex Bezæ, it formerly belonged to Beza, having been found at Clermont (whence its name), in France, and in 1656 it was bought for the Royal Library. Like the Codex Bezæ, again, it contains both Greek and Latin texts, written on opposite pages. Each leaf measures $9\frac{3}{4}$ by $7\frac{3}{4}$ inches, with very wide margins. It is written on beautifully fine vellum, in a very handsome style of writing, and (still like D of the Gospels) it is arranged in lines of irregular length, corresponding to the pauses in the sense. It is generally assigned to the sixth century, and may have been written in Sardinia, since its Latin text is nearly identical with that used by Lucifer, bishop of Cagliari, in the fourth century. The Greek text is correctly written, the Latin has many blunders, and is more independent of the Greek than is the case in Codex Bezæ, belonging to the African type of the Old Latin version. Hence Africa has also been suggested for its place of origin. It has been corrected by no less than nine different hands, the fourth of which (about the ninth century) added the breathings and accents, as they appear in the plate. The text of this Codex is distinctly Western, as might be expected from its containing a Latin version; but Western readings in the Epistles are not so striking as we have seen them to be in the Gospels and Acts.

The remaining uncial manuscripts of the New Testament may, and indeed must, be described more briefly; but as they are sometimes referred to in the Variorum Bible, and of course oftener in critical editions of the Greek, a short notice of them seems to be necessary.

E of the Gospels (*Codex Basiliensis*) is an eighth-century copy of the four Gospels, at Basle, in Switzerland, containing a good representation of the Syrian type of text, so that it will often be found siding with A.

E of the Acts (E_2), the *Codex Laudianus*, is much more valuable, and is the most important Biblical MS. in the Bodleian Library at Oxford. It is a manuscript of the seventh century, containing both Latin and Greek texts, the Latin being on the left and the Greek on the right (unlike D and D_2). It is written in large rough uncials, in lines of varying length, but containing only one to three words each. Its text is Western, with a large admixture of Alexandrian readings. The history of this volume is interesting. An inscription contained in it shows that it was in Sardinia at some time in the seventh century. It was brought to England probably either by Theodore of Tarsus, Archbishop of Canterbury, in 668, or by Ceolfrid, Abbot of Wearmouth and

Jarrow, in the early part of the eighth century. It was probably deposited in one of the great monasteries in the north of England, for it is practically certain that it was used by Bede in writing his commentary on the Acts. At the dissolution of the monasteries it must have been turned loose on the world, like so many other treasures of inestimable value; but ultimately it came into the hands of Archbishop Laud, and was included by him, in 1636, in one of his splendid gifts to the University of Oxford. It is the earliest MS. which contains Acts viii. 37 (the eunuch's confession of faith), D being deficient here.

E of the Pauline Epistles (E_3) is merely a copy of D_2, made at the end of the ninth century, when the text of D_2 had already suffered damage from correctors. Hence it is of no independent value.

Of the remaining manuscripts we shall notice only those which have some special value or interest. Many of them consist of fragments only, and their texts are for the most part less valuable. Most of them contain texts of the Syrian type, and are of no more importance than the great mass of cursives. They prove that the Syrian text was predominant in the Greek world, but they do not prove that it is the most authentic form of the text. Some of the later uncials, however, contain earlier texts to a greater or less degree; and these deserve a separate mention.

F_2 and G_3, of the Pauline Epistles, belong to the same textual group as D_2.

H_3. Forty-three leaves of the Pauline Epistles, divided between Paris, Leningrad, Moscow, Kieff, Turin, and Mount Athos, where the whole MS. once was. Sixth century, written in short sense-lines according to an edition prepared by Euthalius in the fourth century.

I. *Codex Washingtonianus II.* Portions of the Pauline Epistles in the Freer Collection at Washington. Probably seventh century. Definitely " Neutral " or Alexandrian in character, and agrees more with ℵ and A than with B.

K. *Codex Cyprius*, at Paris, is a ninth or tenth century copy of the Gospels, with a typically " Syrian " or Byzantine text.

L. *Codex Regius*, in the National Library at Paris, is conspicuous among the later uncials for the antiquity of the text which it preserves, and it was probably copied from a very early manuscript. It is assigned to the eighth century, and contains the Gospels complete, except for a few small lacunæ. It has a large number of Alexandrian readings in the modern sense of that term (having in fact probably been written in Egypt), and it is very frequently found in conjunction with B in readings which are now generally accepted as the best. One notable case in which its evidence is of special interest is at the end of St.

Mark's Gospel. Like B and ℵ, it breaks off at the end of verse 8; but unlike them it proceeds to give two alternative endings. The *second* of these is the ordinary verses 9-20, but the first is a shorter one, which is also found in a small number of minor authorities: "But they told to Peter and his companions all the things that had been said unto them. And after these things the Lord Jesus himself also, from morning even until evening, sent forth by them the holy and imperishable proclamation of eternal salvation." It is certain that this is not the original ending of St. Mark's Gospel, but it is very probably an early substitute for the true ending, which may have been lost through some accident,[1] or else not written at all. In any case it is interesting as showing the independent character of L and increasing the general value of its testimony elsewhere.

N. *Codex Purpureus Petropolitanus*. Mainly at Leningrad, but with some leaves at Patmos, the Vatican, the British Museum, Vienna and Genoa. About half of a fine copy of the Gospels, written in the sixth century in silver letters upon purple vellum, with a Byzantine text. The Leningrad portion was discovered at Cæsarea in Cappadocia in 1896. Akin to O, Φ and Σ, especially the last.

O. *Codex Sinopensis*. Forty-three leaves of St. Matthew, written in the sixth century in gold letters upon purple vellum, with five illustrations. Acquired at Sinope in Asia Minor by a French officer in 1899, and now in the Bibliothèque Nationale at Paris.

P_2. *Codex Porphyrianus*, a palimpsest of the ninth century at Leningrad, containing Acts, Epistles, and Revelation, and valuable as one of the few uncials of the last book.

R. *Codex Nitriensis*, a palimpsest in the British Museum (Add. MS. 17211). It was brought from the convent of St. Mary Deipara, in the Nitrian Desert of Egypt. It contains 516 verses of St. Luke in a fine large hand of the sixth century, over which a Syriac treatise by Severus of Antioch has been written in the eighth or ninth century. Its text is distinctly valuable, and it contains a large proportion of pre-Syrian readings.

T. *Codex Borgianus*, in the Propaganda at Rome; peculiar as containing both Greek and Coptic texts, the latter being of the Thebaic or Sahidic version. It is only a fragment, or rather several small fragments, containing 179 verses of St. Luke and St. John. It is of the fifth century, and contains an almost

[1] Dr. Hort suggests that a leaf containing verses 9-20 may have been lost from an early copy of the second century; but it must be observed that this implies that the manuscript was written in book form, which is just possible at that date, but not (according to our present knowledge) earlier. If it were a papyrus roll, the end would be in the *inside* of the roll, and therefore not exposed to much risk of damage, unless, as is possible, rolls after reading were left with the end outside.

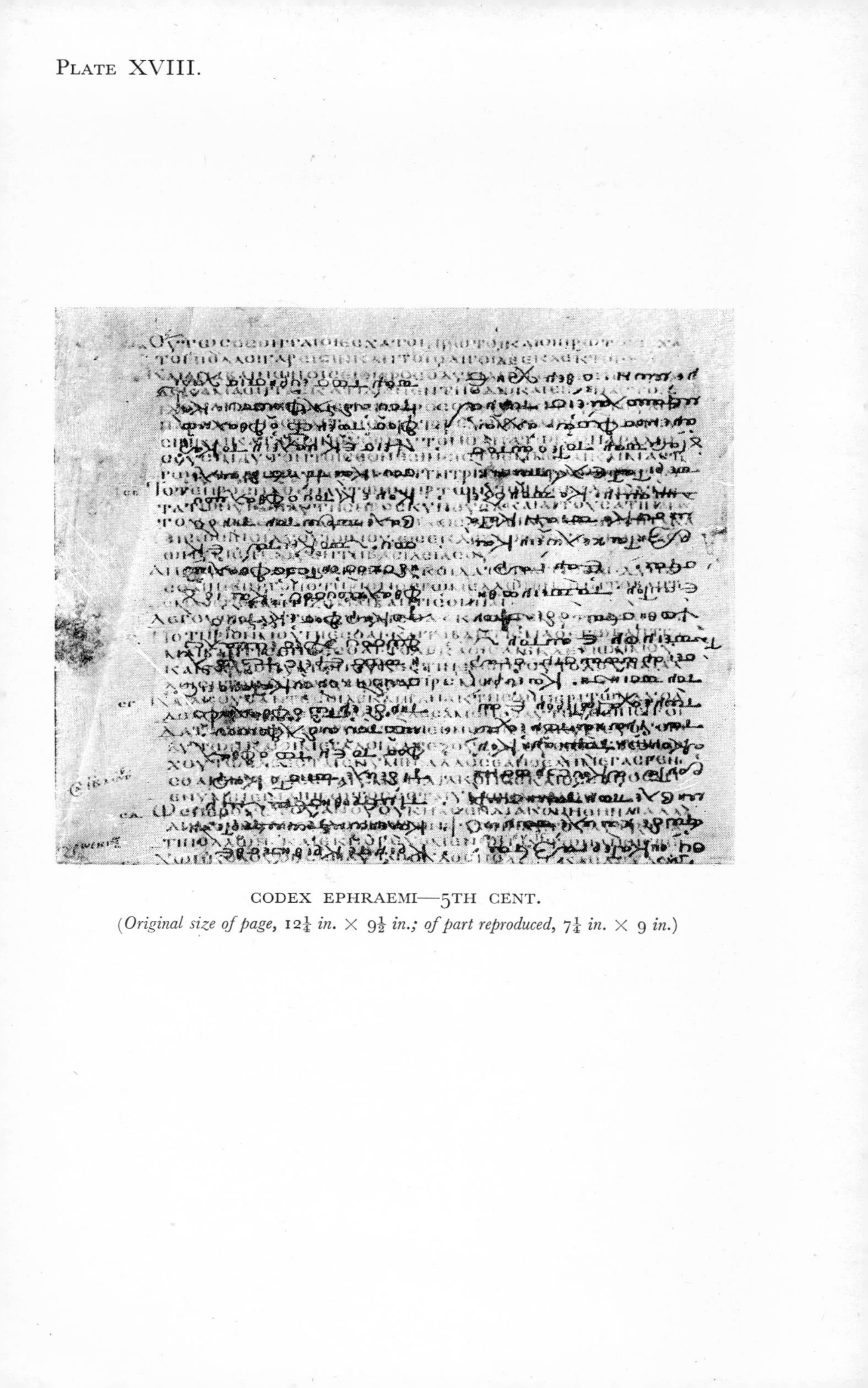

CODEX EPHRAEMI—5TH CENT.

(Original size of page, 12¼ in. × 9½ in.; of part reproduced, 7¼ in. × 9 in.)

PLATE XIX.

ΚΑΤ ΛΟΥΚ

ΤΗΡΟΥΝΤΑΙ ΚΑΙΕΓΕΝΕΤΟΑΥΤΟΝ
ΕΝϹΑΒΒΑΤΩΔΕΥΤΕΡΟΠΡΩΤΩΔΙΑ
ΠΟΡΕΥΕϹΘΑΙΔΙΑΤΩΝϹΠΟΡΙΜΩΝ
ΟΙΔΕΜΑΘΗΤΑΙΑΥΤΟΥΗΡΞΑΝΤΟΤΙΛΛΕΙΝ
ΤΟΥϹϹΤΑΧΥΑϹΚΑΙΨΩΧΟΝΤΕϹΤΑΙϹΧΕΡϹΙΝ
ΗϹΘΙΟΝ ΤΙΝΕϹΔΕΤΩΝΦΑΡΙϹΑΙΩΝ
ΕΛΕΓΟΝΑΥΤΩ ΕΙΔΕΤΙΠΟΙΟΥϹΙΝΟΙ
ΜΑΘΗΤΑΙϹΟΥΤΟΙϹϹΑΒΒΑϹΙΝΟΟΥΚΕΞΕϹΤΙΝ
ΑΠΟΚΡΙΘΕΙϹΔΕΟΙΗϹΕΛΕΓΕΝΠΡΟϹΑΥΤΟΥϹ
ΟΥΔΕΠΟΤΕΤΟΥΤΟ ΑΝΕΓΝΩΤΑΙΟΕΠΟΙΗϹΕΝ
ΔΑΥΕΙΔ ΟΤΕΕΠΕΙΝΑϹΕΝΑΥΤΟϹ
ΚΑΙΟΙΜΕΤΑΥΤΟΥΕΙϹΕΛΘΩΝΕΙϹΤΟΝΟΙΚΟΝ
ΤΟΥΘΥ ΚΑΙΤΟΥϹΑΡΤΟΥϹΤΗϹΠΡΟΘΕϹΕΩϹ
ΕΦΑΓΕΝΚΑΙΕΔΩΚΕΝΚΑΙΤΟΙϹΜΕΤΑΥΤΟΥ
ΟΙϹΟΥΚΕΞΟΝΗΝΦΑΓΕΙΝΕΙΜΗΜΟΝΟΙϹ
ΤΟΙϹΙΕΡΕΥϹΙΝ ΤΗΑΥΤΗΗΜΕΡΑΘΕΑϹΑΜΕΝΟϹ
ΤΙΝΑΕΡΓΑΖΟΜΕΝΟΝΤΩϹΑΒΒΑΤΩΕΙΠΕΝΑΥΤΩ
ΑΝΘΡΩΠΕ ΕΙΜΕΝΟΙΔΑϹΤΙΠΟΙΕΙϹ
ΜΑΚΑΡΙΟϹΕΙ ΕΙΔΕΜΗΟΙΔΑϹ ΕΠΙΚΑΤΑΡΑΤΟϹ
ΚΑΙΠΑΡΑΒΑΤΗϹΕΙΤΟΥΝΟΜΟΥ
ΚΑΙΕΙϹΕΛΘΟΝΤΟϹΑΥΤΟΥΠΑΛΙΝΕΙϹΤΗΝ
ϹΥΝΑΓΩΓΗΝϹΑΒΒΑΤΩΕΝΗΗΝΑΝΘΡΩΠΟϹ
ΞΗΡΑΝΕΧΩΝΤΗΝΧΕΙΡΑ ΠΑΡΕΤΗΡΟΥΝΤΟ
ΑΥΤΟΝΟΙΓΡΑΜΜΑΤΕΙϹΚΑΙΟΙΦΑΡΙϹΑΙΟΙ
ΕΙΤΩϹΑΒΒΑΤΩΘΕΡΑΠΕΥΕΙΙΝΑΕΥΡΩϹΙΝ
ΚΑΤΗΓΟΡΗϹΑΙΑΥΤΟΥ ΑΥΤΟϹΔΕ ΓΕΙΝΩϹΚΩΝ
ΤΟΥϹΔΙΑΛΟΓΙϹΜΟΥϹΑΥΤΩΝΛΕΓΕΙΤΩ
ΤΗΝΧΕΙΡΑΕΧΟΝΤΙΞΗΡΑΝ ΕΓΕΙΡΟΥ ΚΑΙϹΤΗΘΙ
ΕΝΤΩΜΕϹΩ ΚΑΙΑΝΑϹΤΑϹΕϹΤΑΘΗ
ΕΙΠΕΝΔΕΟΙΗϹΠΡΟϹΑΥΤΟΥϹ ΕΠΕΡΩΤΗϹΩ
ΥΜΑϹΕΙΕΞΕϹΤΙΝΤΩϹΑΒΒΑΤΩ ΑΓΑΘΟ
ΠΟΙΗϹΑΙΗΚΑΚΟΠΟΙΗϹΑΙΨΥΧΗΝϹΩϹΑΙ
ΗΑΠΟΛΕϹΑΙ ΟΙΔΕΕϹΙΩΠΩΝ

SEC LUCAN

SERUANTUR ETFACTUMESTEUM
INSABBATOSECUNDOPRIMO
ABIRE PERSEGETES
DISCIPULIAUTEMILLIUS COEPERUNTUELLERE
SPICAS ETFRICANTESMANIBUS
MANDUCABANT QUIDAMAUTEMDEFARISAEIS
DICEBANTEI ECCEQUIDFACIUNT
DISCIPULITUISABBATISQUODNONLICET
RESPONDENSAUTEMIHSDIXITADEOS
NUMQUAMHOCLEGISTISQUODFECIT
DAUIDQUANDOESURIITIPSE
ETQUICUMEOERATINTROIBITINDOMUM
DEIETPANESPROPOSITIONIS
MANDUCAUITETDEDITETQUICUMERANT
QUIBUSNONLICEBATMANDUCARESINONSOLIS
SACERDOTIBUS EODEMDIE UIDENS
QUENDAMOPERANTEMSABBATOETDIXITILLI
HOMOSIQUIDEMSCISQUODFACIS
BEATUSES SIAUTEMNESCISMALEDICTUS
ETTRABARICATORLEGIS
ETCUMINTROISSETITERUMIN
SYNAGOGAMSABBATOINQUAERATHOMO
ARIDAMHABENSMANUM OBSERUABANT
EUMSCRIBAEETPHARISAEI
SISABBATOCURARET UTINUENIRENT
ACCUSAREEUM IPSEAUTEMSCIENS
COGITATIONESEORUMDICITILLI
QUIMANUMARIDAMHABIBATSURGEETSTA
INMEDIO ETSURGENSSTETIT
DIXITAUTEMIHS ADEOS INTERROGABO
UOSSILICETSABBATO BEN
FACEREAUTMALEFACERE ANIMAMSALUARE
AUTPERDERE ADILLITACUERUNT

CODEX BEZÆ—6TH CENT.

(*Original size of each page,* 10 *in.* × 8½ *in.; of column of writing,* 7½ *in.* × 6 *in.*)

entirely Neutral text, with a few Alexandrian corrections. Dr. Hort ranks it next after B and ℵ for excellence of text. Several fragments of other Græco-Coptic MSS. have since been discovered of lesser size and importance.

W. *Codex Washingtonianus I*, in the Freer Collection at Washington. Acquired by Mr. C. L. Freer in Egypt in 1906. Apparently late fourth or fifth century. It contains four Gospels in an order common in the West, Matthew, John, Luke, Mark. Its text varies in character, as if it had been copied from several different MSS. In Matthew, John i. 1–v. 12 (a quire added in the seventh century to replace one that had been damaged), and Luke viii. 13 to the end, it is of the common Byzantine type, but the rest of John and Luke are Alexandrian, Mark i. 1–v. 30 is Western, and the rest of Mark is Cæsarean. After Mark xvi. 14 there is a remarkable insertion, part of which is quoted by Jerome from "some copies, chiefly Greek": "And they answered and said, This generation of lawlessness and faithlessness is under Satan, who doth not allow the truth of God to prevail over the unclean things of the spirits. Therefore make manifest thy righteousness. So spake they now to Christ, and Christ said unto them, The tale of the years of the dominion of Satan is fulfilled, but other terrible things draw near, and by reason of the sins of them I was delivered over unto death, that they may return to the truth and sin no more; that they may inherit the spiritual and incorruptible glory of righteousness which is in heaven." Plate XX shows this passage.

Z. *Codex Dublinensis*, a palimpsest, consisting of thirty-two leaves, containing 295 verses of St. Matthew in writing of the sixth or possibly the fifth century, over which some portions of Greek Fathers were written in the tenth century. It was evidently written in Egypt, in a very large and beautiful hand. Its text is decidedly pre-Syrian, but it agrees with ℵ rather than with B.

Δ (Delta, the fourth letter in the Greek alphabet) (*Codex Sangallensis*) is a nearly complete copy of the Gospels in Greek, with a Latin translation between the lines, written in the ninth century by an Irish scribe at the monastery of St. Gall in Switzerland. It was originally part of the same manuscript as G_3 of the Pauline Epistles. Its text, except in St. Mark, is of the ordinary Syrian type and calls for no special notice, but in St. Mark it is decidedly Neutral or Alexandrian, of the same type as L.

Θ (Theta, the eighth letter in the Greek alphabet) (*Codex Koridethianus*). This letter, which was formerly given to a number of uncial fragments, has now been transferred to a curious new discovery, to which attention was first called by von Soden in 1906. It is a manuscript of the Gospels, of uncouth appearance, probably of the ninth century, written in late, rough uncials by a scribe who knew very little Greek, which formerly belonged to the monastery of Koridethi, near the Caspian, and is now at Tiflis. In most of the Gospels its text is not far removed from the common Byzantine type, but in Mark it is quite different. Here it is so nearly akin to the two groups of minuscules, 1-118-131-209 and 13-69-124-346, referred to above (p. 117), that the whole may be regarded as a single family, Family Theta; and it is to this family that Streeter gave the name of the Cæsarean text.

Λ (Lambda, the eleventh letter in the Greek alphabet) (*Codex Tischendorfianus III*, in the Bodleian). A copy of Luke and John which has been shown to have been originally part of the same manuscript as minuscule 566, at Leningrad. Like E of the Septuagint, it was written partly in uncials and partly in minuscules, in the ninth or tenth century, when the change from one style of writing to the other was taking place; and as with E, Tischendorf divided the two portions and disposed of them to different libraries. It has a note, also found in twelve minuscules, to the effect that its text was derived " from the ancient copies at Jerusalem."

Ξ (Xi, the fourteenth letter of the Greek alphabet) (*Codex Zacynthius*) is a palimpsest containing 342 verses of St. Luke, written in the eighth century, but covered in the thirteenth with a lectionary. It is now in the library of the British and Foreign Bible Society in London, whither it was brought from the island of Zante in 1820. Its text belongs to the same class as L, having a large number of Alexandrian readings, and also some of Western type. Dr. Hort places it next to T.

Π (Pi, the sixteenth letter in the Greek alphabet) (*Codex Petropolitanus*, at Leningrad). A copy of the Gospels, formerly at Smyrna, of the ninth century, which has recently been made the subject of a special study by Mrs. Kirsopp Lake, who regards it as the head of a sub-family of the Byzantine type, akin to, but not descended from, the Codex Alexandrinus (A).

Σ (Sigma,the eighteenth letter of the Greek alphabet) (*Codex Rossanensis*). A copy of Matthew and Mark, written in the sixth century in silver letters on purple vellum, with illustrations. Found at Rossano in Calabria in 1879. In text it is closely akin to N.

Φ (Phi, the twenty-first letter of the Greek alphabet) (*Codex Beratinus*). The fourth of the group of purple manuscripts, N-O-Σ-Φ, at Berat in Albania. Contains only Matthew and Mark, with a note saying that it was mutilated " by the Franks of Champagne "—*i.e.*, probably some of the Crusaders. Its text is generally Byzantine, but it contains the long addition after Matt. xx. 28, already quoted as occurring in D.

Ψ (Psi, the twenty-third letter of the Greek alphabet) (*Codex*

Laurensis). A copy of the Gospels (from Mark ix. 5 onwards), Acts, and Epistles, of the eighth or ninth century, in the monastery of the Laura on Mount Athos. Like L, it inserts the shorter ending to Mark before the longer one. Examined in 1899 by Lake, who showed that its text in Mark is an early one, with readings both Alexandrian and Western, but chiefly akin to the group ℵ C L Δ.

3. *Minuscules.*

Of the great mass of the minuscules it is not proposed to give any detailed description; but a few may be mentioned as of some individual importance. The total now included in the official list is 2429, besides 1678 Lectionaries.

First there is the group 1-118-131-209, known as Family 1, investigated by Lake in 1902, and now forming part of the Cæsarean text. MS. 1 is also notable as having been one of the MSS. used by Erasmus in preparing the first printed Greek New Testament. But in the main he followed MS. 2 in the Gospels, a fifteenth-century copy of the Byzantine text in its latest form.

Next there is the other group, 13-69-124-346, with a number of other MSS. showing more or less affinity with them, which is known as the Ferrar group, from its first identifier and editor, or Family 13. This also has now been subsumed into the Cæsarean text.

33. A MS. of the Gospels, Acts, and Epistles, at Paris, of the ninth century, with a text akin to B, and considered by Hort to be the best of the cursives.

81. A MS. of Acts, written in 1044, in the British Museum. One of the best minuscules of the Acts, ranking in quality with the leading uncials.

157. In the Vatican. Said by Hort to be in the same class as 33 and claimed by Streeter for the Cæsarean group.

565. At Leningrad, written in gold letters on purple vellum. It has the same subscription with reference to copies at Jerusalem as Λ, and in Mark is akin to the Cæsarean type.

Of the rest we cannot say anything here. For the most part they do but produce, with less and less authority as they become later in date, the prevailing Syrian type of text. No doubt good readings *may* lurk here and there among them, but the chances against it are many; and the examination of them belongs to the professional student of Biblical criticism, and not to those who desire only to know the most important of the authorities upon which rests our knowledge of the Bible text. Only for completeness' sake, and as an example of the smaller form of writing prevalent in Greek manuscripts from the ninth century to the fifteenth, is a plate given here of one of these "cursive" MSS.

(Plate XXI). The manuscript here reproduced was written in the year 1022, and is now in the Ambrosian Library at Milan. It contains the Gospels only, and its official designation in the list of New Testament MSS. is Evan. 348. The page of which the upper half is here produced, on the same scale as the original, contains the beginning of St. Luke's Gospel. Its text is of no special interest; it is simply an average specimen of the Greek Gospels current in the Middle Ages, in the beautiful Greek writing of the eleventh century.

The most important authorities for the text of the Greek Testament have now been described in some detail; and it is to be hoped that the reader to whom the matter contained in these pages is new will henceforth feel a livelier interest when he strolls through the galleries of one of our great libraries and sees the opened pages of these ancient witnesses to the Word of God. These are no common books, such as machinery turns out in hundreds every day in these later times. Each one of them was written by the personal labour and sanctified by the prayers of some Egyptian or Syrian Christian of the early days, some Greek or Latin monk of the Middle Ages, working in the writing-room of some great monastery of Eastern or Western Europe, some scribe in a professional scriptorium. Each has its own individuality, which must be sought out by modern scholars with patient toil and persevering study. And from the comparison of all, from the weighing, and not counting merely, of their testimony, slowly is being built up a purer and more accurate representation of the text of our sacred books than our fathers and our forefathers possessed, and we are brought nearer to the very words which Evangelist and Apostle wrote, more than eighteen hundred years ago.

CHAPTER VIII

THE ANCIENT VERSIONS OF THE NEW TESTAMENT

WE have now completed the survey of the primary sources of our knowledge of the text of the Greek New Testament. We go out into a wider territory. Not Greek alone, but all the tongues of Pentecost—the dwellers in Mesopotamia, in Pontus and Asia, in Phrygia and Pamphylia, in Egypt and the parts of Libya about Cyrene, sojourners in Rome, and Arabians—are now laid under contribution. We go to Syrian, and Egyptian, and Roman, and ask them when the sacred Scriptures were translated into their language, and what information they can give us as to the character and exact words of the Greek text from which their translations were originally made. And the answer is that the Word of God was delivered to the dwellers in some at least of these lands before the date at which the oldest of our Greek manuscripts were written. The Vatican and Sinaitic manuscripts carry us back, as we have just seen, to about the middle of the fourth century—say, to A.D. 350—and the papyri a century or more earlier. But the New Testament was translated into Syriac and into Latin by about A.D. 150, and into Egyptian somewhere about A.D. 200; and the copies which we now possess of these versions are lineal descendants of the original translations made at these dates. The stream of textual tradition was tapped at these points, higher in its course than the highest point at which we have access to the original Greek. If we can ascertain with certainty what were the original words of the Syriac or Latin translations, we can generally know what was the Greek text which the translator had before him; we know, that is, what words were found in a Greek manuscript which was extant in the first half of the second century, and which cannot have been written very far from A.D. 100. Of course variations and mistakes crept into the copies of these translations, just as they did into the Greek manuscripts, and much skill and labour are necessary to establish the true readings in these passages; but we have the satisfaction of knowing that we are working back at the common object (the recovery of the original text of the Bible) along an independent line; and when many of these lines converge on a single point, our confidence in the accuracy of our conclusions is enormously increased.

§ 1.—Eastern Versions.

I. *Syriac Versions.*

The Gospel was first preached in the East, and we will therefore take first the versions in the languages of those countries which lay nearest to Judæa. Of these, none can take precedence of the Syriac version. Syriac, as has been already stated (p. 80), is the language of Mesopotamia and Syria, and was likewise (with some variety of dialect) the current language of everyday life in Palestine in the time of our Lord. More than one translation of the Bible was made into this language, and these will be described in order.

(*a*) *The Diatessaron of Tatian.*—Although Syriac is a dialect of Aramaic, akin to that in use in Palestine at the time of our Lord, the Gospels were not written in that language, and had therefore to be translated from the Greek for the benefit of the Christians of the Syriac Church. The headquarters of Syriac Christianity was at Edessa, capital of an independent principality east of the great bend in the upper Euphrates. Now it is known that from about the third quarter of the second century the Gospel story circulated here in the form of a Gospel Harmony, known as the *Diatessaron*, from a Greek phrase meaning " harmony of four," the work of one Tatian, who died about A.D. 180. The story of this work, its circulation, its disappearance, and its partial recovery in our own day, is one of the romances of textual history.

Tatian was a native of the Euphrates valley, born about A.D. 110, who after travels in many lands was converted to Christianity and lived for many years in Rome as a disciple of Justin Martyr. He wrote a vehement defence of Christianity against the Greeks, but after the martyrdom of Justin in A.D. 165 he was charged with heresy on account of his extremely ascetic views, and returned to his native land. Either before or after leaving Rome he compiled his Harmony. Whether the original language was Greek or Syriac is a matter of dispute. In favour of Syriac is the fact that its main circulation was in Syria; but against it are the weighty considerations (*a*) that its title is Greek; (*b*) that a Latin translation was made of it, which is not very likely if it were of purely Syrian origin; (*c*) that it never fell under suspicion of heresy, which suggests that it was produced before Tatian left Rome; (*d*) that its textual affinities are with the Western type; (*e*) that, as there is no evidence of a pre-existing Syriac version of the separate Gospels, the natural course would have been to make the harmony first and then to translate it. It therefore seems probable that Tatian made his harmony in Rome, but took it with him to Syria and there translated it into

Syriac. What is certain is that it was in this form that the Gospel story principally circulated in Syria until the fourth century. After the adoption, however, of the Peshitta (see below) as the official Bible of the Syriac Church it fell into complete obscurity. In the sixth century Bishop Victor of Capua found an anonymous Harmony of the Gospels in Latin, which he guessed to be that of Tatian mentioned in the Church historians. His edition of it (with a Vulgate text unfortunately substituted for that which he found) is extant in the Codex Fuldensis (see below, p. 176), written in A.D. 541-6. A Dutch version also exists which seems to have been made from a Latin text in which the pre-Vulgate text was preserved. But apart from these evidences of precarious survival in the Middle Ages, which have only been recognised as such in the light of modern discoveries, the Diatessaron had wholly disappeared.

Its recovery is a literary curiosity. During the controversy concerning the dates of the New Testament books arising out of the destructive criticism of Baur in the middle of the nineteenth century, there was much discussion of the Diatessaron and its character. Our earliest informant on the subject, the great Church historian Eusebius, in the fourth century, described it as " a sort of patchwork combination of the Gospels "; and if it were compiled, as its name seemed to imply, from the four canonical Gospels, it was decisive evidence that in the third quarter of the second century these four Gospels already stood out by themselves as the recognised and authoritative records of the life of Christ. Such a conclusion was, however, unacceptable to those who, like Baur, contended that the Gospels were not written till between A.D. 130 and 170; and consequently the statement of Eusebius was disputed. The expressions used by Eusebius might be taken to imply that he had not himself seen the work; and another early writer, Epiphanius, towards the end of the fourth century, stated that " some people " called it the Gospel according to the Hebrews. Hence it was maintained by some (notably by the anonymous author of *Supernatural Religion*, 1876, a controversial work which had considerable vogue for a time) that no such thing as a harmony by Tatian existed at all, and that Tatian's Gospel was identical with the Gospel according to the Hebrews, and that again with the Gospel according to Peter—both of them known then only by name and affording no evidence as to the date and authority of the canonical books.

St. Ephraem's Commentary.

The controversy on this subject was at its height in 1877 when Bishop Lightfoot wrote his well-known *Essays on " Supernatural*

Religion," in the course of which he stated the arguments for the common-sense view of the Diatessaron. These arguments were as strong as could reasonably be expected, so long as the Diatessaron itself was lost; yet at that very time demonstrative evidence on the point was in existence, though unknown to either party in the controversy. So long ago as 1836 the Fathers of an Armenian community in Venice had published an Armenian version of the works of St. Ephraem of Syria (a writer of the fourth century), among which was a commentary on the Diatessaron; but Armenian was then a language little known, and no attention was paid to it. In 1876, however, the Armenian Fathers employed Dr. George Moesinger to revise and publish a Latin version of it which had been prepared by the original editor, Dr. Aucher. Why so important a discovery still continued unnoticed is a puzzle which has never been solved; but unnoticed it remained until 1880, when attention was called to it by Dr. Ezra Abbot, in America, whereby it shortly became known to scholars in general. Ephraem's commentary included very large quotations from the work itself, so that its general character was definitely established, and no responsible scholar could question the fact that the Diatessaron was actually a harmony of (or, more accurately, a narrative compiled from) the four canonical Gospels.

Discovery of the Diatessaron.

If matters had stopped there, the discovery, though of great importance for the "higher criticism" of the New Testament, would have had little bearing upon textual questions; but further developments were in store. In the course of the investigations to which Aucher's discovery gave rise it was pointed out that a work purporting to be an Arabic translation of the Diatessaron itself was mentioned in an old catalogue of the Vatican Library; and, on search being made, the description was found to be correct. The series of discoveries did not even end here; for the Vatican manuscript chancing to be shown to the Vicar-Apostolic of the Catholic Copts, while on a visit to Rome, he observed that he had seen a similar work in Egypt, which he undertook to obtain. The second manuscript proved to be better than the first, and from the two in conjunction the Diatessaron was at last edited by Ciasca in 1888, and dedicated to Pope Leo XIII, in honour of his Jubilee.

The Text of the Diatessaron.

The importance of this final publication lies in the fact that it enables us to learn something of the state of the text of the Gospels at the time when Tatian made his compilation from

PLATE XX.

ΕΞΑΥΤ[illegible]ΠΕΡΙΠΑΤΟΥΣΙΝΕΦΑΝΕΡ[illegible]
ΕΤΕΡΑΜΟΡΦΗΠΟΡΕΥΟΜΕΝΟΙΣΕΙΣΑΓΡΟΝ
ΚΑΚΕΙΝΟΙΑΠΕΛΘΟΝΤΕΣΑΠΗΓΓΕΛΟΝΤΟΙΣΛΟΙ
ΠΟΙΣ ΟΥΔΕΕΚΕΙΝΟΙΣΕΠΙΣΤΕΥΣΑΝ ΥΣΤΕΡΟΝ
ΑΝΑΚΕΙΜΕΝΟΙΣΤΟΙΣΙΑΕΦΑΝΕΡΩΘΗΚΑΙΩΝΕΙ
ΔΙΣΕΝΤΗΝΑΠΙΣΤΙΑΝΑΥΤΩΝΚΑΙΣΚΛΗ
ΡΟΚΑΡΔΙΑΝ ΟΤΙΤΟΙΣΘΕΑΣΑΜΕΝΟΙΣΑΥΤΟΝ
ΕΓΗΓΕΡΜΕΝΟΝΟΥΚΕΠΙΣΤΕΥΣΑΝ
ΚΑΚΕΙΝΟΙΑΠΕΛΟΓΟΥΝΤΕΛΕΓΟΝΤΕΣ ΟΤΙΟ
ΑΙΩΝΟΥΤΟΣΤΗΣΑΝΟΜΙΑΣΚΑΙΤΗΣΑΠΙΣΤΙΑΣ
ΥΠΟΤΟΝΣΑΤΑΝΑΝΕΣΤΙΝ ΟΜΗΕΩΝΤΑΥΠΟ
ΤΩΝΠΝΑΤΩΝΑΚΑΘΑΡΤΑ ΤΗΝΑΛΗΘΕΙΑΝ
ΤΟΥΘΥΚΑΤΑΛΑΒΕΣΘΑΙΔΥΝΑΜΙΝ ΔΙΑ
ΤΟΥΤΟΑΠΟΚΑΛΥΨΟΝΣΟΥΤΗΝΔΙΚΑΙΟΣΥ
ΝΗΝΗΔΗ ΕΚΕΙΝΟΙΕΛΕΓΟΝΤΩΧΩ ΚΑΙΟ
ΧΣΕΚΕΙΝΟΙΣΠΡΟΣΕΛΕΓΕΝ ΟΤΙΠΕΠΛΗΡΩ
ΤΑΙΟΟΡΟΣΤΩΝΕΤΩΝΤΗΣΕΞΟΥΣΙΑΣΤΟΥ
ΣΑΤΑΝΑ ΑΛΛΑΕΓΓΙΖΕΙΑΛΛΑΔΕΙΝΑΚΑΙΥ
ΠΕΡΩΝΕΓΩΑΜΑΡΤΗΣΑΝΤΩΝΠΑΡΕΔΟΘΗΝ
ΕΙΣΘΑΝΑΤΟΝ ΙΝΑΥΠΟΣΤΡΕΨΩΣΙΝΕΙΣΤΗΝ
ΑΛΗΘΕΙΑΝΚΑΙΜΗΚΕΤΙΑΜΑΡΤΗΣΩΣΙΝ
ΙΝΑΤΗΝΕΝΤΩΟΥΡΑΝΩΠΝΙΚΗΝ ΚΑΙΑ
ΦΘΑΡΤΟΝΤΗΣΔΙΚ ΑΙΟΣΥΝΗΣΔΟΞΑΝ
ΚΛΗΡΟΝΟΜΗΣΩΣΙΝ ΑΛΛΑΠΟΡΕΥΘΕΝ
ΤΕΣΕΙΣΤΟΝΚΟΣΜΟΝΑΠΑΝΤΑΚΗΡΥΞΑΤΕ
ΤΟΕΥΑΓΓΕΛΙΟΝΠΑΣΗΤΗΚΤΙΣΕΙ ΟΠΙΣΤΕΥ
ΣΑΣΚΑΙΒΑΠΤΙΣΘΕΙΣΣΩΘΗΣΕΤΑΙ ΟΔΕΑ
ΠΙΣΤΗΣΑΣΚΑΤΑΚΡΙΘΕΙΣ ΟΥΣΩΘΗΣΕΤΑΙ
ΣΗΜΙΑΔΕΤΟΙΣΠΙΣΤΕΥΣΑΣΙΝΤΑΥΤΑΠΑΡΑ
ΚΟΛΟΥΘΗΣΕΙΕΝΤΩΟΝΟΜΑΤΙΜΟΥ

WASHINGTON CODEX OF GOSPELS—LATE 4TH OR 5TH CENT.

(Original size, 8¼ in. × 5¾ in.)

PLATE XXI.

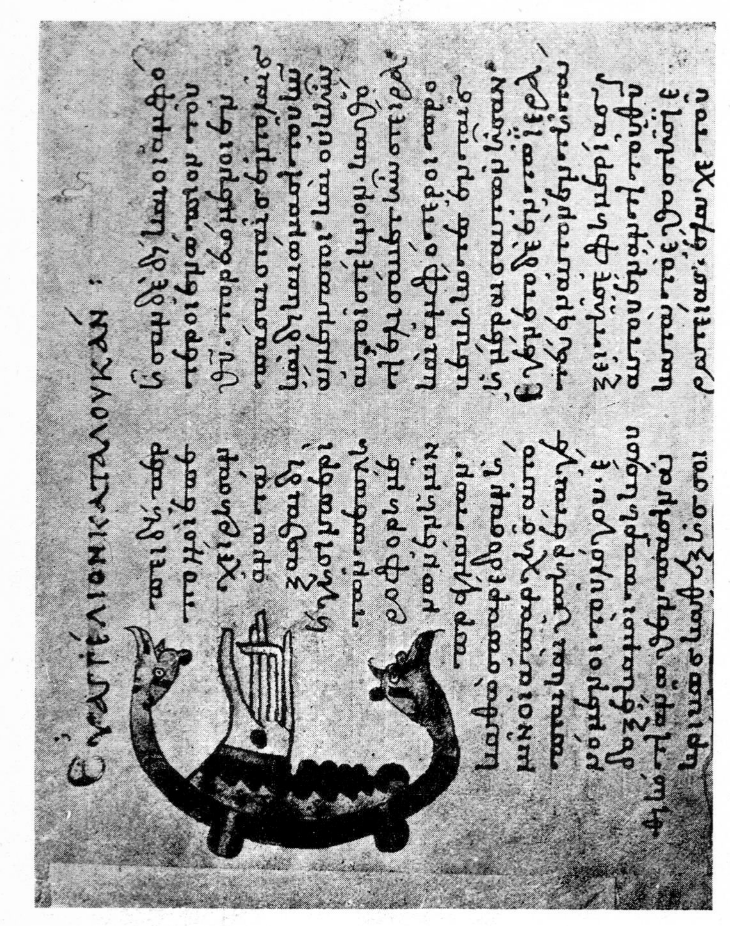

ΕΥΑΓΓΕΛΙΟΝ ΚΑΤΑ ΛΟΥΚΑΝ :

CURSIVE GREEK MS.—A.D. 1022.

(*Unreduced; full page, 8 in. × 6 in.*)

Plate XXII.

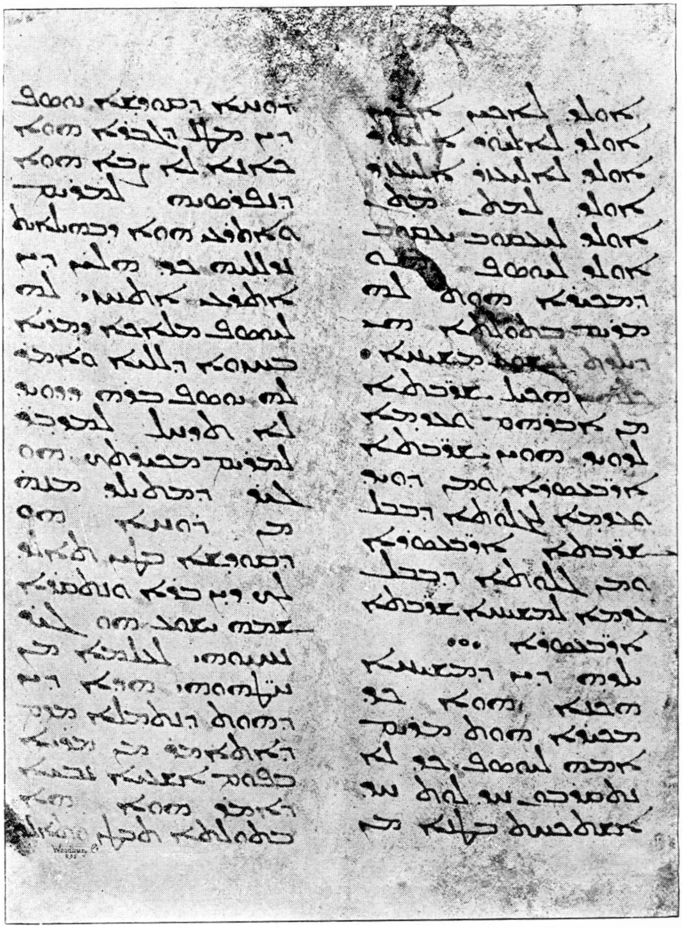

CURETONIAN SYRIAC MS.—5TH CENT.

(Original size of page, $11\frac{3}{4}$ in. × 9 in.; without margins, as here, $9\frac{1}{2}$ in. × $7\frac{1}{4}$ in.)

SAHIDIC CODEX OF ACTS—4TH CENT.

(*Original size,* $12\frac{1}{2}$ *in.* $\times$ $6\frac{1}{2}$ *in.*)

them. It is true that we only possess the Diatessaron in Arabic, but it is affirmed by competent scholars that the Arabic shows evident signs of being a very close rendering of the Syriac, and the character of the text supports this view. If the text of the Diatessaron had been altered at all, it would almost inevitably have been in the direction of assimilating it to the current text of the Gospels, as was actually done in Latin by Bishop Victor of Capua. The text of the Gospels in the Arabic Diatessaron has not, however, undergone this process of assimilation to any great extent; and it is therefore fair to accept it as at any rate an approximation to the text of Tatian. And here lies the gist of the whole discovery from the textual point of view; for the text of the Diatessaron is evidently of a distinctly Western type. There is also some kinship between it and the Old Syriac version, to be mentioned presently; but it will be better to reserve the discussion of this until that version has been described.

The Dura Fragment.

There is, however, yet another discovery, very recent in date, to be mentioned in connection with the Diatessaron. In 1920 British troops were in occupation at a place called Salihiyah on the western bank of the upper Euphrates, and there some English officers discovered the remains of a Roman fortress, on the walls of which were remains of ancient paintings. They reported their find to headquarters, and Miss Gertrude Bell, realising their importance, urged the American archæologist Professor J. H. Breasted to visit the site. The troops were, however, on the eve of being withdrawn, and Professor Breasted was only able to have a single day there. Without that one day, all interest in the site might have been lost; but Professor Breasted and his colleagues were able to realise the value of the paintings and to take notes and photographs, and subsequently, when Salihiyah had come within the area of the French mandate, detailed excavations were undertaken by Professor Franz Cumont and Professor Breasted, subsequently continued by Yale University, under the direction of Professor M. Rostovzeff. These excavations revealed that the site was that of Dura-Europos, a Roman fortified frontier city, which after various vicissitudes had been captured by the Persians in A.D. 256. Just before the final siege, the walls had been strengthened by a huge ramp on the inside, which sealed up the ruins of a quantity of buildings, including a Christian church and a Jewish synagogue; and among them was a room with a number of papyrus and vellum fragments. One of these vellum fragments, when examined at Yale in 1933, proved to contain fourteen imperfect lines of the Diatessaron in Greek. The document is necessarily earlier than

A.D. 256, and may be assigned with certainty to the first half of the third century.

This is the only extant fragment of the Diatessaron itself, as distinct from translations; and the fact that it is in Greek, although found in the extreme corner of Syria, has been used as an argument in favour of Greek being the original. This, however, cannot be pressed; for Dura was a commercial town and a military fortress, and there must have been many there, whether soldiers or civilians, who were unacquainted with Syriac. This is shown by the documents among which the fragment was found, which are commercial documents in Greek and military documents in Latin. The arguments for a Greek original are not therefore materially strengthened by this find.

The text of the fragment contains the narrative of the petition of Joseph of Arimathea for the body of Jesus, and even within these fourteen lines all four canonical Gospels are employed, while two words are grammatically altered to suit the combination of phrases from different Gospels. This shows with what caution the evidence of Tatian, even when we can ascertain it, must be used; for we have to allow for editorial rehandling as well as the combination of words from the different Gospels in an intricate mosaic. It is the belief of von Soden that Tatian's Harmony exercised a very disturbing influence on the Gospel text; and this fragment indicates that this theory (which has not been favourably received) may need examination. It is only to be hoped that future discoveries will provide more material for its determination.

(*b*) *The Old Syriac.*—It has been seen that our knowledge of the Diatessaron, apart from references to it in Church historians such as Eusebius, is the fruit of modern discoveries. The same is true of the version which ranks next in time among the Syriac authorities. A century ago its very existence was unknown. Some acute critics had indeed guessed that there must have been a version in Syriac older than that which bears the name of the Peshitta, but no portion of it was known to exist. In 1842, however, a great mass of Syriac manuscripts reached the British Museum from the library of a monastery in the Nitrian Desert in Egypt—the result of long negotiations with the monks by various travellers. Among them was the palimpsest under whose Syriac text is the copy of the Greek Gospels known as R (see p. 150), many copies of the ordinary Syriac Bible, and other precious documents. But among them also were some eighty leaves of a copy of the Gospels in Syriac which Dr. Cureton, one of the officers of the Museum, recognised as containing a completely different text from any manuscript previously known. These leaves were edited by him, with a preface in which he contended that in this version we have the very words of our Lord's discourses, in the identical language in which they were originally spoken. The manuscript itself (of which a facsimile may be seen in Plate XXII) is of the fifth century, practically contemporary with the earliest manuscripts which we possess of the Peshitta Syriac; but Cureton argued that the character of the translation showed that the original of his version (which from the name of its discoverer is often known as the Curetonian Syriac, and is so referred to in the Variorum Bible) must have been made earlier than the original of the Peshitta, and that, in fact, the Peshitta was a revision of the Old Syriac, just as the Vulgate Latin was in part a revision of the Old Latin.

On this point a hot controversy raged for some time, since scholars familiar with the Peshitta, some of whom had even been inclined to regard it as being as early as the second century, were not inclined to yield the primacy to the newcomer. This controversy, however, is now over. No one now doubts that the Curetonian MS. represents a version earlier than the Peshitta. On the one hand, as will appear shortly, the origin of the Peshitta is now almost certainly established; and, on the other, additional evidence has come to light with regard to the version represented by the Curetonian MS.

A new copy of the Old Syriac Gospels was discovered, and its text published at the very time when the first edition of this book was being written. In 1892 two enterprising Cambridge ladies, Mrs. Lewis and her sister, Mrs. Gibson, visited the Monastery of St. Catherine, on Mount Sinai, the place where Tischendorf made his celebrated discovery of the Codex Sinaiticus, and where Professor Rendel Harris had quite recently found a Syriac copy of a very early Christian work, hitherto supposed to be lost, the "Apology" of Aristides. These ladies photographed a number of manuscripts, among them a Syriac palimpsest which they had noticed as containing a Gospel text; and when they brought their photographs home, the underlying text of this palimpsest was recognised by two Cambridge Orientalists, Mr. Burkitt and Professor Bensly, as belonging to the Old Syriac version, hitherto known only in the fragments of Cureton. The palimpsest contains the greater part (about three-fourths, the rest being undecipherable) of the four Gospels. Naturally enough the announcement of the discovery aroused much interest, and another expedition was made to Sinai to copy the MS. in full, after which the half-obliterated writing had to be painfully deciphered and edited. The results are now part of the permanent stock of textual criticism.

It is clear, in the first place, that the Sinaitic MS. does not represent precisely the same text as the Curetonian. The differences between them are much more marked than, say, between any two manuscripts of the Peshitta or of the Greek Testament. One striking proof of this may be found in the first chapter of St. Matthew; for whereas the Curetonian MS. emphasises the fact of the Miraculous Conception, reading in verse 16[1] "Jacob begat Joseph, to whom was betrothed Mary the Virgin, who bare Jesus Christ" (thus avoiding even the word "husband," which occurs in the Greek), the Sinaitic MS. appears at first sight even to deny it, reading "Jacob begat Joseph, and Joseph, to whom was betrothed Mary the Virgin, begat Jesus who is called Christ." It is not surprising that some scholars were eager to claim this as the original form of the narrative, the story of the Divine Conception being (in their view) a later excrescence. It was, however, soon pointed out by Mr. Burkitt, one of the first editors of the Sinai manuscript, and eventually editor of the authoritative edition of the Old Syriac version, that the reading is not in fact unorthodox. It has long been recognised that the genealogy in St. Matthew is not the record of an actual line of descent, but rather of an official line of succession. Thus Salathiel was not the son of Jechonias, and the kings of Judah from Solomon to Jechonias, who figure in St. Matthew's genealogy, were not ancestors of Joseph. Hence there is no more reason for pressing the literal meaning of the word "begat" in the statement of the relationship between Joseph and our Lord, than there is elsewhere in the record. This explanation accounts for the fact that in other respects the language of the Sinaitic Syriac implies the Virgin Birth,[2] while the very fact of the ambiguity of the phrase accounts for the alteration introduced into the Curetonian copy. It does not necessarily follow that the Sinaitic Syriac represents the original words of the Evangelist more accurately than the Greek text; but the former can be relieved from the charge of deliberate alteration of the text with a polemical motive.

In other passages also the Sinaitic MS. shows noteworthy divergences from the Curetonian. Thus Sin. (to use its common abbreviation) omits Matt. xxiii. 14 (one of the woes pronounced against the scribes and Pharisees), while Cur. has it. Cur. had the last twelve verses of St. Mark (only a portion survives, but enough to prove that it was there), but Sin. omits them. In Luke xi. 2-4 Sin. gives a shorter version of the Lord's Prayer than Cur. In the narrative of the institution of the Lord's

[1] Plate XXII exhibits this portion of the Curetonian MS., the page containing Matt. i. 14-23.

[2] The title "Mary the Virgin" itself implies a comparatively late origin; and the phrase "before they came together," the quotation from Isaiah referring to the Virgin Birth, and the narrative of Joseph's doubts and behaviour are meaningless and unintelligible on the unorthodox interpretation.

Supper (Luke xxii.) Sin. gives the verses in the order 19, 20*a*, 17, 20*b*, 18, Cur. in the order 19, 17, 18, omitting 20, each representing a different attempt to get rid of the apparent double mention of the Cup. In Luke xxii. 43, 44, Cur. gives the episode of the Angel and the Bloody Sweat, while Sin. omits it; and similarly Sin. omits, while Cur. has, the Word from the Cross, "Father, forgive them," etc., in xxiii. 24. In John xi. 39 Sin. has a curious addition, which is found nowhere else, after "Martha . . . saith unto him," "Why are they taking away the stone?" Cur. is defective here, so it is impossible to say whether it agreed or differed.

In spite of such not unimportant differences, there is no doubt that the two MSS. represent the same version, and that one of great antiquity. Its Syriac title, "The Gospel of the Separated," is evidently given to it by contrast with Tatian's Harmony, and seems to show that it is later than the Diatessaron. This is the conclusion of Burkitt, the best authority on the subject. He would assign it to a date about A.D. 200, and believes that its original text was akin to, but not directly descended from, that found in א B, but modified by the insertion of Western readings derived from the Diatessaron. The Sinaitic represents the earlier form of the version, the Curetonian having been to some extent revised from later Greek MSS. It is probable that Old Syriac versions of other books than the Gospels originally existed, since St. Ephraem, whose date precedes the Peshitta, is known to have written commentaries on the Acts and Pauline Epistles, which implies the existence of Syriac translations. It is moreover unlikely that the Syriac Church, which appears to have possessed the Old Testament in its own language from the third century at latest, would have been content with a New Testament consisting only of the Gospels. But no trace has survived of an Old Syriac version of these books.

(*c*) *The Peshitta* (*Pesh.* in Variorum Bible).—This is the great standard version of the ancient Syriac Church, current and in general use from the fifth century onwards. Its history has only recently been elucidated by Burkitt. It was formerly supposed to have been used by St. Ephraem, who died in A.D. 373, and some scholars put it back to the third, or even the second, century. Burkitt, however, showed that this belief was unfounded, and that there was no evidence of the use of this version before the fifth century, to which the earliest extant MSS. of it belong. Now it is on record that Rabbula, Bishop of Edessa from A.D. 411-435, translated the New Testament from Greek into Syriac, and ordered a copy to be placed in every church in his diocese. It is therefore natural to conclude that the Peshitta, which is found in circulation in the generation after Rabbula, is in fact his translation, the prompt acceptance of which would be due to his authority. Rabbula is, in fact, the Jerome of the Syriac Church.

The name means "simple" or "common," but the origin of it is unknown. The Peshitta (or Peshitto, as it is often less correctly written) is known to us in a much greater number of manuscripts than the Old Syriac, the total hitherto recorded being 243. Nearly half of these, including the most ancient, formed part of the splendid collection of Syriac MSS. from the Nitrian Desert to which allusion has already been made (p. 150), and are now in the British Museum. Of some of these, containing parts of the Old Testament, we have spoken above (p. 80). Of those which contain the New Testament, two are of the fifth century (the oldest being Add. MS. 14,459, in the British Museum, containing the Gospels of St. Matthew and St. Mark), and at least a dozen more are not later than the sixth century, three of them bearing precise dates in the years 530-39, 534, and 548. The Peshitta was first printed by Widmanstadt, in 1555, from only two manuscripts, both of late date. It was re-edited by Mr. Gwilliam in 1902-20 from some forty MSS., many of them of very early date, as shown above; but so carefully were the later copies of the Peshitta made, between the fifth and twelfth centuries, that the substantial difference between these two editions is very slight.

That the foundations of the Peshitta go back to a very early date is shown by the fact that it does not contain those books of the New Testament which were the last to be generally accepted. All copies of it omit 2 Peter, 2 and 3 John, Jude, and the Apocalypse. It is a smooth, scholarly, accurate version, free and idiomatic, without being loose, and Greek texts of the Syrian family have evidently been used for it. Its relations with the Old Syriac have been discussed above. It appears to be not so much a revision of it (at any rate as it appears in the Curetonian and Sinaitic MSS.) as a later version based in part upon it, but upon other materials as well. On the whole it represents the Byzantine text in an early stage, but more ancient elements can sometimes be discerned in it.

(*d*) *The Philoxenian* or *Harkleian Syriac*.—In the year 508, Philoxenus, Bishop of Mabug, in Eastern Syria, thinking the current Peshitta version did not represent the original Greek accurately enough, caused it to be revised throughout by one Polycarp; and in A.D. 616 this version was itself revised, with the assistance of some Greek manuscripts in Alexandria, by Thomas of Harkel, himself also subsequently Bishop of Mabug. This version had practically escaped notice until 1730, when four copies of it were sent from the East to Dr. Ridley, of New College, Oxford, from which, after his death, an edition was printed by

Professor J. White in 1778-1803. It is now known to us in many more manuscripts, a total of about fifty (all in the Harkleian revision) being recorded. A large proportion of these are in England. The best is said to be one in the Cambridge University Library, written in 1170, but a copy of the seventh century and another of the eighth century exist at Rome, another at Florence bears the date A.D. 757, and there are two of the tenth century in the British Museum.

The original Philoxenian version was written in idiomatic Syriac, but of this only the four minor Catholic Epistles were known, these having been adopted into the Syriac New Testament after being omitted in the Peshitto. They were edited by Pococke in 1630. A copy of the Apocalypse in this version was, however, discovered in a MS. in the John Rylands Library at Manchester by Dr. Gwynn of Dublin, and published in 1897. The Harkleian revision was of a totally different character, being literal in the extreme, and made from MSS. of a Western type. It is therefore of some use as evidence of Western readings.

(*e*) *The Palestinian Syriac.*—There is yet another version of the New Testament in Syriac, known to us only in fragments, in a different dialect of Syriac from all the other versions. It is believed to have been made at Antioch in the sixth century, and to have been used exclusively in Palestine. It was originally discovered at the end of the eighteenth century by Adler in a Lectionary (containing lessons from the Gospels only) in the Vatican Library, and was fully edited by Erizzo in 1861-64 and by Lagarde in 1892. Since then fragments of the Gospels and Acts have come to light in the British Museum and at Leningrad; fragments of the Pauline Epistles in the Bodleian and at Mount Sinai; and two additional Lectionaries were found at the latter place by Mrs. Lewis, and edited by her. The text of this version is mixed.

This closes the list of Syriac Versions,[1] which rank among the oldest and most interesting of all translations of the New Testament. From Syria and Mesopotamia we pass now to the neighbouring country of Egypt.

II. *Egyptian Versions.*

The history of the Coptic language, as it existed in Egypt at the time when the Christian Scriptures were translated in that country, has been told in a previous chapter (p. 81). There can be no doubt that Christianity spread into Egypt at a very early

[1] Another Syriac version is sometimes enumerated, styled the *Karkaphensian*; but this is not a continuous version at all, but a collection of passages on which annotations are made dealing with questions of spelling and pronunciation. It is like the Massorah on the Hebrew Old Testament, and probably derives its name from the monastery in which it was compiled.

date. Alexandria, then the headquarters of Greek literature, possessed a large colony of Jews, by and for whom the Septuagint version of the Hebrew Scriptures had been made; and religious thought and philosophy flourished among them. Apollos, the disciple of St. Paul, was a Jew of Alexandria; and the intercourse of Alexandria with Palestine, with Syria, and with Asia Minor made it inevitable that the new religion should spread thither soon after it had overleapt the boundaries of Palestine itself. At what precise date the New Testament books were translated into the native language of Egypt we cannot tell. Some time would elapse before the faith spread from the Greek-speaking population to the Coptic natives; some time more before oral teaching was superseded by written books. But by or soon after the end of the second century it is probable that the first Coptic versions had been made. Our knowledge of these versions is, for the most part, of quite recent growth, and is growing still through the discovery of manuscripts in Egypt. Different dialects were spoken in different parts of the country, and each of these came in course of time to have its own version of the Scriptures. Until recently only two of these versions were known; we are now acquainted, more or less, with five, but whether each of them possessed a complete Bible of its own is quite uncertain.

(*a*) *The Memphitic* or *Bohairic Version* (*Memph.* in Variorum Bible) was the version current in Lower (*i.e.*, Northern) Egypt, of which the principal native town was Memphis. Originally, however, the dialect in which it is written belonged only to the coast district near Alexandria, and another dialect was in use in Memphis itself; hence it is better to avoid the term Memphitic, and use the more strictly accurate name *Bohairic* (from Bohaïrah, the Arabic name of Lower Egypt). This was the most developed and most literary dialect of the Egyptian language, and ultimately spread up the country and superseded all the other dialects. The consequence of this is that the Bohairic is the Coptic of to-day, so far as the language still exists, and that in the Bohairic dialect alone was the complete New Testament known before the discoveries of the last generation. All the other Coptic versions existed in fragments only.

The Bohairic version was first made known by some Oxford scholars at the end of the seventeenth century, and the first printed edition of it was published at Oxford by Wilkins in 1716. Neither in this nor in any subsequent edition was sufficient use made of the manuscripts available for comparison, until the production by the Rev. G. Horner of a full critical edition in 1898-1905. Over a hundred manuscripts exist and have been examined, and of these Horner used forty-six in the Gospels and thirty-four in the other books. None of them is very early.

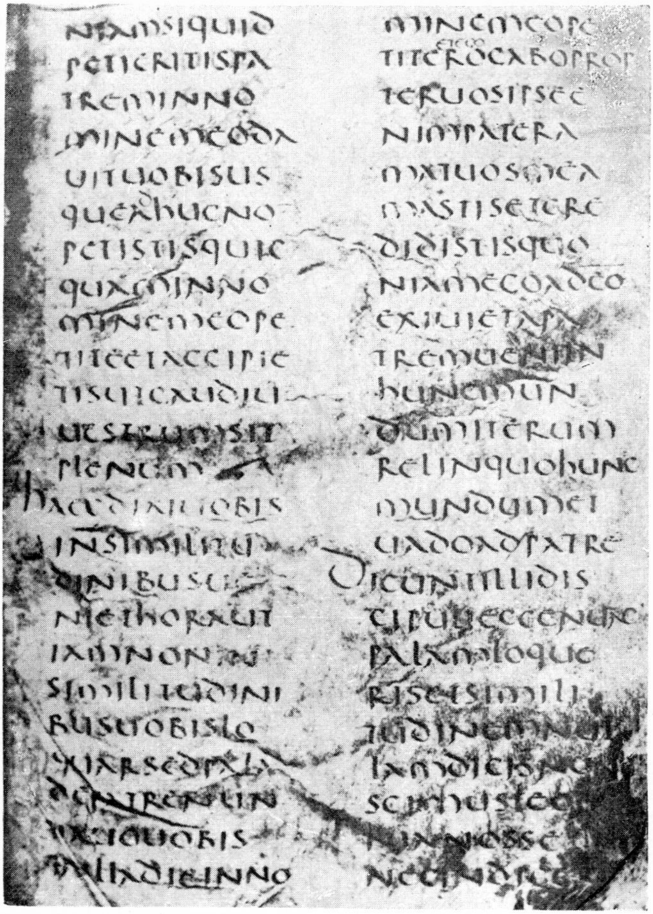

Plate XXIV.

CODEX VERCELLENSIS—4TH CENT.

(*Original size of page,* $9\frac{1}{2}$ *in.* × $6\frac{1}{2}$ *in.; without margins, as here,* $7\frac{1}{4}$ *in.* × $4\frac{1}{4}$ *in.*)

PLATE XXV.

quod est hoc uerbum
quia in potestate et uirtute
imperat spiritibus
inmundis et exeunt
et diuulgabatur fama de illo
in omnem locum regionis
XIII Surgens autem de synagoga
introiuit in domum simonis
socrus autem simonis
tenebatur magnis febrib(us)
et rogauerunt illum pro ea
et stans super illam impera
uit febri et dimisit illam
et continuo surgens
ministrabat illis
Cum sol autem occidisset
omnes qui habebant infir
mos uariis languoribus
ducebant illos ad eum
at ille singulis manus impo
nens curabat eos
Exiebant etiam daemonia
a multis clamantia et di
centia quia tu es filius di
et increpans non sinebat
ea loqui

et uidit duas naues stantes
secus stagnum
piscatores autem discende
rant et lauabant retia
ascendens autem in unam
nauem quae erat
simonis
rogauit autem a terra
reducere pusillum
et sedens docebat
de nauicula turbas
Ut cessauit autem loqui
dixit ad simonem
duc in altum et laxate retia
uestra in capturam
et respondens simon
dixit illi
praeceptor per totam
noctem laborantes
nihil cepimus
in uerbo autem tuo
laxabo rete
et cum hoc fecissent
concluserunt piscium
multitudinem copiosam
rumpebatur autem rete eorum

CODEX AMIATINUS—*circ.* A.D. 715.

(*Original size of page*, 19½ *in.* × 13½ *in.* ; *of part reproduced*, 8½ *in.* × 10½ *in.*)

The oldest and best is a MS. of the Gospels at Oxford, which is dated A.D. 1173-4; there is one at Paris dated in 1178-80; there is another, in the British Museum, of the year 1192; others are of the thirteenth and later centuries. There is indeed a single leaf of the Epistle to the Ephesians which may be as early as the fifth century (in the British Museum), but this exception is too small to be important. The Apocalypse was not originally included in this version, and we know that in the third century its authenticity was questioned in Egypt. The translation is generally good and careful, so that it is easy to see what was the Greek which the translator had before him in any particular passage. The text, too, is of an excellent type. Excluding passages which appear only in the later MSS., and which evidently were not in the original version, the Bohairic text is mainly of a Neutral or Alexandrian type, with not much mixture of Western readings, and little or nothing of Syrian. The doubt about the last twelve verses of St. Mark appears in the best MS., which gives the shorter alternative ending (as in L, see p. 150) in the margin. Otherwise all the Bohairic MSS. have the usual verses 9-20. The passage John vii. 53—viii. 11 is omitted by all the best MSS. In Acts also the Bohairic text is definitely Alexandrian. The date of the version is probably in the first half of the third century.

(*b*) *The Thebaic* or *Sahidic Version* (from Es-sa'id, the Arabic name of Upper Egypt) (*Theb.* in Variorum Bible).—Again, Thebaic is the older name, Sahidic the more accurate and the one now in general use. This is the version which was current in Upper (*i.e.* Southern) Egypt, of which the chief town was Thebes. Its existence was not noticed until the end of the eighteenth century, and the first printed edition of a few fragments of it was that of Woide, published at Oxford, after his death, in 1799. Since that date our knowledge of the Sahidic version has enormously increased. It exists only in fragments, but these fragments are now very numerous indeed, so that it has been possible for Mr. Horner to put together a practically complete Sahidic New Testament, with, at any rate in the Gospels, not less than three witnesses for almost every passage. Many of the fragments are of very early date, going back to the fifth, and even to the fourth, century. The British Museum acquired in 1911 a copy of Acts (with Deuteronomy and Jonah) which can be securely dated to the first half of the fourth century; and the British and Foreign Bible Society has a copy of St. John's Gospel, probably of the second half of the same century, discovered by Mr. J. L. Starkey when working for one of Sir Flinders Petrie's expeditions in 1923. The Sahidic version is probably somewhat earlier than the Bohairic, but there need not be much interval between them. It was formerly supposed that it leant rather to the Western type of text, but fuller knowledge has shown that, while it contains some readings which are also found in Western MSS., it is fundamentally and preponderantly of the same family as ℵ B. In Acts less than one-eighth of the characteristically "Western" readings have Sahidic support.

The specimen shown in Plate XXIII is taken from the MS. of Acts mentioned above, which is the oldest substantial MS. of the Sahidic version. It is a papyrus codex, and a note at the end is written in a common non-literary hand of about the middle of the fourth century. The MS. itself, therefore, is not later than that date. The page reproduced contains Acts viii. 34–ix. 3. Verse 37 (the eunuch's declaration of faith) is omitted, as it is by ℵ A B C, etc.

The remaining Coptic versions may be dismissed very briefly. They have only recently been discovered, they are known as yet only in a few fragments, and their characteristics cannot yet be said to be established. Hence they have not yet made their appearance in critical editions of the New Testament, and may for the present be disregarded. They are (*c*) the *Fayumic*, or version current in the district of the Fayum, west of the Nile and south of the Delta, from which an enormous number of Greek and Coptic papyri have reached Europe in recent years. It appears to be related to the Sahidic, being probably descended from an early form of the same version. (*d*) The *Middle Egyptian*, found in manuscripts from the region of Memphis, related, like the Fayumic, to the Sahidic. (*e*) The *Akhmimic*, found in a number of fragments from the neighbourhood of Akhmim, the ancient Panopolis, from which also came the manuscript containing the extraordinarily interesting portions of the apocryphal Gospel and Revelation of Peter which were published in 1892. This is said to be the earliest dialect of the Coptic language, but at present only a few small fragments of the New Testament have been published, the first to appear being the discovery of Mr. W. E. Crum. It is as certain as such speculations can be that our knowledge of the Egyptian versions will be very greatly increased within the next few years, but whether any of them will be found to have a text to any material extent independent of the Sahidic is at present doubtful.

The remaining Oriental versions of the New Testament may be dismissed with a very short notice. Their evidence may sometimes be called into court, but it is seldom of much importance.

The *Armenian* version, as we have it now, dates from the fifth century. Up to about the year 390 Armenia, the country to the east of Asia Minor and north of Mesopotamia, lying between the Roman and Persian empires, possessed no version of its own; but between that date and A.D. 400 translations of both Old and New Testaments were made, partly from Greek and partly from Syriac. This version shows a marked affinity with the Old Syriac in the Gospels. About the year 433 these translations were revised with the help of Greek manuscripts brought from Constantinople, presumably of the Byzantine type. The result was the existing Armenian version, which consequently has, as might be expected, a very mixed kind of text. One very interesting piece of evidence has, however, been preserved in an Armenian manuscript. Most of the oldest MSS. of the Gospels in this version omit the last twelve verses of St. Mark; but one of them, written in the year 989, contains them, with a heading stating that they are " of the Elder Ariston."[1] This has been taken to mean Aristion, who lived in the first century, and is mentioned by Papias, his younger contemporary, as having been a disciple of the Lord. If the tradition which assigns to him the authorship of Mark xvi. 9-20 could be accepted, it would clear up the doubts surrounding that passage in a satisfactory way. It would show that St. Mark's Gospel was left unfinished, or was mutilated at a very early date, and that a summary of the events following the Resurrection, written by Aristion, was inserted to fill the gap; and we gain the evidence of another witness of our Lord's life on earth. There is, however, no confirmation of this story. The earliest MS. of the Armenian Gospels is dated in the year 887; there are probably two others of the ninth century and six of the tenth. The rest of the New Testament is only found in copies containing the whole Bible, which are rare and never older than the twelfth century.

The *Georgian* version deserves brief mention here, since modern scholars (principally F. C. Conybeare in England and R. P. Blake in America) have shown that it was made from an Armenian text older and better than any extant Armenian MS.; and Blake concludes that the Greek text on which it is ultimately based was of the Cæsarean type. It is therefore a useful witness for the reconstitution of the Cæsarean text.

The *Gothic* version, as has already been stated (p. 83), was made for the Goths in the fourth century, while they were settled in Mœsia, before they overran Western Europe. It was made by their Bishop Ulfilas, and was translated directly from the Greek. We know it now only in fragments, more than half of the Gospels being preserved in a magnificent manuscript at Upsala, in Sweden,

[1] The credit of this discovery belongs to Mr. F. C. Conybeare, of University College, Oxford.

written (in the fifth or sixth century) in letters of gold and silver upon purple vellum. Some portions of the Epistles of St. Paul are preserved in palimpsest fragments at Milan; but the Acts, Catholic Epistles, and Apocalypse are entirely lost. The Greek text used by Ulfilas seems to have been of the Syrian type in the New Testament, just as it was of Syrian (Lucianic) type in the Old.

The *Ethiopic* version belongs to the country of Abyssinia, and was probably made about the year 600; but most of the existing manuscripts (of which there are over a hundred) are as late as the seventeenth century, only a few going back as early as the fifteenth, the oldest of all (at Paris) being of the thirteenth century. Little is known about the character of the text, as it has never been critically edited.

Several *Arabic* versions are known to exist, some being translations from the Greek, some from Syriac, and some from Coptic, while others are revisions based upon some or all of these. None is earlier than the seventh century, perhaps none so early; and for critical purposes none is of any value.

Other Oriental versions (Slavonic, Persian) are of still later date, and may be ignored.

§ 2.—The Western Versions.

We now pass to the Western world, and trace the history of the New Testament as it spread from its obscure home in Palestine to the great capital of the world, and to the countries in its neighbourhood which owned its sway and spoke its language. In speaking of the Latin Bible we are at once taking a great step nearer home; for Latin was the literary language of our own forefathers, it was in Latin that the Bible first reached our land, and the Latin Bible was for centuries the official Bible of our country. Nay, more, it was from the Latin Bible that the first English Bibles were translated. Therefore we have a special interest in the history of this version, an interest which is still further increased by the remarkable character which it possessed in its earlier stages, and by the minuteness with which we are able to trace its fortunes in later days. We have already described the Latin versions in relation to the Old Testament; we have now to speak of them in relation to the New.

In the Old Testament we have seen that there are two Latin versions, known as the Old Latin and the Vulgate; and we have seen that of these the Vulgate is the more important as an aid to the recovery of the original Hebrew text, because it was translated directly from the Hebrew, while the Old Latin was translated from the Septuagint; and also because the Vulgate is complete, while the Old Latin has come down to us only in fragments. In respect of the New Testament the relative importance of the two is somewhat different. Here we possess both versions practically complete: and whereas the Old Latin was translated direct from the original Greek, the Vulgate was only a revision of the Old Latin. Moreover, we possess a few manuscripts of the original Greek which are as early as the Vulgate; but the Old Latin was made long before all but a few of our manuscripts were written, and takes us back to within a generation or two of the time at which the sacred books were themselves composed.

The *Old Latin Version* is consequently one of the most valuable and interesting evidences which we possess for the condition of the New Testament text in the earliest times. It exists, however, in a variety of forms, and its precise history is obscure. The conclusions at which Hort arrived were as follows. It has already been said (p. 84) that it was originally made in the second century, perhaps not very far from A.D. 150, and probably, though not certainly, in Africa. Another version, apparently independent, subsequently appeared in Europe; and the divergences between these rival translations, as well as the extensive variations of text which found their way into both, made a revision necessary, which was actually produced in Italy in the fourth century, and to which Augustine refers as superior to its competitors. Hence it is that three different families or groups can be traced—the *African*, the *European*, and the *Italian*. We are able to identify these several families by means of the quotations which occur in the writings of the Latin Fathers. Thus the quotations of Cyprian, who died in 258, give us a representation of the African text; the European text is found in the Latin version of the works of Irenæus, which was probably made at the end of the second century, or very shortly afterwards; while the Italian text appears conspicuously in Augustine (A.D. 354-430). By the help of such evidence as this we can identify the texts which are found in the various manuscripts of the Old Latin which have come down to us.

This distinction into three families, though accepted by Wordsworth and White, the editors of the Vulgate, has not been universally approved. Bentley in the past and Burkitt in our own day disputed the existence of the Italian revision, the latter arguing with much force that Augustine's "Italian" text was in fact Jerome's Vulgate, which he certainly used in his longer quotations (such as could not be made from memory) in the latter part of his life. What is certain is that a distinction can be drawn between an extremer and a less extreme form of the Old Latin, and that the former is found in authorities connected with Africa (such as the manuscript mentioned below as *k*, and the quotations in Cyprian), and the latter in authorities connected with

Europe (such as *a* and *b*). But the manuscripts differ very much among themselves (as Jerome complained), and probably no coherent history can be made of them.

Owing to the fact that the Vulgate eventually superseded the Old Latin as the Bible of the Western Church, manuscripts of the latter are scarce, but when they exist are generally very old. No copy contains the whole of the New Testament, and very few are perfect even in the books which they contain. Thirty-eight manuscripts of the Old Latin exist; of these, twenty-eight contain the Gospels, four the Acts, five the Catholic Epistles, eight the Pauline Epistles, and three the Apocalypse, of which a practically complete text is also preserved to us in the commentary of Primasius, an African Father of the sixth century. Manuscripts of the Old Latin are indicated in critical editions by the small italic letters of the alphabet. One of the oldest and best is the Codex Vercellensis (*a*), of which a facsimile is given in Plate XXIV. It contains the four Gospels, in the order usual in the Western Church—namely, Matthew, John, Luke, Mark. It is written in silver letters, in very narrow columns, on extremely thin vellum stained with purple. The passage shown in the Plate is John xvi. 23-30. In verse 26 this MS. has a curious reading, due to an accidental omission of words: instead of " Ye shall ask in my name; and I say not unto you that I will pray the Father for you," it has " ask in my name, and I will pray for you." The passage may be seen at the top of the second column: " in nomine meo petite et ego rogabo propter vos," the words " et ego " being added above the line. This manuscript was written in the fourth century, and is consequently as old as the oldest Greek uncials of the Bible. It is now at Vercelli in Italy.

Other important MSS. of the Old Latin are, for the Gospels, the Codex Veronensis (*b*), of the fourth or fifth century, one of the most valuable of all; Codex Colbertinus (*c*), an extraordinarily late copy, having been written in the twelfth century, in Languedoc, where the tradition of the Old Latin text lingered very late, but containing a good text; Codex Palatinus (*e*), fourth or fifth century, very incomplete, containing a distinctly African type of text; Codex Brixianus (*f*), sixth century, with an Italian text; Codex Bobiensis (*k*), fifth or sixth century, containing the last half of Mark and the first half of Matthew in a very early form of the African text; the Latin text of the Codex Bezæ (*d*), for which see p. 144. In the Acts, there are Codex Bezæ (*d*), as before; the Latin text of the Codex Laudianus (*e*), see p. 148; Codex Gigas (*g*), of the thirteenth century, the largest manuscript in the world, containing the Acts and Apocalypse in the Old Latin version, the rest in the Vulgate; and some palimpsest fragments (*h* and *s*) of the fifth or sixth century. The Catholic

Epistles are very imperfectly represented, being contained only in the CODEX CORBEIENSIS, of St. James (*ff*), of the tenth century, and portions of the other epistles in other fragmentary MSS. The Pauline Epistles are known in the Latin version of the CODEX CLAROMONTANUS (d_2), for which see p. 148; *e*, *f*, *g* are similarly Latin versions of other bilingual manuscripts; and the remaining authorities are fragments. The Apocalypse exists only in *m* of the Gospels and *g* and *h* of the Acts. It must be remembered, however, that these MSS. are supplemented by the quotations in Latin Fathers, which are very numerous, and which show what sort of text each of them had before him when he wrote.

It may be interesting to mention which manuscripts represent the various families of the Old Latin text. The African text is found in *k* and (in a somewhat later form) *e* of the Gospels, *h* of the Acts and Apocalypse, in Primasius on the Apocalypse, and in Cyprian generally. The Italian text, which is the latest of the three, appears in *f* and *q* of the Gospels, *q* of the Catholic Epistles, *r* of the Pauline Epistles, and in Augustine. The remaining MSS. have, on the whole, European texts (*b* being an especially good example), but many of them are mixed and indeterminate in character, and some have been modified by the incorporation of readings from the Vulgate.

It has been said above (p. 111) that the Old Latin version testifies to a type of Greek text of the class which has been described as "Western." This applies especially to the African group of the Old Latin, which is often found in alliance with Codex Bezæ. The European MSS. have less strongly marked divergences from the ordinary text, and may perhaps have been affected by comparison with Greek MSS. The earlier forms of the Old Latin, however, are distinctly Western, as has been shown in describing the peculiar readings of this class of text; and since the original translation into Latin was made in the second century, and perhaps early in that century, it shows how soon considerable corruptions had been introduced into the text of the New Testament. It is, indeed, especially in the earliest period of the history of the text that such interpolations as those we have mentioned can be introduced. At that time the books of the New Testament had not come to be regarded as on a level with those of the Old. They were precious as a narrative of all-important facts; but there was no sense of obligation to keep their language free from all change, and additions or alterations might be made without much scruple. Hence arose the class of manuscripts of which the Old Latin version is one of the most important representatives.

The Vulgate.—The history of this version has already been narrated in connection with the Old Testament. It was in the year 382 that Pope Damasus entrusted Jerome with the task of producing an authoritative revision of the Latin Bible which should supersede the innumerable conflicting copies then in existence. A settled version of the Gospels was naturally regarded as the prime need, and this was the first part of the work to be undertaken. Jerome began cautiously. A wholly new version of the familiar text would have provoked much opposition, and Jerome consequently contented himself, as Damasus had intended, with merely revising the existing Old Latin translation. He compared it with some ancient Greek manuscripts, and only made alterations where they were absolutely necessary to secure the true sense of a passage. Minor corrections, though in themselves certain, he refrained from introducing, in order that the total change might be as little as possible. The Gospels were completed in 384, and the rest of the New Testament, revised after the same manner, but still more slightly, appeared later (the exact date is not known). The Old Testament, which, as we have seen, was an altogether new translation from the Hebrew, was not finished until twenty years after this date.

The New Testament was consequently a distinct work from the Old, and was made on a different principle. It was based on the "Italian" type of the Old Latin, from which it differs less than the Italian differs from the primitive "African" text. The revision which produced the Italian text consisted largely, as we have seen, in the introduction of Syrian readings into a text which was mainly Western in character. Jerome's revision, which was based on MSS. of a "Neutral" (or, as it seems preferable to call it, Alexandrian) character, removed many of the Syrian interpolations, but still left the Vulgate a mixed text. Its evidence is, consequently, of less value than that of the earlier versions; but it must be remembered that all the authorities used by Jerome in the production of the Vulgate must have been as old as, or older than, the oldest manuscripts which we now possess.

Manuscripts of the Vulgate are countless. There is no great library in Western Europe which does not possess them by scores and by hundreds. After existing side by side with the Old Latin version for some centuries it became universally adopted as the Bible of Western Christendom, and was copied repeatedly in every monastery and school until the invention of printing. Hence when we come now to try to recover the original text of the Vulgate, we are confronted with a task at least as hard as that of recovering the original text of the Greek Bible itself. It is believed that over 8,000 manuscripts exist in Europe, and the majority of these have never been fully examined.[1] It is only

[1] Dr. Gregory (1909) gives a list amounting to 2,472, but his enumeration does not pretend to be anything like exhaustive.

PLATE XXVI.

THE LINDISFARNE GOSPELS—*circ.* A.D. 690.

(*Original size*, $13\frac{1}{2}$ *in.* × 10 *in.*)

PLATE XXVII.

credimus caritati qua habet ds in nob
Ds caritas e et qui manet in caritate in do manet et ds
in eo. Jn hoc pfecta e caritas nobiscum ut fiducia habea
mus in die iudicii. Quia sicut ille e et nos sumus in hoc
mundo. timor non e in caritate sed perfecta caritas
foras mittit timore qnm timor poena habet qui aute
timet non e pfectus in caritate. Nos ergo diligamus
dm qnm ds prior dilexit nos. Si quis dixerit qnm di
ligo dm et fratre suu oderit mendax e. Qui aut non
diligit fratre suu que uidet. dm que non uidet quomo
do potest diligere. et hoc mandatu a do habemus ut
qui diligit dm diligat et fratrem suum.
Omnis qui credit qnm ihs e xps ex do natus e. et omnis
qui diligit eu qui genuit. diligit et eu qui natus e ex do
Jn hoc cognouimus qnm diligimus natos di cu dm dili
gamus et mandata eius faciamus. haec e eni caritas
di ut mandata eius custodiamus. et mandata eius
grauia non sunt qnm omne quod natu e ex do uincit
mundu et haec e uictoria quae uincit mundu fides
nra. quis e qui uincit mundu nisi qui credit qnm ihs e
filius di. hic e qui uenit per aqua et sanguine ihs
xps. non in aqua solu sed in aqua et sanguine. et sps
est qui testificatur qnm xps e ueritas. qnm tres sunt
qui testimoniu dant. sps aqua et sanguis. et tres unu sunt
Si testimoniu hominu accipimus testimoniu di maius
est. qnm hoc e testimoniu di quod maius e quia testi
ficatus e de filio suo. Qui credit in filio di habet tes
timoniu di in se. qui non credit filio mendacem facit
eu in qnm non credit in testimonio quod testificatus e
ds de filio suo. et hoc testimoniu e qm uita aeterna.

ALCUIN'S VULGATE—9TH CENT.

(*Original size of page*, 20 *in.* × 14½ *in.*; *of part reproduced*, 8½ *in.* × 5 *in.*)

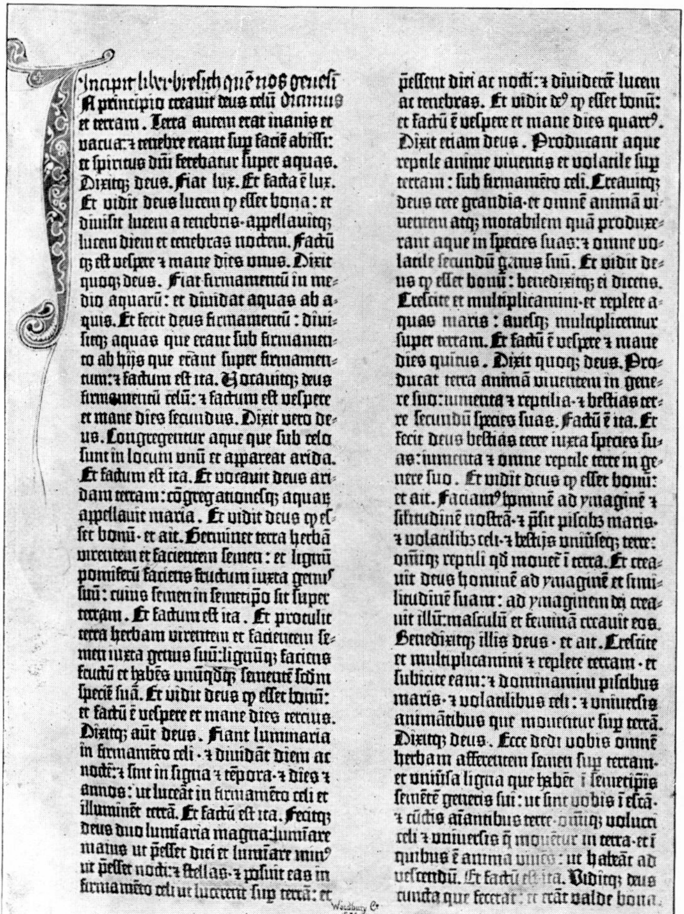

PLATE XXVIII.

Incipit liber bresith quē nos genesī
In principio creauit deus celū dicimus
et terram. Terra autem erat inanis et
vacua: ⁊ tenebre erant sup faciē abissi:
et spiritus dñi ferebatur super aquas.
Dixitq; deus. Fiat lux. Et facta ē lux.
Et vidit deus lucem q̄ esset bona: et
diuisit lucem a tenebris. appellauitq;
lucem diem et tenebras noctem. Factū
q; est vespere ⁊ mane dies unus. Dixit
quoq; deus. Fiat firmamentū in me-
dio aquarū: et diuidat aquas ab a-
quis. Et fecit deus firmamentū: diui-
sitq; aquas que erant sub firmamen-
to ab hijs que erant super firmamen-
tum: ⁊ factum est ita. Vocauitq; deus
firmamentū celū: ⁊ factum est vespere
et mane dies secundus. Dixit vero deus. Congregentur aque que sub celo
sunt in locum unū et appareat arida.
Et factum est ita. Et vocauit deus ari-
dam terram: cōgregacionesq; aquaȝ
appellauit maria. Et vidit deus q̄ esset bonū. et ait. Germinet terra herbā
virentem et facientem semen: et lignū
pomiferū faciens fructum iuxta genus
suū: cuius semen in semetipō sit super
terram. Et factum est ita. Et protulit
terra herbam virentem et facientem semen iuxta genus suū: lignūq; faciens
fructū et habēs unūqdq; sementē sc̄dm
speciē suā. Et vidit deus q̄ esset bonū:
et factū ē vespere et mane dies tercius.
Dixitq; aūt deus. Fiant luminaria
in firmamēto celi. ⁊ diuidāt diem ac
noctē: ⁊ sint in signa ⁊ tēpora. ⁊ dies ⁊
annos: ut luceāt in firmamēto celi et
illuminēt terrā. Et factū est ita. Fecitq;
deus duo luminaria magna: luminare
maius ut p̄eesset diei et luminare min9
ut p̄eesset nocti: ⁊ stellas. ⁊ posuit eas in
firmamēto celi ut lucerent sup terrā: et

p̄eessent diei ac nocti: ⁊ diuiderēt lucem
ac tenebras. Et vidit de9 q̄ esset bonū:
et factū ē vespere et mane dies quart9.
Dixit etiam deus. Producant aque
reptile anime viuentis et volatile sup
terram: sub firmamēto celi. Creauitq;
deus cete grandia. et omnē animā viuentem atq; motabilem quā produxe-
rant aque in species suas: ⁊ omne volatile secundū genus suū. Et vidit deus q̄ esset bonū: benedixitq; ei dicens.
Crescite et multiplicamini. et replete a-
quas maris: avesq; multiplicentur
super terram. Et factū ē vespere ⁊ mane
dies quintus. Dixit quoq; deus. Pro-
ducat terra animā viuentem in gene-
re suo: iumenta ⁊ reptilia. ⁊ bestias terre secundū species suas. Factū ē ita. Et
fecit deus bestias terre iuxta species suas: iumenta ⁊ omne reptile terre in ge-
nere suo. Et vidit deus q̄ esset bonū:
et ait. Faciam9 hominē ad ymaginē ⁊
similitudinē nostrā. ⁊ p̄sit piscib3 maris.
⁊ volatilib3 celi. ⁊ bestijs uniūseq; terre:
omniq; reptili qđ mouet̄ i terra. Et creauit deus hominē ad ymaginē et similitudinē suam: ad ymaginem dei creauit illū: masculū et feminā creauit eos.
Benedixitq; illis deus. et ait. Crescite
et multiplicamini ⁊ replete terram. et
subicite eam: ⁊ dominamini piscibus
maris. ⁊ volatilibus celi: ⁊ uniuersis
animātibus que mouentur sup terrā.
Dixitq; deus. Ecce dedi vobis omnē
herbam afferentem semen sup terram.
et uniūsa ligna que habēt i semetipis
sementē generis sui: ut sint vobis i escā.
⁊ cūctis aīantibus terre. omniq; volucri
celi ⁊ uniuersis q̄ mouentur in terra. et i
quibus ē anima viuēs: ut habeāt ad
vescendū. Et factū est ita. Viditq; deus
cuncta que fecerat: et erāt valde bona.

THE MAZARIN BIBLE—A.D. 1456.

(Original size, 15 in. × 11 in.)

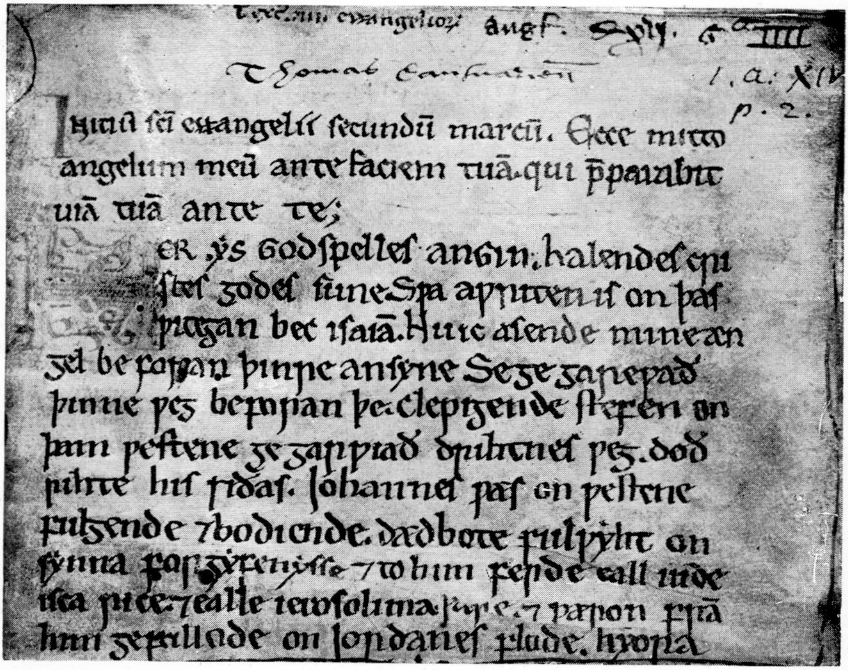

PLATE XXIX.

ENGLISH GOSPELS OF THE TENTH CENTURY—12TH CENT.

(*Original size of page*, $8\frac{1}{4}$ *in.* × $5\frac{3}{4}$ *in.* ; *of part reproduced*, $4\frac{1}{4}$ *in.* × 5 *in.*)

known that the text has been very considerably corrupted, partly by intermixture with the Old Latin version during the time when both translations were simultaneously in use, partly by the natural accidents attending the text of any book which has been repeatedly copied. We shall see in the next chapter what attempts were made to correct it during the Middle Ages. In modern times no complete critical edition has yet been produced. Our great English scholar Richard Bentley examined and caused to be examined a considerable number of manuscripts, but never advanced so far as to form a revised text of any part of the Bible. At last, about 1877, the work was undertaken at Oxford, being planned by John Wordsworth, with whom, on his appointment to be Bishop of Salisbury in 1885, was associated H. J. White, afterwards Dean of Christ Church. The Gospels appeared in 1889-98, and Acts in 1905. Bishop Wordsworth died in 1911, but White carried on the work as far as Ephesians before his death in 1934. Philippians, Colossians and Thessalonians have since appeared (1937) under the editorship of the Rev. H. F. D. Sparks, and it is hoped that the completion of the New Testament is in sight. Meanwhile very serviceable pocket editions have been produced by White (1911) and Nestle (1906; twelfth edition, 1937), the former giving the revised text of the large Oxford edition and the latter the official Clementine text, both with brief critical apparatus.

The best manuscript of the Vulgate is the Codex Amiatinus, of which a reduced facsimile, showing the lower half of the page, is given in Plate XXV. This has a special interest for Englishmen, apart from the value of the text contained in it, as having been produced in England at the beginning of the eighth century. Its English origin was only discovered about fifty years ago, and in a curious way. On its second page is an inscription stating that it was presented to the abbey of Monte Amiata by Peter of Lombardy, and it was always supposed to have been written in Italy. But Peter's name was obviously written over an erasure, and, besides, spoilt the metre of the verses in which the inscription is composed. Still, the truth was never suspected until a brilliant conjecture by the Italian G. B. de Rossi, confirmed by a further discovery by Professor Hort, showed that the original name was not Peter of Lombardy, but Ceolfrid of England. Then the whole history of the MS. was made clear. It was written either at Wearmouth or at Jarrow, famous schools in the north of England in the seventh and eighth centuries (having probably been copied from MSS. brought from Italy by Ceolfrid), and was taken by Abbot Ceolfrid as a present to Pope Gregory II in the year 716. It was used in the revision of the Vulgate by Pope Sixtus V in 1585-90, and its present home is in the great Laurentian Library at Florence. It is a huge volume, each leaf measuring 19½ by 13½ inches, written in large and beautifully clear letters. The passage shown in the Plate is Luke iv. 32–v. 6. An example of a correction may be seen in column 2, thirteen lines from the bottom, where the singular imperative *laxa* has been altered by a corrector to the plural *laxate*, which corresponds more exactly with the original Greek. The text is carefully and accurately written, and it is taken by Wordsworth and White as their first and most important authority.

An interesting addition has lately been made to its history. It is recorded by Bede that Ceolfrid had two other copies of the Bible made, besides that which he took as a gift to the Pope. In 1909 a single leaf, in writing closely resembling that of the Amiatinus, was discovered by the Rev. W. Greenwell in a curiosity shop in Newcastle, and within this last year eleven more leaves, which had been utilised to form the covers of estate accounts in the north of England, were (largely through the agency of Viscount Wakefield and the Friends of the National Libraries) secured for the nation. All twelve leaves, which include parts of 1 and 2 Kings, and unquestionably form part of one of the sister codices of the Amiatinus, are now in the British Museum, where they are a monument of the time when, under the leadership of Benedict Biscop, Ceolfrid, and especially Bede, the north of England led the Western world in scholarship.

Among the other most important MSS. of the Vulgate are the CODEX FULDENSIS, written in A.D. 546 for Bishop Victor of Capua, containing the whole New Testament (together with the apocryphal Epistle of St. Paul to the Laodiceans), the Gospels being arranged in a consecutive narrative, based on the Diatessaron of Tatian (see above, p. 156); CODEX CAVENSIS (ninth century), witten in Spain, and with a Spanish type of text; CODEX TOLETANUS (eighth century), very similar to the Cavensis; the LINDISFARNE GOSPELS (about A.D. 690), a splendid north English copy, resembling the Codex Amiatinus in text, described more fully on pp. 184-6; the HARLEIAN GOSPELS (sixth or seventh century), in the British Museum; the STONYHURST GOSPELS (seventh century), formerly at Durham, now at Stonyhurst, written in a beautiful little uncial hand; and the manuscripts exhibiting the revision by Alcuin, described in the following chapter.

Wordsworth and White classify them into the following groups: (1) Northumbrian, headed by the Amiatinus, with the Lindisfarne and Stonyhurst Gospels, which they regard as the best, and which Dom Chapman would trace back to the edition prepared by Cassiodorus in the sixth century; (2) a less good group headed by the Harleian Gospels, regarded by C. H. Turner as representing non-Cassiodorian texts from Italy; (3) an Irish group, headed by the Book of Armagh (eighth or ninth century); (4) a group, of which a seventh-century MS. in the Bodleian is the chief representative, intermediate between groups 2 and 3; (5) a Spanish group, headed by the Cavensis and Toletanus; and (6) texts representing the revisions of Alcuin and Theodulf, to be described in the next chapter.

§ 3.—Summary.

Such, then, is the list of the witnesses on whom, together with the quotations in the Fathers, we have to depend for the establishment of the best attainable text of the New Testament. It will have been seen that the picture presented by Westcott and Hort in 1881, though in the main holding its ground, has undergone certain modifications as the result of the discoveries of the last fifty years. It would be rash to claim that finality has yet been reached; but at each stage of the journey it is useful to sum up the results which *appear* to have been reached, if only to serve as a basis for further examination, or as an hypothesis by which future discoveries may be tested.

The classification now suggested is as follows:

(α) *Byzantine*, a title which seems preferable to Hort's "Syrian," as avoiding confusion with "Syriac" and as more descriptive of the text which came to be generally adopted in the Byzantine Church. This is the text found in the vast majority of later MSS., which from them passed into the earliest printed texts, and which was the universally "received text," until it was challenged by modern scholarship and by the results of modern discoveries. Its characteristic features are verbal revision in the direction of smoothness, intelligibility, ease of comprehension, concordance between different narratives of the same event. It seems to be the result of a long-continued process of minor revision in the interests of the ordinary reader. The earliest traces of it appear in the quotations of Chrysostom, who worked at Antioch until 398 and then at Constantinople until 407, and it seems to have established itself in the Metropolitan Church in the course of the next centuries, until by the eighth it is found in practically complete possession of the Greek world. The oldest and most important MSS. which show readings of this type are A and C in the Gospels, W except in Mark, and the purple MSS. N, O, Σ, Φ; after these follow the great mass of later uncials and minuscules. It can now, however, generally be discarded when it comes into competition with the earlier families.

(β) *Alexandrian*, substantially identical with Hort's "Neutral." The latter title is better avoided, since it now appears that this type of text cannot claim an uncontaminated descent from the originals, but is rather the result of skilled editorial handling of good materials; also that it is not a text universally current in Egypt (though that is its main home), but is rather the product of a well-equipped scriptorium in a particular place, which can hardly be other than Alexandria. To this family belong in the first line the great uncials B and ℵ, often supported by L R T Z, also by A and C except in the Gospels, by the minuscules 33, 81 and 157, and the Coptic versions, both Sahidic and Bohairic. Of the Fathers, Origen is the one who most often has readings of this type.

(γ) *Cæsarean.*—The discovery of this family of text has been described above (p. 117). So far, its character has only been established in Mark, the Gospel which (being the shortest and containing the least of our Lord's teaching) appears to have had the least circulation in the early Church, and so escaped revision and corruption. Here it is found in the Codex Koridethianus (Θ), the groups of minuscules known as Family 1 and Family 13, the Chester Beatty papyrus P^{45}, the Armenian and Georgian versions, and the quotations in the later works of Origen and in Eusebius. It clearly established itself in the library at Cæsarea, where Origen and Eusebius worked, but there is evidence, especially in P^{45}, of its circulation in Egypt, and that may well be its original home. In character it lies between the Alexandrian and Western.

(δ) *Western.* As stated above, it was formerly the custom to label as " Western " any reading which was earlier than " Syrian," but was not found in the " Neutral " authorities. In this way it was argued that the Western text was in early times prevalent, not only in the West, but also in Syria and even in Egypt; that it was in fact the original form of text, from which the " Neutral " was derived by drastic editorial revision. But the growth of evidence and investigation has shown that in this sense no such thing as a Western text exists at all. The Syriac and Egyptian variants from the " Neutral " or Alexandrian text do not by any means always or generally coincide with those of the Latin authorities; and it is not possible to trace them to a common source, or reconstruct a Western text on these lines at all. On the other hand, if it is once recognised that it is not necessary to group in a single family all readings with early attestation which do not belong to the Alexandrian family, it is easy to segregate one group of these which have a common character, and whose attestation is definitely Western. This is the type of text found in Codex Bezæ and the other Græco-Latin uncials D_2 E_3 F_2 G_3, the African form of the Old Latin version, especially in the MSS. *k* and *e*, and the quotations in Cyprian, Priscillian,

Tyconius and Primasius. It is a type marked by striking variations from all other groups, especially in the Gospels and Acts. In the Acts especially it abounds with variants which some have thought superior to the Alexandrian and Byzantine texts, and which, if not original, must be due to deliberate alterations by someone who regarded himself as having authoritative information. Specimens of these variants will be found in Appendix I.

(ε) *Syriac.*—It seems necessary to separate the Old Syriac version from the Western family with which it was formerly associated. It is in fact nearer akin to the Alexandrian type, though independent of it; and such infusion of Western readings as it has may well be attributed to the influence of Tatian's Diatessaron. It may therefore be regarded rather as the local text of the Church of Edessa, influenced at first by the Western text imported by Tatian from Rome, and eventually revised under Byzantine influences by Rabbula into the form of the Peshitta, which became the authorised Bible of the Syrian Church.

When, however, all these families have been marked off and labelled, it must be recognised that they have not exhausted the early history of the New Testament text. No one of these families can be taken as containing the whole authentic truth; all reach back to a period of uncertainty out of which they gradually emerged; and they do not all between them cover the whole of the material. In addition to the readings which can be attributed with some certainty to one or the other family, there is a residue of unassigned readings, relics of a time when there was much variation among the texts of the sacred books (especially the Gospels) circulating among the widely scattered Christian communities, out of which the families or types which we have now learned to discern were gradually formed. If this be so, we must recognise that absolute certainty in details is unattainable; that even if the Alexandrian type (or the Western or Cæsarean, if anyone prefers it) is generally superior, it cannot always be right, and we must be prepared to consider alternative readings on their merits. We must be content to know that the general authenticity of the New Testament text has been remarkably supported by the modern discoveries which have so greatly reduced the interval between the original autographs and our earliest extant manuscripts, and that the differences of reading, interesting as they are, do not affect the fundamental doctrines of the Christian faith.

CHAPTER IX

THE VULGATE IN THE MIDDLE AGES

In the preceding chapters the attempt has been made to narrate the history of the Greek text of the New Testament. It is the history of the text of the New Testament in its original tongue, to which all translations into other languages must look back, and on which our knowledge of the life and teaching of our Lord and His disciples ultimately rests. But it by no means completes the story of the way in which the Bible reached our people. In the chapters that follow we have to explain how the Bible circulated in what was at first the western portion of the Roman Empire, and then was the western portion of Europe as transformed by the irruption of barbarians from the East; how it reached our distant corner of this European world; how it was translated into English and won its way into the heart of our English people; and how it has been retranslated in our own day in the light of the discoveries of new material and new evidence which we have been describing. So we shall link in one continuous chain the original Hebrew and Greek Scriptures with the Bible which we read in our churches and homes today.

Importance of the Vulgate.

The history of the Bible in Western Europe is for a thousand years the history of the Vulgate, and of the Vulgate alone. In the East the Scriptures circulated in Greek, in Syriac, in Coptic, in Armenian, in Georgian, in Æthiopic, in Arabic, in Persian. In the West, Latin was the only language of literature. The Latin language was carried by the Roman legionaries into Africa, into Gaul, into Spain, into parts of Germany, and even to distant Britain; and wherever the Latin language went, thither, after the conversion of the Empire to Christianity, went the Latin Bible. Throughout the period which we know as the Middle Ages, which may roughly be defined as from A.D. 500 to 1500, almost all books were written in Latin. Latin was the language in which different nations communicated with one another. Latin was the language of the monasteries; and the monasteries were the chief centres of the learning which existed during those centuries. An educated man, speaking Latin, was a member of a society which included all educated men in Western Europe, and might be equally at home in Italy, in Gaul, and in Britain.

We shall see in the next chapter that translations of parts of the Bible into English existed from a very early time; but these were themselves translations from the Latin Bible, and for every copy of the Bible in English there were scores, or even hundreds, in Latin. The same was the case on the Continent. Translations were made, in course of time, into French, Italian, and other languages; but the originals of these translations were always Latin Bibles. Every monastery had many copies; and the relics of these, the remnant which escaped from the vast destructions of the Reformation and all the other chances of time, fill our museums and libraries to-day. To the Latin Bible we owe our Christianity in England; and in tracing its fortunes during the Middle Ages we are but supplying the link between the early narrative of the spread of the Bible throughout Europe and its special history in our own islands.

Simultaneous Use of Old Latin and Vulgate.

We have said that the form in which the Bible was first made known to the Latin-speaking people of the West was that of the Old Latin version. The African form of this version spread along the Roman provinces which occupied the north of the continent in which it was produced; the European variety of it was propagated throughout Gaul and Spain; while a revised and improved edition was current in Italy in the fourth century. But these different editions, if indeed they ever amounted to distinct editions, did not remain distinct long. They were so intermingled that nearly every MS. represents some different combination of influences. Then came the Vulgate, the revised Latin Bible of St. Jerome. Undertaken though it was at the express request of the Pope, it yet did not win immediate acceptance. Even so great an authority as St. Augustine objected to the extensive departures from the current version which Jerome had made in his Old Testament. For some centuries the Vulgate and the Old Latin existed side by side. Complete Bibles were then rare. More commonly, a volume would contain only one group of books, such as the Pentateuch or the Prophets, the Gospels or the Pauline Epistles; and it would very easily happen that the library of any one individual would have some of these groups according to the older version and others according to the Vulgate. Hence we find Christian writers, even as late as the eighth century, using sometimes one version and sometimes the other;[1] and when complete copies of the Bible came to be written, some books might be copied from manuscripts of the one type and others from those of the other. Special

[1] Old Latin quotations are found in Aldhelm (late seventh century) and Bede.

familiarity with particular books was a strong bar to the acceptance of the new text. Thus the Gospels continued to circulate in the Old Latin much later than the Prophets, and the old version of the Psalms was never superseded by Jerome's translation at all, but continues to this day to hold its place in the received Bible of the Roman Church.

Consequent Mixture of Texts.

One unfortunate result followed from this long period of simultaneous existence of two different texts—namely, the intermixture of readings from one with those of the other. Scribes engaged in copying the Vulgate would, from sheer familiarity with the older version, write down its words instead of those of St. Jerome; and on the other hand a copyist of the Old Latin would introduce into its text some of the improvements of the Vulgate. When it is remembered that this was in days when every copy had to be written by hand, when the variations of one manuscript were perpetuated and increased in all those which were copied from it, it will be easier to understand the confusion which was thus introduced into both versions of the Bible text. It is as though every copy of our Revised Version were written by hand, and the copyists were to substitute, especially in the best known books, such as the Gospels, the more familiar words of the Authorised Version. Very soon no two copies of the Bible would remain alike, and the confusion would only be magnified as time went on.

So it was with the Latin Bible in the Middle Ages. The fifth and sixth centuries are the period during which the old and new versions existed side by side. In Italy the final acceptance of the Vulgate was largely due to Gregory the Great (590-604). In Gaul, in the sixth century, certain books, especially the Prophets, were habitually known in Jerome's translation; the rest were still current mainly in the old version. In the seventh century the victory of the Vulgate was general. But it was a sadly mutilated and corrupted Vulgate which emerged thus victorious from the struggle; and the rest of the Middle Ages is the history of successive attempts to revise and reform it, and of successive decadences after each revision, until the invention of printing made it possible to fix and maintain a uniform text in all copies of the Bible.

The Vulgate in Spain and Ireland.

The truest text of the Vulgate was no doubt preserved in Italy. The worst was unquestionably in Gaul, which we may now begin to call France. But two countries, situated at different extremes of Western Christendom, preserved somewhat distinct types of text, which eventually had considerable influence upon the history of the Vulgate. These were Spain and Ireland. Each was, for a considerable period, cut off from communication with the main body of Christendom: Spain, by the Moorish invasion, which for a time confined the Christian Visigoths to the north-western corner of the peninsula; Ireland, by the English conquest of Britain, which drove the ancient Celtic Church before it, and interposed a barrier of heathendom between the remains of that Church and its fellow Christians on the Continent. The consequence of this isolation was that each Church preserved a distinct type of the Vulgate text, recognisable by certain special readings in many passages of the Bible. The Spanish Bible was complete, and its text, though of very mixed character, contains some good and early elements; witness the Codex Cavensis and the Codex Toletanus, mentioned on p. 176. The Irish Bible as a rule consists of the Gospels alone, and its text is likewise mixed, containing several remarkable readings; but its outward form and ornamentation had a special character and a peculiar beauty, the connection of which with the Bibles produced in northern England forms an intriguing problem.

Anglo-Celtic MSS.

The seventh century is the most glorious period in the history of the Irish Church. Thanks chiefly to the efforts of St. Patrick, Ireland was not only itself mainly a Christian land, but was sending out missionaries into other countries. One of the most important of these missions was that of Columba, who settled at Iona, off the coast of Mull, and thence evangelised the Picts of Scotland. Here the young prince Oswald, expelled from Northumbria by the heathen Britons under Penda, took refuge, and hence, on recovering his kingdom, he summoned missionaries to preach the Gospel in northern England from the centre which he gave them at Lindisfarne. Thus there grew up, under the leadership of Aidan and Cuthbert, a Northumbrian Church in close association with the Church in Ireland. Visible evidence of this community remains in the illuminated copies of the Scriptures which have come down to us from both Ireland and Northumbria. The special feature of this style is its extraordinarily intricate system of interlacing patterns, sometimes geometric and sometimes including animal forms, combined and continued with marvellous precision over a whole page throughout the pattern of a huge initial letter. Looked at from a little distance, a page of one of these manuscripts resembles a harmonious mosaic or enamelled pattern in soft and concordant colours. Examine it closely, even with a magnifying glass, and the eye wearies itself in following the intricacy of its pattern, and the hand strives in vain to reproduce its accuracy even for a few inches of its course. The use of gold gives to later illuminations a greater splendour of appearance at first sight; but no other style shows a quarter of the inexhaustible skill and patient devotion which is the glory of the Anglo-Celtic school.

Until recently it has been assumed that this school had its origin in Ireland, and was carried by the Irish missionaries through Scotland into Northumbria. But lately good authorities have argued that the influence was the other way; that it was evolved from Continental influences in northern England, and was thence carried back by the Irish to their own land, where it developed certain national characteristics of its own. The one fixed point is the great Lindisfarne Gospels, which, being written in honour of St. Cuthbert (d. 687), cannot be materially later than A.D. 700. This (of which a fuller description is given below) is the finest example of the Anglo-Celtic school, and is certainly of English origin; and there is no MS. of definitely Irish origin which can be assigned to an earlier date. The most notable example of Irish decoration is the famous Book of Kells, which is believed to have been produced at Iona; but there is no reason to give it a date earlier than the eighth century. It is more barbaric in colouring than the English school, its reds and yellows contrasting with the soberer lilacs and pale greens of the Lindisfarne book; and its interlacements and figure-drawings are also more extravagant. Splendid as it is in its wealth of ornament, it lacks the restraint and good taste of the English style.

Texts of English MSS. derived from Italy.

But whatever be the artistic relationships of the manuscripts of Ireland and North England, there is no doubt as to their textual characters. The Irish text is a considerably contaminated Vulgate, while the English texts are the best Vulgate texts extant. This they owe to their direct descent from Italian MSS. of the best quality. As we have seen (p. 175), the Codex Amiatinus was copied at Wearmouth or Jarrow, shortly before the year 716, from a MS. or MSS. brought over by Benedict Biscop or Ceolfrid, which apparently represents the text of the scholar-statesman Cassiodorus. With regard to the Lindisfarne MS., we have further evidence connecting it with Italy.

The Lindisfarne Gospels.

It is a copy of the four Gospels, written in a fine and bold uncial hand, with magnificent ornamentation at the beginning of each book. The main text is that of the Latin Vulgate; but between the lines a later hand has written a paraphrase of the Latin into the primitive English which we commonly call Anglo-Saxon. Of this paraphrase more will be said in the next chapter; at present our concern with it lies in the fact that the author of it has added at the end of the volume a history of the manuscript. He tells us that it was written by Eadfrith, Bishop of Lindisfarne, in honour of St. Cuthbert, the great saint of Lindisfarne and Northumbria, who died in A.D. 687; that it was covered and "made firm on the outside" by Ethilwald; that Billfrith the anchorite wrought in smith's work the ornaments on its cover; and that he himself, Aldred, "an unworthy and most miserable priest," wrote the English translation between the lines. We know, therefore, that the volume was written shortly after the year 687. Now before each Gospel is placed a list of festivals on which lessons were read from that book; and, strange as it may seem at first sight, it has been shown that these festivals are unquestionably festivals of the Church of Naples. What is still more remarkable, this strange fact can be completely explained. When Theodore of Tarsus was sent by Pope Vitalian to England in 669 to be Archbishop of Canterbury, he brought with him, as his companion and adviser, one Hadrian, the abbot of a monastery near Naples. Theodore visited the whole of England, including Northumbria; and there can be no reasonable doubt that these tables of lessons were copied from a manuscript which Abbot Hadrian had brought with him from Italy. The text itself may have been copied from the same manuscript, or from one of those brought over by Biscop or Ceolfrid. In any case it is practically the same text as the Amiatinus.

The plate opposite this page is a much reduced copy of the first words of the Gospel of St. Luke in the Lindisfarne book; and even in this reduction the beauty and elaboration of the intricately interlaced design which composes the initial Q can be fairly seen. Between the lines of the original writing is the English paraphrase, in a minute cursive hand, without pretensions to ornament. The history of the MS. after its completion deserves a word of mention, for a special romance attaches to it. Written in honour of St. Cuthbert, it was preserved at Lindisfarne along with the Saint's body; but in the year 875 an invasion of the Danes drove the monks to carry away both body and book. For several years they wandered to and fro in northern England; then, in despair, they resolved to cross over to Ireland. But the Saint was angry at being taken from his own land, and a great storm met the boat as it put out; and as the boat lay on its side in the fury of the storm the precious volume was washed overboard and lost. Realising the Saint's displeasure, the monks put back, in a state of much penitence and sorrow for their loss; but at last the Saint encouraged one of them in a dream to search for the book along the shore, and on a day of exceptionally low tide they found it, practically uninjured by its immersion. The story is told by the chronicler Simeon of Durham, writing about 1104; and it need not be dismissed as a mere medieval legend. Precious volumes, according to the Irish practice, were carried in special cases or covers, which might well defend them from much damage from the sea; and it is certain that several pages of this book (which was regularly known in medieval times as "the book of St. Cuthbert which fell into the sea") show to this day the marks of injury from water which has filtered in from without. The subsequent history of the MS. may be briefly told. Always accompanying the Saint's body, it found homes at Chester-le-Street, Durham, and finally at Lindisfarne once more. At the dissolution of the monasteries it was cast abroad into the world and stripped of its jewelled covers; but was rescued by Sir Robert Cotton, and passed with his collection into the British Museum, where it now rests in peace and safety.

Eminence of English Scholarship in Eighth and Ninth Centuries.

But this is a digression. The point which we have established is the formation of an excellent text of the Vulgate in northern England, by means of copies brought from Italy. During the eighth and ninth centuries northern England was the most flourishing home of Christian scholarship in western Europe. The twin houses of Wearmouth and Jarrow were the headquarters of the school; and the great names in it are those of Ceolfrid, Bede and Alcuin. Ceolfrid's services in the bringing of manuscripts from Italy, and in the production of the Codex Amiatinus, have been mentioned above (p. 175). Bede (A.D. 674-735), the first great historian of England, lived and died at Jarrow. Of him we shall have more to say in the next chapter, in connection with the earliest translations of the Bible into English. Alcuin (A.D. 735-805), on the other hand, is intimately connected with the most important stage of the history of the Vulgate in the Middle Ages.

Alcuin invited by Charlemagne to Revise Vulgate in France.

While Ireland and England were taking the lead in promoting the study and circulation of the Bible, the Bible in France was sinking deeper and deeper into the confusion and corruption which have been described above. No one who has not worked among manuscripts can know the endless degrees of deterioration to which a much-copied text can sink, or realise the hopelessness of maintaining for long a high or uniform standard of correctness. Nothing but the strong hand of a reformer could check the progress of decay; and that was at last found in the great emperor Charlemagne. From the beginning of his reign this monarch manifested great concern for the reformation of the text of the Scriptures. He forbade them to be copied by inexperienced boys at schools; and when he cast his eyes round for a scholar who might undertake the revision of the corrupted text, he naturally looked to England, and there found the man whom he required in the person of Alcuin of York, the most distinguished scholar of the day. Alcuin was invited to France; was attached to the court at Aix and made master of the schools which Charlemagne established in his palace, with the title and revenues of the abbot of St. Martin of Tours; and subsequently retiring to Tours, inaugurated there a great school of copyists and scholars, and there received the commission of the emperor to prepare a revised and corrected edition of the Latin Bible.

Alcuin's Vulgate.

Two families of texts were then widely represented in France, the Spanish and the Irish. These, coming respectively from south and north, met in the region of the Loire, and both were known to Alcuin. Probably he realised that both were more or less corrupt. In 796 we find him sending to York for manuscripts, showing how highly he valued the text preserved in the copies of northern England; in 801 the revision was complete, and on Christmas Day in that year a copy of the restored Vulgate was presented by him to Charlemagne. We have evidence of several copies having been made under Alcuin's own direction during the short remainder of his life, and, although none of these has actually come down to us, we yet possess several manuscripts which contain Alcuin's text more or less perfectly preserved. The best of these is the Codex Vallicellianus, containing the whole Bible, now in the library of the Oratory adjoining the Church of Sta. Maria in Vallicella, at Rome, but written at Tours in the ninth century, probably in or soon after the lifetime of Alcuin. Another fine copy (Brit. Mus. Add. MS. 10546, sometimes known as the Bible of Charlemagne), likewise containing the whole Bible, may be seen in one of the showcases in the British Museum, and of this a reproduction is given in Plate XXVII. It is an excellent specimen of the style of writing introduced in France during the reign of Charlemagne, the special headquarters of which was the school of Tours, over which Alcuin presided. It marked a new departure in the history of Latin writing, and it was this style of writing that indirectly formed the model from which our modern printed types are taken. The MS. in question is written in double columns on a page measuring 20 by 14½ inches. Here only part of one column can be shown (and that much reduced in scale), containing 1 John iv. 16–v. 10, and it will be seen that the famous interpolation in verse 8 relating to the

Three Witnesses is here absent. As stated in the Variorum Bible, this text is found in no Greek manuscript, with the exception of two, in which it is manifestly inserted from the Latin. It is a purely Latin interpolation, though one of early origin, and it finds no place in Alcuin's corrected Vulgate. There the text runs, "For there are three that bear witness, the spirit, the water, and the blood; and the three are one."

The Golden Gospels of Charlemagne.

The zeal of Charlemagne for the Bible was not manifested in his encouragement of Alcuin's revision alone. From his reign date a series of splendid manuscripts of the Gospels, written in gold letters upon white or purple vellum, and adorned with magnificent decorations. The artistic inspiration of these highly decorated copies is clearly derived from the Anglo-Celtic manuscripts of which we have spoken above, and it is probable that here again Alcuin was the principal agent in carrying the English influence into the Continent. It has at least been shown to be probable that the centre from which these "Golden Gospels," as they are sometimes called, took their rise, was in the neighbourhood of the Rhine, where Alcuin was settled as master of the palace schools before his retirement to Tours; and the earliest examples of this style appear to have been written during the time of his residence in that region. In any case they are a splendid evidence of the value in which the sacred volume was held, and they show how the tradition of the English illumination was carried abroad into France. The characteristic interlacings of the style are plainly evident, but the extent to which they are employed has diminished; and although the profuse employment of gold lends these books a gorgeousness which their predecessors do not possess, yet the skill and labour bestowed upon them cannot be ranked so high, and the reader who will compare the best examples of either class will probably agree that, while both are splendid, the Books of Kells and of Lindisfarne are even more marvellous as works of art than the Golden Gospels of Charlemagne. The texts of these Gospels differ from those of the Tours manuscripts in being closer to the Anglo-Saxon type, and this is quite in accordance with the theory which assigns their origin to the influence of Alcuin, but at a period earlier than that of his thorough revision of the Vulgate. Manuscripts of this class continued to be written under the successors of Charlemagne, especially in the reign of Charles the Bald (843-81); but after that date they disappear, and a less gorgeous style of illumination takes the place of these elaborate and beautiful volumes.

The Revision of Theodulf.

It was not only under the immediate direction of Charlemagne that the desire for an improved text of the Vulgate was active. Almost simultaneously with Alcuin, Theodulf. Bishop of Orleans, was undertaking a revision upon different lines. Theodulf was probably a Visigoth by birth—a member, that is, of the race of Goths which had occupied Spain, and from which the Spaniards are in part descended. He came from the south of France, and hence all his associations were with the districts on either side of the Pyrenees. Thus, while Alcuin represented the English and Irish traditions of the Bible text, Theodulf embodies the traditions of Spain. At Orleans, however, of which see he was bishop about the year 800, he stood at the meeting-place of the two streams; and his revised Vulgate, though mainly Spanish in type, shows also traces of Irish influence, as well as of the use of good Alcuinian MSS. His revision is very unequal in value, and its importance is by no means so great as that of Alcuin's work. Undertaken apart from the influence of Charlemagne, it was never generally adopted, and now survives in comparatively few manuscripts, the best of which is in the National Library at Paris.[1]

The School of St. Gall.

One other school of Biblical study at this period deserves notice. Not far from the Lake of Constance lies the monastery of St. Gall, now a comparatively obscure and unvisited spot, but formerly a great centre of study and of penmanship. At this day it is almost, if not quite, unique in retaining still in the twentieth century the library which made it famous in the ninth. At a still earlier period it was a focus of Irish missionary effort. Irish monks made their way to its walls, bringing with them their own peculiar style of writing; and manuscripts in the Irish style still exist in some numbers in the library of St. Gall. The style was taken up and imitated by the native monks; and in the ninth century, under the direction of the scribe and scholar Hartmut, the school of St. Gall was definitely established as a prominent centre of activity in the work of copying MSS. His successors, towards the end of the century, developed a distinct style of writing, which became generally adopted in the districts bordering on the Rhine. The *text* of these St. Gall manuscripts, on the other hand, looks southwards for its home, not north, and is derived from Milan, with some traces of Spanish influence, instead of from Ireland.

[1] The British Museum possesses a copy (Add. MS. 24124), known as the Bible of St. Hubert, which is at present exhibited in one of the show-cases.

Subsequent Deterioration.

Thus in the ninth century a healthy activity prevailed in many quarters, directed towards the securing of a sound text of the Bible. But permanence in goodness cannot be maintained so long as books are copied by hand alone. The errors of copyists undo the labours of scholars, and in a short time chaos has come again. The Alcuinian text was corrupted with surprising rapidity, and the private labours of Theodulf had even less lasting an effect. The decadence of the house of Charlemagne was reflected in the decadence of the Bible text which he had striven to purify and establish. The invasion of the Normans broke up the school of Tours, as the invasion of the Danes broke up the school of Wearmouth and Jarrow in Northumbria. In these wars and tumults scholarship went to the ground. A few individuals, such as our Norman Archbishop Lanfranc, tried to check the growing corruption of the Bible text, but with only temporary effect. It was not until four centuries had passed away that a real and effectual attempt was made to restore the Vulgate to something like its ancient form.

The Revision of the Thirteenth Century.

England had led the way in the ninth century; but in the thirteenth the glory belongs almost entirely to France. It is to the influence of the French king St. Louis, and the scholarship of the newly established University of Paris that the revision of the thirteenth century is due. Those who are acquainted with the manuscripts of the Vulgate in any of our great libraries will know what a remarkable proportion of them were written in this century. The small, compressed writing, arranged in double columns, with little decoration except simple coloured initials, becomes very familiar to the student of manuscripts, and impresses him with a sense of the great activity which must have prevailed at that period in multiplying copies of the Bible. Very many of them are small volumes, evidently intended for private use; and their number is a proof of a great growth of the study of the Bible at this time. For us at the present day the principal result of the labours of the Paris doctors is the division of our Bible into chapters. Divisions of both Old and New Testaments into sections of various sizes existed from very early times; but our modern chapter-division was the work of Stephen Langton, then a doctor of the University of Paris, afterwards Archbishop of Canterbury and leader of the barons in the struggle which gave birth to Magna Charta. The *texts* of these Parisian Bibles are not, it must be admitted, of any very remarkable excellence; but they are very important in the history of the Vulgate, because it is virtually upon them that the printed text of the Bible of the Roman Church is based to this day.

Printed Latin Bibles.

We are going ahead too fast, and shall have to retrace our steps in the next chapter; but it will be convenient to conclude here the history of the Latin Bible. It has been made evident that, so long as Bibles continued to be copied by hand, no stability or uniformity of text could be maintained. As with the Greek Bible, so with the Latin, the later copies become progressively worse and worse. Hence the enormous importance of the invention of printing, which made it possible to fix and stereotype a form of text, and secure that it should be handed on without substantial change from one generation to another. The first book printed in Europe, it is pleasant to know, was the Latin Bible—the splendid Mazarin Bible (so called from the fact that the first copy which attracted much attention in later times was that in the library of Cardinal Mazarin) issued by Gutenberg in 1456, of which a copy may be seen exhibited in the British Museum, and from which the first page is here given in reduced facsimile (Plate XXVIII). But this edition, and many others which followed it, merely reproduced the current form of text, without revision or comparison with the best manuscripts. Ximenes and Erasmus, the first editors of the Greek printed Bible, also bestowed much labour on the Latin text; but the first really critical edition was that prepared by Stephanus in 1528, and revised by himself in 1538-40. No authoritative edition, however, was forthcoming until the accession to the Papal chair of Sixtus V in 1585.

The Sixtine Bible.

Immediately on his accession, this energetic Pope appointed a commission to revise the text of the Bible, and in the work of revision he himself took an active part. Good manuscripts were used as authorities, including notably the Codex Amiatinus; and in 1590 the completed work issued from the press in three volumes. The text resembles generally that of Stephanus, on which it was evidently based. But hardly had Pope Sixtus declared his edition to be the sole authentic and authorised form of the Bible, when he died; and one of the first acts of Clement VIII, on his accession in 1592, was to call in all the copies of the Sixtine Bible. The alleged reason was that the edition was full of errors, but Dr. White, the editor of the Oxford Vulgate, has shown that this charge is baseless. It is true that some errors in the prefaces have been corrected in hand-stamped type; but the Bible text is remarkably accurate.

The Clementine Bible.

It is believed, however, that Clement was incited to this attack on his predecessor's memory by the Jesuits, whom Sixtus had offended. In any case the fact remains that Clement caused a new edition to be prepared, which appeared towards the end of 1592. This edition was not confined to a removal of the errors of the press in the Sixtine volumes, but presents a considerably altered text, differing, it has been estimated, from its predecessor in no less than 3,000 readings. Here at last we reach the origin of the text of the Latin Bible current today; for the Clementine edition, sometimes appearing under the name of Clement, sometimes (to disguise the appearance of difference between two Popes) under that of Sixtus, was constituted the one authorised text of the Vulgate, from which no single variation is permitted.

It cannot be pretended that the Clementine text is satisfactory from the point of view of history or scholarship. The alterations which differentiate it from the Sixtine edition, except where they simply remove an obvious blunder, are, for the most part, no improvement; and in any case, the circumstances of the time did not permit so full and scientific an examination of all the evidence as is possible now. The task of revising the Vulgate text in accordance with modern knowledge was for a long time left almost entirely to scholars outside the pale of the Roman Church. Of these the most conspicuous have been Richard Bentley in the past, Bishop Wordsworth, Mr. White, M. Berger, and Dr. Corssen in the last fifty years. More recently the Vatican has itself taken the matter in hand. Under the auspices of Pope Leo XIII a new critical edition of the Vulgate was planned, and search was made, especially in Spain, for manuscripts hitherto unexamined. The conduct of the work was entrusted by Pope Pius XI (himself formerly a librarian and a lover of manuscripts as well as of the Bible) to the English Cardinal F. A. Gasquet, under whose direction the main editorial labour was carried out by Dom Henri Quentin. The New Testament being already far advanced in the Oxford edition, it was decided to deal first with the Old Testament. The first volume, containing Genesis, appeared in 1926, and now the Pentateuch is complete. Dom Quentin, in an elaborate study of the MSS. of the Pentateuch (of which thirty-three were used for Genesis), came to the conclusion that they fall into three groups, headed respectively by the Tours Pentateuch (sixth or seventh century), the Ottobianus of the Vatican (an Octateuch, lacking Ruth and part of Judges, of the seventh century), and the Amiatinus (early eighth century, see p. 175); and he forms his text by following the majority of these three, of which he regards the Tours MS. as the best.

Since the lamented death of Dom Quentin in 1935, the work has been entrusted by the Pope to a Benedictine community established in a monastery bearing the name of St. Jerome, on the Janiculan hill. This will ensure the continuance of the work, under successive editors as may be necessary, until its completion. When the Vatican Old Testament and the Oxford New Testament are complete, scholars will at last have a scientifically established text of the Vulgate, secured by the permanence of print.

CHAPTER X

THE ENGLISH MANUSCRIPT BIBLES

We take another step forward in our story, and narrow still further the circle of our inquiry. It is no longer the original text of the Bible with which we have to deal, nor even the Bible of Western Europe. Our step is a step nearer home; our subject is the Bible of our own country and in our own language. For nearly a thousand years, from the landing of Augustine to the Reformation, the official Bible, so to speak, the Bible of the Church services and of monastic usage, was the Latin Vulgate. But although the monks and clergy learnt Latin, and a knowledge of Latin was the most essential element of an educated man's culture, it was never the language of the common people. To them the Bible, if it came at all, must come in English, and from almost the earliest times there were churchmen and statesmen whose care it was that, whether by reading it for themselves, if they were able, or by hearing it read to them, the common people should have at least the more important parts of the Bible accessible to them in their own language. For twelve hundred years one may fairly say that the English people has never been entirely without an English Bible.

The Conversion of England.

It was in the year 597 that Augustine landed in Kent, and brought back to that part of the island the Christianity which had been driven out of it by our Saxon, Jute, and Engle forefathers. In 634, Birinus, a Roman priest from Gaul, converted the West Saxons; and in 635 came Aidan from Iona to preach Christianity in Northumbria, as related in the last chapter. Soon after the middle of the century all England had heard the Word of Christ, proclaimed by word of mouth by the missionaries of Rome or of Ireland. At first there would be no need of a written Bible for the common people. As in the days of Christ and His Apostles, men heard the Word of God by direct preaching. Most of them could not read, and the enthusiasm of a convert requires personal instruction rather than study of a written book. Yet it was not long before the story of the Bible made its appearance in English literature.

The Bible Paraphrase of Cædmon.

In the abbey of the Lady Hilda at Whitby was a brother named Cædmon, who had no skill in making songs, and would therefore leave the table when his turn came to sing something for the pleasure of the company. But one night when he had done so, and had lain down in the stable and there fallen asleep, there stood One by him in a dream, and said, "Cædmon, sing Me something." And he answered, "I cannot sing, and for that reason I have left the feast." But He said, "Nevertheless, thou canst sing to Me." "What," said he, "must I sing?" And He said, "Sing the beginning of created things." So he sang; and the poem of Cædmon is the first native growth of English literature. It is a paraphrase in verse of the Bible narrative, from both Old and New Testaments, written in that early dialect which we call Anglo-Saxon, but which is really the ancient form of English.

The Psalter of Aldhelm.

Cædmon's Bible paraphrase was written about 670, a generation after the coming of Aidan; and another generation had not passed away before part of the Bible had been actually translated into English. Aldhelm, Bishop of Sherborne, who died in 709, translated the Psalms, and thereby holds the honour of having been the first translator of the Bible into our native tongue. It is uncertain whether we still possess any part of his work, or not. There is a version of the Psalms in Anglo-Saxon, preserved in a manuscript at Paris, which has been supposed to be the Psalter of Aldhelm; but the manuscript was only written in the eleventh century, and the language of the translation seems to contain forms which had not come into existence in the time at which Aldhelm lived. If, therefore, this version, which gives the first fifty Psalms in prose and the rest in verse, really belongs to Aldhelm at all, the language must have been somewhat modified in later copies.

Bede.

The next translator of whom we hear is the greatest name in the history of the early English Church. Bede (673-735) was the glory of the Northumbrian school, which, as we have seen, was the most shining light of learning in western Europe during the eighth century. In addition to his greatest work, the *History of the English Church*, he wrote commentaries on many of the books of the Bible. These works, which were intended primarily for scholars, were written in Latin; but we know that he also took care that the Scriptures might be faithfully delivered to the common people in their own tongue. He translated the Creed and the Lord's Prayer, as the first essentials of the Christian faith; and at the time of his death he was engaged on a translation of the Gospel of St. John. The story of its completion, told by his disciple, Cuthbert, is well known, but it never can be omitted in a history of the English Bible. On the Eve of Ascension Day, 735, the great scholar lay dying, but dictating, while his strength allowed, to his disciples; and they wrote down the translation of the Gospel as it fell from his lips, being urged by him to write quickly, since he knew not how soon his Master would call him. On Ascension morning one chapter alone remained unfinished, and the youth who had been copying hesitated to press his master further; but he would not rest. "It is easily done," he said; "take thy pen and write quickly." Failing strength and the last farewells to the brethren of the monastery prolonged the task, till at eventide the boy reminded his master: "There is yet one sentence unwritten, dear master." "Write it quickly," was the answer; and it was written at his word. "It is written now," said the boy. "You speak truth," answered the saint; "it is finished now." Then he bade them lay him on the pavement of his cell, supporting his head in their hands; and as he repeated the Gloria, with the name of the Holy Spirit on his lips, he passed quietly away.

Of Bede's translation no trace or vestige now remains; nor are we more fortunate when we pass from the great scholar of the early Church to the great statesman, King Alfred. Alfred, by far the finest name among the early sovereigns of England, careful for the moral and intellectual welfare of his people, did not neglect the work which Aldhelm and Bede had begun. He prefixed a translation of the Ten Commandments and other extracts from the Law of Moses to his own code of laws, and translated, or caused to be translated, several other parts of the Bible. He is said to have been engaged on a version of the Psalms at the time of his death; but no copy of his work has survived, although a manuscript (really of later date) now in the British Museum,[1] and containing the Latin text with an English translation between the lines, has borne the name of King Alfred's Psalter. Still, though nothing has come down to us from Bede or Alfred, the tradition is valuable, as assuring us of the existence of English Bibles, or parts of Bibles, in the eighth and ninth centuries. From the end of this period we have an actual example of an English Psalter still extant; for a manuscript in the British Museum, containing the Psalms in Latin, written about A.D. 700 (though formerly supposed to have belonged to St. Augustine himself), has had a word-for-word translation in the Kentish dialect inserted about the end of the ninth century. In the tenth century we stand on firmer ground, for, in addition to similar translations, we reach the date of independent versions, known to us from copies still extant in several of our public libraries.

[1] Stowe MS. 2, of the eleventh century.

Interlinear Glosses.

It is indeed possible that the Gospels were rendered into English earlier than the tenth century, since one would naturally expect them to be the first part of the Bible which a translator would wish to make accessible to the common people; but we have no actual mention or proof of the existence of such a translation before that date. As in the case of the Psalter, the earliest form in which the Gospels appear in the English language is that of glosses, or word-for-word translations written between the lines of Latin manuscripts; and the oldest copy of such a gloss now in existence is that of which mention has already been made in describing the Lindisfarne book of the Gospels. That magnificent volume was originally written in Latin about the year 700; and about 950 Aldred the priest wrote his Anglo-Saxon paraphrase between the lines of the Latin text. Some words of this translation may be seen in the facsimile given in Plate XXVI; and we may regard them with a special interest as belonging to the oldest existing copy of the Gospels in the English language. The dialect in which this translation is written is naturally Northumbrian, which differed in some respects from that spoken in other parts of the island. Another gloss of the Gospels is found in a manuscript at Oxford, known as the Rushworth MS. It is of somewhat later date than the Lindisfarne book, and in the Gospels of St. Mark, St. Luke, and St. John it follows that manuscript closely; but the gloss on St. Matthew is in the Old Mercian dialect, which was spoken in the central part of England.

The Gospels of the Tenth Century.

These glosses were, no doubt, originally made in order to assist the missionaries and preachers who had to instruct their congregations in the message of the Gospel; and the same must have been the object of the earliest independent translations of the Bible books. Few, if any, of the ordinary English inhabitants would be able to read; but the monks and priests who preached to them would interpret the Bible to them in their own tongue, and their task would be rendered easier by the existence of written English Gospels. We know, moreover, that during the latter part of the Anglo-Saxon period the culture and scholarship of the English clergy declined greatly, so that the preachers themselves would often be unable to understand the Latin Bible, and needed the assistance of an English version. It is in the south that we first meet with such a translation of the Gospels existing by itself, apart from the Latin text on which it was based. There are in all six copies of this translation now extant, two at Oxford, two at Cambridge, and two in the British Museum, with a fragment of a seventh at Oxford. All these are closely related to one another, being either actually copied from one another or taken from a common original without much variation. The oldest is a manuscript in the library of Corpus Christi College, Cambridge, which was written by one Ælfric, at Bath, about the year 1000. There can be no doubt that the original translation, of which these are copies, was made in the south-west of England, in the region known as Wessex, not later than about the middle of the tenth century. It may have been made earlier, but we have no evidence that it was so, and the total absence of such evidence must be taken as an unfavourable sign.

In Plate XXIX is given a facsimile of one of the British Museum copies of this first independent version of the Gospels in English. The manuscript, which was written in the early part of the twelfth century, has an interest of its own, even apart from its contents; and its history is partly told by the inscriptions which it bears on its first page, here reproduced. This page contains the beginning of St. Mark's Gospel, which holds the first place in the Anglo-Saxon Gospels, and is headed "Text[us] iiii. evangelior[um]"—*i.e.*, "The text of the four Gospels." To the right of this are the words "ang^{l}. d xvi. G^{a} IIII." Below is the name "Thomas Cantuarien[sis]" and the figures "1 A xiv."; and at the bottom of the page (not included in the plate) is the signature "Lumley." What do all these inscriptions tell us of the history of the MS.? They tell us first that it is a copy of the four Gospels in English; next that it bore the press-mark "D[istinctio] xvi, G[r]a[dus] IV," a press-mark of a form which we know to have been used in the library of Canterbury Cathedral; and when we turn up the catalogue of that library, made in the time of Prior Henry of Eastry, we find among the English books a "Textus iv evangeliorum, anglice," which it is safe to assume is the same book. After the dissolution of the monasteries it passed into the possession of Archbishop Thomas Cranmer, whose secretary wrote his name (in a hand closely resembling the prelate's own writing) at the head of the page; and after Cranmer's death it was acquired, with many others of his books, by Henry Fitz-Alan, Earl of Arundel, from whom it descended to his son-in-law, John, Lord Lumley. Lumley died in 1609, and his library was bought for Henry, Prince of Wales, eldest son of James I. Thereby this volume entered the Royal Library, in which it bore the press-mark 1 A xiv.; and when that library was presented to the nation by George II in 1757, it passed into the keeping of the British Museum, then newly established; and there, retaining the same press-mark, it still remains. So much history may a few notes of ownership convey to us.

Some readers may be curious to see the form of the language in which this first English Bible is written. It is unlike enough to our modern English, yet it is its true and direct ancestor. After quoting the first words of the Gospel in Latin, the translation begins thus: "Her ys Godspelles angin, halendes cristes godes sune. Swa awriten ys on thaswitegan bec isaiam. Nu ic asende mine ængel beforan thinre ansyne. Se gegarewath thinne weg beforan the. Clepigende stefen on tham westene gegarwiath drihtnes weg. Doth rihte his sythas. Iohannes wæs on westene fulgende & bodiende. Dædbote fulwyht on synna forgyfenysse."

The Old Testament of Ælfric.

This specimen will probably be enough for those who have no special acquaintance with Anglo-Saxon. Shortly after the date at which this version of the Gospels was probably made, in or about the year 990, Ælfric, Archbishop of Canterbury, translated a considerable part of the Old Testament—namely, the Pentateuch, Joshua, Judges, Kings, Esther, Job, Judith, and Maccabees, omitting such passages as seemed to him less necessary and important. Two copies of this version are known, at Oxford and in the British Museum. This completes the history of the English Bible before the Norman Conquest. That catastrophe seems to have crushed for a time the literary development of the English people. The upper class was overthrown and kept in subjection; the lower orders were too ignorant to carry on the work for themselves. It is true that the existence of the manuscript described just above is a proof that the early English version of the Gospels continued to be copied, and presumably read, in the twelfth century; but it is not until the century after this that we find any resumption of the task of translating the Scriptures into the language of the common people.

Verse Translations in the Thirteenth Century.

In the reigns of John and Henry III the intermixture between Norman and English was progressing fast, and the English element was beginning to assert its predominance in the combination. English poetry begins again with Layamon about the year 1205. Ten years later religious verse made its reappearance in the "Ormulum," a metrical version of the daily services of the Church, including portions of Scripture from the New Testament. About the middle of the century the narratives of Genesis and Exodus were rendered into rhyming verse; and towards its end we find a nearer approach to regular translation in a metrical version of the Psalter which has come down to us in several copies. It is curious that, at this time, the Psalter seems to have been in especial favour in England, almost to the exclusion of the other books of the Bible. For about a century, from 1250 to 1350, no book of the Bible seems to have been translated into English except the Psalter; and of this there were no less than three distinct versions within that period. In addition to the verse translation just mentioned, of which the author is unknown, a prose version exists, written in the first half of the fourteenth century, which has been attributed to one William of Shoreham, Vicar of Chart Sutton, in Kent. The attribution, however, rests solely on the fact that it occurs in the same volume as some poems by William of Shoreham; and since the dialect is not Kentish but of West Midlands, the attribution is improbable. At about the same time another prose version, accompanied by a verse-by-verse commentary, was produced by Richard Rolle, a hermit of Hampole, near Doncaster, which had a wide circulation, and that not only in the north, since copies are extant in the other dialects of the kingdom.

The Psalters of William of Shoreham—

Some specimens of these translations will show the progress of the English language, and carry on the history of the English Bible. The following is the beginning of the 56th Psalm as it appears in the version attributed to William of Shoreham: "Have mercy on me, God, for man hath defouled me. The fende trubled me, fe*gh*tand[1] alday o*gh*ayns me. Myn enemys defouled me alday, for many were fe*gh*tand o*gh*ains me. Y shal dred the fram the he*gh*t of the daye; y for sothe shal hope in the. Hii shal hery my wordes, what manes flesshe doth to me. Alday the wicked acurseden myn wordes o*gh*ains me; alle her thoutes ben in ivel."

And of Richard Rolle of Hampole.

In Richard Rolle of Hampole the verses are separated from one another by a commentary, much exceeding the original text in length. Many copies of this version exist, but they differ considerably from one another, so that it is difficult to say which represents best the author's original work. Here is the same passage as it appears in one of the manuscripts (Brit. Mus. Arundel MS. 158): "Have mercy of me, God, for man trad me, al day the fy*gh*tynge troublede me. Myn enemys me trede al day for many fy*gh*tynge a*gh*enes me. Fro the hy*gh*nesse of the day schal I drede: I sothly schal hope in the. In God I schal preyse my wordes, in God I hopede. I schal no*gh*t drede what flesch doth to me. Al day my wordes thei cursede a*gh*enes me, alle the tho*gh*tes of hem in yvel."

[1] The letter represented by *gh* sometimes corresponds to our y, sometimes to g or gh.

Revival of Religion in the Fourteenth Century.

Such was the knowledge of the Bible in England on the eve of the great revival which took place in the fourteenth century. The old Anglo-Saxon version of the Gospels had dropped out of use, as its language gradually became antiquated and unintelligible; and no new translation had taken its place. The Psalms alone were extant in versions which made any pretence to be faithful. The remaining books of the Bible were known to the common people only in the shape of rhyming paraphrases, or by such oral teaching as the clergy may have given. But with the increase of life and interest in the lower classes, and with the revival of literary activity in the English language, this condition of things could not last. The end of the thirteenth century had seen the first recognition of the right of the common folk to representation in the national Council, which thenceforward became a Parliament. The reigns of Edward II and Edward III saw the steady growth of a spirit of healthy life and independence in the people. They saw also the rise of literature, in Langland and Gower, and above all in Chaucer, to a position of real influence in the national life. And with this quickening interest in their surroundings on the part of the common people, there came a quickening interest in religion, which was met and answered by the power and the will to provide religious teaching for them in their own language. The tragedy of the Black Death also, in 1348-9, may well have deepened the national feeling. Thus was the way prepared for the religious movement which makes the fourteenth century so important a period in the history of our Church and Bible. In France, under the stimulus of the University of Paris, and perhaps of the king, St. Louis, the awakening had come a century sooner, and had manifested itself alike in a revised edition of the current Vulgate text, with a great multiplication of copies for common and private use, and in the preparation of the first complete version of the Bible in French. In England the result of the movement was likewise an increased circulation of the Bible, but it was a Bible in the language of the people.

The movement of which we are speaking is commonly connected in our minds, and quite rightly, with the name of Wycliffe; but it is impossible to define exactly the extent of his own personal participation in each of its developments. The movement was at first discountenanced, and presently persecuted, by the leading authorities in Church and State; and hence the writers of works in connection with it were not anxious to reveal their names. Most of the publications on the Wycliffite side are anonymous; and the natural consequence of this is that nearly all of them have been, at one time or another, attributed to Wycliffe himself. So far, however, as our immediate subject, the translation of the Bible, is concerned, there is no reason to doubt the personal responsibility of Wycliffe; nor is there any sufficient reason for the opinion, which has been sometimes held, that a complete English Bible existed before his time. It rests mainly on the statement of Sir Thomas More, in his controversy with Tyndale, the author of the first printed English New Testament, that he had seen English Bibles of an earlier date than Wycliffe's. The nearest approach to a justification of this claim is a version of the Pauline Epistles and the four larger Catholic Epistles (1 John, James, 1 and 2 Peter), to which were subsequently added the minor Catholic Epistles, the Acts, and Matt. i.–vi. 8, extant in a small group of MSS., of which the earliest (now at Cambridge) was written about the year 1400. This version (the credit for the publication of which in 1902 is due to Miss A. Paues) is said in the prologue to have been made at the request of a monk and a nun by their superior; and that it belongs to a time of controversy is shown by the fact that the author says that he wrote it at the risk of his life. It therefore does not satisfy the requirements of More's statement at all. It is far more probable that More was not aware that there were *two* Wycliffite translations, and had mistaken the date of the earlier one. This would be all the easier since the earlier version had no preface (as the second had) which definitely identified it with Wycliffe's views. To the history of these translations, the first complete Bible in the English language, we may now proceed.

Wycliffe.

John Wycliffe was born in Yorkshire about the year 1320. He entered Balliol College at Oxford, and presently became Fellow and, for a short time, Master of that College; but resigned the latter post when, in 1361, he was presented to the living of Fillingham, in Lincolnshire. It was not until he had passed middle life that he began to take part in public controversies; but when he did so, he at once became the most prominent leader of the party of reform. It was a period of discontent in England; discontent at the long and costly war with France, discontent at the demands of the Pope for money, discontent at the wealth of the higher dignitaries and corporations of the Church, who, in the main, supported the claims of the Pope. Wycliffe's first work was a treatise justifying the refusal of Parliament to pay the tribute claimed by the Pope in 1366; and from 1371 he was in the forefront of the religious and social disturbance which now began to rage. Papal interference and Church property were the main objects of his attack, and his chief enemies were the bishops. He was supported in most of his struggles by John of Gaunt, who wished to humiliate the Church; by the University of Oxford, consistently faithful to him except when he committed himself to theological opinions which it held heretical; and by the great mass of the common people, whose views he reflected with regard to the Pope and the Papal supporters.

With the political and religious controversy we have here nothing to do. Whether Wycliffe was right or wrong in his attack on Church property or in his generally socialistic schemes concerns us not now. Reformers are often carried to extremes which dispassionate observers must condemn. But his championship of the common people led him to undertake a work which entitles him to honourable mention by men of all parties and all opinions—the preparation of an English Bible which every man who knew his letters might read in his own home. And that even those who could not read might receive the knowledge of the teachings of this Bible, he instituted his order of "poor priests" to go about and preach to the poor in their own tongue, working in harmony with the clergy if they would allow them, but against them or independent of them if they were hostile.

The Earlier Wycliffite Bible.

The exact history of Wycliffe's translation of the Bible is uncertain. Separate versions of the Apocalypse and of a Harmony of the Gospels have been attributed to him, with more or less probability, but with no certainty. In any case these were but preludes to the great work. The New Testament was first finished, about the year 1380; and in 1382, or soon afterwards, the version of the entire Bible was completed. He was now rector of Lutterworth, in Leicestershire, living mainly in his parish, but keeping constantly in touch with Oxford and London. Other scholars assisted him in his work, and we have no certain means of knowing how much of the translation was actually done by himself. The New Testament is attributed to him, but we cannot say with certainty that it was entirely his own work. The greater part of the Old Testament was certainly translated by Nicholas Hereford, one of Wycliffe's most ardent supporters at Oxford. Plate XXX gives a reproduction of a page of the very manuscript written under Hereford's direction, now in the Bodleian Library at Oxford (Bodl. 959). The manuscript itself seems to tell something of its history. It breaks off quite abruptly at Baruch iii. 20, in the middle of a sentence, and it is evident that Hereford carried on the work no further; for another manuscript at Oxford, copied from it, ends at the same place, and contains a contemporaty note assigning the work to Hereford. It may be supposed that this sudden break marks the time of

Hereford's summons to London in 1382, to answer for his opinions, which resulted in his excommunication and retirement from England. The manuscript is written by five different scribes. The page exhibited, which contains Ecclesiasticus xlvii. 6–xlviii. 17, shows the change from the fourth hand to the fifth, with corrections in the margin which may be those of Hereford himself. After Hereford's departure the translation of the Old Testament was continued by Wycliffe himself or his assistants, and so the entire Bible was complete in its English dress before the death of Wycliffe in 1384.

A marked difference in style distinguishes Hereford's work from that of the other translators. Their style is free and colloquial, as is Wycliffe's own in his other works. There can be little doubt that he had in his mind the common people, for whom his version was specially intended, and that he wrote in a style which they would understand and appreciate. Hereford, on the other hand, was a scholar, perhaps a pedant, trained in University ideas of exactness and accuracy. He clung too closely to the exact words of the Latin from which his translation was made, and hence his style is stiff and awkward, and sometimes even obscure from its too literal faithfulness to the original.

The Later Wycliffite Bible.

The rest of the translation also was capable of improvement, and the strong contrast in style with the work of Hereford called aloud for a revision of the whole version. Such a revision was taken in hand, shortly after Wycliffe's death, by one of his followers, and was completed probably about the year 1388. The pupil who executed it has left a preface, in which he describes the principles upon which his revision was made, but he has not told us his name; from internal evidence, however, and especially from the verbal resemblance between this preface and other writings of which the author is known, he is believed to have been John Purvey, one of Wycliffe's most intimate friends during the latter part of his life, and a sharer in the condemnation of Nicholas Hereford. The Old Testament, which stood most in need of revision, was completed first, and the reviser's preface relates to that alone. The New Testament followed later. This revised version rapidly supplanted its predecessor, and became the current form of the Wycliffite Bible during the fifteenth century.

About a hundred and seventy copies of the Wycliffite Bible are now known to be in existence; and of these, five-sixths contain the revised edition by Purvey, while less than thirty have the original form of the translation. The following instance will show the character of this, the first complete English Bible, and the extent of the alterations made by Purvey. In the first passage the author of the older version is Hereford; in the second it is Wycliffe or one of his unnamed assistants.

EARLIER VERSION

ISAIAH xxxv. 1-6.

Gladen shal desert and the with oute weie, and ful out shal ioyen the wildernesse, and flouren as a lilie. Buriownynge it shal burioune, and ful out ioyen, ioyeful and preising. The glorie of Liban is youe to it, the fairnesse of Carmel and of Saron; thei shul see the glorie of the Lord, and the fairnesse of oure God. Coumforteth the hondes loosid atwynne, and the feble knees strengtheth. Seith, yee of litil corage, taketh coumfort, and wileth not dreden; lo ! oure God veniaunce of yelding shal bringe, God he shal come and sauen us. Thanne shul ben opened the eyen of blynde men, and eres of deue men shal ben opened. Thanne shal lepe as an hert the halte, and opened shal be the tunge of doumbe men; for kut ben in desert watris, and stremes in wildernesse.

LATER VERSION

ISAIAH xxxv. 1-6.

The forsakun *Judee* and with outen weie schal be glad, and wildirnisse schal make ful out ioye, and schal floure as a lilie. It buriownynge schal buriowne, and it glad and preisinge schal make ful out ioie. The glorie of Liban is youun to it, the fairnesse of Carmele and of Saron; thei schulen se the glorie of the Lord, and the fairnesse of oure God. Coumforte ye comelid hondis, and make ye strong feble knees. Seie ye, men of litil coumfort, be ye coumfortid, and nyle ye drede; lo ! oure God schal brynge the veniaunce of yelding, God hym silf schal come, and schal saue us. Thanne the iyen of blynde men schulen be openyd, and the eeris of deef men schulen be opyn. Thanne a crokid man schal skippe as an hert, and the tunge of doumbe men schal be openyd; for whi watris ben brokun out in desert, and stremes in wildirnesse.

EARLIER VERSION

HEBREWS i. 1-3.

Manyfold and many maners sum tyme God spekinge to fadris in prophetis, at the laste in thes daies spak to us in the sone: whom he ordeynede eyr of alle thingis, by whom he made and the worldis. The which whanne he is the schynynge of glorie and figure of his substaunce, and berynge alle thingis bi word of his vertu, makyng purgacioun of synnes, sittith on the righthalf of mageste in high thingis; so moche maad betere than aungelis, by how moche he hath inherited a more different, *or excellent*, name bifore hem.

LATER VERSION

HEBREWS i. 1-3.

God, that spak sum tyme bi prophetis in many maneres to oure fadris, at the laste in these daies he hath spoke to us bi the sone; whom he hath ordeyned eir of alle thingis, and bi whom he made the worldis. Which whanne also he is the brightnesse of glorie, and figure of his substaunce and berith all thingis bi word of his vertu, he makyth purgacioun of synnes and syttith on the righthalf of the maieste in heuenes; and so much is maad betere than aungels, bi hou myche he hath enerited a more dyuerse name bifor hem.

Such is the first complete English Bible, the first Bible which we know to have circulated among the common people of England. Many of the copies which now remain testify that they were intended for private use. They are not large and well-written volumes, such as would be placed in libraries or read to a congregation. Such copies there were, indeed—volumes which were found in kings' houses and in monastic libraries, as we shall see presently; but those of which we are now speaking are small, closely written copies, with no ornamentation, such as a man would have for his own reading and might carry in his pocket. In this form the Bible reached those who could not read Latin. It had indeed travelled a long way. It was no careful rendering of an accurately studied and revised Greek text, such as we have to-day. The original Greek had been translated into Latin long centuries before; the Latin had become corrupted and had been revised and translated anew by St. Jerome; St. Jerome's version had become corrupted in its turn, and had suffered many things of editors and copyists; and from copies of this corrupted Latin the English translation of Wycliffe and Purvey had been made. Still, through all these changes and chances, the substance of the Holy Scriptures remained the same; and, with whatever imperfections, the entire Bible was now accessible to the English in their own language, through the zeal and energy of John Wycliffe.

Is the Wycliffite Bible really Wycliffe's?

So, at least, it has always been held; and it is only because erroneous statements, once issued, may continue to mislead if not constantly corrected that it is necessary to refer to the assertion put forward in 1894 by the well-known Roman Catholic scholar Dr. (afterwards Cardinal) F. A. Gasquet to the effect that the Wycliffite Bible is not Wycliffe's at all, but is the work of his bitterest opponents, the bishops of the English Church who represented the party of Rome.

Theory that it was an Authorised Version issued by the Bishops.

Gasquet's main arguments are as follows: (1) The evidence connecting Wycliffe with an English version of the Bible is very slight; (2) the hostility of the bishops to an English Bible has been much exaggerated, and there is no sign that the possession or use of such a Bible was commonly made a subject of inquiry in the examinations of Wycliffe's adherents; (3) the character of the extant copies, and the rank and known opinions of their original owners, are such as to be inconsistent with the idea that they were the work of a poor and proscribed sect, as the Wycliffites are represented to have been; (4) there are indications of the existence of an authorised translation of the Bible at this period, and this we must conclude to be the version which has come down to us. The Bible of Wycliffe, if it ever existed, must have been completely destroyed.

Examination of this Theory.

Now on the first of these points, Dr. Gasquet seems to ignore the strength of the evidence which connects Wycliffe and his supporters, not merely with *a* translation of the Bible, but with *these* translations. That they were responsible for *a* translation is proved by the contemporary evidence of Archbishop Arundel, Knyghton, and a decree of the Council held at Oxford in 1408—all witnesses hostile to the Wycliffites. If that translation is not the one commonly known as the Wycliffite Bible, then no trace of it exists at present, which is in itself improbable. But of the actually extant translations, the Old Testament in the earlier version, as we have seen, is shown to be the work of Nicholas Hereford by the evidence of the note in the Oxford manuscript; while the later version is obviously based upon the earlier, and was, moreover, certainly the work of someone who held identical views with Purvey; further, in a manuscript of the earlier version at Dublin Purvey's own name is written as the owner, and (what is more important) the prologues to the several books commonly found in the later version have been inserted in Purvey's own writing. Dr. Gasquet says " whether Hereford or Purvey possibly may have had any part in the translation does not so much concern us "; but he cannot seriously mean to maintain that an authorised version of the English Bible, existing (as on his theory it existed) in direct opposition to the Wycliffite Bible, could itself be the work of Hereford and Purvey, the two most conspicuous adherents and companions of Wycliffe. Moreover, the last words of the preface to the revised version show that the author did not know how his work might be received by those in power, and looked forward to the possibility of being called upon to endure persecution for it: " God graunte to us alle grace to kunne [understand] wel and kepe wel holi writ, and suffre ioiefulli sum peyne for it at the laste." This evidence, taken together with the proved connection of Hereford and Purvey with the extant translation, is sufficient to establish that it is, as has always been believed, the Wycliffite Bible.

Still more disastrously does Gasquet's case break down in respect of his assertion that there is no evidence that Wycliffe's followers were persecuted for the possession of the Scriptures in English; for in fact the depositions of the witnesses against the Lollards (as Wycliffe's followers were called) repeatedly make mention of the possession of vernacular Bibles. Dr. Gasquet finally ruined his case by referring to the prosecution of Richard Hun in 1514. He admits that Hun was charged with the possession of a vernacular Bible, the prologue to which contained heretical errors; but he affirms that " we shall look in vain in the edition of Wycliffite Scriptures published by Forshall and Madden for any trace of these errors." He maintains therefore that the Bible for the possession of which Hun was persecuted was not that which we know as Wycliffe's. It is to be feared that Gasquet had not himself looked at the edition to which he refers; for there, in the preface to the second Wycliffite Bible, which we know as Purvey's, are precisely the statements which are cited verbatim in the charges against Hun. If Dr. Gasquet had read it, he could not possibly have attributed to the official heads of the English Church a translation the prologue to which speaks of "the pardouns of the bisschopis of Rome, that ben opin leesingis," and affirms that "to eschewe pride and speke onour of God and of his lawe, and repreve synne bi weie of charite, is matir and cause now whi prelatis and summe lordis sclanndren men, and clepen hem lollardis, eretikis, and riseris of debate and of treson agens the king." There can in fact be no doubt that the Bibles which we possess are in fact the translation produced by Wycliffe and his followers, and are those for the possession of which they were condemned by some at least of the heads of the English Church.[1]

The whole suggestion is in truth a mare's nest, probably due to the fact that Dr. Gasquet, at the time when he first promulgated it, was daily passing, on his way to the Manuscript Department of the British Museum, a handsome copy of the earlier Wycliffite Bible, which had once been the property of Thomas of Woodstock, Duke of Gloucester, uncle of Richard II. Dr. Gasquet was fully justified in emphasising the fact that copies of this Bible are known to have been in the possession of members of the Royal Family, such as Henry VI, Henry VII, and Humphrey, Duke of Gloucester, and of many religious houses, which were never charged with heresy on that account. But the fact is that the persecution of the Lollards was partial and intermittent. Much of it was due to the activity of particular bishops, such as Archbishop Arundel, under whose influence a Provincial Council at Oxford in 1408 forbade the production of any translation of the Scriptures into English, or any use of the translation lately composed in the time of John Wycliffe; but not all the bishops were of Arundel's way of thinking. Wycliffe had powerful supporters, notably John of Gaunt and the University of Oxford, so that there would have been no difficulty in the way of the production of fine copies, or their possession by eminent persons. As time went on, moreover, the charge of Lollardism or of heresy probably became weaker. Unless a copy contained Purvey's prologue (and most of them do not) there was nothing to connect it with Lollardism; and individuals and religious houses may

[1] Gasquet's article, originally printed in the *Dublin Review* (July, 1894), was reprinted in his volume, *The Old English Bible* (1897). The most complete and fully documented refutation of it was in the *Church Quarterly Review* for January, 1901.

have possessed them in all innocence of heart. It is quite probable that in the fifteenth and sixteenth centuries many people (including the royal owners mentioned above) used them without suspicion of their connection with Wycliffe. Among them may well have been Sir Thomas More himself (see above, p. 202); otherwise we should have to suppose that the orthodox Bibles of which he speaks, and which he expressly distinguishes from the Bible which caused the condemnation of Richard Hun, have wholly disappeared. It is contrary to all reason to suppose that the condemned Bible has survived in many scores of copies, while the orthodox one has perished without leaving a trace. The only rational explanation is that Sir Thomas More, whose good faith no one would question, was mistaken; that Cardinal Gasquet's revival of his contention was an unfortunate lapse on the part of a scholar who did much good work for Biblical studies; and that the manuscript Bibles of which we have been speaking were in truth the work of John Wycliffe and his disciples, and were the first and only complete Bibles in the English tongue before the invention of printing.

CHAPTER XI

THE ENGLISH PRINTED BIBLE

In the fifteenth century, then, the Bible was circulating, to a limited extent, in the Wycliffite translations, tolerated, though not encouraged, by the powers of Church and State; but the middle of the century was barely passed when two events took place which, though totally unconnected with one another, by their joint effects revolutionised the history of the Bible in Western Europe. In May 1453 the Turks stormed Constantinople; and in November 1454 the first dated product of the printing press in Europe was issued to the world.[1] The importance of the latter event is obvious, and has been already explained. Not only did the invention of printing do away, once and for all, with the progressive corruption of texts through the inevitable errors of copyists, but it also rendered it possible to multiply copies to an indefinite extent and to make learning accessible to every man who could read. Knowledge need no longer " rest in moulded heaps " in the monastic libraries, but could freely " melt in many streams to fatten lower lands." All that was required was that men should be found willing and able to make use of the machinery which the discovery of Gutenberg had put into their hands.

It was the other of the two events above recorded which, in great measure, provided the inspiration that was needful in order to make the invention of printing immediately fruitful. The Turkish invasion of Europe, culminating in the capture of Constantinople and the final fall of the Eastern Empire, drove to the West numberless scholars able and willing to teach the Greek language to the people among whom they took refuge. Greek, almost forgotten in Western Europe during many centuries, had always been a living language in the East, and now, journeying westwards, it met a fresh and eager spirit of inquiry, which welcomed joyfully the treasures of the incomparable literature enshrined in that language. Above all, it brought to the West the knowledge of the New Testament in its original tongue; and with the general zeal for knowledge came also a much increased study of Hebrew, which was of equal value for the Old Testament. Thus at the very moment when the printing press was ready to

[1] There are some fragments of printed editions of the grammar of Donatus which may be as early as 1450.

spread instruction over the world a new learning was springing up, which was only too glad to take advantage of the opportunity thus presented to it.

The revival of learning affected the Bible in three ways. In the first place it led to a multiplication of copies of the then current Bible, the Latin Vulgate. It is said that no less than 124 editions of it were issued before the end of the fifteenth century. Next, and far more important, it produced a study of the Scriptures in their original languages; and though the Greek and Hebrew manuscripts then available were by no means perfect, they at least served to correct and explain the more corrupt Latin. Finally—the point with which we are especially concerned in the present chapter—it promoted a desire to make the Scriptures known to all classes of men directly, and not through the medium of men's instruction; and this could only be done by having the Bible translated in each country into the common language of the people. The earliest vernacular Bibles were not connected with the Reformation controversy. A German Bible was printed at Strassburg by Mentelin in 1466, and eighteen others (besides Psalters and other separate books) appeared before the publication of the first part of Luther's translation in 1522. An Italian Bible was printed at Venice in 1471, and a Dutch one in 1477. A French Bible was printed at Lyons about 1478, and another about 1487. Even in England the greater part of the Bible narrative was available in Caxton's version of the Golden Legend, printed in 1483. But with the outbreak of the Reformation, Bible translation took on a new and controversial aspect. The reformers held that the best method of overthrowing the power of the monasteries and of the Roman Church was to enable the common people to read the Bible for themselves and learn how much of the current teaching of the priest and friar had no basis in the words of Scripture. The leaders of the Roman Church, on the other hand, doubted the advisability of allowing the Scriptures to be read by uneducated or half-educated folk without the accompaniment of oral instruction. With some this was a perfectly honest belief, for which there was much to be said; some, on the other hand, may have known that certain current practices could not be justified out of the Bible; others may have feared that the reformers would introduce heretical teaching into their translations. So it fell out that the struggle of the Reformation period was largely concerned with the question of the translation of the Bible. In Germany the popular version was made, once and for all, by the great reformer Luther; but in England, where parties were more divided, the translation of the Bible was the work of many years and many hands. In this chapter we shall narrate the history of the successive translations which were made in England, from the invention of printing to the completion of the Authorised Version in 1611, and in conclusion shall give some account of the Revised Version of 1881-5.

1. *Tyndale's Bible*, 1525.

The true father of the English Bible is William Tyndale, who was born in Gloucestershire about the year 1490. He was educated at Oxford, where he was a member of Magdalen Hall, then a dependency of Magdalen College. Here he may have begun his studies of Biblical interpretation and of the Greek language under the great leaders of the new learning at Oxford, Colet of Magdalen and Grocyn of New College. He graduated as B.A. in 1512, as M.A. in 1515; and at some uncertain date he is said to have gone to Cambridge, probably too late to have found Erasmus there, whose Greek New Testament he was destined to translate. When exactly he decided to devote himself to this task is unknown; but while he was resident tutor in the house of Sir John Walsh, at Little Sodbury in Gloucestershire, between 1520 and 1523, he is recorded to have said, in controversy with an opponent, " If God spare my life, ere many years I will cause a boy that driveth the plough shall know more of the Scripture than thou doest."[1] He had hoped that this might be accomplished under the patronage of the leaders of the Church, notably Tunstall, Bishop of London, to whom he applied in 1523 for countenance and support. Tunstall, however, refused his application, and although Humphrey Monmouth, an alderman of London, took him into his house for several months, it was not long before Tyndale understood " not only that there was no room in my lord of London's palace to translate the New Testament, but also that there was no place to do it in all England."

Accordingly in 1524 he left England and took up his abode in the free city of Hamburg. Here his translation of the New Testament was completed, and in 1525 he transferred himself to Cologne in order to have it printed. Meanwhile rumours of his work had got abroad. He was known to belong to the reforming party; in translating the Bible he was following the example of Luther; he may even have met Luther himself at Wittenburg,

[1] Consciously or otherwise, Tyndale was repeating the sentiments of Erasmus: " I totally disagree with those who are unwilling that the sacred scriptures, translated into the vulgar tongue, should be read by private individuals. . . . I wish they were translated into all languages of all peoples, that they might be read and known not merely by the Scotch and Irish, but even by the Turks and Saracens. . . . I wish that the ploughman might sing parts of them at his plough and the weaver at his shuttle, and that the traveller might beguile with their narration the weariness of his way " (Preface to N.T. of 1516).

which is not far from Hamburg. His translation was probably part of a design to convert England to Lutheranism; and clearly it must not be allowed to go forward if it were possible to stop it. The secret of the printing was, however, well kept; and it was not until the printing had made considerable progress that Cochlæus, an active enemy of the Reformation, obtained the clue to it. Hearing boasts from certain printers at Cologne of the revolution that would shortly be made in England, he invited them to his house; and having made them drunk, he learnt that three thousand copies of an English translation were being printed, and that some ten sheets of it had already been struck off. Having, in this truly creditable manner, obtained the information he required, he at once set the authorities of the town in motion to stop the work; but Tyndale secured the printed sheets and fled with them to Worms. At Worms he not only finished the edition partly printed at Cologne, which was in small quarto form and accompanied by marginal notes (or, as some think without much reason, printed a similar edition *de novo*), but also, knowing that a description of this edition had been sent by Cochlæus to England, in order that its importation might be stopped, had another edition struck off in octavo form and without notes. The printer was Peter Schoeffer.

Both editions were completed in 1525, which may consequently be regarded as the birth-year of the English printed Bible, though it was probably not until the beginning of 1526 that the first copies reached this country. Money for the work had been found by a number of English merchants, and by their means the copies were secretly conveyed into England, where they were eagerly bought and read on all sides. The leaders of the Church, however, declared against the translation from the first. Archbishop Warham, a good man and a scholar, issued a mandate for its destruction. Tunstall preached against it, declaring that he could produce 3,000 errors in it. Sir Thomas More wrote against it with much bitterness, charging it with wilful mistranslation of ecclesiastical terms with heretical intent. The book was solemnly burnt in London at Paul's Cross, and the bishops subscribed money to buy up all copies obtainable from the printers; a proceeding which Tyndale accepted with equanimity, since the money thus obtained enabled him to proceed with the work of printing a revised edition.[1] At the same time

[1] The account of this transaction given by the old chronicler Hall is very quaint. After describing how a merchant named Packington, friendly to Tyndale, introduced himself to Tunstall and offered to buy up copies of the New Testament for him, he proceeds thus: " The Bishop, thinking he had God by the toe, when indeed he had the devil by the fist, said, ' Gentle Mr. Packington, do your diligence and get them; and with all my heart I will pay for them whatsoever they cost you, for the books are erroneous and

one reprint of the New Testament after another was issued by Dutch printers, and, in spite of all efforts of the Bishops, copies continued to pour into England as fast as they were destroyed.

The English New Testament was thus irrevocably launched upon the world; yet so keen was the search for copies, both then and afterwards, and so complete the destruction of them, that barely a trace of these earliest editions remains to-day. Of the quarto edition, begun at Cologne and ended at Worms, only one solitary fragment exists, comprising eight out of the ten leaves printed at Cologne, with the text of Matt. i. 1–xxii. 12. It is now in the Grenville collection in the British Museum, and from it is taken the half-page reproduced in Plate XXXI, showing the beginning of the Sermon on the Mount. Of the octavo, one perfect copy exists in the library of the Baptist College at Bristol,[1] another, imperfect, in St. Paul's Cathedral. This is all that is left of the six thousand copies which Tyndale is said to have printed in 1525 at Worms, while of all the editions that followed up to 1534 no fragment has survived.

Tyndale's New Testament differs from all those that preceded it in being a translation from the original Greek, and not from the Latin. He made use of such other materials as were available to assist his judgment—namely, the Vulgate, the Latin translation which Erasmus published along with his Greek text, and the German translation of Luther; but these were only subordinate aids, and his main authority was unquestionably the Greek text which had been published by Erasmus in 1516 and revised in 1522. This was a new departure, and some of the "mistakes" which Tunstall and others professed to find in Tyndale's work may have been merely cases in which the Greek gave a different sense from the Latin to which they were accustomed. The amount of actual errors in translation would not appear to be at all such as to justify the extremely hostile recep-

nought, and I intend surely to destroy them all, and to burn them at Paul's Cross.' Packington came to William Tyndale and said, 'William, I know thou art a poor man, and hast a heap of New Testaments and books by thee, for the which thou hast both endangered thy friends and beggared thyself, and I have now gotten thee a merchant which, with ready money, shall despatch thee of all that thou hast, if you think it so profitable for yourself.' 'Who is the merchant?' said Tyndale. 'The Bishop of London,' said Packington. 'Oh, that is because he will burn them,' said Tyndale. 'Yea, marry,' quoth Packington. 'I am the gladder,' said Tyndale, 'for these two benefits shall come thereof: I shall get money to bring myself out of debt, and the whole world will cry out against the burning of God's Word; and the overplus of the money that shall remain to me shall make me more studious to correct the said New Testament, and so newly to imprint the same once again, and I trust the second will much better like you than ever did the first.' And so forward went the bargain, the Bishop had the books, Packington had the thanks, and Tyndale had the money."

[1] This copy was discovered in 1740 by an agent of the Earl of Oxford who bestowed on the fortunate discoverer an annuity of £20.

PLATE XXX.

solempnytes ... [illegible] to þis ende he preiside þe name
... and þat ben lered in þe pees in songis and in prouerbis and
comparisouns and in remenyngis wondreden þe londis
and in þe name of þe lord to whom is þe to name god of
israel. þou gedridist as latoun gold and as leed þou fulfil
dist siluer and þou bowedist þin þiȝis to wymmen
power þou haddist in þi bodi þou ȝeue a wem in þi glorie.
and defoulidist þi seed to bringe in wraþþefulnesse to þi fre
children. and in oþer þingis þi folie þat þou shuldist maken þe
empire partid on two. and of Effraym to comaun
den an hard maundement. god forsoþe shal not le
uen his merci and he shal not spille ne don awei his wer
kis ne leesen fro þe stok his chosene sones sones and
þe seed of him þat loueþ þe lord he shal not shenden.
he ȝaf forsoþe remnaunt to iacob and dauid of þat lynage. and Salo
mon hadde ende wiþ his fadris. and he lafte after him
of his seed þe folie of þe folc and þe mynushid fro þe
prudence roboam. þe which turnede awei þe folc bi
his counseil. and ieroboam þe sone of nabaþ þat made
to synnen israel and ȝaf þe weie of synnyng to effraym
and ful manye ben redundeden þe synnes of hem. forsoþe
þei turneden hem awei fro þe lond. and he souȝte alle wicke
nesses vn to þe tyme þat defendyng ful cam to hem.
and fro alle synnes he delyuerede hem.

And helias þe prophete roos as fier and his word as a
brond brende þe which brouȝte in to hem hungir
and folewinge him bi þer envie he maden fewe. forsoþe þei
myȝten not suffre þe heestis of þe lord. bi þe
word of þe lord he wiþhelde heuene and caste doun fro
him þe fier þries. so maad large is helie in his
merueilis. and who mai in lijc manere glorien to þee. þat
reiside vp þe deede fro helle fro þe lot of deþ in þe
word of þe lord god. þe which puttide doun kingis
to deþ and þou brekist liȝtli þe myȝt of hem and þe glorious

caste awei fro þe lond and ben scaterid in to eche
lond. and þer is lafte ful fewe folc and a prince in þe
hous of dauid. summe of hem diden þat shulde
plesen to god. oþere forsoþe diden many
synnes. Ezechias strengþide his citee and brouȝte
in to þe myddil of it water. and dolue wiþ iren
þe roche and bilde vp to þe water a pit. in his
dayes steȝede vp sennacherib and sente rapsa
cen and vnderputte his hond aȝen hem and putte
out his hond in to syon and proud is maad in his
myȝt. þanne moued ben þe hertis and þe
hondis of hem and þei sorewiden as wymmen
trauailinge wiþ childe. and þei inwardli clepeden
þe merciful lord and strechinge out hondis þei
rereden vp to heuene. and þe holi lord god herde
anoon þe vois of hem. he remembride not þe
synnes of hem ne ȝaf hem to þer enemys. but
purgide hem in þe hond of ysaie þe holi prophete.
he þrew doun þe tentis of assiries and hem to
brosede þe aungil of þe lord. for whi ezechie
dide þat pleside to þe lord and strongli he wente
in þe weie of dauid his fader þat ysaie þe grete prophete
and feiþful in þe siȝte of god sente to him. in his
dayes bacward wente aȝen þe sunne and addi
de to þe king lijf. wiþ a greet spirit he saw
þe laste þingis and counfortide þe weilinge men
in syon vn to euermor. he shewide þingis to co
men and hid er þat þei fellen.

The mynde of Josie maad in makinge of
smelling is a werk of a pyment makere. in eche
mouþ as hony shal ben inwardli swete þe
mynde of him and as melodie in þe feste of wyn.
he is euene riȝt goodli in þe penaunce of folc and

WYCLIFFE'S BIBLE—A.D. 1382.

(Original size of page, 13 in. × 9¼ in.; of part reproduced, 5¾ in. × 7½ in.)

u. vi.

The fyfth Chapter.

When he sawe the people / he went vp into a mountaine/and wen he was sett/ hys disciples cam vnto him / and he opened his mouth/and taught them sayinge: Blessed are the povre in sprete: for thers is the kyngdom of heven. Blessed are they that mourne: for they shalbe comforted. Blessed are the meke: for they shall inheret ✕ the erthe. Blessed are they which hũger and thurst for rightewesnes: for they shalbe fylled. Blessed are the mercyfull: for they shall obteyne mercy. Blessed are the pure in hert: for they shall se god. Blessed are the maynteyners of peace: for they shalbe called the chyldren of god. Blessed are they which suffre persecucion for righttewesnes sake: for thers is the kyngdom of heven. Blessed are ye whẽ men shall revyle you/and persecute you/ and shal falsly saye all manner of evle sayings agaynst you for my sake. Reioyce ãd be gladde/for greate is youre rewarde in heven. For so persecuted they the prophetts which were before youre dayes.

All these dedes here rehearsed as to norisshe peace/ to shewe mercy/ to suffre psecuciõ/ and so forth/make not a man happye and blessed/ nether deserve the rewarde of heven: but declare and testifie that we are happy and blessede and that we shall have greate pmociõ ĩ heven. and certyfyeth vs ĩ oure hertes that we are goddes sonnes/ & that the holy gost is in vs. for all good thynges are geven to vs frely of god for christes bloudes sake ãd his merittes

TYNDALE'S NEW TESTAMENT—A.D. 1525.

(Unreduced; size of whole page, $7\frac{1}{2}$ in. × $5\frac{1}{2}$ in.)

tion which the leaders of the Church gave to the English Bible. More may or may not have been right in holding that the old ecclesiastical terms, such as "church," "priest," "charity," round which the association of centuries had gathered, should not be set aside in favour of "congregation," "senior," "love," and the like: there is much to be said on both sides of the question; but certainly this was no just reason for proscribing the whole translation and assailing its author. Nor can such treatment be explained on the ground of Tyndale's marginal comments, controversial though they unquestionably were, and, in part, derived from those of Luther; for measures were taken to suppress the book before its actual appearance, and the proscription was not confined to the quarto, which alone contained the comments, but was extended to the octavo, in which the sacred text stood by itself. The reception which the heads of the English Church, Henry VIII included, gave to Tyndale's Testament can only be attributed to a dislike of the very existence of an English Bible.

Tyndale's labours did not cease with the appearance of his New Testament. His hope was to complete the translation of the whole Bible; and although other works, chiefly of a controversial character, occupied some portion of his time, he now set himself to work on the Old Testament. The first instalment occupied him for four years, and in 1530 the Pentateuch, translated from the original Hebrew and accompanied by strongly controversial marginal notes, was printed at Marburg. The five books must have been separately printed, since Genesis and Numbers are printed in black letter, and the others in Roman (or ordinary) type; but there is no sufficient evidence of separate publication. Only one perfect copy of this edition is known, in the British Museum. The Pentateuch was followed in 1531 by the Book of Jonah, of which also only one copy is now known to exist, likewise in the British Museum. But Tyndale had not said his last word on the New Testament. Like a good scholar, he was as fully aware as his critics could be that his version admitted of improvement, and he undertook a full and deliberate revision of it, striving especially after a more exact correspondence with the Greek. The publication of his labours was hastened by the appearance of an unauthorised revision in 1534, the work of one George Joye. Since the original publication in 1526, the printers of Antwerp had been issuing successive reprints of it, each less correct than its predecessor, and at last Joye had consented to revise a new edition for the press. Joye had taken Tyndale's version, altered it considerably, especially by comparison with the Latin Vulgate, had introduced variations of translation in accordance with his own theological opinions, and had published the whole without any indication of a change of authorship. Tyndale was justly indignant at this act of combined piracy and fraud; but his best antidote was found in the publication of his own revised edition in the autumn of the same year. It is this edition of 1534, printed at Antwerp, which is the true climax of Tyndale's work on the New Testament. The text had been diligently corrected; introductions were prefixed to each book; the marginal commentary was rewritten in a less controversial spirit; and at the end of the volume were appended certain extracts from the Old Testament which were read as "Epistles" in the Church services for certain days of the year.

With the appearance of this edition Tyndale's work was practically at an end. The battle was substantially won; for although he himself was held in no greater favour in England than before, the feeling against an English Bible had considerably abated, and the quarrel with Rome had reached an open rupture. As early as 1530 an assembly convoked by Archbishop Warham, while repeating the official condemnation of Tyndale, announced that the king would have the New Testament faithfully translated "as soon as he might see their manners and behaviour meet, apt and convenient to receive the same." By 1535 Cromwell and Cranmer were convinced of the desirability of having the Bible translated by authority; and Tyndale was able to present a magnificent copy of his new edition to Queen Anne Boleyn,[1] who had constantly favoured the undertaking of the English Bible. But the enmity of the Romanist party against Tyndale himself was not abated; and his labour for the diffusion of God's Word was destined to receive the crown of martyrdom. He was now residing at Antwerp, a free city, and was safe as an inmate of the "English House," an established home of English merchants in that city. But in 1535 a traitor, named Henry Philips, wormed himself into his confidence and used his opportunity to betray him into the hands of some officers of the Emperor Charles V, by whom he was kidnapped and carried out of the city. The real promoters of this shameful plot have never been known. It is certain that Philips was well supplied with money, which must have come from the Romanist party, to which he belonged. Henry VIII, who was now at open war with this party, can have had no share in the treachery. The most that can be said against him is that he took no steps to procure Tyndale's release. Cromwell used his influence to some extent; but from the moment of the arrest the prisoner's fate was certain. Charles V had set himself to crush heresy by stringent laws; and there was no doubt that, from Charles's point of view, Tyndale was a heretic. After a long imprisonment at Vilvorde, in Belgium, he was brought to

[1] This copy is now in the British Museum.

trial, and in October 1536 he suffered martyrdom by strangling at the stake and burning, crying "with a fervent, great, and a loud voice, 'Lord, open the King of England's eyes.'"

Before his arrest Tyndale had once more revised his New Testament, which passed through the press during his imprisonment. This edition, which appeared in 1535, differs little from that of 1534, and the same may be said of other reprints which appeared in 1535 and 1536. These cannot have been supervised by Tyndale himself, and the eccentricities in spelling which distinguish one of them are probably due to Flemish compositors. We shall see in the following pages how his work lived after him, and how his translation is the direct ancestor of our Authorised Version. The genius of Tyndale shows itself in the fact that he was able to couch his translations in a language perfectly understanded of the people and yet full of beauty and of dignity. If the language of the Authorised Version has deeply affected our English prose, it is to Tyndale that the praise is originally due. He formed the mould, which subsequent revisers did but modify. A specimen of his work may fitly close our account of him.[1] It is his version of Phil. ii. 5-13 as it appears in the edition of 1534, and readers will at once recognise how much of the wording is familiar to us in the rendering of the Authorised Version:

"Let the same mynde be in you the which was in Christ Jesu. Which beynge in the shape of God, and thought yt not robbery to be equal with God. Neverthelesse, he made hymsilfe of no reputacion, and toke on him the shape of a servaunte, and becam lyke unto men, and was founde in his apparell as a man. He humbled hym sylfe and becam obedient unto the deeth, even the deeth of the crosse. Wherfore God hath exalted hym, and gyven hym a name above all names, that in the name of Jesus shulde every knee bowe, both of thingis in heven and thingis in erth and thingis under erth, and that all tonges shulde confesse that Jesus Christ is the lorde, unto the prayse of God the father. Wherfore, my dearly beloved: as ye have alwayes obeyed, not when I was present only, but nowe moche more in myne absence, even so performe youre owne health with feare and tremblynge. For yt is God which worketh in you, both the wyll and also the dede, even of good wyll."

2. *Coverdale's Bible*, 1535.

Tyndale was burnt; but he, with even greater right than Latimer, might say that he had lighted such a candle, by God's grace, in England, as should never be put out. His own New

[1] Another specimen will be found in Appendix II, where it can be compared with the versions of his successors.

Testament had been rigorously excluded from England, so far as those in authority could exclude it; but the cause for which he gave his life was won. Even before his death he might have heard that a Bible, partly founded on his own, had been issued in England under the protection of the highest authorities. In 1534 the Upper House of Convocation of Canterbury had petitioned the king to authorise a translation of the Bible into English, and it was probably at this time that Cranmer proposed a scheme for a joint translation by nine or ten of the most learned bishops and other scholars. Cranmer's scheme came to nothing; but Cromwell, now Secretary of State, incited Miles Coverdale to publish a work of translation on which he had been already engaged. Coverdale had known Tyndale abroad, and is said to have assisted him in his translation of the Pentateuch; but he was no Greek or Hebrew scholar, and his version, which was printed abroad in 1535 (probably, according to the latest expert view, at Marburg) and appeared in England in that year or the next, professed only to be translated from the Dutch [*i.e.*, German] and Latin. Coverdale, a moderate, tolerant, earnest man, claimed no originality, and expressly looked forward to the Bible being more faithfully presented both " by the ministration of other that begun it afore " (Tyndale) and by the future scholars who should follow him; but his Bible has two important claims on our interest. Though not expressly authorised, it was undertaken at the wish of Cromwell, and a dedication to Henry VIII, printed apparently by Nycholson of Southwark, was inserted among the prefatory matter of the German-printed sheets, which were no doubt imported unbound. It is thus the first English Bible which circulated in England without let or hindrance from the higher powers. It is also the first complete English printed Bible, since Tyndale had not been able to finish the whole of the Old Testament. A page of it is shown in Plate XXXII. In the Old Testament Coverdale depended mainly on the Swiss-German version published by Zwingli and Leo Juda in 1524-9, though in the Pentateuch he also made considerable use of Tyndale's translation. The New Testament is a careful revision of Tyndale by comparison with the German. It is to Coverdale therefore that our English versions of the poetical and prophetical books are primarily due, and in handling the work of others he showed great skill. Many of Coverdale's phrases have passed into the Authorised Version. In one respect he departed markedly from his predecessor—namely, in bringing back to the English Bible the ecclesiastical terms which Tyndale had banished.

In addition to the Bible issued in 1535-6, Coverdale, in 1538, published a revised New Testament with the Latin Vulgate in parallel columns.[1] Meanwhile the demand for the Bible continued unabated, and a further step had been made in the direction of securing official authorisation. Two revised editions were published in 1537, this time printed in England by Nycholson; and one of these, in quarto, bore the announcement that it was "set forth with the king's most gracious license." The bishops in Convocation might still discuss the expediency of allowing the Scriptures to circulate in English, but the question had been decided without them. The Bible circulated, and there could be no returning to the old ways.

Coverdale's Treatment of the Apocrypha.

One important characteristic of our English Bible makes its first appearance in Coverdale's Bible of 1535. This is the segregation of the books which we call the Apocrypha. As has been stated above (p. 54), these books formed an integral part of the Greek Old Testament, being intermixed among the books which we know as canonical. They were, however, rejected from the Hebrew Canon as formed about A.D. 100. Many of the early Fathers concurred in this rejection. The Syrian version omitted them; in the Canon of Athanasius they were placed in a class apart; and Jerome refused to include them in his Vulgate. They had, however, been included in the Old Latin version, which was translated from the Septuagint; and the Roman Church was reluctant to abandon them. The provincial Council of Carthage in 397, under the influence of Augustine, expressly included them in the Canon; and in the Latin Bible they remained, the Old Latin translation of them being incorporated in Jerome's Vulgate. When the Reformation came, however, Luther reverted to the Hebrew Canon, and placed these books apart under the title of "Apocrypha." At the same time he segregated Hebrews, James, Jude and Revelation at the end of the New Testament, as books of lesser value. Tyndale followed this arrangement in his New Testament, and would probably have done the same in the Old, since he was translating from the Hebrew and was much under the influence of Luther. Certainly Coverdale does so. His Old Testament is divided into five parts: (1) Pentateuch; (2) Joshua-Esther; (3) Job-"Solomon's Balettes" (*i.e.*, Song of Solomon); (4) Prophets; (5) "Apocripha, the bokes and treatises which amonge the fathers of olde are not rekened to be of like authorite with the other bokes of the

[1] This was printed in England, but so inaccurately that Coverdale had a second edition printed at once in Paris. This no doubt led to a coolness with his English printer, Nycholson, of Southwark, who issued another edition, also very inaccurate, substituting the name of "Johan Hollybushe" for that of Coverdale on the title-page.

byble, nether are they founde in the Canon of the Hebrue." This example was followed in all subsequent English Bibles, though without going to the length, now unfortunately common, of omitting altogether these books, which the Articles of our Church (agreeing in this with both Jerome and Luther) prescribe to be read for example of life and instruction of manners. The Roman Church, on the other hand, at the Council of Trent in 1546, adopted by a majority the opinion that all the books of the larger Canon should be received as of equal authority, making this for the first time a dogma of the Church, in spite of Jerome, and enforcing it by anathema.

The Apocrypha in Subsequent English Bibles.

To complete the story it may be noted that the Puritan party always manifested dislike for these books. They were omitted from some editions of the Geneva Bible. Copies of the Authorised Version without the Apocrypha are known as early as 1629, though the numeration of the sheets shows that the books were printed, but omitted in binding up. This practice must have existed earlier, for it was forbidden by Archbishop Abbot in 1615. Copies of which it never formed part are known from 1642 onwards. In 1644 the Long Parliament forbade the reading of lessons from it in public; but the lectionary of the English Church has always included lessons from it. The first edition printed in America (apart from a surreptitious printing in 1752), in 1782, is without it. In 1826 the British and Foreign Bible Society, which has been one of the principal agents in the circulation of the Scriptures throughout the world, resolved never in future to print or circulate copies containing the Apocrypha; and this resolution has recently debarred the Society from assisting in the printing of the Bible for the Church in Abyssinia, because the Ethiopic Bible, being translated from the Septuagint, has always contained the Apocryphal books.

3. *Matthew's Bible*, 1537.

Fresh translations, or, to speak more accurately, fresh revisions, of the Bible now followed one another in quick succession. The first to follow Coverdale's was that which is known as Matthew's Bible, but which is in fact the completion of Tyndale's work. Tyndale had only published the Pentateuch, Jonah, and the New Testament, but he had never abandoned his work on the Old Testament, and he had left behind him in manuscript a version of the books from Joshua to 2 Chronicles. The person into whose hands this version fell, and who was responsible for its publication, was John Rogers, a disciple of Tyndale and an earnest Reformer; and whether "Thomas Matthew," whose name stands at the foot of the dedication, was an assistant of Rogers, or was Rogers himself under another name, has never been clearly ascertained.[1] There is, however, no doubt that Rogers was the person responsible for it, and that " Matthew " has no other known existence. The Bible which Rogers published in 1537, at the expense of two London merchants, consisted of Tyndale's version of Genesis to 2 Chronicles, Coverdale's for the rest of the Old Testament (including the Apocrypha), and Tyndale's New Testament according to his final edition in 1535; the whole being very slightly revised, and accompanied by introductions, summaries of chapters, woodcuts, and copious marginal comments of a somewhat contentious character. It was printed abroad, probably at Antwerp, was dedicated to Henry VIII, and was cordially welcomed and promoted by Cranmer. Cromwell himself, at Cranmer's request, presented it to Henry and procured his permission for it to be sold publicly; and so it came about that Tyndale's translation, which Henry and all the heads of the Church had in 1525 proscribed, was in 1537 sold in England by leave of Henry and through the active support of the Secretary of State and the Archbishop of Canterbury.

4. *The Great Bible*, 1539-1541.

The English Bible had now been licensed, but it had not yet been commanded to be read in churches. That honour was reserved for a new revision which Cromwell (perhaps anxious lest the substantial identity of Matthew's Bible with Tyndale's, and the controversial character of the notes, should come to the king's knowledge) employed Coverdale to make on the basis of Matthew's Bible. It was decided to print it in Paris, where better paper and more sumptuous printing were to be had. The French king's licence was obtained, and printing was begun in 1538. Before it was completed, however, friction arose between the English and French courts, and on the suggestion of the French ambassador in London the Inquisition was prompted to seize the sheets. Coverdale, however, rescued a great number of the sheets, conveyed printers, presses, and type to London, and there completed the work, of which Cromwell had already in September, 1538, ordered that a copy should be put up in some convenient place in every church. The Bible thus issued in the spring of 1539 is a splendidly printed volume of large size, from

[1] It has also been suggested that Matthew stands for Tyndale, to whom the greater part of the translation was really due. The appearance of Tyndale's name on the title-page would have made it impossible for Henry VIII to admit it into England without convicting himself of error in proscribing Tyndale's New Testament.

which characteristic its popular name was derived. Prefixed to it is a fine engraved title-page (reproduced as the frontispiece to the present volume), believed (though not with certainty) to be the work of Holbein. It represents the Almighty at the top blessing Henry, who hands out copies of the Bible to Cranmer and Cromwell on his right and left. Below, the archbishop and the Secretary of State, distinguished by their coats of arms beneath them, are distributing copies to the clergy and laity respectively, while the bottom of the page is filled with a crowd of people exclaiming *Vivat Rex!* ("Long live the King!"). Cromwell's own copy, on vellum with illuminations, is now in the library of St. John's College, Cambridge. In contents, it is Matthew's Bible revised throughout, the Old Testament especially being considerably altered in accordance with Munster's Latin version, which was greatly superior to the Zurich Bible on which Coverdale had relied in preparing his first translation. The New Testament was also revised, with special reference to the Latin version of Erasmus. Coverdale's characteristic style of working was thus exhibited again in the formation of the Great Bible. He did not attempt to contribute independent work of his own, but took the best materials which were available at the time and combined them with the skill of a master of language. He had intended to add notes, and with this view inserted marginal marks, which he explains in his prologue; but the Privy Council refused to sanction them, and after standing in the margin for three editions these signposts were withdrawn.

In accordance with Cromwell's order, which was repeated by royal proclamation in 1541, copies of the Great Bible were set up in every church; and we have a curious picture of the eagerness with which people flocked to make acquaintance with the English Scriptures in the complaint of Bishop Bonner that "diverse wilful and unlearned persons inconsiderately and indiscreetly read the same, especially and chiefly at the time of divine service, yea in the time of the sermon and declaration of the word of God." One can picture to oneself the great length of Old St. Paul's (of which the bishop is speaking) with the preacher haranguing from the pulpit at one end, while elsewhere eager volunteers are reading from the six volumes of the English Bible which Bonner had put up in different parts of the cathedral, surrounded by crowds of listeners who, regardless of the order of divine service, are far more anxious to hear the Word of God itself than expositions of it by the preacher in the pulpit. Over all the land copies of the Bible spread and multiplied, so that a contemporary witness testifies that it had entirely superseded the old romances as the favourite reading of the people. Edition after edition was required from the press. The first had appeared in 1539; a second (in which the books of the Prophets had again been considerably revised by Coverdale) followed in April 1540, with a preface by Cranmer, and a third in July. In that month Cromwell was overthrown and executed, and his arms were excised from the title-page in subsequent editions; but the progress of the Bible was not checked. Another edition appeared in November, and on the title-page was the authorisation of Bishop Tunstall of London, who had thus lived to sanction a revised form of the very work which, as originally issued by Tyndale, he had formerly proscribed and burnt. Three more editions appeared in 1541, all substantially reproducing the revision of April 1540, though with some variations; and by this time the immediate demand for copies had been satisfied, and the work alike of printing and of revising the Bible came for the moment to a pause.[1]

It is worth noting that the Great Bible, in spite of its size, was not confined to use as a lectern Bible in churches. There is good evidence that it was also bought for private study. A manuscript in the British Museum (Harl. MS. 590, f. 77) contains the narrative of one W. Maldon of Newington, who states that he was about fifteen years of age when the order for the placing of the Bible in churches was issued: "and immediately after divers poor men in the town of Chelmsford in the county of Essex . . . bought the New Testament of Jesus Christ, and on Sundays did sit reading it in the lower end of the Church, and many would flock about them to hear their reading." He describes how his father took him away from listening to these readings: "then thought I, I will learn to read English, and then will I have the New Testament and read thereon myself; and then had I learned of an English primer as far as *patris sapientia*, then on Sundays I plied my English primer. The Maytide following I and my father's prentice, Thomas Jeffery, laid our money together and bought the New Testament in English, and hid it in our bedstraw"; for which, on discovery by his father, he was soundly thrashed. The price of the folio Great Bible, which the printers had wished to fix at 13s. 4d., was reduced at Cromwell's request to 10s. in sheets or 12s. bound. A New Testament might therefore have cost about 2s. 6d.—which, of course, meant far more then than now.

It is from the time of the Great Bible that we may fairly date the origin of the love and knowledge of the Bible which has characterised, and which it may be hoped will always characterise,

[1] Several of the editions of the Great Bible were printed by Whitchurch, and it is under the name of Whitchurch's Bible that the rule laid down for the guidance of the revisers of 1611 refers to it. The rule (which instructs the revisers to refer to "Tindale's, Matthew's, Coverdale's, Whitchurch's" and the "Geneva" translations) is quoted in the preface to the Revised New Testament of 1881.

the English nation. The successive issues of Tyndale's translation had been largely wasted in providing fuel for the opponents of the Reformation; but every copy of the seven editions of the Great Bible found, not merely a single reader, but a congregation of readers. The Bible took hold of the people, superseding, as we have seen, the most popular romances; and through the rest of the sixteenth and the seventeenth centuries the extent to which it had sunk into their hearts is seen in their speech, their writings, and even in the daily strife of politics. And one portion of the Great Bible has had a deeper and more enduring influence still. When the first Prayer Book of Edward VI was drawn up, directions were given in it for the use of the Psalms from the Great Bible; and from that day to this the Psalter of the Great Bible has held its place in our Book of Common Prayer. Just as, eleven hundred years before, Jerome's rendering of the Psalter from the Hebrew failed to supersede his slightly revised edition of the Old Latin Psalms, to which the ears of men were accustomed, so the more correct translation of the Authorised Version has never driven out the more familiar Prayer-Book version which we have received from the Great Bible. It may be, it certainly is, less accurate; but it is smoother in diction, more evenly balanced for purposes of chanting; above all, it has become so minutely familiar to us in every verse and phrase that the loss of old associations, which its abandonment would produce, would more than counterbalance the advantage of any gain in accuracy.

5. *Taverner's Bible*, 1539.

One other translation should be noticed in this place for completeness sake, although it had no effect on the subsequent history of the English Bible. This was the Bible of R. Taverner, an Oxford scholar, who undertook an independent revision of Matthew's Bible at the same time as Coverdale was preparing the first edition of the Great Bible under Cromwell's auspices. Taverner was a good Greek scholar, but not a Hebraist; consequently the best part of his work is the revision of the New Testament, in which he introduces not a few changes for the better. The Old Testament is more slightly revised, chiefly with reference to the Vulgate. Taverner's Bible appeared in 1539, and was once reprinted; but it was entirely superseded for general use by the authorised Great Bible, and exercised no influence upon later translations.

6. *The Geneva Bible*, 1557-1560.

The closing years of Henry's reign were marked by a reaction against the principles of the Reformation. Although he had thrown off the supremacy of the Pope, he was by no means favourably disposed towards the teachings and practices of the Protestant leaders, either at home or abroad; and after the fall of Cromwell his distrust of them took a more marked form. In 1543 all translations of the Bible bearing the name of Tyndale were ordered to be destroyed; all notes or comments in other Bibles were to be obliterated; and the common people were forbidden to read any part of the Bible either in public or in private. In 1546 Coverdale's New Testament was joined in the same condemnation with Tyndale's, and a great destruction of these earlier Testaments then took place. Thus, in spite of a resolution of Convocation, instructing certain of the bishops and others to take in hand a revision of the errors of the Great Bible, not only was the work of making fresh translations suspended for several years, but the continued existence of those which had been previously made seemed to be in danger.

The accession of Edward VI in 1547 removed this danger, and during his reign all the previous translations were frequently reprinted. It is said that some forty editions of the existing translations—Tyndale's, Coverdale's, Matthew's, the Great Bible, and even Taverner's—were issued in the course of this short reign; but no new translation or revision made its appearance. It is true that Sir John Cheke, whose memory is preserved by Milton as having "taught Cambridge and King Edward Greek," prepared a translation of St. Matthew and part of St. Mark, in which he avoided, as far as possible, the use of all words not English in origin, substituting (for example) "gainrising" for "resurrection" and "biword" for "parable"; but this version was not printed, and remains as a mere linguistic curiosity. Under Mary it was not likely that the work of translation would make any progress. Two of the men most intimately associated with the previous versions, Cranmer and Rogers, were burnt at the stake, and Coverdale (who under Edward VI had become Bishop of Exeter) escaped with difficulty. The public use of the English Bible was forbidden, and copies were removed from the churches; but beyond this no special destruction of the Bible was attempted.

Meanwhile the fugitives from the persecution of England were gathering beyond sea, and the more advanced and earnest among them were soon attracted by the influence of Calvin to a congenial home at Geneva. Here the interrupted task of perfecting the English Bible was resumed. The place was very favourable for the purpose. Geneva was the home, not only of Calvin, but of Beza, the most prominent Biblical scholar then living. Thought was free, and no considerations of state policy or expediency need affect the translators. Since the last revision of the English translation much had been done, both by Beza and by others, to improve and elucidate the Bible text. A company of Frenchmen was already at work in Geneva on the production of a revised translation of the French Bible, which eventually became the standard version for the Protestants of that country. Amid such surroundings a body of English scholars took in hand the task of revising the Great Bible. The firstfruits of this activity was the New Testament of W. Whittingham, brother-in-law of Calvin's wife and a Fellow of All Souls College, Oxford, which was printed in 1557 in a convenient small octavo form; but this was soon superseded by a more comprehensive and complete revision of the whole Bible by Whittingham himself and a group of other scholars. Taking for their basis the Great Bible in the Old Testament, and Tyndale's last revision in the New, they revised the whole with much care and scholarship. In the Old Testament the changes introduced are chiefly in the Prophetical Books and the Hagiographa (which had not been translated by Tyndale, but had mainly been taken from the Latin), and consist for the most part of closer approximations to the original Hebrew. In the New Testament they took Beza's Latin translation and commentary as their guide, and by far the greater number of the changes in this part of the Bible are traceable to his influence. The whole Bible was accompanied by explanatory comments in the margin, of a somewhat Calvinistic character, but without any excessive violence or partisanship. The division of chapters into verses, which had been introduced by Whittingham from Stephanus' Græco-Latin New Testament of 1551, was here for the first time adopted for the whole English Bible. In all previous translations the division had been into paragraphs, as in our present Revised Version. For the Old Testament, the verse division was that made by Rabbi Nathan in 1448, which was first printed in a Venice edition of 1524, and was adopted by Pagninus in a Latin Bible in 1528, with a different division in the New Testament. Stephanus' Latin Bible of 1555 is the first to show the present division in both Testaments, and it was this that was followed in the Geneva Bible.

Next to Tyndale, the authors of the Geneva Bible have exercised the most marked influence of all the early translators on the Authorised Version. Their own scholarship, both in Hebrew and in Greek, seems to have been sound and sober; and Beza, their principal guide in the New Testament, was unsurpassed in his own day as an interpreter of the sacred text. Printed in legible Roman type and in a convenient quarto or smaller form, with a few illustrative woodcuts, and accompanied by an intelligible and sensible commentary, the Geneva Bible (either as originally published in 1560, or with the New Testament further revised by Tomson, in fuller harmony with Beza's views, in 1576) became the Bible of the household, as the Great Bible was the Bible of the church. It was never authorised for use in churches, and Archbishop Parker, who was interested in its rival, described below, seems to have obstructed the printing of it in England; but there was nothing to prevent its importation from Geneva, and up to 1617 there was hardly a year which did not see one or more reprints of it. The bishops in general seem to have welcomed it, and it was powerfully supported by Walsingham; and until the final victory of King James's Version it was by far the most popular Bible in England for private reading. Many of its improvements, in phrase or in interpretation, were adopted in the Authorised Version.[1]

7. *The Bishops' Bible*, 1568.

With the accession of Elizabeth a new day dawned for the Bible in England. The public reading of it was naturally restored, and the clergy were required once more to have a copy of the Great Bible placed in their churches, which all might read with due order and reverence. But the publication of the Geneva Bible made it impossible for the Great Bible to maintain its position as the authorised form of the English Scriptures. The superior correctness of the Geneva version threw discredit on the official Bible; and yet, being itself the Bible of one particular party in the Church, and reflecting in its commentary the views of that party, it could not properly be adopted as the universal Bible for public service. The necessity of a revision of the Great Bible was therefore obvious, and it happened that the Archbishop of Canterbury, Matthew Parker, was himself a textual scholar, a collector of manuscripts, an editor of learned works, and consequently fitted to take up the task which lay ready to his hand. Accordingly, about the year 1563, he set on foot a scheme for the revision of the Bible by a number of scholars working separately. Portions of the Bible were assigned to each of the selected divines for revision, the Archbishop reserving for himself the task of editing the whole and passing it through the press. A considerable number of the selected revisers were bishops,[2] and

[1] It is the Geneva Bible to which the popular title of the "Breeches Bible" is given, from its translation of Gen. iii. 7. It has been observed that the "Soldier's Pocket Bible," printed for the Parliamentary armies in 1643, consists of a number of passages taken from the Geneva Bible.

[2] Alley, Bishop of Exeter; Davies, Bishop of St. David's; Sandys, Bishop of Worcester; Barlow, Bishop of Chichester; Horne, Bishop of Winchester; Bentham, Bishop of Lichfield and Coventry; Grindal, Bishop of London; Parkhurst, Bishop of Norwich; Scambler, Bishop of Peterborough; Cox, Bishop of Ely; Guest, Bishop of Rochester (who, however, did not perform the part allotted to him); and probably Bullingham, Bishop of Lincoln, and Jones, Bishop of Llandaff. The other revisers were Pierson, Canon of Canterbury; Perne, Dean of Ely; Goodman, Dean of Westminster; and probably Thomas Bickley, Chaplain to Parker.

hence the result of their labours obtained the name of the Bishops' Bible.

The Bishops' Bible was published in 1568, and it at once superseded the Great Bible for official use in churches. No edition of the earlier text was printed after 1569, and the mandate of Convocation for the provision of the new version in all churches and bishops' palaces, though not as imperative as the injunctions in the case of the Great Bible, must have eventually secured its general use in public services. Nevertheless, on the whole, the revision cannot be considered a success, and the Geneva Bible continued to be preferred as the Bible of the household and the individual. In the forty-three years which elapsed before the appearance of the Authorised Version, nearly 120 editions of the Geneva Bible issued from the press, as against twenty of the Bishops' Bible, and while the former are mostly of small compass, the latter are mainly the large volumes which would be used in churches. The method of revision did not conduce to uniformity of results. There was, apparently, no habitual consultation between the several revisers. Each carried out his own assigned portion of the task, subject only to the general supervision of the Archbishop. The natural result is a considerable amount of unevenness. The historical books of the Old Testament were comparatively little altered; in the remaining books changes were much more frequent, but they are not always happy or even correct. The New Testament portion was better done, Greek being apparently better known by the revisers than Hebrew. Like almost all its predecessors, the Bishops' Bible was provided with a marginal commentary, on a rather smaller scale than that in the Geneva Bible, and mainly merely explanatory. A large quarto edition was published in 1569, and a second folio in 1572, in which the New Testament was once more revised, while the Old Testament was left untouched; but the total demand for the Bishops' Bible, being probably confined to the copies required for public purposes, can never have been very great.

8. *The Rheims and Douai Bible*, 1582-1609.

Meanwhile the zeal of the reformed churches for the possession of the Bible in their own languages drove the Romanists into competition with them in the production of translations. For each of the principal provinces of the Latin Church a translation was provided conformable to the views of that Church on the text and interpretation of Scripture. It was not that the heads of the Roman Church believed such translations to be in themselves desirabl; but since there was evidently an irrepressible popular demand for them, it was clearly advisable, from the

Roman point of view, that the translated Bible should be accompanied by a commentary in accordance with Roman teaching, rather than by that of the Genevan Calvinists or the English bishops. The preparation of an English version naturally fell to the scholars of the English seminary which had lately been established in France. The original home of this seminary was at Douai, but in 1578 it was transferred for a time to Rheims; and it was during the sojourn at Rheims that the first part of the English Bible was produced. This was the New Testament, which was published in 1582. The Old Testament, for lack of funds, did not appear until 1609, when the seminary had returned to Douai; and consequently the completed Bible goes by the name of the Rheims and Douai version.

The most important point to observe about this Roman Catholic Bible is that the translation is made, not from the original Hebrew and Greek, but from the Latin Vulgate. This was done deliberately, on the ground that the Vulgate was the Bible of Jerome and Augustine, that it had ever since been used in the Church, and that its text was preferable to the Greek wherever the two differed, because the Greek text had been corrupted by heretics. Furthermore, the translators (of whom the chief was Gregory Martin, formerly Fellow of St. John's College, Oxford) held it their duty to adhere as closely as possible to the Latin words, even when the Latin was unintelligible. Bishop Westcott quotes an extraordinary instance in Ps. lvii. 10: "Before your thorns did understand the old briar; as living so in wrath he swalloweth them." The general result is that the translation is almost always stiff and awkward, and not unfrequently meaningless. As a contribution to the interpretation of Scripture it is of slight importance; but, on the other hand, its systematic use of words and technical phrases taken directly from the Latin has had a considerable influence on our Authorised Version. Many of the words derived from the Latin which occur in our Bible were incorporated into it from the Rheims New Testament.

The Romanist Bible had no general success, and its circulation was not large. The New Testament was reprinted four times (1600, 1621, 1633, 1749) between 1582 and 1750; the Old Testament only once (1635). Curiously enough, the greater part of its circulation was in the pages of a Protestant controversialist, Fulke, who printed the Rheims and the Bishops' New Testaments side by side, and also appended to the Rheims commentary a refutation by himself. Fulke's work had a considerable popularity, and it is possibly to the wider knowledge of the Rheims version thus produced that we owe the use made of it by the scholars who prepared the Authorised Version: to which version, after our long and varied wanderings, we are now at last come.

9. *The Authorised Version.*

The attempt of Archbishop Parker and the Elizabethan bishops to provide a universally satisfactory Bible had failed. The Bishops' Bible had replaced the Great Bible for use in churches, and that was all. It had not superseded the Geneva Bible in private use; and faults and inequalities in it were visible to all scholars. For the remaining years of Elizabeth's reign it held its own; but in the settlement of religion which followed the accession of James I, the provision of a new Bible held a prominent place. At the Hampton Court Conference in 1604, to which bishops and Puritan clergy were alike invited by James in order to confer on the subject of religious toleration, Dr. Reynolds, President of Corpus Christi College, Oxford, raised the subject of the imperfection of the current Bibles. Bancroft, Bishop of London, supported him; and although the Conference itself arrived at no conclusion on this or any other subject, the King had become interested in the matter, and a scheme was formulated shortly afterwards for carrying the revision into effect. It appears to have been James himself who suggested the leading features of the scheme—namely, that the revision should be executed mainly by the Universities; that it should be approved by the bishops and most learned of the Church, by the Privy Council, and by the King himself, so that all the Church should be concerned in it; and that it should have no marginal commentary, which might render it the Bible of a party only. To James were also submitted the names of the revisers; and it is no more than justice to a king whose political misconceptions and mismanagements have left him with a very indifferent character among English students of history, to allow that the good sense on which he prided himself seems to have been conspicuously manifested in respect of the preparation of the Authorised Version, which, by reason of its after effects, may fairly be considered the most important event of his reign.

It was in 1604 that the scheme of the revision was drawn up, and some of the revisers may have begun work upon it privately at this time; but it was not until 1607 that the task was formally taken in hand. The body of revisers was a strong one. It included the professors of Hebrew and Greek at both Universities, with practically all the leading scholars and divines of the day. There is a slight uncertainty about some of the names, and some changes in the list may have been caused by death or retirement, but the total number of revisers was from forty-eight to fifty. These were divided into six groups, of which two sat at Westminster, two at Oxford, and two at Cambridge. In the first instance each group worked separately, having a special part of

The first boke of Moses, called Genesis.

Fo. i.

The first dayes worke. The seconde dayes worke. The thirde dayes worke.

The fourth dayes worke. The fifth dayes worke. The sixte dayes worke.

The first Chapter.

A
Esd.6.d
Eccli.18.a
Iere.10.b
Heb.11.a
Esa.44.c

N ỹ begynnynge God created heauen ꝛ earth: and ỹ earth was voyde and emptie, and darcknes was vpon the depe, ꝛ ỹ sprete of God moued vpō the water.

And God sayde: let there be light, ꝛ there was light. And God sawe the light that it was good. Then God deuyded ỹ light from the darcknes, and called the light, Daye: and the darcknes, Night. Then of the euenynge and mornynge was made the first daye.

And God sayde: let there be a firmament betwene the waters, and let it deuyde ỹ waters a sunder. Then God made ỹ firmamēt, and parted the waters vnder the firmamēt, from the waters aboue the firmament: And so it came to passe. And God called ỹ firmament, Heauen. Then of the euenynge ꝛ mornynge was made the seconde daye.

And God sayde: let the waters vnder heauen gather thē selues vnto one place, ỹ the drye londe maye appeare. And so it came to passe. And God called ỹ drye londe, Earth: and the gatheringe together of waters called he, ỹ See. And God sawe ỹ it was good. (Iob 26.b; Pro.8.c)

B

And God sayde: let ỹ earth bringe forth grene grasse and herbe, that beareth sede: ꝛ frutefull trees, that maye beare frute, every one after his kynde, hauynge their owne sede in them selues vpon the earth. And so it came to passe. And the earth brought forth grene grasse and herbe, ỹ beareth sede every one after his kynde, ꝛ trees bearinge frute, ꝛ

a

COVERDALE'S BIBLE—A.D. 1535.

(*Original size*, 10¾ *in.* × 6⅝ *in.*)

the Bible assigned to it. The two Westminster groups revised Genesis—2 Kings, and Romans—Jude; the Oxford groups Isaiah—Malachi, and the Gospels, Acts, and Apocalypse; while those at Cambridge undertook 1 Chronicles—Ecclesiastes and the Apocrypha. Elaborate instructions were drawn up for their guidance, probably by Bancroft. The basis of the revision was to be the Bishops' Bible, though the earlier translations were to be consulted; the old ecclesiastical terms (about which Tyndale and More had so vehemently disagreed) were to be retained; no marginal notes were to be affixed, except necessary explanations of Hebrew and Greek words; when any company had finished the revision of a book, it was to be sent to all the rest for their criticism and suggestions, ultimate differences of opinion to be settled at a general meeting of the chief members of each company; learned men outside the board of revisers were to be invited to give their opinions, especially in cases of particular difficulty.

With these regulations to secure careful and repeated revision, the work was earnestly taken in hand. It occupied two years and nine months of strenuous toil, the last nine months being taken up by a final revision by a committee consisting of two members from each centre. (Nothing, it may be observed, is heard of revision by the bishops, the Privy Council, or the King.) It was seen through the press by Dr. Miles Smith and Bishop Bilson, the former of whom is believed to have been the author of the valuable preface of the Translators to the Reader;[1] and in the year 1611 the result of the revisers' labours issued from the press.[2] It was at once attacked by Dr. Hugh Broughton, a Biblical scholar of great eminence and erudition, who had been omitted from the list of revisers on account of his violent and impracticable disposition. Broughton had, so far back as 1593, tried hard to secure Burghley's support for a translation to be produced by himself, which, as he declared, sundry bishops, doctors, "and other inferior of all sort" were pressing him to undertake; but Burghley does not seem to have been responsive, and Archbishop Whitgift actively opposed it, so much so that Broughton threatened to bestow his favours upon the Scots, who, he asserts, were ready to pay him far more liberally than the English. But even this hope had come to nothing. His disappointment vented itself in a very hostile criticism of the new version; but this had very little effect, and the general reception

[1] This preface is not printed in the Bibles in ordinary circulation, but may be found in the Variorum Bible.

[2] The price of these large folio copies appears to have been 25s. in sheets and 30s. bound. A Cambridge edition in 1629, in small folio, was priced at 10s., and the King's Printers tried to drive the University Press off the market by undercutting their price, but without success.

of the revised Bible seems to have been eminently favourable. Though there is no record whatever of any decree ordaining its use, by either King, Parliament, or Convocation, the words "Appointed to be read in churches" appear on its title-page; and there can be no doubt that it at once superseded the Bishops' Bible (which, except for some half-dozen reprints of the New Testament, was not reprinted after 1606) as the official version of the Scriptures for public service. Against the Geneva Bible it had a sharper struggle, and for nearly half a century the two versions existed side by side in private use. From the first, however, the version of 1611 seems to have been received into popular favour, and the reprints of it far outnumber those of its rival. Three folio editions and at least fourteen in quarto or octavo appeared in the years 1611-14, as against six of the Geneva Bible. Between 1611 and 1644, the *Historical Catalogue* of the British and Foreign Bible Society enumerates fifteen editions of the Geneva and 182 of the Authorised. After 1616, however, English-printed editions of the Geneva cease almost entirely, and this may be due to pressure from above. Nevertheless, it would be untrue to say that the version of 1611 owed its success to official backing from the authorities of Church or State, for its victory became complete just at the time when Church and State were overthrown, and when the Puritan party was dominant. It was its superior merits, and its total freedom from party or sectarian spirit, that secured the triumph of the Authorised Version, which from the middle of the seventeenth century took its place as the undisputed Bible of the English nation.

Its Excellence and Influence.

The causes of its superiority are not hard to understand. In the first place, Greek and Hebrew scholarship had greatly increased in England during the forty years which had passed since the last revision. It is true that the Greek text of the New Testament had not been substantially improved in the interval, and was still very imperfect; but the chief concern of the revisers was not with the readings, but with the interpretation of the Scriptures, and in this department of scholarship great progress had been made. Secondly, the revision was the work of no single man and of no single school. It was the deliberate work of a large body of trained scholars and divines of all classes and opinions, who had before them, for their guidance, the labours of nearly a century of revision. The translation of the Bible had passed out of the sphere of controversy. It was a national undertaking, in which no one had any interest at heart save that of producing the best possible version of the Scriptures. Thirdly, the past forty years had been years of extraordinary growth in English literature. Prose writers and poets—Spenser, Sidney, Hooker, Marlowe, Shakespeare, to name only the greatest—had combined to spread abroad a sense of literary style and to raise the standard of literary taste. Under the influence, conscious or unconscious, of masters such as these, the revisers wrought out the fine material left to them by Tyndale and his successors into the splendid monument of Elizabethan prose which the Authorised Version is universally admitted to be.

Into the details of the revision it is hardly necessary to go far. The earlier versions of which the revisers made most use were those of Rheims and Geneva. Tyndale no doubt fixed the general tone of the version more than any other translator, through the transmission of his influence down to the Bishops' Bible, which formed the basis of the revision; but many improvements in interpretation were taken from the Geneva Bible, and not a few phrases and single words from that of Rheims. Indeed, no source of information seems to have been left untried; and the result was a version at once more faithful to the original than any translation that had preceded it, and finer as a work of literary art than any translation either before or since. In the Old Testament the Hebrew tone and manner have been admirably reproduced, and have passed with the Authorised Version into much of our literature. Even where the translation is wrong or the Hebrew text corrupt, as in many passages of the Prophets or the last chapter of Ecclesiastes, the splendid stateliness of the English version makes us blind to the deficiency in the sense. And in the New Testament, in particular, it is the simple truth that the English version is a far greater *literary* work than the original Greek. The Greek of the New Testament is a language which had passed its prime and had lost its natural grace and infinite adaptability. The English of the Authorised Version is the finest specimen of our prose literature at a time when English prose wore its stateliest and most majestic form.

The influence of the Authorised Version, alike on our religion and our literature, can never be exaggerated. Not only in the great works of our theologians, the resonant prose of the seventeenth-century Fathers of the English Church, but in the writings of nearly every author, whether of prose or verse, the stamp of its language is to be seen. Milton is full of it; naturally, perhaps, from the nature of his subjects, but still his practice shows his sense of the artistic value of its style. So deeply has its language entered into our common tongue, that one probably could not take up a newspaper or read a single book in which some phrase was not borrowed, consciously or unconsciously, from King James's version. No master of style has been blind to its charms; and those who have recommended its study most strongly have often been those who, like Carlyle and Matthew Arnold, were not prepared to accept its teaching to the full.

But great as has been the literary value of the Authorised Version, its religious significance has been greater still. For nearly three centuries it has been the Bible, not merely of public use, not merely of one sect or party, not even of a single country, but of the whole nation and of every English-speaking country on the face of the globe. It has been the literature of millions who have read little else, it has been the guide of conduct to men and women of every class in life and of every rank in learning and education. No small part of the attachment of the English people to their national church is due to the common love borne by every party and well-nigh every individual for the English Bible. It was a national work in its creation, and it has been a national treasure since its completion. It was the work, not of one man, nor of one age, but of many labourers, of diverse and even opposing views, over a period of ninety years. It was watered with the blood of martyrs, and its slow growth gave time for the casting off of imperfections and for the full accomplishment of its destiny as the Bible of the English nation.

The Authorised Version Accepted as Final.

With the publication of the Authorised Version the history of the English Bible closes for many a long year. Partly, no doubt, this was due to the troubled times which came upon England in that generation and the next. When the constitutions of Church and State alike were being cast into the melting-pot, when men were beating their ploughshares into swords, and their pruning-hooks into spears, there was little time for nice discussions as to the exact text of the Scriptures, and little peace for the labours of scholarship. But the main reason for this pause in the work was that, for the moment, finality had been reached. The version of 1611 was an adequate translation of the Greek and Hebrew texts as they were then known to scholars. The scholarship of the day was satisfied with it as it had been satisfied with no version before it; and the common people found its language appeal to them with a greater charm and dignity than that of the Genevan version, to which they had been accustomed. As time went on the Authorised Version acquired the prescriptive right of age; its rhythms became familiar to the ears of all classes; its language entered into our literature; and Englishmen became prouder of their Bible than of any of the creative works of their own literature.[1]

[1] A few bibliographical details may be added. The first edition was generally well printed, but errors began to creep in at once; and the history has been inextricably confused by the printers' habit of binding up together

Need of a Revision in our own Time.

What, then, were the causes which led to the revision of this beloved version after it had held its ground for nearly three hundred years? They may be summed up in a single sentence: The increase of our knowledge concerning the original Hebrew and Greek texts, especially the latter. The reader who will glance back at our history of the Greek texts in Chapters VI—VIII will see how much of our best knowledge about the text of the New Testament has been acquired since the date of the Authorised Version. Of all the manuscripts described in Chapter VII scarcely one was known to the scholars of 1611; of all the versions described in Chapter VIII not one was known except the Vulgate, and that mainly in late and corrupt manuscripts. The editions of the Greek text chiefly used by the translators of 1611 were those of Erasmus, Stephanus, and Beza, and these had been formed from a comparison of only a few manuscripts, and those mostly of the latest period.[1] The translators used the best materials that they had to their hands, and with good results, since their texts were substantially true, though not in detail; but since their time the materials have increased to such an extent as to revolutionise the situation entirely.

The Authorised Version had, indeed, hardly seen the light when a beginning was made in a movement which was ultimately to undermine it. Only sixteen years after its publication the Codex Alexandrinus (see p. 135) reached England; and the inclusion of the more important of its variant readings in Walton's Polyglot of 1657 showed scholars that it was not safe to depend on manuscripts of the fifteenth century when manuscripts of the fifth century were available. Thenceforth there began the search for manuscripts, the results of which provided the materials for our Chapters VII and VIII, and the labours of scholars

---

sheets from different printings. In 1629 a group of Cambridge scholars superintended a carefully printed edition, and this salutary revision was carried further in 1638. Meanwhile an edition in 1631 earned the title of the "Wicked Bible" by omitting the word "not" in the Seventh Commandment. In 1701 Bishop Lloyd superintended an edition at Oxford, in which Archbishop Usher's dates for Scripture chronology were added in the margin. In 1717 a fine but inaccurate edition printed by Baskett at Oxford acquired notoriety as the "Vinegar Bible," from the misprint *Vinegar* for *Vineyard* in the headline to Luke xx. Editions carefully revised for the removal of printers' errors were produced in 1762 at Cambridge under the editorship of Dr. T. Paris, and in 1769 at Oxford under the editorship of Dr. B. Blayney. In 1833 the Oxford University Press produced a line-for-line reprint of the *editio princeps*, and at the tercentenary in 1911 a facsimile in a reduced size, with a bibliographical introduction by A. W. Pollard, subsequently expanded into his *Records of the English Bible* (1911), which remains the most authoritative treatment of the subject.

[1] Stephanus consulted two good uncials, D and L, but only to a slight extent.

which were summarised in the appendix to Chapter VII. The climax was reached in the work of Tischendorf and Tregelles in the middle of the nineteenth century, and especially in the publication by the former of the two great fourth-century manuscripts, the Codex Sinaiticus and the Codex Vaticanus. It was then obvious that the time had come for the preparation of a new Greek text, established on critical principles on a mass of evidence far older and better than that which King James's translators had before them. The successive editions of Tischendorf and Tregelles showed what such a revised text would be, and the climax was reached in the New Testament of Westcott and Hort, published in 1881.

In the matter of a revised English translation a move had been made even before the discovery of the Sinaiticus. About the year 1855 the subject began to be mooted in magazine articles and in motions in Convocation. The way was paved by the enterprise of a small group of scholars, Dr. Ellicott, afterwards Bishop of Gloucester, Dr. Moberly, head master of Winchester and afterwards Bishop of Salisbury; Dr. Barron, Principal of St. Edmund's Hall, Oxford; the Rev. H. Alford, afterwards Dean of Canterbury; the Rev. W. G. Humphry and the Rev. E. Hawkins, who in 1857 published a revision of the Authorised Version for the Gospel of St. John, following it up with six of the Epistles in 1861 and 1863. This gave the general public an idea of what revision would mean, and prepared men's minds for the operations which eventually led to the production of the Revised Version.

The history of the revision is told at sufficient length in the preface to the New Testament. The initiative was taken by the Convocation of the Province of Canterbury. In February of the year 1870 a definite proposal was made that a revision of the Authorised Version should be taken into consideration. In May the broad principles of the revision were laid down in a series of resolutions, and a committee of sixteen members was appointed to execute the work, with power to add to its numbers. The committee divided itself into two companies, one for each Testament, and invitations were issued to all the leading Biblical scholars of the United Kingdom to take part in the work. The invitations were not confined to members of the Church of England. The English Bible is the Bible of Nonconformists as well as of the Established Church, and representatives of the Nonconformist bodies took their seats among the revisers. Thus were formed the two companies to whom the Revised Version is due. Each company consisted originally of twenty-seven members, but deaths and resignations and new appointments caused the exact numbers to vary from time to time; and it cannot be questioned that most of the leading Biblical scholars of the day were included among them. Further, when the work had barely begun, an invitation was sent to the churches of America asking their co-operation; and in accordance with this invitation two companies were formed in America, to whom all the results of the English companies were communicated. The suggestions of the American revisers were carefully and repeatedly considered, and those of their alterations on which they desired to insist, when they were not adopted by their English colleagues, were recorded in an appendix to the published version.[1] The Revised Version is, consequently, the work not of the English Church alone, nor of the British Isles alone, but of all the English-speaking Churches throughout the world; only the Roman Catholics taking no part in it.

The methods of the revision left little to be desired in the way of care and deliberation. The instructions to the Revisers (which are given in full in their preface) required them to introduce as few alterations as possible consistently with faithfulness; to use in such alterations the language of the Authorised or earlier versions, where possible; to go over their work twice, in the first revision deciding on alterations by simple majorities, but finally making or retaining no change except two-thirds of those present approved of it. Thus the Revised Version represents the deliberate opinions of a large majority of the best scholars of all English-speaking Churches in the last quarter of the nineteenth century.

It was on the 22nd of June, 1870, that the members of the New Testament Company, having first received the Holy Communion in Westminster Abbey, held their first meeting in the Jerusalem Chamber; the Old Testament company entered on their work eight days later. The New Testament Company met on 407 days in the course of eleven years, the Old Testament Company on 792 days in fifteen years. It was on the 11th of November, 1880, that the New Testament Revisers set their signatures to the preface of their work, and the Revised New Testament was issued to a keenly expectant world on the 17th of May, 1881. The Old Testament followed almost exactly four years later, the preface being signed on July 10th, 1884, and the volume published on May 19th, 1885. The revision of the Apocrypha was not part of the undertaking of Convocation, but was commissioned by the two University Presses. The work was shared by the two companies, the New

[1] An edition (unauthorised) incorporating the readings of the American revisers in the New Testament was issued in 1881, and an authorised edition in 1898. A further revision was made in 1901. But it does not appear that any of these editions had much success.

Testament Company, which was the first to be set free from its main task, distributing Ecclesiasticus, Tobit, Judith, Wisdom, and 1 and 2 Maccabees among three groups of its members, while the Old Testament Company appointed a small committee to deal with the remaining books. The work dragged on over many years, involving some inequalities in treatment, and the book was finally published in November, 1895. It may be observed that the Revisers incorporated the missing fragment of 2 Esdras (vii. 36-105) which is not in the Authorised Version, but which was discovered in 1875 by R. L. Bensly in a manuscript at Amiens. Curiously enough, after Professor Bensly had made his discovery public, it turned out that nearly fifty years earlier Professor Palmer had actually transcribed the fragment from another MS. at Madrid, but had never announced or published it.

What, then, of the result of this prolonged and conscientious labour? Is the Revised Version a worthy successor to the Authorised Bible, which has entered so deeply into the life of Englishmen? Has it added fresh perfection to that glorious work, or has it laid hands rashly upon sacred things? What, in any case, are the characteristics of the revision of 1881-5 as compared with the version on which it is based?

Characteristics of the Revised Version.

A. *Changes in Text.*—The first class of changes introduced in the Revised Version consists of those which are due to a difference in the text translated; and these are most conspicuous and most important in the New Testament. The version of 1611 was made from a Greek text formed by a comparison of very few manuscripts, and those, for the most part, late (see pp. 103, 235). The version of 1881, on the other hand, was made from a Greek text based upon an exhaustive examination, extending over some two centuries, of all the best manuscripts in existence. In Dr. Hort and Dr. Scrivener the New Testament Company possessed the two most learned textual critics then alive; and when it is remembered that no change was finally accepted unless it had the support of two-thirds of those present, it will be seen that the Greek text underlying the Revised Version has very strong claims on our acceptance. No one edition of the Greek text was followed by the Revisers, each reading being considered on its own merits; but it is certain that the edition and the textual theories of Drs. Westcott and Hort, which were communicated to the Revisers in advance of the publication of their volumes, had a great influence on the text ultimately adopted, while very many of their readings which were not admitted into the text of the Revised Version yet find a place in the margin. The Greek text of the New Testament of 1881 has been estimated to differ from that of 1611 in no less than 5,788 readings, of which about a quarter are held notably to modify the subject-matter; though even of these only a small proportion can be considered as of first-rate importance. The chief of these have been referred to on p. 17, but the reader who wishes for a fuller list may compare the Authorised and Revised readings in such passages as: Matt. i. 25; v. 44; vi. 13; x. 3; xi. 23; xvii. 21; xviii. 11; xix. 17; xx. 22; xxiii. 14; xxiv. 36; xxvii. 35. Mark vii. 19; ix. 44, 46, 49; xv. 28; xvi. 9-20. Luke i. 28; ii. 14; ix. 35, 54, 55; xi. 2-4; xvii. 36; xxiii. 15, 17. John iv. 42; v. 3, 4; vi. 69; vii. 53–viii. 11; viii. 59. Acts iv. 25; viii. 37; ix. 5; xv. 18, 34; xviii. 5, 17, 21; xx. 15; xxiv. 6-8; xxviii. 16, 29. Rom. iii. 9; iv. 19; vii. 6; viii. 1; ix. 28; x. 15; xi. 6; xiv. 6; xvi. 5, 24. 1 Cor. ii. 1; vi. 20; viii. 7; xi. 24, 29; xv. 47. 2 Cor. i. 20; xii. 1. Gal. iii. 1, 17; iv. 7; v. 1. Eph. iii. 9, 14; v. 30. Phil. i. 16, 17. Col. i. 2, 14; ii. 2, 18. 1 Thess. i. 1. 1 Tim. iii. 3, 16; vi. 5, 19. 2 Tim. i. 11. Heb. vii. 21. 1 Peter iv. 14. 1 John iv. 3; v. 7, 8, 13. Jude 23. Rev. i. 8, 11; ii. 3; v. 10; xi. 17; xiv. 5; xvi. 7; xxi. 24; xxii. 14. This list, which any reader of the Variorum Bible may extend indefinitely for himself (with the advantage of having the evidence for and against each change succinctly stated for him), contains some of the more striking passages in which the Revised Version is translated from a different Greek text from that used in the Authorised Version, and few scholars will be found to deny that in nearly every case the text of the Revised Version is certainly superior.

In the Old Testament the case is different. This is not because the translators of the Old Testament in the Authorised Version were more careful to select a correct text than their colleagues of the New Testament, but simply because our knowledge of the Old Testament text has not increased since that date to anything like the extent that it has in respect of the New Testament. As we have seen in the earlier chapters, all extant manuscripts of the Hebrew Scriptures contain what is known as the Massoretic text, and they do not greatly differ among themselves. Such differences of reading as exist are traced by a collation of the early versions—*e.g.*, the Septuagint or the Vulgate; but we know too little as yet of the character and history of these versions to follow them to any great extent in preference to the Hebrew manuscripts. The Revisers, therefore, had no choice but to translate, as a rule, from the Massoretic text; and consequently they were translating substantially the same text as that which the authors of King James's Version had before them. This is one explanation of the fact, which is obvious to every reader, that the Old Testament is much less altered in the Revised Version than the New;[1] and

[1] A well-known example of an altered reading occurs in Isa. ix. 3 (the first lesson for Christmas Day), " Thou hast multiplied the people and *not* increased

the reader who wishes to learn the improvements which might be introduced by a freer use of the ancient versions must be referred to the notes in the Variorum Bible.

B. *Changes in Interpretation.*—The situation is reversed when we come to consider the differences, not of text but of interpretation, between the Authorised Version and the Revised. Here the advance is greater in the Old Testament than in the New, and again the reason is plain. The translators of the New Testament in the Authorised Version were generally able to interpret correctly the Greek text which they had before them, and their work may, except in a few passages, be taken as a faithful rendering of an imperfect text. On the other hand, Hebrew was less well known in 1611 than Greek, and the passages in which the Authorised Version fails to represent the original are far more numerous in the Old Testament than in the New. The reader who will take the trouble to compare the Authorised and Revised Versions of the prophetical and poetical books will find a very considerable number of places in which the latter has brought out the meaning of passages which in the former were obscure. To some extent the same is the case with the Epistles of St. Paul, where, if we miss much of the familiar language of the Authorised Version, we yet find that the connection between the sentences and the general course of the argument are brought out more clearly than before. But it is in the Old Testament, in Job, in Ecclesiastes, in Isaiah and the other Prophets, that the gain is most manifest, and no one who cares for the meaning of what he reads can afford to neglect the light thrown upon the obscure passages in these books by the Revised Version.[1]

C. *Changes in Language.*—Besides differences in text and differences in interpretation, we find in the Revised Version very many differences in language. By far the greater number of the changes introduced by the Revisers are of this class, and it is on them that the general acceptance, or otherwise, of the new translation very largely depends. Sometimes these changes embody a slight change of meaning, or remove a word which has acquired in course of time a meaning different from that which it originally had. Such are the substitution of "Sheol"

---

the joy; they joy before thee according to the joy in harvest," etc.; the marginal reading being *to him*. In the Revised Version these readings change places, "his" (lit. *to him*) being in the text, and *not* in the margin. The note in the Variorum Bible explains that in the Hebrew both readings are pronounced alike.

[1] The most striking single passage in the New Testament where the Revised Version has altered the interpretation of the Authorised Version is Acts xxvi. 28, where for the familiar "almost thou persuadest me to be a Christian" we find "With but little persuasion thou wouldest fain make me a Christian" —unquestionably a more correct translation of the Greek.

or "Hades" for "hell," "condemnation" for "damnation," and "love" for "charity" (notably in 1 Cor. xiii.). Others are attempts at slightly greater accuracy in reproducing the precise tenses of the verbs used in the Greek, as when in John xvii. 14 "the world hated them" is substituted for "the world hath hated them." Others, again, are due to the attempt made to represent the same Greek word, wherever it occurs, by the same English word, so far as this is possible. The translators of the Authorised Version were avowedly indifferent to this consideration; or, rather, they deliberately did the reverse. Where there were two or more good English equivalents for a Greek word, they did not wish to seem to cast a slight upon one of them by always using the other, and so they used both interchangeably.[1] The Revisers of 1881-5 took a different view of their duty. Sometimes the point of the passage depends on the same or different words being used, and here it is misleading not to follow the Greek closely. So much weight is laid on the exact words of the Bible, so many false conclusions have been drawn from its phrases by those who are not able to examine the meaning of

[1] See the Translators' Preface (unfortunately omitted from our ordinary Bibles, but very rightly inserted in the Variorum Bible, p. xxiii): "Another thing we think good to admonish thee of, gentle Reader, that we have not tied ourselves to an uniformity of phrasing, or to an identity of words, as some peradventure would wish that we had done, because they observe, that some learned men somewhere have been as exact as they could that way. Truly, that we might not vary from the sense of that which we had translated before, if the word signified the same thing in both places, (for there be some words that be not of the same sense every where,) we were especially careful, and made a conscience, according to our duty. But that we should express the same notion in the same particular word; as, for example, if we translate the *Hebrew* or *Greek* word once by *purpose*, never to call it *intent*; if one where *journeying*, never *travelling*; if one where *think*, never *suppose*; if one where *pain*, never *ache*; if one where *joy*, never *gladness*, &c. thus to mince the matter, we thought to savour more of curiosity than wisdom, and that rather it would breed scorn in the atheist, than bring profit to the godly reader. For is the kingdom of God become words or syllables? Why should we be in bondage to them, if we may be free? use one precisely, when we may use another no less fit as commodiously? . . . Now if this happen in better times, and upon so small occasions, we might justly feel hard censure, if generally we should make verbal and unnecessary changings. We might also be charged (by scoffers) with some unequal dealing towards a great number of good *English* words. For as it is written of a certain great Philosopher, that he should say, that those logs were happy that were made images to be worshipped; for their fellows, as good as they, lay for blocks behind the fire: so if we should say, as it were, unto certain words, Stand up higher, have a place in the Bible always; and to others of like quality, Get you hence, be banished for ever; we might be taxed peradventure with St. *James's* words, namely, *To be partial in ourselves, and judges of evil thoughts.* Add hereunto, that niceness in words was always counted the next step to trifling; and so was to be curious about names too: also that we cannot follow a better pattern for elocution than God Himself; therefore He using divers words in His holy writ, and indifferently for one thing in nature: we, if we will not be superstitious, may use the same liberty in our *English* versions out of *Hebrew* and *Greek*, for that copy or store that He hath given us."

those phrases in the original Greek and Hebrew, that minute accuracy in reproducing the exact language of the original is highly desirable, if it can be had without violence to the idioms of the English tongue. One special class of passages to which this principle has been applied occurs in the first three Gospels. In these the same events are often recorded in identical words, proving that the three narratives have some common origin; but in the Authorised Version this identity is often obscured by the use of different renderings of the same words in the various Gospels. The Revisers have been careful to reproduce exactly the amount of similarity or of divergence which is to be found in the original Greek of such passages.

Reception of the Revised Version.

What, then, is the final value of the Revised Version, and what is to be in future its relation to the Authorised Version to which we have been so long accustomed? On the first appearance of the Revised New Testament it was received with much unfavourable criticism. Dean Burgon of Chichester, occupying towards it much the same position as Dr. Hugh Broughton in relation to the Authorised Version, assailed it vehemently in the *Quarterly Review* with a series of articles, the unquestionable learning of which was largely neutralised by the extravagance and intemperance of their tone. The Dean, however, was not alone in his dislike of the very numerous changes introduced by the Revisers into the familiar language of the English Bible, and there was a general unwillingness to adopt the new translation as a substitute for the Authorised Version in common use. When, four years later, the revision of the Old Testament was put forth, the popular verdict was more favourable. The improvements in interpretation of obscure passages were obvious, while the changes of language were less numerous; moreover, the language of the Old Testament books being less familiar than that of the Gospels, the changes in it passed with less observation. Scholars, however, were not by any means universally satisfied with it, and the reviews in the principal magazines, such as the *Quarterly* and *Edinburgh*, were not favourable. It must be remembered, however, that most of the leading scholars of the country were members of the revision companies, and that the reviews, as a rule, were necessarily written by those who had not taken part in the work. The grounds of criticism, in the case of both Testaments, were two-fold: either the critics objected on scientific grounds to the readings adopted by the Revisers, or they protested against the numerous changes in the language, as making the Revised Version less suitable than its predecessor to be the Bible of the people. But with respect to the first class of criticisms, it may fairly be supposed that the opinion of the Revisers is entitled to greater weight than that of their critics. In a work involving thousands of details, concerning many hundreds of which the evidence is nearly equally balanced, it was not to be supposed that a result could be reached which would satisfy in every point either each member of the revision companies themselves, or each critic outside; and consequently the less weight can be attached to the fact that reviewers, who themselves had taken no direct part in the work, found many passages on which their own opinion differed from that to which the majority of the Revisers had come.

More than fifty years have now passed since the publication of the Revised Version, and the dust of the original controversy has had time to die down. In less than that time the Authorised Version drove the Geneva Bible from the field; but there is no sign of a similar victory of the Revised over the Authorised. The general verdict is, we think, this. There is no doubt that the Revised represents, in the New Testament, a very superior Greek text. There is no doubt that in very many places, especially in the prophetical and poetical books of the Old Testament and in the Epistles in the New, it makes the meaning clearer and represents the original more accurately. On both these grounds the Revised Version is indispensable for anyone who really wishes to study the Bible. On the other hand, it is universally felt that very many of the verbal changes introduced by the Revisers, especially in the Gospels (where they are more noticeable because of the greater familiarity of these books), are unnecessary and disturbing. Their principle, that the same English word should always be used to represent the same Greek word, introduced in order to meet the then common habit of text-hunting and verbal quibbling, is in fact unsound. No two languages are so identical that the corresponding words are interchangeable. There are nuances of meaning and usage which defeat the word-for-word translator, and render his results unidiomatic or stiff or pedantic. The task of translation is a delicate one, and the Victorian scholars had not the same innate sense of style and verbal felicity as the Elizabethan and Jacobean. Further, the Revisers were misled by their own scholarship. They applied (in such matters as the rendering of the tenses of the verb) the principles of Attic Greek. The discoveries of Greek papyri that have been made since their time have taught us much about the Hellenistic Greek of the period of the Septuagint and the New Testament; and we realise that it had its own usages which were not so strict as those of the great classical authors. We can safely be more idiomatic in our translation, without departing from faithfulness.

A distinction must accordingly be drawn between the Old Testament and the New, and even between the Gospels and the other books. In the Gospels the sense of discomfort from the constant changes of the familiar words is too great, and the changes, where they do not rest on a change in the text translated, are unnecessary. In the Old Testament, however, and in many passages in the Epistles, the reader who uses the Revised Version will often not be aware that a change has been made, while he will find that he understands what he is reading better than he did before. It is true that the Authorised Version has struck its roots too deeply into our language and literature, and is itself too great a monument of literary art, to be dispossessed without a preponderating balance of loss. We can no more do without the Authorised Version than we can do without Shakespeare and Bacon. Nevertheless we have every reason to be grateful to the Revised Version, which puts at the English reader's disposal the results of generations of devoted labour, and supplies him with a text of the Scriptures of his faith, on the soundness of which he can rely. Both are now essential parts of our heritage; and the final verdict must be: the Revised for study, the Authorised for reading.

Of late years there has been a demand for translations of the Bible, and especially the New Testament, into the language of our own day. Some of these err on the side of excessive colloquialism. The Greek of the New Testament is not colloquial. It is literary Greek, though the amount of literary skill and conscious art varies greatly from the rough and almost illiterate Greek of the Apocalypse and the simplicity of St. Mark, to the greater mastery of style of St. Luke and the more individual mannerisms of St. John and St. Paul. The danger of these attempts is a loss of dignity, which detracts from the impressiveness of the books. On the other hand, a paraphrase into the language of our own day may often make a difficult passage more intelligible. As commentaries, therefore, and aids to study, these versions may serve a useful purpose. The best are probably those of R. F. Weymouth (1903), E. J. Goodspeed (1923), and especially J. Moffatt (1901, 1935). A handy modernised New Testament, keeping closer to the Revised Version and not aiming at colloquialism, is that of E. E. Cunnington (1926), which also has a useful appendix of selected "Western" readings. Still more recently a version on somewhat similar lines has been produced by the United Society for Christian Literature (*The Book of Books*, 1938).

If, in conclusion, the question be asked, What has been the general effect on our view of the Bible of the discoveries of the last fifty years?, the answer would seem to be this. The discoveries of Greek papyri in Egypt have materially reduced the gap between the earliest extant manuscripts of the New Testament and Septuagint and the date at which the original books were written. They have established, with a wealth of evidence which no other work of ancient literature can even approach, the substantial authenticity and integrity of the text of the Bible as we now possess it. They have also thrown much light on the conditions under which the books of the Bible circulated in the earliest Christian centuries. They have shown how different these were from the conditions applying to the works of pagan literature, and have made it easier to understand how the immense variety of readings, which we find in the extant manuscripts, came into existence. They have made us realise that there is no hard-and-fast rule for determining the original reading in every case; that the classification of authorities into separate families needs qualification, at least in the sense that the edges of such classifications must be smoothed off, and that though it is possible to decide that one group of authorities is on the whole superior, it is not possible to affirm that the truth is always to be found there and there exclusively. Our knowledge of the ancient versions, especially the Syriac and Coptic, and to a lesser degree the Armenian and Georgian, has been materially increased; and much valuable work has been done on the great mass of later manuscripts.

For all this we have every reason to be thankful. There is much work left for scholars to do; further discoveries of early manuscripts may yet be hoped for; but the general reader may await all such developments in security, confident that he has nothing to fear from the fullest and freest research; that he may, on the contrary, expect a constant accession of knowledge and of interest, and that in the end truth will prevail.

APPENDIX I

NOTABLE VARIOUS READINGS

In this appendix a selection is given of a hundred of the most notable various readings in the Gospels and Acts, in order that the reader may have some idea of the character and importance of these variants. In the fifty examples taken from the Gospels, the contrast is between the "received" or Byzantine text, which is translated in the Authorised Version, on the one hand, and the readings of the earlier manuscripts, which are for the most part followed in modern editions and in the Revised Version, on the other. In those taken from the Acts, it is between the great mass of manuscripts, both early and late, on the one hand, and the peculiar readings of the Western group of authorities (principally Codex Bezæ and its allies) on the other.

The symbols used are as follows:

- ℵ A B C D, etc. Greek uncial MSS. (see pp. 128-153).
- Fam. 1, fam. 13, 33. Greek minuscule MSS. (see pp. 153-4).
- OL. Old Latin version.
- a, b, c, gig, etc. Old Latin MSS.
- Diat. Diatessaron.
- OS. Old Syriac version.
- OS^s. Sinaitic MS. of Old Syriac.
- OS^c. Curetonian MS. of Old Syriac.
- Sah. Sahidic version.
- TR. The Received or Byzantine text, found in the vast majority of later Greek MSS., and translated in the AV.
- AV. Authorised Version of 1611.
- WH or WH^1. Westcott and Hort's edition of the Greek text, 1881.
- WH^2. Readings regarded by Westcott and Hort as possible, but less probable.
- RV or RV^1. Revised Version of 1881.
- RV^2. Margin of Revised Version.

	Authorised Version.	*Other Readings.*
1.	Mt. i. 16. Jacob begat Joseph the husband of Mary, of whom was born Jesus, who is called Christ: ℵB, TR, WH, RV.	(*a*) Jacob begat Joseph, to whom the Virgin Mary being espoused bore Jesus who is called Christ: fam. 13, OL, OS^c. (*b*) Jacob begat Joseph, and Joseph, to whom was betrothed Mary the Virgin, begat Jesus, who is called Christ, OS^s.

Authorised Version.	*Other Readings.*
2. Mt. iii. 16. Jesus when he was baptized, went up straightway out of the water.	OL (a, g), Diat., and Justin add "and a great light shone around."
3. Mt. v. 44. Bless them that curse you, do good to them that hate you: D, TR, OL (some MSS.).	Om. ℵ B, fam. 1, OS, Sah, WH, RV.
4. Mt. vi. 13. For thine is the kingdom, etc.: L W, TR, OL (some MSS.), RV².	Om. ℵ B D, fam. 1, WH, RV¹.
5. Mt. xvi. 2, 3. When it is evening . . . the signs of the times: C D W, fam. 1, TR, OL, WH², RV¹.	Om. ℵ B, fam. 13, OS, Sah, WH¹. RV².
6. Mt. xvii. 21. Howbeit this kind goeth not out but by prayer and fasting: C D W, TR, OL, RV².	Om. ℵ B, 33, OL (e), OS, Sah, WH, RV¹.
7. Mt. xviii. 11. For the Son of man is come to save that which was lost: D W, OL, OSᶜ, TR, RV² (*cf.* Lk. xix. 10).	Om. ℵ B L, fam. 1, fam. 13, 33, OL (e), OSˢ, Sah, WH, RV¹.
8. Mt. xx. 16. For many be called, but few chosen: C D W, fam. 1, TR, OL, OS. From xxii. 14.	Om. ℵ B L, Sah, WH, RV.
9. Mt. xx. 28.	D Φ, OL, OSᶜ add "But seek ye to increase from that which is little, and to become less from that which is greater. But when ye enter in and are invited to dine, sit not down in the higher places, lest perchance one more honourable than thou shall come, and he that invited thee come and say to thee, Go down lower, and thou be shamed. But if thou liest down in the worse place, and one worse than thou come in, he that invited thee will say, Go up higher, and that shall be to thine advantage."
10. Mt. xx. 33.	OL (c) adds: "And Jesus said to them, Believe ye that I can do this? And they answered him, Yea, Lord." OSᶜ adds "and we may see thee."
11. Mt. xxi. 44. And whosoever shall fall on this stone . . . grind him to powder: ℵ B C W, fam. 1, TR, OSᶜ, Sah, WH¹, RV¹.	Om. D, 33, OL, OSˢ, WH², RV².
12. Mt. xxiii. 27. Which indeed appear beautiful outward, but are within full of dead men's bones: ℵ B etc., TR, WH, RV.	Without the tomb appears beautiful, but within it is full of dead men's bones: D, Diat.
13. Mt. xxiv. 36. Of that day and hour knoweth no man, no, not the angels of heaven: LW, fam. 1, TR, OSˢ, Sah, RV².	ℵ B D Φ, fam. 13, OL, WH, RV¹ add "neither the Son."
14. Mt. xxv. 41. Everlasting fire, prepared for the devil and his angels: ℵ B etc., TR, WH, RV.	Everlasting fire, which my Father hath prepared for the devil and his angels, D, fam. 1, OL.
15. Mt. xxvii. 49. Let us see whether Elias will come to save him: A D W, fam. 1, TR, OL, OSˢ, WH¹, RV¹.	ℵ B C L, WH², RV² add "And another took a spear, and pierced his side, and there came out water and blood" (from Jn. xix. 34).

Authorised Version.	*Other Readings.*
16. Mk. i. 2. In the prophets: A W, TR, RV^2. [Correction of an error, the quotation being from Malachi as well as Isaiah.]	In Isaiah the prophet: א B D L, fam. 1, 33, OL, Sah, WH, RV^1.
17. Mk. ix. 44, 46. Where their worm dieth not, and the fire is not quenched: A D W, TR, OL. [Repeated from verse 48.]	Om. א B C L, fam. 1, OL (k), OS^s, Sah, WH, RV.
18. Mk. ix. 49. And every sacrifice shall be salted with salt: A C D, TR, OL, RV^2 (*cf.* Lev. ii. 13).	Om. א B L W, fam. 1, OL (k), OS^s, Sah, WH, RV^1.
19. Mk. x. 27. With men it is impossible, but not with God; for with God all things are possible: א A B etc., TR, WH, RV.	(*a*) With men it is impossible, but with God it is possible: D, OL (a, k). (*b*) Famm. 1 and 13 omit "for with God all things are possible."
20. Mk. xiii. 2. There shall not be left one stone upon another that shall not be thrown down: א A B etc., TR, WH, RV.	D, OL add "and in three days another shall rise up (or 'shall be raised up') without hands."
21. Mk. xvi. 3.	OL (k) adds "But suddenly at the third hour of the day darkness was made throughout the whole world, and angels descended from heaven, and the Son of God arose in splendour, and the angels ascended with him, and immediately it was made light."
22. Mk. xvi. 9-20. Now when Jesus was risen . . . Amen: A C D L W, TR, OL, OS^c, Sah (some MSS.), RV^1.	(*a*) Om. א B, OS^s, WH, RV^2. (*b*) And they reported briefly to those who were with Peter all that had been enjoined on them. And after this Jesus himself appeared, and from the rising to the setting of the sun sent forth through them the holy and imperishable proclamation of eternal salvation: L, OL (k), Sah.
23. Lk. iv. 18. To heal the broken-hearted: A, fam. 1, TR, OL (f). From Isa. lxi. 1.	Om. א B D L W, fam. 13, OL, OS^s, Sah, WH, RV.
24. Lk. v. 10, 11. And so was also James and John, the sons of Zebedee, which were partners with Simon. And Jesus said unto Simon, Fear not; from henceforth thou shalt catch men. And when they had brought their ships to land, they forsook all, and followed him: So nearly all authorities.	And there were partners with him, James and John, sons of Zebedee; and he said unto them, Come hither, and be not fishers of fish, for I will make you fishers of men. And they when they heard this left all their gear on the beach and followed him: D, OL (e).
25. Lk. vi. 4.	D adds the following verse: "The same day, beholding one working on the sabbath, he saith unto him, Man, if thou knowest what thou doest, thou art blessed; but if thou knowest not, thou art accursed and a transgressor of the law."
26. Lk. vi. 48. For it was founded upon a rock: A C D, TR, OL, RV^2. From Mt. vii. 25.	Because it had been well builded: א B L W, 33, Sah, WH, RV^1. OS^s omits the clause.
27. Lk. ix. 54. Even as Elias did: A C D W, TR, OL, RV^2.	Om. א B L, OL (e), OS, Sah, WH, RV^1.

Authorised Version.	*Other Readings.*
28. Lk. ix. 55. And said, Ye know not what manner of spirit ye are of; for the Son of man is not come to destroy men's lives, but to save them: D, TR, OL, OS^{c}, with some varieties in detail, RV^{2}.	Om. ℵ A B C L W, OL (l), OS^{s}, Sah, WH, RV^{1}.
29. Lk. xi. 2-4. Our Father, which art in heaven: A C D W, TR, OL, OS^{c}, Sah, RV^{2}.	Father: ℵ B L, fam. 1, OS^{s}, WH, RV^{1}.
Thy will be done, as in heaven, so in earth: ℵ A C D W, TR, OL, RV^{2}.	(*a*) Thy will be done: OL (a), Sah. (*b*) Om. B L, famm. 1, 13, OS, WH, RV^{1}.
But deliver us from evil: A C D W, TR, OL, OS^{c}, RV^{2}. [Expanded in accordance with Mt. vi. 9-13.]	Om. ℵ B L, fam. 1, OS^{s}, Sah.
30. Lk. xi. 35, 36. Take heed therefore that the light which is in thee be not darkness. If thy whole body therefore be full of light, having no part dark, the whole shall be full of light, as when the bright shining of a candle doth give thee light: So nearly all authorities.	(*a*) If therefore the light that is in thee be darkness, how great is that darkness: D, OL [from Mt. vi. 23*b*]. (*b*) Take heed therefore that the light that is in thee be not darkness. If the body that is in thee hath no lamp shining, it is dark to thee; how much more when the lamp shineth doth it lighten thee: OL (f, q), OS^{s}. (*c*) Take heed therefore that the light that is in thee be not darkness. If the light that is in thee be darkness, how great is that darkness: OS^{c}.
31. Lk. xi. 53, 54. And as he said these things unto them, the scribes and the Pharisees began to urge him vehemently, and to provoke him to speak of many things: laying wait for him, and seeking to catch something out of his mouth, that they might accuse him: A etc., TR.	(*a*) And when he was come out from thence, the scribes and the Pharisees began to press upon him vehemently, and to provoke him to speak of many things; laying wait for him, to catch something out of his mouth: ℵ B L, WH, RV. (*b*) And as he said these things unto them before all the people, the Pharisees and the lawyers began to be vehement, and to converse with him about many things, seeking to take some occasion against him, that they might find something whereof to accuse him: D, OL, OS, Diat.
32. Lk. xxii. 17-20. (The Last Supper) And he took the cup . . . and he took bread . . . Likewise also the cup after supper . . . which is shed for you: ℵ A B etc., TR, WH^{2}, RV^{1}.	(*a*) Omit 19*b*, 20 "which is given for you . . . which is shed for you": D, OL (a, d, ff, etc.), WH^{1}, RV^{2}. (*b*) Omit 19*b*, 20, and prefix 19*a* to 17, 18: OL (b, e). (*c*) Omit 20, and prefix 19 to 17, 18: OS^{c}. (*d*) Arrange in order 19, 20*a*, 17, 20*b*, 18: OS^{s}. (*e*) Omit 17, 18: Syr (Peshitta). All apparently attempts to get rid of the double mention of the Cup.

	Authorised Version.	*Other Readings.*
33.	Lk. xxii. 43, 44. And there appeared an angel . . . drops of blood falling down to the ground: ℵ* D L, fam. 1, TR, OL, OS^c, WH^2, RV^1.	Om. ℵ^a A B W, fam. 13, OL (f), OS^s, Sah, WH^1, RV^2.
34.	Lk. xxiii. 34. Then said Jesus, Father, forgive them; for they know not what they do: ℵ* A C L, fam. 1, TR, OL (c, e), OS^c, WH^2, RV^1.	Om. ℵ^a B D W, OL (a, b), OS^s, Sah, WH^1, RV^2.
35.	Lk. xxiii. 38. In letters of Greek and Latin and Hebrew: ℵ* A D, fam. 1, TR, OL. [Cf. Jn. xix. 19.]	Om. ℵ^{ca} B C L, OL (a), OS, Sah, WH, RV.
36.	Lk. xxiii. 42, 43. And he said unto Jesus, Lord, remember me when thou comest into thy kingdom. And Jesus said unto him, Verily I say unto thee, To-day shalt thou be with me in paradise: So nearly all authorities.	And turning unto the Lord, he said unto him, Remember me in the day of thy coming. And Jesus answered and said unto him that rebuked him, Be of good cheer, to-day shalt thou be with me in paradise: D.
37.	Lk. xxiii. 53.	(*a*) Fam. 13 adds " and he rolled a great stone to the door of the sepulchre." (*b*) D, OL (c), Sah add " and when he had laid him, he placed a great stone on the sepulchre which twenty men could scarce have rolled."
38.	Lk. xxiv. 6. He is not here, but is risen: Nearly all authorities, WH^2, RV^1.	Om. D, OL, OS, WH^1, RV^2.
39.	Lk. xxiv. 12. Then arose Peter . . . come to pass: Nearly all authorities, WH^2, RV^1.	Om. D, OL (a, b, e, l), OS, WH^1, RV^2.
40.	Lk. xxiv. 36. And saith unto them, Peace be unto you: Nearly all authorities, WH^2, RV^1.	Om. D, OL, OS, WH^1, RV^2.
41.	Lk. xxiv. 40. And when he had thus spoken, he showed them his hands and his feet: Nearly all authorities, WH^2, RV^1.	Om. D, OL, OS, WH^1, RV^2.
42.	Lk. xxiv. 51. And carried up into heaven: Nearly all authorities, WH^2, RV^1.	Om. ℵ* D, OL, OS^s, WH^1, RV^2,
43.	Jn. i. 18. The only begotten Son: A, fam. 1, TR, OL, OS^c, RV^1.	The only begotten God: ℵ B C L, Sah, WH, RV^2.
44.	Jn. v. 3. Waiting for the moving of the water: A^2 D, fam. 1, TR, OL, RV^2.	Om. ℵ A* B C L, OL (q), OS, Sah, WH, RV^1.
45.	Jn. v. 4. For an angel . . . whatsoever disease he had: A L, fam. 1, TR, OL, RV^2.	Om. ℵ B C D W, OL (f, l, q), OS, Sah, WH, RV^1.
46.	Jn. vi. 56.	D, and in part OL (a, ff^2) add: As the Father is in me and I in the Father. Verily, verily, I say unto you, If ye receive not the body of the Son of man as the bread of life, ye have not life in him.
47.	Jn. vii. 53—viii. 11. The Woman taken in Adultery: D, TR, OL (b e), RV^2.	Om. ℵ A B C L W, OL (a, f, q), OS, Sah, WH, RV^1. Fam. 1 places at end of Gospel, fam. 13 after Lk. xxi. 38.

Authorised Version.	*Other Readings.*
48. Jn. viii. 59. Going through the midst of them, and so passed by: ℵ[ca] A C L, fam. 1, TR, OL (f, q), RV².	Om. ℵ* B D, OL, OS[s], Sah, WH, RV¹.
49. Jn. xi. 39.	OS[s] adds: Why are they taking away the stone?
50. Jn. xii. 8. For the poor always ye have with you, but me ye have not always: Nearly all authorities.	Om. D, OS[s].

In the following selection of readings from Acts (except where otherwise stated; see viii. 37, xviii. 21, xxiv. 6-8, xxviii. 16, 29) the text translated in the left-hand column is that of the great mass of authorities, both Alexandrian and Byzantine. Those in the right-hand column are readings of the Western type, found in D and some OL MSS., as indicated.

51. Acts i. 2. Until the day in which he was taken up, after that he through the Holy Ghost had given commandments unto the apostles whom he had chosen.	Until the day in which he chose the apostles through the Holy Ghost, and commanded them to preach the Gospel: D (in part), Sah.
52. Acts i. 5. Not many days hence.	Which also ye shall receive not many days hence at the Pentecost: D, Sah (in part).
53. Acts iv. 18. And they called them.	And when they were agreed in their judgement they spake unto them: D, OL (h, gig).
54. Acts v. 15.	Add: For they were relieved from every sickness that each of them had: D, OL (gig, p).
55. Acts v. 18.	Add: And each of them went his way to his own place: D.
56. Acts v. 39. Ye cannot overthrow them; lest haply ye be found even to fight against God.	Ye cannot overthrow them, neither you nor kings nor tyrants. Refrain therefore from these men, lest haply, etc.: D, OL (h).
57. Acts vi. 10.	Add: because they were confounded by him with all boldness. Being unable therefore to look the truth in the face: D, OL (h).
58. Acts vii. 24.	Add: and hid him in the sand: D (from LXX).
59. Acts viii. 24.	Add: and he ceased not to weep much: D.
60. Acts viii. 37. And Philip said, If thou believest with all thine heart, thou mayest. And he answered and said, I believe that Jesus Christ is the Son of God: E (D is defective here), TR, OL, RV².	Om. ℵ A B C, most other MSS., Sah, WH, RV¹.
61. Acts viii. 39. The Spirit of the Lord caught away Philip.	The Holy Spirit descended on the eunuch. But the angel of the Lord caught away Philip from him: A¹ (D is defective here) and a few other MSS., OL (p).

62. Acts ix, 4, 5. Why persecutest thou me? And he said, Who art thou, Lord? And he said, I am Jesus whom thou persecutest. But arise.

Why persecutest thou me? It is hard for thee to kick against the pricks [from xxvi. 14]. And he said, Who art thou, Lord? And the Lord said unto him, I am Jesus of Nazareth [from xxii. 8], whom thou persecutest. And he, trembling and astonished at that which had happened unto him, said, Lord, what wilt thou have me to do? And the Lord said unto him, Arise: OL (with variations; D is defective). Partly in AV.

63. Acts ix. 7, 8. Hearing a voice, but seeing no man. And Saul arose from the earth; and when his eyes were opened, he saw no man [*or* nothing, ℵ A B].

Hearing a voice, but seeing no man with whom he spoke: OL (gig). And he said to them, Raise me up from the earth. And when they had raised him, when his eyes were opened, he saw nothing: OL (h).

64. Acts x. 25. And as Peter was coming in, Cornelius met him.

And as Peter drew near to Cæsarea, one of the servants ran before him and made known that he was there. And Cornelius sprang forth and met him: D, OL (gig).

65. Acts xi. 2. And when Peter was come up to Jerusalem.

Peter therefore long time desired to journey to Jerusalem; and exhorting the brethren and confirming them, speaking many words, <he went forth> through the regions, teaching them: who also met with them and declared unto them the grace of God: D, OL (p, w).

66. Acts xi. 17. What was I, that I could withstand God?

Add: that I should not give the Holy Spirit to them that believed on him: D, OL (w).

67. Acts xi. 27, 28. And in these days came prophets from Jerusalem unto Antioch. And there stood up one of them, named Agabus, and signified.

And in these days came prophets from Jerusalem unto Antioch, and there was much joy. And when we were gathered together, one of them, named Agabus, spake signifying: D, OL (p, w).

68. Acts xii. 10. And they went out, and passed on through one street.

And they went out, and descended the seven steps, and passed on through one street: D, OL (p).

69. Acts xii. 23. And he was eaten of worms, and gave up the ghost.

And coming down from his throne, he was eaten of worms while yet living, and so gave up the ghost: D.

70. Acts xiii. 33.

Add: Desire of me and I will give thee the heathen for thine inheritance, and the uttermost parts of the earth for thy possession: D (from Ps. ii. 8).

71. Acts xiii. 43.

Add: And it came to pass that the word of God went through all the city: D E, OL (w).

72. Acts xiv. 2. But the unbelieving Jews stirred up the Gentiles, and made their minds evil affected against the brethren.

But the chiefs of the synagogues of the Jews and the rulers stirred up persecution against the righteous, and made the minds of the Gentiles evil affected against the brethren; but the Lord speedily gave peace: D, and partially E.

73. Acts xiv. 7.	Add: And the whole multitude was stirred up at the teaching. But Paul and Barnabas abode still in Lystra: D E, OL (h, w).
74. Acts xv. 2. When therefore Paul and Barnabas had no small dissension and disputation with them, they determined that Paul and Barnabas, and certain other of them, should go up to Jerusalem unto the apostles and elders about this question.	When therefore Paul and Barnabas had no small dissension and disputation together with them,—for Paul spake, affirming vehemently that they should remain as they had believed, but they that had come from Jerusalem brought word to Paul and Barnabas and certain others that they should go up to Jerusalem unto the apostles and elders, to be judged among them about this question: D.
75. Acts xv. 5. But there rose up certain of the sect of the Pharisees which believed.	But those that brought word to them that they should go up to the elders rose up, being certain of the sect of the Pharisees: D.
76. Acts xv. 20.	Add: And do not unto others what you would not should be done unto you: D, Sah. So also in verse 29.
77. Acts xvi. 4. And as they went through the cities, they delivered them the decrees for to keep that were ordained of the apostles and elders which were at Jerusalem.	And passing through the cities they preached and delivered to them with all boldness the Lord Jesus Christ, at the same time delivering also the commandments of the apostles and elders which were at Jerusalem: D.
78. Acts xvi. 35. And when it was day, the magistrates sent the serjeants.	And when it was day the magistrates came together in the market-place, and remembering the earthquake that had taken place they were afraid, and sent the serjeants: D.
79. Acts xvi. 39. And they came and besought them, and brought them out, and desired them to depart out of the city.	And they came with many friends to the prison, and besought them to depart, saying, We knew not concerning you that you are righteous men. And they brought them out and besought them, saying, Depart out of this city, lest they gather together again crying out against you: D, and partially a few other MSS.
80. Acts xvii. 15. Unto Athens.	Add: But he passed by Thessaly, for he was prevented from preaching the word to them: D.
81. Acts xviii. 21. But bade them farewell, saying, I must by all means keep this feast that cometh in Jerusalem; but I will return again unto you, if God will: D, TR, OL (gig). AV has the Western reading here, exceptionally. A few authorities (but not D) add, "But Aquila he left in Ephesus."	But bade them farewell and said, I will return again unto you, if God will: ℵ A B E, Sah, WH, RV.
82. Acts xviii. 27. And when he was disposed to pass into Achaia, the brethren wrote, exhorting the disciples to receive him: who, when he was come, helped them	And certain Corinthians who were dwelling in Ephesus, when they had heard him, besought him to go with them to their country. And when he consented, the Ephesians wrote

much which had believed through grace. — to the disciples in Corinth to receive him; who, when he had taken up his abode in Achaia, helped much in the churches: D, *P*[38].

83. Acts xix. 1. And it came to pass that, while Apollos was at Corinth, Paul having passed through the upper coasts came to Ephesus. — But when Paul desired after his own judgement to journey to Jerusalem, the Spirit bade him turn aside into Asia. And passing through the upper coasts he cometh to Ephesus: D, *P*[38].

84. Acts xix. 9. Disputing daily in the school of one Tyrannus. — Add: from the fifth hour till the tenth: D, two other MSS., OL (gig).

85. Acts xix. 14. And there were seven sons of one Sceva, a Jew, and chief of the priests, which did so. — Among whom also the sons of one Sceva, a priest, desired to do the same thing; (for) it was their custom to exorcise such persons. And entering in to the man that was possessed they began to call upon him the name, saying, We adjure thee by Jesus, whom Paul preacheth, to come forth: D, *P*[38].

86. Acts xxi. 16. And brought with them one Mnason of Cyprus, an old disciple, with whom we should lodge. And when we were come to Jerusalem. — And these brought us to those with whom we should lodge. And coming to a certain village, we were with one Mnason, of Cyprus, an old disciple. And departing thence we came to Jerusalem: D.

87. Acts xxi. 25. As touching the Gentiles which believe, we have written and concluded that they [observe no such thing, save only that] they keep themselves: so TR, AV; ℵ A B, Sah., WH, RV, omit the words in brackets. — As touching the Gentiles which believe, they have nothing to say against thee, for we have written and concluded that they observe no such thing, save only that they keep themselves: D, and partly C, Sah.

After Acts xxii. 28, D is defective. The readings of the Western text are given from other authorities.

88. Acts xxiii. 15. Now therefore ye with the council signify to the chief captain. — Now therefore we ask you to do this for us; gather the council together, and signify to the chief captain: *P*[49], OL (h, gig), Sah.

89. Acts xxiii. 23, 24. Make ready . . . at the third hour of the night, and provide them beasts, that they may set Paul on, and bring him safe unto Felix the governor. — Make ready . . .; and at the third hour of the night he commands them to be ready to set forth. And he gave orders to the centurions to provide beasts, that they might set Paul on, and bring him safe by night to Cæsarea unto Felix the governor. For he was afraid less perchance the Jews might seize him and slay him, and he himself might therewithal incur the charge of having received money: *P*[49], one minuscule, OL (some MSS.).

90. Acts xxiii. 27. Rescued him, having understood that he was a Roman. — Rescued him, crying out and saying that he was a Roman: *P*[49], OL (gig).

91. Acts xxiv. 6-8. Whom we took: ℵ A B etc., OL (some MSS.), Sah, WH, RV[1]. — Add: and would have judged . . . to come unto thee: E, some other MSS., TR, OL (some MSS.), AV, RV[2].

92. Acts xxiv. 10. Beckoned unto him to speak.	Beckoned unto him to make his defence for himself. And he, taking on him the appearance of one inspired, said: Syr (Harkl. marg.).
93. Acts xxiv. 24. With his wife Drusilla, which was a Jewess, he sent for Paul.	With his wife Drusilla, which was a Jewess, who also asked to see Paul and hear his word. Being willing therefore to gratify her, he sent for Paul: Syr (Harkl. marg.).
94. Acts xxiv. 27. And Felix, willing to show the Jews a pleasure, left Paul bound.	But Paul he left in custody by reason of Drusilla: one minuscule, Syr (Harkl. marg.).
95. Acts xxv. 24, 25. Crying that he ought not to live any longer. But when I found that he had committed nothing worthy of death, and that he himself hath appealed to Augustus, I have determined to send him.	That I might give him over to torture without defence. But I could not give him up, by reason of the commands which we have from Augustus. But I bade them, if anyone desired to accuse him, to follow me to Cæsarea, where he was under guard; who, coming thither, cried out that he might be removed from life. And when I had heard both parties, I perceived that he was in no way worthy of death; but when I said, Wilt thou be judged among them at Jerusalem? he appealed unto Cæsar.
96. Acts xxvii. 1. And when it was determined that we should sail into Italy, they delivered Paul and certain other prisoners unto one named Julius, a centurion of Augustus' band.	So therefore the governor ordained to send him to Cæsar. And on the next day he called a certain centurion, named Julius, of Augustus' band, and delivered Paul to him, with other prisoners also. And we went on board the boat and began the voyage to Italy: one OL MS., Syr (Harkl. marg.).
97. Acts xxviii. 16. Paul was suffered to dwell by himself: ℵ A B, WH, RV[1].	The centurion delivered the prisoners to the captain of the guard; but Paul was suffered to dwell by himself without the camp: TR, OL, AV, RV[2] (except the last three words, which are in OL and one Greek MS.).
98. Acts xxviii. 19.	Add: but that I may deliver my soul from death: OL and two Greek MSS.
99. Acts xxviii. 29. Verse omitted by ℵ A B E etc., WH, RV[1].	Verse included in TR, AV, RV[2].
100. Acts xxviii. 31.	Add: that this is Jesus the Son of God, by whom all the world will be judged: a few Latin MSS.

APPEN

SPECIMENS OF THE ENGLISH

This Table contains Heb. i. 1-9 as translated in all the principal versions descr
Bibles has already been given on p. 205. A comparison of these passages wil
Authorised Version is found to be in Tyndale. The Wycliffite versions stan
even in his earliest New Testament, we find already the cadences and the ph
revised by him, and all the other translations are plainly nothing but revision
of the Bristol copy; the rest are from originals in the British Museum.

Tyndale, 1525.

God in tyme past diversly and many wayes, spake vnto the fathers by prophetes: but in these last dayes he hath spoken vnto vs by hys sonne, whom he hath made heyre of all thyngs: by whom also he made the worlde. Which sonne beynge the brightnes of his glory, and very ymage off his substance, bearynge vppe all thyngs with the worde of his power, hath in his awne person pourged oure synnes, and is sytten on the right honde of the maiestie an hye, and is more excellent then the angels in as moche as he hath by inheritaunce obteyned an excellenter name then have they.

For vnto which off the angels sayde he at eny tyme: Thou arte my sonne, this daye begate I the? And agayne: I will be his father, and he shalbe my sonne. And agayne when he bryngeth in the fyrst begotten sonne in the worlde, he sayth: And all the angels of god shall worshippe hym. And vnto the angels he sayth: He maketh his angels spretes, and his ministers flammes of fyre. But vnto the sonne he sayth: God thy seate shal be for ever and ever. The cepter of thy kyngdom is a right cepter. Thou hast loved rightewesnes and hated iniquitie: Wherfore hath god, which is thy god, anoynted the with the oyle off gladnes above thy felowes.

Coverdale, 1535.

God in tyme past dyuersly and many wayes, spake vnto ye fathers by prophetes, but in these last dayes he hath spoken vnto vs by his sonne, whom he hath made heyre of all thinges, by whom also he made the worlde. Which (sonne) beynge the brightnes of his glory, and the very ymage of his substaunce, bearinge vp all thinges with the worde of his power, hath in his owne personne pourged oure synnes, and is set on the righte hande of the maiestie on hye: beynge even as moch more excellent then ye angels, as he hath obtayned a more excellent name then they.

For vnto which of the angels sayde he at eny tyme: Thou art my sonne, this daye have I begotten the? And agayne: I will be his father, and he shalbe my sonne: and agayne, whan he bryngeth in the fyrst begotten sonne in to the worlde, he sayeth: And all the angels of God shal worshippe him. And of the angels he sayeth: He maketh his angels spretes, and his mynisters flammes of fyre. But vnto ye sonne he sayeth: God, y^t seate endureth for ever and ever: the cepter of y^t kyngdom is a right cepter. Thou hast loved righteousnes, and hated iniquyte: wherfore God (which is thy God) hath anoynted the with the oyle of gladnesse above y^t felowes.

Matthew, 1537.

God in tyme past dyuersly and many wayes, spake vnto the fathers by ye Prophetes but in these last dayes he hath spoken vnto vs by hys sonne, whom he hath made heyre of all thinges: by whom also he made ye worlde. Which sonne beynge the brightnes of his glory, and very ymage of hys substance, bearynge vp all thynges wyth the worde of hys power, hath in hys awne person purged oure synnes, and is sytten on the righte hande of the maiestye on hye, and is more excellent then the angels, in as moche as he hath by inherytaunce obteyned an excellenter name then haue they.

For vnto whych of the angels sayde he at eny tyme: Thou arte my sonne, this daye begate I the? And agayne: I will be his father, and he shalbe my sonne. And agayne when he bryngeth in the fyrst begotten sonne into the worlde, he sayth: And all the angels of God shall worshyppe hym. And of the angels he sayth: He maketh hys angels spretes, and hys ministres flammes of fyre. But vnto ye sonne he sayth: God, thy seate shalbe for ever and ever. The scepter of thy kyngdome is a ryght scepter. Thou hast loved ryghtewesnes and hated iniquyte. Wherefore God whych is thy God, hath anoynted the with the oyle of gladnes aboue thy felowes.

Great Bible (*Cromwell's*), 1539.

God in tyme past diuersly and many ways, spake vnto the fathers by Prophetes: but in these last dayes he hath spoken vnto vs by hys awne sonne, whom he hath made heyre of all thinges, by whom also he made the worlde. Whych (sonne) beinge the brightnes of hys glory, and the very ymage of hys substance rulynge all thynges wyth the worde of hys power, hath by hys awne person pourged oure synnes, and sytteth on the righte hande of the maiestye on hye: beynge so moch more excellent then the angels, as he hath by inherytaunce obteyned a more excellent name then they.

For vnto whych of the angels sayde he at eny tyme: Thou art my sonne, this daye have I begotten the? And agayne: I will be his father, and he shalbe my sonne. And agayne, when he bryngeth in the fyrst begotten sonne into the worlde, he sayth: And let all the angels of God worshyppe hym. And vnto the angels he sayth: He maketh hys angels spretes, and hys ministres a flamme of fyre. But vnto the sonne he sayth: Thy seate (O God) shalbe for ever and ever. The scepter of thy kingdome is a ryght scepter. Thou hast loved ryghtewesnes, and hated iniquyte. Wherfore, God, even thy God hath anoynted the with the oyle of gladnes aboue thy felowes.

The Bible

1. At sc
and in di
God spak
time to *o*
the Proph
2. In th
he hathe
us by his S
he hathe
all things
also he
worldes,
3. Who
brightnes
rie, and
forme of
and bea
things by
worde, h
self purg
and sitte
hand of
in the hi
4. And
much m
then the
muche
obteined
lent nam
5. For
the Ang
anie tim
my Son
begate I
gaine, I
ther, an
my sonn
6. And a
bringeth
begotten
the wor
And let
of God
7. And
he saith
the Spir
gers, an
a flame
8. But
he saith,
throne i
euer: th
thy kin
scepter
nes.
9. Tho
righteou
ted iniq
fore G
God, h
thee wi
gladnes
lowes.

‹ANSLATIONS OF THE BIBLE.

›d in Chapter XI. A portion of the same passage as it appears in the Wycliffite llustrate the truth of the statement made in the text, that the foundation of the apart, and have had no influence upon subsequent translations; but in Tyndale, es of the Authorised Version. Matthew's Bible gives Tyndale's version as finally f this model. The extract from Tyndale is taken from Mr. F. Fry's facsimile reprint

---

neva 560.

ie times s maners ye olde athers by : ast dayes ken vnto e, whome le heir of whome ade the

ing the the glo- ingraued persone, vp all s mightie by him ur sinnes, the right maiestie places, made so excellent gels in as ie hathe ore excel- en thei.

which of aid he at Thou art this day ? and a- e his Fa- e shalbe

e when he *his* first nne into he saith, ne Angels ip him. ne Angels maketh s messen- ministers e.

the Sonne God, thy euer and cepter of ne *is* a righteous-

ast loued and ha- Where- *euen* thy anointed oyle of e thy fel-

The Bishops' Bible, 1568.

1\. God which in tyme past, at sundrie tymes, and in diuers maners, spake vnto the fathers in the prophetes:

2\. Hath in these last dayes, spoken vnto vs in the sonne, whom he hath appoynted heyre of all thynges, by whom also he made the worldes.

3\. Who beyng the bryghtnesse of the glorie, and the very image of his substaunce, vpholdyng all thynges with the worde of his power, hauing by himselfe pourged our sinnes, hath syt on the ryght hande of the maiestie on hye:

4\. Beyng so much more excellent then the Angels, as he hath by inheritaunce obtayned a more excellent name then they.

5\. For vnto which of the Angels sayde he at any tyme: Thou art my sonne, this day haue I begotten thee?

6\. And agayne, I wyll be to hym a father, and he shalbe to me a sonne? and agayne, when he bryngeth in the first begotten sonne into the worlde, he saith: And let all the Angels of God worship hym.

7\. And vnto the Angels he sayth: He maketh his Angels spirites, and his ministers a flambe of fyre.

8\. But vnto the sonne [he sayth] Thy seate O God [shalbe] for euer and euer: The scepter of thy kingdome [is] a scepter of ryghteousnesse.

9\. Thou hast loued ryghteousnesse, and hated iniquitie: Therfore God, euen thy God, hath annoynted thee with the oyle of gladnesse, aboue thy felowes.

The Rheims New Testament, 1582.

1 Diversely and many vvaies in times past God speaking to the fathers in the pro- 2 phets: last of al in these daies hath spoken to vs in his Sonne, vvhome he hath appointed heire of al, by vvhome he made also the vvorldes. 3 VVho being the brightnesse of his glorie, and the figure of his substaunce, and carying al things by the vvord of his povver, making purgation of sinnes, sitteth on the right hand of the Maiestie in the high places: 4 being made so much better then Angels, as he hath inherited a more excellent name aboue them.

5 For to vvhich of the Angels hath he said at any time, *Thou art my sonne, to day haue I begotten thee?* and againe, *I vvil be to him a father, and he shal be to me a* 6 *sonne.* And vvhen againe he bringeth in the first begotte into the vvorld, he saith, *And let al the Angels of God adore* 7 *him.* And to the Angels truely he saith, *He that maketh his Angels, spirites: and his ministers, a* 8 *flame of fyre.* But to the Sonne: *Thy throne ô God for euer and euer: a rod of equitie, the rod of* 9 *thy kingdom. Thou hast loued iustice, and hated iniquitie: therfore thee, God, thy God hath anointed vvith the oil of exultation aboue thy fellovves.*

The Authorised Version, 1611.

1 God who at sundry times, and in diuers manners, spake in time past vnto the Fathers by the Prophets,

2 Hath in these last dayes spoken vnto vs by *his* Sonne, whom he hath appointed heire of all things, by whom also he made the worlds,

3 Who being the brightnesse of his glory, and the expresse image of his person, and vpholding all things by the word of his power, when hee had by himselfe purged our sinnes, sate down on yᵉ right hand of the Maiestie on high,

4 Being made so much better then the Angels, as hee hath by inheritance obtained a more excellent Name then they.

5 For vnto which of the Angels said he at any time, Thou art my sonne, this day haue I begotten thee? And again, I will be to him a Father, and he shall be to me a Sonne.

6 And again, when he bringeth in the first begotten into the world, hee saith, And let all the Angels of God worship him.

7 And of the Angels he saith: Who maketh his Angels spirits, and his ministers a flame of fire.

8 But vnto the Sonne, *he saith*, Thy throne, O God, *is* for euer and euer: a scepter of righteousnesse *is* the scepter of thy kingdome.

9 Thou hast loued righteousnesse, and hated iniquitie, therefore God, *euen* thy God hath anointed thee with the oyle of gladnesse aboue thy fellowes.

The Revised Version, 1881.

1 God, having of old time spoken unto the fathers in the prophets by divers portions and in di- 2 vers manners, hath at the end of these days spoken unto us in *his* Son, whom he appointed heir of all things, through whom also he made 3 the worlds; who being the effulgence of his glory, and the very image of his substance, and upholding all things by the word of his power, when he had made purification of sins, sat down on the right hand of the Majesty on high; 4 having become by so much better than the angels, as he hath inherited a more excellent name than 5 they. For unto which of the angels said he at any time,

Thou art my Son,
This day have I begotten thee?

and again,

I will be to him a Father,
And he shall be to me a Son?

6 And when he again bringeth in the firstborn into the world, he saith, And let all the angels of God worship him. 7 And of the angels he saith,

Who maketh his angels winds,
And his ministers a flame of fire;

8 but of the Son *he saith*,

Thy throne, O God, is for ever and ever;
And the sceptre of uprightness is the sceptre of thy kingdom.

9 Thou hast loved righteousness, and hated iniquity:
Therefore God, thy God, hath anointed thee
With the oil of gladness above thy fellows.

INDEX